ENCYCLOPEDIA OF AUSTRALIAN
CRIME

A calendar of murder, mayhem, rape, robbery and much, much more

JIM MAIN & BEN COLLINS

First printed 2006. Reprinted 2007.

Published by:

Bas Publishing
ABN 30 106 181 542
F16/171 Collins Street
Melbourne Vic. 3000
Tel: (03) 9650 3200
Fax: (03) 9650 5077
Web: www.baspublishing.com.au
Email: mail@baspublishing.com.au

The National Library of Australia Cataloguing-in-Publication entry

Main, Jim, 1943- .
   Encyclopedia of Australian crime : a calendar of murder, mayhem, rape,
   robbery and much, much more

   ISBN 1 920910 76 X.

   1. Crime - Australia - Encyclopedias. I. Collins, Ben. II.
   Title.

364.99403

Design & Layout: Ben Graham

Introduction

The history of Australian crime might stretch back only 200-odd years, but for intrigue, cunning and savagery, it matches many of the world's more ancient and feudal nations. In fact, lurking in our relatively brief past are crimes that many would believe unthinkable, and perhaps unspeakable, in so-called civilised, genteel, Western society.

For example, the abhorrent, seemingly inhuman act of cannibalism would appear, to the average Australian, to be the domain of primitive headhunting tribes in deepest, darkest Africa or New Guinea – and probably a myth at that. However, we have at least one chilling story of cannibalism of our own that makes the skin crawl.

On September 20, 1822, eight convicts escaped from the penitentiary at Tasmania's Macquarie Harbour, and, when the food became scarce in dense forest, they began murdering each other and feasting on the corpses. Irishman Alexander Pearce was the sole survivor and his account of events outraged the colony. Pearce later coaxed another inmate to abscond and was caught after cannibalising his body. Before his execution, Pearce further repulsed his captors by remarking: "Man's flesh is delicious. It tastes far better than fish or pork."

Whether we like it or not – and many Australians probably prefer to ignore this unflattering part of our history – Australia, as we now know it today, was formed on the backs of convicts. From 1788 to 1868, about 800 ships transported 162,000 British convicts Down Under.

Australia was a frontier society and some convicts possessed an overwhelming urge to escape the shackles of discipline, food rations and road gangs to explore for themselves what life was like on the other side of the frontier. Often, they discovered the harsh Australian bush was even more unforgiving.

Australia's first bushranger was a West Indian man-mountain named John 'Black' Caesar, who came to Australia as a convict on the First Fleet in 1788 and proved a rather distinctive fugitive in New South Wales for much of the 1790s until he was shot dead by a free settler-turned-bounty-hunter.

Bushranging evolved with the discovery of gold and improved horsemanship, with the likes of 'Mad' Dan Morgan and Ben Hall relieving numerous travellers of their finery on the roadways in the 1860s.

The individual who towers above all Aussie criminals before, and probably since, was another bushranger, Ned Kelly, whose name and legacy continues to be, in various quarters, revered, reviled and revised more than 125 years after his execution. Unbeknown to many people is the fact that the Kelly Gang's shootout with police at Glenrowan in 1880 lasted 12 hours, whereas the legendary, almost mythological Wild West showdown between the Earp brothers and the Dalton Gang at the OK Corral was over in a mere 30 seconds.

Drawing attention to such a detail is not meant to glorify criminals and their illegal exploits – that is not the intention of this book – but to simply illustrate that our criminal history makes for fascinating reading.

While America had Al Capone and John Dillinger and the United Kingdom had the notorious Kray brothers, we had gangsters of our own in Melbourne's 'Squizzy' Taylor and Sydney's Darcy Dugan, who, despite their small stature, assumed celebrity status while they were, in 'Squizzy's' words, "living in clover". Underworld wars have claimed many lives over the decades, with Melbourne alone contributing the lion's share in recent years.

We have also had our share of serial killers and an unnerving number of utterly baffling unsolved cases such as the disappearance of the Beaumont children, the Bogle-Chandler murder mystery and the triple-homicide of the Murphy siblings at Gatton in Queensland. And let's not forget the 'Great Bookie Robbery' - our equivalent to Britain's Great Train Robbery.

While this book does not claim to be definitive, it stands as a document of public record. Within these pages, you will also find at least one crime – from the famous to the not-so-well-known-but-equally-intriguing – for each day of the calendar year. The diversity from one day to the next is quite remarkable. What crime(s) do you share your birthday with?

Numerous anniversary milestones will be clocked up in 2007 alone. It will mark, among others, 150 years since John Price, the Inspector General of Prisons in Victoria, was bashed to death by convicts at Williamstown; 100 years since the imprisonment of West Australian 'baby farmer' Alice Mitchell; 80 years since the fatal shooting of 'Squizzy' Taylor; 50 years since the Sundown Murders in South Australia; 25 years since Lindy Chamberlain was jailed for life; 20 years since the Hoddle Street and Queen Street massacres; and 10 years since the disappearance of Jaidyn Leskie and the murder of Melbourne mother Jane Thurgood-Dove in front of her children in the family driveway.

Unfortunately, it is inevitable that this list will continue to grow. But, judging by the number of television programs devoted to factual and fictional crime, and the reams of pages that murder and underworld 'hits' fill in our major daily newspapers, so too will our almost voyeuristic fascination with crime and the individuals who commit it.

Ben Collins and Jim Main

JANUARY

Death takes no holidays, not even on New Year's Day or Australia Day (January 26). Murder, mayhem and madness can occur at any time of the year and, in the hot summer days of January, Australia has been rocked by horrific crimes, with poisonings, rapes, shootings, multiple murders and even cannibalism. Crimes this month include:

THE BOGLE-CHANDLER MYSTERY
THE CONVICT CANNIBAL
THE THAI HEROIN BUST
THE ELOISE WORLEDGE MYSTERY
THE WANDA BEACH MURDERS
THE BABY FARMER
And, much, much more.

JANUARY 1

THE BATTLE OF BROKEN HILL (1915)

Technically, Australia already was at war with Turkey when *January 1* dawned in the Outback in 1915, but no shots had been fired in anger — until camel driver Mulla Abdulla and ice-cream vendor Gaol Mahomed that day launched a private guerrilla war just outside the New South Wales mining town of Broken Hill. Picnicking families were travelling to nearby Silverton in open-air ore trucks when they noticed an ice-cream van by the side of the tracks. From it fluttered the red and white Turkish flag. Almost immediately, they had to duck for cover as two shots rang out from a nearby trench. Police and soldiers rushed to the scene, where they surrounded the two gunmen.

Finally, after several hours, the siege was ended when Abdulla was shot dead and Mahomed mortally wounded. They had killed Elma Cowie, Albert Millar, William Shaw and James Greig and the wounded included a police constable, Robert Mills. Abdulla had been armed with a Snider rifle, while Mahomed had been firing a Martini Henry rifle.

The *Barrier Mail* reported that the murderers had been "riddled with bullets". It is believed that after Abdullah had been convicted for slaughtering sheep illegally, Mahomed had convinced him that neither had a future in Australia and it would be better to die as Muslim patriots. Although Abdullah was from north-west India (now Pakistan) and Mahomed an Afghan, they had sworn allegiance to the Sultan of Turkey as the leader of their faith. Their ambush sparked outrage in Broken Hill and a mob, believing the German community was behind the outrage, set alight the German Club before marching towards a camel drivers' camp. Police stopped them, but tension in Broken Hill was high for many weeks.

WHO KILLED LITTLE JAIDYN? (1998)

The death of 14-month Jaidyn Leskie shocked the state of Victoria. His little body was found in the Blue Rock Dam, near the Gippsland town of Moe, on *January 1*, 1998. Police were horrified by Jaidyn's injuries as his skull had been smashed and one of his arms broken. Despite intensive police investigations and DNA testing, the toddler's death remains a mystery. Little Jaidyn was left in the care of a friend of his mother, Bilynda Williams. That friend, then 29-year-old unemployed mechanic Greg Domaszewicz, was charged with Jaidyn's murder, but on *December 4*, 1998, was found not guilty of either murder or manslaughter.

Domaszewicz told the jury that at two o'clock on the day Williams had left Jaidyn with him, he left the boy alone to pick up Williams from a pub. When he returned, Jaidyn was missing and a pig's head had been left on the front lawn. He did not tell Williams until two hours later that her son was missing. Also, the investigation was muddied by claims that two DNA samples were contaminated at the Victorian Forensic Science laboratory. DNA traces found on Jaidyn's bib matched that of the DNA of a rape victim, who has never been a suspect in the toddler's death. The mystery therefore remains.

THE BOGLE-CHANDLER MYSTERY (1963)

The bodies of Dr Gilbert Bogle and Mrs Margaret Chandler were found early on *January 1*, 1963, in the Sydney suburb of

Chatswood. The two had been at a party given by a CSIRO scientist and police were baffled as there was no evident cause of death. Both bodies were covered, Dr Bogle's by his jacket and Mrs Chandler's by cardboard beer cartons. The director of the NSW Department of Forensic Medicine, Dr John Lang, testified at the coroner's court inquest in May, 1963, that the couple had died from acute circulatory failure, but could not explain why the circulatory systems had failed. There were no marks on either body and no poisonous substances were found in either body's internal organs.

However, government analyst Mr Ernest Ogg did not rule out the possibility of chemical poisoning. He also indicated: "I can see no prospect of this mystery being solved so far as chemical poisons are concerned." It was suggested that Mrs Chandler wanted to take Dr Bogle, an eminent scientist, as her lover, but there was no evidence she had had sexual intercourse just before her death. And her husband, Dr Geoffrey Chandler, had left the party earlier than his wife and had picked up his two children at his in-laws' home in Granville. No satisfactory theory has been put forward as a solution to the Bogle-Chandler mystery and no one even knows for sure whether it was a case of murder at all.

JANUARY 2

THE SHOOTING MYSTERY (1909)

Constable William Hyde was on foot patrol in the Adelaide suburb of Kensington on the night of Saturday, *January 2*, 1909, when a woman told him she had seen three men acting suspiciously. Despite the heat of summer, the men were wearing overcoats and had hats pulled down over their faces. Constable Hyde went to investigate and noticed three men break cover. He therefore walked up to them and told them he wanted to know what they were doing. The men ran off, but Constable Hyde managed to grab one of them.

One of the two men who had run off, stopped and produced a pistol. He fired twice at the police officer, but did not hit him. Constable Hyde, who was unarmed, then tried to pull something from a pocket in an attempt to fool the men into thinking he too had a pistol. However, the only item of note in his pocket was a pipe. The man he had apprehended then shouted to his companions that the police officer did not have a gun. Several more shots were fired and Constable Hyde took a bullet to the face.

The dying police officer was placed on a window shutter which was used as a makeshift stretcher and taken to the nearest police station. From there, he was taken to the Adelaide Hospital, but died of his wound two days later. Police launched a massive man-hunt but, despite finding two hats, two overcoats and a pistol, the trail went cold. The men were described as being aged between 25 and 30, ranging in height from short to tall, but were never apprehended. The Adelaide police shooting therefore remains a mystery.

CRUSHED LIKE A PUMPKIN (2005)

Jarrad Francis Matthews was a 19-year-old male prostitute who had a regular client in 71-year-old grandfather Howard Ambrose. Matthews had met Ambrose for sex numerous times and, after the third encounter, was in the habit of going to Ambrose's home at Warrion, near the western Victorian town of Colac, for sex. In December, 2004, Matthews copied telephone numbers from Ambrose's contact book and told the elderly man, who had been married with four children, that he would telephone his friends and tell them he was a paedophile. Ambrose agreed to pay the young man $1000, but received a phone call from Matthews on *January 2*, 2005. Matthews said he was sorry for what he had done and suggested they meet again. The couple drove in Ambrose's car from Melbourne to Warrion and the other man stripped down to shorts in preparation for sex.

While lying on his front, Matthews came from behind and struck Ambrose numerous times with an axe to the back of the head. He then wrapped a towel around Ambrose's head as he did not like to look at what he had done as the head resembled "a crushed pumpkin". Matthews then tried to drive Ambrose's car back to Melbourne, but did not know how to drive a manual vehicle. Two days later, police interviewed him after tracing the call he had made to Ambrose. Also, Matthews had rifled his victim's wallet and later cashed $2000 from the dead man's credit card account. Matthews pleaded guilty to Ambrose's murder and Justice Teague sentenced him to 18 years' jail, with a non-parole period of 13 years.

✳✳

JAILED (1879): Sympathisers of the Kelly Gang were thrown in jail on *January 2*, 1879, for an indefinite period. The authorities were determined to dismantle the gang's power base of supporters and informants on police movements, its 'bush telegraph', but they made themselves decidedly unpopular by locking up certain people who had nothing to do with the gang's activities. Amid a public outcry, the so-called sympathisers were all released three weeks later.

JANUARY 3

POISON AT THE PARSONAGE (1928)

Parson's wife Ethel Constance Griggs died of arsenic poisoning in the tiny Gippsland town of Omeo on *January 3*, 1928, and within weeks, her death was the subject of considerable speculation, not only in Gippsland, but also in Melbourne. Had Mrs Griggs been murdered, or had she committed suicide. Or had her death been an accident?

Mrs Griggs was the unhappy wife of Omeo's Methodist parson, Ronald Geeves Griggs, a man who wore his calling like a badge. He started studying for the Methodist ministry as soon as he returned to Australia from the battlefields of World War I and, at the same time, started courting Ethel White, the daughter of a Tasmanian farmer. They had known each other from childhood and, significantly, she was from a religious family. On completion of his theological studies at Queen's College, Melbourne, they were married. That was in 1926, shortly before the Methodist church appointed him licentiate (a preacher yet to be ordained) at Omeo. Griggs, then 26, and his wife, 20, moved into the tidy weatherboard parsonage and, two years later, their names would be known in every household in Victoria.

Although the Griggs' marriage was not an outwardly happy one, there was little reason to suspect that Griggs would fall prey to the sins of the flesh which he denounced with such fervour from the pulpit. However, soon after his arrival in Omeo he became infatuated with 20-year-old farmer's daughter Lottie Condon, a vivacious churchgoer. Griggs and the pretty Miss Condon were often seen together, invariably with the parson riding his motorcycle with the girl as a sidecar passenger. At first there was no hint that Mrs Griggs objected to the friendship and she even invited Miss Condon to stay at the parsonage for the final week of 1926. However, Mrs Griggs soon detected small signs of familiarity and affection and, at the end of the week, ordered the girl out of the parsonage, ending an outburst by describing Miss Condon as "a hussy".

Griggs denied to his wife that he had committed adultery and although he probably was telling the truth, it was not long before he and the delectable Miss Condon became lovers and he often stayed over at her father's farmhouse. This clandestine relationship lasted several months before the couple became more and more open and even were seen cuddling in the bush surrounding Omeo.

When Mrs Griggs gave birth to a daughter, she hoped her husband would come to his senses, but it had the opposite effect and Griggs even sent mother and baby to Tasmania for a holiday. They were absent for almost six months and, during that time, Mrs Griggs even asked for a divorce. However, she returned to Omeo with her baby on *December 31*, 1927, in perfect health. Yet she was dead just three days later. In fact, Mrs Griggs complained of being ill almost as soon as she returned to the parsonage. She vomited and Griggs later prepared her a snack, including a pot of tea. Mrs Griggs drank some of the tea and ate half a sandwich, but would not drink any more of "that tea".

Mrs Griggs' condition worsened and, soaked in sweat, she eventually went into a state of delirium and a doctor was called twice. At one o'clock on the morning of *January 3*, Griggs knocked on the door of neighbour Herbert Mitchell to ask if he could have a look at his wife as she appeared to be in a very heavy state of sleep. Mrs Griggs was dead and when the doctor arrived, Griggs asked him: "Will you give a death certificate?" He said he could not bear the thought of his wife's body "cut up" for an autopsy.

Mrs Griggs' body was buried without the slightest police suspicion, but the swishing of tongues reached even Melbourne and the police and the Methodist hierarchy became increasingly interested in Mrs Griggs' death. The church acted first and asked Griggs to attend a special committee meeting at which he was asked about his relationship with Miss Condon. Griggs swore he had not committed adultery but, meanwhile, the police started investigating Mrs Griggs' death and sent a vastly experienced officer, Detective Sergeant Danial Mulfahey, to Omeo. Almost immediately, Miss Condon admitted she and Griggs had been having an affair and she even told detectives the parson had promised to marry her.

Griggs eventually was charged with his wife's murder and Mrs Griggs' body was exhumed to become the subject of scientific testing for arsenic poisoning. The examination was conducted by State pathologist Dr Crawford Mollison, while portions of the body were tested chemically by government analyst Mr C.A. Taylor for traces of arsenic. The poison, apart from being virtually tasteless, can be administered with lethal results through several doses. The amount of arsenic found in Mrs Griggs' body could have killed several men.

Although the prosecution had no difficulty proving that Mrs Griggs died of arsenic poisoning, it was another matter to prove that Griggs had deliberately poisoned his wife, especially as police could not find a trace of arsenic at the parsonage. This was a critical point as Griggs claimed that his wife had committed suicide and once had tried to throw herself on to a fire. The problem with this theory was that it would have been impossible for Mrs Griggs, on her deathbed, to remove traces of poison.

The evidence at Griggs' trial in Gippsland was conflicting and the jury, after a long deliberation, returned to say it could not agree on a verdict, although 10 of the 12 were in favour of convicting Griggs. A new trial in Melbourne was ordered in this sensational case. Again the evidence seemed conflicting, with even a suggestion a pharmacist might have made a mistake with a prescription, and the jury deliberated for six hours and 20 minutes before returning its verdict. Griggs gripped a rail as he turned his head to hear the jury foreman say "not guilty".

Griggs, of course, wanted to marry Miss Condon, but her father shifted the family to New South Wales and the parson never saw his beloved Lottie again. Although Griggs was found not guilty of murdering his wife, his life was almost beyond repair. He tried to enter the Presbyterian Ministry in South Australia under a false name but, after being uncovered, faded from public record, presumably under another assumed name. Griggs might have been found not guilty of poisoning his wife, but his own life had been poisoned and the mystery of Ethel Griggs' death has gone to the grave with her.

THE TIN SOLDIER (1931)

Residents of the Sydney suburb of Waverley knew Thomas Kennedy as either "the tin soldier" or "the mad general" because of his obsession with marching drills and target practice with a .22 rifle. Kennedy twice was rejected for service in the Great War because of varicose veins and this affected him to the degree that he felt persecuted, while neighbours thought he was a returned serviceman who had not recovered from shellshock. On the morning of *January 3*, 1931, Kennedy, armed with his rifle, refused to pay for a packet of cigarettes in busy Bondi Junction and told the shopkeeper to "charge them to the Governor".

The shopkeeper immediately rushed out to notify traffic policeman Constable Norman Allan that Kennedy not only was armed but appeared to be in a dangerous mood. Constable Allan sprinted after Kennedy and then told him it would be best if he handed over the rifle. Kennedy fired three bullets into the policeman's chest and then warned bystanders to "back off". With Allan dead in the street, police reinforcements were sent to the scene. However, Kennedy raced home and locked the front door before a police officer, Constable Ernest Andrews, unlocked the back door of the cottage and confronted Kennedy. Two shots rang out and, as the policeman clutched his stomach, Kennedy stabbed him to finish him off. A policeman at the front gate spotted Kennedy through the shattered glass of the front door and shot him in the stomach. "The tin soldier" died in hospital a few hours later. Thousands lined streets for the funerals of Constables Allan and Andrews.

JANUARY 4

HANGED AT ARARAT (1870)

Andrew Vair, 33, had the dubious distinction of being the first man hanged at Ararat, Victoria. He had been found guilty of the murder of business colleague Amos Cheale at St Arnaud on *January 4*, 1870. Vair had confronted Cheale about their business dealings and, when he did not get a satisfactory response, shot him dead. The Scot fled to Adelaide and then to Yankalilla, South Australia, where he was captured and charged with murder. Vair was executed at the Ararat jail on *August 15*, 1870, and, before he dropped to his death, admitted his guilt and that he hoped for mercy.

JANUARY 5

THE KILLING CLARKES (1867)

Brothers Thomas and John Clarke were bushrangers who terrorised the area around where they lived at Braidwood, New South Wales, in the 1860s. There was another brother, James, but in 1865 he was jailed for seven years for the robbery of the Cowra mail. Also, with patriarch John Clarke Senior dying in jail while awaiting trial for murder, Thomas and John Clarke embarked on a massive crime wave which involved nine mail robberies and more than 30 hold-ups. They had accomplices, but the police were more interested in arresting the Clarke brothers.

On *January 5*, 1867, special constables John Carroll, Patrick Kennagh, Eneas McDonnell and John Phegan set out in search of the Clarkes but were ambushed and shot dead. Pound notes were pinned to their bodies to signify 'blood money'. The discovery of their bodies sparked outrage and, while the brothers continued their crime wave, a tip-off led police to trap them in their hide-out. A shoot-out ensued but, when more troopers, joined the fight, the Clarke brothers surrendered. They were tried in Sydney for their crimes and sentenced to death. Thomas and John Clarke were hanged at Darlinghurst jail on *June 25*, 1867.

THE COWARDLY BUSHRANGER (1899)

Alexander Fordyce, a farmer and part-time barman, was a member of the gang which staged the Eugowra gold escort robbery of *June 15*, 1862, which netted the bushrangers almost 4000 pounds in cash and 10,000 pounds worth of gold — a massive heist in those days. After the robbery, in which the bushrangers exchanged gunfire with the troopers aboard the coach, gang leader Frank Gardiner discovered that the 42-year-old Fordyce had not fired a shot and branded him a coward. Gardiner told Fordyce there would be no rations for him and, although the man who did not fire a shot in the robbery, believed this meant food, it actually meant there would be no share of the gold or cash haul.

Police eventually caught up with most of the gang and Fordyce and several others who had taken part in the robbery were tried in Sydney. Fordyce was sentenced to death, but this eventually was commuted to life imprisonment. It is believed Fordyce spent more than seven years in jail and, when eventually released, was a mere shadow of the man who had taken part in one of Australia's most notorious crimes. He died in an asylum on *January 5*, 1899, at 79 years of age.

JANUARY 6

THE PACK-HORSE KILLING (1859)

Police Constable William Green was escorting gold-dealer Cornelius Green from Omeo to Bairnsdale in Victoria's Gippsland region on *January 6*, 1859, when he and his party were ambushed. Both Green and the unrelated Constable

Green were hit by bullets, but survived the attack. The gold-dealer managed to make his way to an inn to raise the alarm, but later found that the pack-horse carrying his gold had bolted and went in search of it.

Next day, the wounded Constable Green and a group of troopers went to the scene of the crime and discovered the body of the gold-dealer. He had been shot numerous times, his head had been bashed in and one of his hands had been near-severed by an axe. Police immediately launched a man-hunt for two men who had briefly joined Green's group. They eventually found George Chamberlain and William Armstrong hiding in a shanty and were arrested with barely any resistance. It was then that Armstrong made the astonishing confession that two years earlier he had killed a man known as "Ballarat" Harry. He was tried for murder, found guilty and executed on *July 12*, 1859.

THE KILLER BARONET (1844)

Although John Knatchbull was the son of baronet Sir Edward Knatchbull, he was a rogue. After being educated at the influential Winchester school, he joined the navy. However, the heavy gambler was arrested for being a pickpocket and was transported to New South Wales in 1825. Knatchbull, despite his fall from grace, found it difficult to change his ways and was sentenced to seven years on Norfolk Island after presenting a forged cheque. He gained his ticket-of-leave in 1842, worked as a sailor in coastal waters and proposed marriage to widow Harriet Craig.

To marry, Knatchbull needed money, so told his fiancée that he would collect debts owed to him. On the night of *January 6*, 1844, he called in at the shop of Mrs Ellen

Jamieson, in Kent Street, Sydney. Not long after, residents heard a cracking and crashing noises. They went to investigate and found Mrs Jamieson, her head smashed in by an axe, in a pool of blood. She was critically injured and, behind a door, the residents found Knatchbull in hiding. He was charged with assault and robbery, but this was changed to a charge of murder when Mrs Jamieson died 12 days later. Knatchbull pleaded not guilty on the grounds of insanity, but was found guilty. He was hanged in front of a crowd estimated at 10,000 on *February 13*, 1844.

**

CAPTURED (1965): Pentridge escapees Ronald Ryan and Peter Walker are captured on *January 6*, 1965, after 17 days on the run. (Refer to *February 3*.)

JANUARY 7

THE PIER MURDER (1885)

Freeland Morell, an American, and John Anderson were shipmates abroad the barque *Don Nicholls,* which had berthed in Adelaide late in 1885. The two occasionally quarrelled, but no one suspected their bickering would result in murder. However, Morell stabbed Anderson in the heart while walking along a pier and, when police arrived, still had the murder weapon in his hand. Amazingly, however, he said he had no recollection of murdering Anderson. Morell was found guilty of murder and sentenced to death. He was hanged on *January 7*, 1886, and said before he faced the drop: "Now you will see how an American dies."

**

HANGED: Four of the nine Mt Rennie gang-rapists were hanged on *January 7*, 1887. (Refer to *September 16*.)

JANUARY 8

THE MISSING BOY (1973)

Late on *January 8*, 1973, Sunshine High School student John Landos, 13, went for a walk from where his family was holidaying at the Erskine River Caravan Park, near Lorne (Victoria). He had been at the beach and was supposed to go rabbit-hunting with his father, Ken, but returned too late and expressed his disappointment at not going shooting with his father. He trudged off to be on his own, and was never seen again. The last confirmed sighting of him was at nearby Dean's Marsh on the day he disappeared.

The Year 8 student was wearing brown corduroy pants, a red shirt and white sandshoes and, after his parents reported him missing, police issued a description. John's parents also launched their own search and spent countless hours combing the Dean's Marsh area in western Victoria. However, neither John nor his clothing has ever been found. There were numerous so-called "sightings" of the boy for several years after his disappearance, but the case remains a mystery.

THE ROAD RAGE DEATH (2002)

Ivan Conabere, 38 years of age, was a decent, law-abiding citizen who liked reading and music. He also was intent on obtaining his motor-cycle licence and, as he rode down

Cornwall Street, West Brunswick around 6pm on *January 8*, 2002, he had L-plates on his 250cc motor-cycle. After an incident involving 27-year-old Thomas Ivanovic, he remonstrated by pointing down the road where a traffic incident had occurred. Ivanovic reacted by shooting Conabere in the chest with a .32 Walther self-loading pistol. Just three seconds later, Ivanovic shot him a second time.

Ivanovic told a man riding behind Conabere: "What are you looking at? He had me by the throat. What did you expect me to do?" Ivanovic then hid the unlicensed gun down a drain before walking back up Cornwall Street and admitting he shot the motor-cyclist. However, he kept insisting: "What else could I do?" He even told a friend: "He threatened to kill me and then go inside and kill my family."

However, Justice Cummins, in the Supreme Court of Victoria, told Ivanovic: "Punishment is so important, because this killing was so cruel and gratuitous. Special deterrence is important because it needs demonstrating to you that human life is not cheap. General deterrence is especially important because others need to be deterred from wreaking cruel violence on persons on our public streets for no cause." He sentenced Ivanovic to 20 years' imprisonment, with a non-parole period of 15 years.

**

HANGED (1889): Louisa Collins, "The Borgia of Botany", on *January 8*, 1889, became the last woman executed in New South Wales after being found guilty of murdering her two husbands and a child. Collins' mode of killing was poisoning with arsenic. It took four trials before she was found guilty.

JANUARY 9

THE MULTIPLE MURDERER (1931)

Arnold Karl Sodeman was married with a two-year-old daughter, but always will be remembered as one of Australia's worst killers, even though he was suffering from a brain disease throughout his spree of death. His trail of human destruction started on *November 9*, 1930, when he abducted and strangled 12-year-old Mena Griffith in an empty house in the Melbourne suburb of Ormond. His second victim was 16-year-old Hazel Wilson, whose body was discovered on a vacant allotment in Oakleigh Road, Ormond, soon after she disappeared on the night of *January 9*, 1931.

Then, on New Year's Day, 1935, Sodeman struck a third time when he abducted and strangled 12-year-old Ethel Belshaw at the Gippsland beach resort of Inverloch. Then, on *December 1*, 1935, he struck for the fourth and final time when he strangled six-year-old Jane Rushmer at Dumbalk, where he was working on roads. The little girl had been seen being "dinked" on a bike and Sodeman flew into a rage when workmates started talking about the girl's death. Police were called to the work camp and, after being arrested, Sodeman confessed to police.

The multiple killer, who had sexually molested at least one of his victims, went on trial before Justice Gavan Duffy and jury at the Melbourne Criminal Court from *January 17*, 1936. He was found guilty of murder and Justice Duffy sentenced him to death. He was hanged at Pentridge on *June 1*, 1936, and a post-mortem revealed that Sodeman had been suffering from a brain disease known as leptomeningitis. This disease rendered him unaccountable for his actions after even just a few glasses of beer, as alcohol inflamed his brain tissues.

JANUARY 10

THE BRISBANE OFFICE KILLING (1946)

Pretty Bronia Armstrong worked as a stenographer for the Brisbane Associated Friendly Societies Institute in an arcade in central Brisbane. The Institute's secretary, Reginald Spence Wingfield Brown, a 49-year-old father of three grown-up children, became infatuated with her, causing Bronia considerable discomfort and anguish. Finally, she resigned her position and was due to leave her job on *January 17*, 1946. However, she was strangled on *January 10*, and her body was discovered in the Institute waiting room the following morning. She was wearing only a bra and slip.

Brown had tried to make the murder look like suicide and told police that Bronia had been unhappy at home and that she talked of jumping off a bridge. However, blood stains were found in his office and police concluded that he had killed the girl there and then dragged the body into the waiting room. There was a long scratch running from his office to the waiting room. Brown, despite insisting he had been framed, was found guilty of murder and was sentenced to life imprisonment. He later hanged himself and left a suicide note which read: "I did not kill Bronia Armstrong. My conscience is clear."

**

GUNNED DOWN (1989): Australian Federal Police Assistant Commissioner Colin Winchester was gunned down in the driveway outside his house Dookie, Canberra, at 9.15pm on *January 10*, 1989. He was shot twice in the head at point-blank range and died at the scene. Mr Winchester, who was a member of the police force for 27 years and was regarded as a tough but compassionate man, was the highest-ranking police officer to be murdered in Australia. David Harold Eastman, a public servant who had been on long-term sick leave, was convicted of his murder on *November 3*, 1995, after a trial lasting 85 days.

JANUARY 11

THE CANNIBAL CONVICT (1824)

When convicts Alexander Pearce and Thomas Cox escaped from the Macquarie Harbour penal settlement, Van Diemen's Land, on *November 13*, 1823, they would have had no idea that they would become part of Australian folklore. The two men ran into the bush armed with an axe, but no food. Several days later, they came across the King's River but, because Cox would not swim, Pearce flew into a rage. He struck his companion several times with the axe and, as he was about to cross the river, Cox shouted to him: "Put me out of my misery." Pearce turned back and again struck Cox over the head, killing him. Pearce, who was desperately hungry, saw his dead companion as a source of food and then committed the unthinkable. He cut a piece from Cox's thigh, roasted it and are it before cutting off another slice for sustenance once he had crossed the river.

However, the remorse of turning cannibal saw him hailing a schooner on *January 11*, 1824, and then confessing to both murder and cannibalism. He said he was "willing to die" for his actions. A search party was sent to look for Cox's body and, when it was found, the head and arms were missing, along with parts of the thighs and calves. When asked about the head, Pearce said he had left it on the body. It was found several yards away, but the hands were never found. Peace also said that after eating part of the thigh — "because no person can tell what he will do when driven by hunger" — he threw the rest into the river. Pearce was found guilty of murder and sentenced to death. His execution on *July 19*, 1824, was watched by a large crowd, with a Rev. Connolly addressing those assembled before the drop. The minister told the crowd that Pearce, standing on the edge of eternity, wanted to acknowledge his guilt. Finally, he asked the crowd to offer their prayers and beg the Almighty to have mercy upon Pearce.

THE THAI HEROIN BUST (1990)

Young Sydneysider Warren Fellows came from a well-known Australian family as his father Bill was a jockey who had ridden 1949 Melbourne Cup winner Foxzami. Warren, the youngest of three children, worked as a barman and hairdresser on leaving school, but soon got caught up in the Sydney drugs scene. He became a drug courier and in October, 1978, was asked to travel to Thailand with well-known sportsman Paul Hayward, a member of the Newtown Jets Rugby League club and a professional boxer.

Fellows was reluctant to make the trip as he had heard that authorities had been tipped off about the run and was worried about being arrested in Thailand. However, he and Hayward were convinced there would be no problems and flew to Bangkok. However, Fellows earlier had obtained a false passport and went to Thailand under the name of Gregory Barker. Then, on *October 11*, 1978, Thai police raided Hayward's room and found 8.5 kilograms of heroin in a suitcase. Both men were arrested and, under physical duress in which they alleged they were threatened with summary execution, they implicated a third man, Bangkok bar owner William Sinclair. Fellows, Hayward and Sinclair spent three years in jail before being convicted of drug offences. They were sentenced to life in jail, but Sinclair was released on appeal two years later. Hayward received a royal pardon and was released on *April 7*, 1989, while Fellows also was released, on *January 11*, 1990, on royal pardon.

THE AMERICAN SERVICEMEN KILLINGS (1945)

Brisbane residents were shocked on the afternoon of *January 11*, 1945, when the sound of a gunshot echoed around the city. The noise was unmistakable and, soon after people put their hands to their ears, an American serviceman staggered from a public toilet shouting that he had been shot. The American, Lieutenant Allen Middleton, died on his way to hospital and police were left to solve the mystery. Why would anyone shoot someone dead in broad daylight? There seemed no motive and there were few clues, except for the description of a man in a grey suit and hat walking from the toilet block seconds after the shot had been heard. Many men wore grey suits at this time, so the police virtually were looking for a needle in a haystack.

Then, on *January 24*, American Petty Officer John McCollum answered the door at his rented home in Alderley and was shot in the stomach. He died shortly after, but this time the police had a lead. The dying American had told them about a "red bread van". A search was launched and, shortly after, a red bread van was found just a few blocks away. When questioned, the bread carter — wearing a grey suit — admitted shooting the American. Ex-Australian soldier Frederick William Everest, who had been dismissed from the army because of schizophrenia, was arrested and told police he had shot Middleton and McCollum because Americans were "out to get him". Everest was tried for murder, but was found not guilty on the grounds of insanity and was committed to an asylum.

**

UNSOLVED (1990): Greek immigrant Ionnnis Fratzeskos was brutally bashed to death in Darwin on *January 11*, 1990, and his murder is still ulsolved. Fratzekos' body was found on the floor of the new Post Office construction site and his attacker had bludgeoned him across the face with a concrete brick before dragging the body to a hiding place behind a pile of bricks. Robbery was ruled out as a motive as his wallet, containing $400, was found near Fratzeskos' body.

JANUARY 12

JAILED, BUT NO BODY (1952)

Store owner William Lavers was feeding horses at his Glenelg, New South Wales, property early on the morning of *September 5*, 1936, when he heard a car approaching. As the store had a petrol bowser, he went to attend the customer.

However, no one saw him again, dead or alive, and his wife contacted police. They found the petrol pump on the ground and blood stains on a heavy piece of metal. Despite every effort, no trace of Lavers was found and the case files gathered dust — until 10 years later when Frederick McDermott was charged with Lavers' murder. The evidence against him was largely circumstantial and was based mainly on someone hearing him admit killing the store owner. According to the police, McDermott killed Lavers over six gallons of petrol he could not afford to buy. It also was alleged that McDermott killed the store owner with a blow to the head, the body chopped up with an axe and buried in the bush.

McDermott, a 38-year-old shearer, was found guilty of murder and sentenced to death. Although this sentence was commuted to one of life imprisonment, McDermott pleaded his innocence. Finally, in 1951, a Royal Commission was appointed to look into the case. More than 100 witnesses were called to give evidence and Mr Justice Kinsella eventually found that McDermott had been convicted on inaccurate evidence "given honestly and in good faith". For his part, McDermott told the hearing: "May the Lord strike me stone dead — I have been in jail for five years for something I never done." The commission findings led to McDermott's release from Long Bay jail on *January 12*, 1952. He was awarded 500 pounds in compensation and died in Sydney, in August, 1977.

THE ELOISE WORLEDGE MYSTERY (1976)

Eloise Worledge was an ordinary eight-year-old who lived with parents Patricia (Patsy) and Lindsay and siblings Anna and Blake in the Melbourne bayside suburb of Beaumaris. Patsy and Lindsay Worledge were on the brink of breaking up and Eloise, understandably was upset over this and, on the warm night of *January 11*, 1976, possibly went to bed worried about what would happen to her family. Wearing two-piece yellow pyjamas, she was last seen by her mother at about 11pm. Patsy Worledge had been to a jazz ballet session and then called into a neighbour's house, but took the time — as usual — to look in on her children and kiss them goodnight. Meanwhile, Lindsay Worledge went to bed at about 11.40pm and said he also checked on the children.

At 4.45am on *January 12*, Patsy Worledge woke and, before going to the toilet, noticed that the passage light, normally left on for the children, was switched off. She again checked on her children and discovered that Eloise was not in her bedroom. Further, the curtains in the room had been pulled aside and she noticed that the fly-wire screen to the window had been cut. Forensic tests later revealed the screen had been cut from the inside.

Patsy Worledge notified her sister and a neighbour of Eloise's disappearance, while her husband rang the police. Sergeant Cyril Wilson, a Beaumaris-based police officer, went to the Worledge home in Scott Street and, on seeing the cut flywire, called for back-up. Police immediately launched a task force and, at one stage, more than 200 police officers were involved in a desperate search for the missing eight-year-old. A $10,000 reward was posted but, despite numerous reports by neighbours of suspicious occurrences in and around Scott Street – including a car that sped down Scott Street at 2am – nothing was found of the cute little blonde with the toothy grin.

Police were convinced the open window and cut flywire were diversions and that Eloise probably had been lured, by someone she knew, through the front door of the family home. Young Blake told police he heard "robbers" kidnap his sister, but that he had been too scared to raise the alarm because he feared for his own safety. Despite every police effort, the mystery of Eloise's disappearance remains.

JANUARY 13

THE LAST BUSHRANGERS (1903)

Brothers Patrick and Jimmy Kenniff were born to a life of crime and, after minor tangles with the law, were jailed in 1895 for horse stealing. On release, they took up grazing in Queensland's Carnarvon district but, in 1902, came under suspicion of stealing a pony. Jimmy Kenniff was apprehended by Police Constable George Doyle, station manager Albert Dahlke and tracker Sam Johnson. However, Johnson had to leave the scene to retrieve a packhorse and, when he returned, there was no sign of Doyle or Dahlke. The Kenniff brothers then rode towards him, but he escaped to raise the alarm.

A search party a few days later made the "ghastly discovery" of two bodies. Doyle and Dahlke had been shot and the *Sydney Morning Herald* of *April 2* reported: "The bodies were taken across a creek by a large log about 20 yards from where the shooting occurred, and had probably been cut up there, rolled in blankets and then conveyed to a rock, where the ghoulish work was resumed. After being burned, all the bones were broken into small pieces with two hardwood sticks and a large round stone like a cannon ball."

Police mounted a huge manhunt for the Kenniffs, but the brothers escaped capture for three months before they were arrested, without a fight, at a camp on the Maranoa River.

They were sent for trial in the Supreme Court at Brisbane, were found guilty and sentenced to death. At the request of the defence, the case went to the Full Court over matters of law and although Patrick Kenniff's sentence was upheld, his brother's sentence was commuted to one of life imprisonment. Patrick was hanged at Boggo Road jail on *January 13*, 1903, while Jimmy served 16 years' jail and died in 1940. They were regarded as Australia's last bushrangers.

THE WANDA BEACH MURDERS (1965)

When 15-year-olds Christine Sharrock and Marianne Schmidt went to Wanda Beach, in Sydney's south, on *January 13*, 1965, they inadvertently ignited one of Australia's greatest murder mysteries. The girls went to the beach with Marianne's brothers Peter (10), Wolfgang (seven) and Norbert (six) and sister Trixie (nine), and travelled by train to Cronulla. The day had started as fine and hot, but a change in the weather saw the group walking along the beach rather than swimming. Christine and Marianne left the little group and walked towards the Wanda sand dunes, never to be seen alive again.

Marianne's brothers and sister waited for her and Christine to return but, at 5pm, decided to leave the beach and return home, where they were told the two 15-year-olds did not return from their walk. Police were notified and, the following afternoon, a man walking along Wanda Beach saw blood in the sand. When he went to investigate, he saw the two dead girls side by side in a shallow grave. There was a considerable amount of blood at the scene and both girls had been sexually assaulted, stabbed and bashed.

Police, naturally, launched an immediate investigation and wanted to speak with a surfer Wolfgang Schmidt had seen in the area. Police also scoured the area for possible clues and discovered a bloodstained knife. However, police were unable to determine whether it was the murder weapon or even if the blood stains were human. In a desperate effort to solve the mystery, police even reconstructed the walk to death, with women police officers dressed as the two girls. However, there were no new leads. An inquest into the death of the two girls was held in April, 1966, but although police had a number of possible suspects, the coroner found that the girls had been murdered by a person or persons unknown. The mystery remains, although one convicted killer remains at the top of the list of suspects.

POOR CHRISTOPHER ROBIN (1977)

Little Christopher Robin Weltman was looking forward to his first camping experience. He was just seven years of age and the YMCA holiday camp at Loftia Park in the Adelaide Hills would provide him with his first experience of the bush. However, Christopher, a mild asthmatic, disappeared from the camp on the evening of *January 12*, 1977.

More than 200 police and volunteers took part in the search for Christopher, a quietly spoken boy who often said he wanted to be a policeman when he grew up. Tragically, his body was found by a volunteer on the afternoon of *January 13*, just 20 hours after the boy had last been seen. The body was found just 50 metres from the camp lavatory block and only 100 metres from the hut Christopher shared with other children.

The boy had been bashed around the head and there was blood around the nose. There was a trail of blood from a nearby track and police correctly assumed the little boy had been attacked on the track and that his body had been dragged into the scrub. Half a brick was found close to the body and, significantly, forensic tests revealed that there were traces of blood and organic material attached to it. There were no indications of a struggle and there was no evidence of sexual assault.

Police, after interviewing the 73 children at the camp, arrested a 12-year-old boy over Christopher's death and he faced the Supreme Court of South Australia in July, 1977. In a sworn statement, the boy told the jury of seven men and five women that he was angry with Christopher for telling other children at the camp that he had "done a poo near a car". Medical evidence was given that Christopher had been struck at least three times to the head and shoulders and that a bruise mark on his chest matched the pattern of the 12-year-old's shoes.

The jury took just 40 minutes to find the boy guilty of Christopher's murder and Justice Mitchell then said that under the South Australian Crimes Act, she could impose only one sentence, for the boy to be detained at the Governor's pleasure. The judge refused an application by the Adelaide *Advertiser* to publish the boy's name.

There was a sad sequel to the case of poor Christopher Robin when, in 1979, his mother, Theresa Dato, armed herself with a knife and went to a reform home "to get the stinking animal who killed my son". Mrs Dato was disarmed, arrested and pleaded guilty in the Adelaide Magistrates' Court of carrying an offensive weapon. She was released on a $250, two-year good behaviour bond.

**

HANGED (1896): Charles Henry Strange was hanged at Melbourne Gaol on *January 13*, 1896, for using a tomahawk to kill Fred Cunningham in Gippsland. An epileptic, Strange was examined to determine his sanity before he was executed.

JANUARY 14

THE BOILED BODY (1926)

Old Bill Oliver was a well-known and well-loved character in outback New South Wales and, when he went missing in January, 1925, there were concerns for his safety. Police made a thorough search of the country near the tiny New South Wales hamlet of Wanaaring and, at an old camp site, came across human remains. The police found a human skull which had been bashed in and they were now convinced Old Bill had been murdered, even though the body was badly decomposed. In fact, the body was been boiled in an attempt to remove identifying features.

Meanwhile, one of Old Bill's cheques had been cashed at Wilcannia, while a man named Walter Harney tried to sell the old man's car. Harney went to trial on *January 14*, 1926, but the jury failed to agree and a new trial was ordered. Harney, a South African who had often been in trouble with the law and, at his retrial, was found guilty of murder. Judge Bevan told him: "If you have a spark of humanity in you, you must show remorse for your cold-blooded crime." He sentenced Harney to death and he was duly executed.

JANUARY 15

THE BABY FARMER (1894)

Frances Knorr, late in the Victorian era, ran a home for unwanted babies and preyed on unmarried mothers. Promising to look after the babies, Knorr quickly realised that it was possible to pocket the money without incurring an expense in feeding and clothing the unfortunate little victims. But, to ply this ghastly trade, she had to stay one step ahead of the law. She moved from her home in Moreland Road, Brunswick, but a new tenant started gardening and discovered the body of a baby which had been battered to death. The bodies of two other babies were discovered and Knorr was arrested in Sydney and sent to trial for murder.

Knorr, 26, and the mother of two children, insisted she knew nothing of the deaths of the three little innocents and claimed they had died of natural causes, but was found guilty and sentenced to death. She was hanged at the Old Melbourne jail on *January 15*, 1894, but not before confessing to killing the three babies. In admitting she had suffocated two and strangled the other, Knorr said she hoped her confession would be a "deterrent to those who perhaps are carrying on the same practice".

JANUARY 16

THE KILLING OF ALPHONSE GANGITANO (1998)

Alphonse Gangitano was a peacock who strutted Lygon Street, Melbourne's "Little Italy", as if he owned it. Always immaculately dressed, it was ironic that the good-looking Gangitano was shot dead at his Melbourne home in 1998 — wearing only underpants. Gangitano's apparent ambition from a very early age was to be a gangster, and, from his late teens to his death, he lived — and died — this dream.

The man who modelled himself on American gangsters — real and celluloid — was involved in a number of criminal activities, including illegal gambling and protection. Gangitano was also a heavy punter, although there were suggestions he lost more than he won, and he was said to have rubbed other criminals up the wrong way. He was the main suspect in a shooting at St Kilda, but police were unable to break the underworld's code of silence and Gangitano walked free. Police later charged Gangitano and fellow gangland identity Jason Moran with a number of offences, including assault charges over a violent incident in a King Street nightclub in which 13 people were injured.

On the evening of *January 16*, 1998, friend Graham Kinniburgh called in to see him at his home in Glen Orchard Close, Templestowe. Gangitano, in his underpants and not expecting visitors, sat where he could see the unlocked front door. An hour later, at about 11pm, another visitor called in to see Gangitano. Kinniburgh later told police he left Gangitano's house to buy cigarettes and, when he returned about 30 minutes later, the 40-year-old was dead, lying in a pool of blood in his laundry. Gangitano, whose body had been discovered by his wife, met his end after being shot several times.

While there was speculation that the assassination of Gangitano was the result of his involvement in a $200 million drug cartel, the identity of his second visitor that night has never been revealed. Gangitano was obsessed with home security, but a surveillance camera he had installed had been turned off before his murder, leading to strong rumours that his killer was someone he knew well. Police believe it was Moran, who was gunned down with associate Pasquale Barbaro at a junior football clinic in Pascoe Vale on *June 21*, 2003. But, officially at least, Gangitano's murder remains unsolved.

**

BLASTED (1964): Fruit and vegetable marketer Vincenzo Muratore was killed by a gunshot blast outside his home in the Melbourne bayside suburb of Hampton on *January 16*, 1964

JANUARY 17

THE OBSESSIVE LOVER (2002)

Craig Steve Rye, 41, was obsessed with former lover Sharon Judd, 39, and repeatedly asked her to return to him after she left him in December, 2001. Judd, the mother of two children, treated Rye like a friend, but had no intention of getting back with him. They had spent three years together after their respective marriages had broken up and Rye refused to accept the separation. On the afternoon of *January 17*, 2002, he visited her at her Melbourne home and suggested they have sex. When Judd refused, Rye contacted friends to say she was worried about her former boyfriend's behaviour.

Rye returned to Judd's home that evening and, after sexually assaulting her, strangled her and the set fire to the house. At his trial, Justice Teague told Rye: "You went to Sharon's home and she let you in. You attacked her sexually.

You inflicted upon her injuries that were found at the autopsy. At one stage, you penetrated her vagina with some object. Only you know what it was, but it was such as to cause a laceration to her vagina that was about 8cm long. You then strangled her."

After killing his former lover, Rye tried to cover his tracks by taking Judd's mobile telephone and new stereo and VCR before starting a fire disfiguring his victim's body. Justice Teague told Rye: "You resented her moving out. You pressed her to return and the pressure you applied was extreme. A Supreme Court of Victoria jury found Rye guilty of murder and the judge, in handing down his sentence, said that he accepted the killing was not premeditated and therefore told Rye he would impose a 20-year prison term, with a non-parole period of 15 years.

THE MOTHER MURDERER (2005)

Phillip Raymond Parkes, 49, bludgeoned his near-blind mother Grace, 83, to death as she watched television in the loungeroom of her home in Collaroy Plateau on Sydney's northern beaches on *January 17*, 2005. Parkes' explanation for the murder was that he was "driven crazy" by the level of care his mother required and couldn't handle the idea that he might become her full-time carer. He also claimed that voices in his head demanded he kill her.

The father-of-three, who had been a long-time user of cannabis and suffered personality disorders, had previously been convicted of committing armed robberies while disguised in womens' clothing and wielding an unloaded gun. He claimed he had resorted to crime to support his children, one of whom was disabled. Parkes and the first of his two wives had lived in a Hari Krishna community for a time, but the union ended when she left him for another member of the sect. He was sentenced to 18 years' jail.

JANUARY 18

GANG RAPE (1835)

Sophie Wordsworth, her husband and three acquaintances — William Woodhead, Peter Gordon and Robert Hutchins — had been drinking at a public house in Maitland on *January 18*, 1835, when they decided to leave at dusk. The Wordsworths suggested the three men join them for tea and, as they travelled through the bush, the husband was knocked to the ground. The three men grabbed his wife and took it in turns to have sex with her. She eventually broke free and, near naked, ran to her home, where she spent the next fortnight in bed. Woodhead, Gordon and Hutchins were charged with rape, a jury found them guilty and they were sentenced to death.

✸✸

THE DEATH OF JIMMY GOVERNOR (1901): Aboriginal bushranger Jimmy Governor was hanged on *January 18*, 1901, for the slaughter of women and children in country New South Wales. (Refer to *July 20*.)

✸✸

SHOT DEAD (1964): Fruiterer Antonio Monaco was shot dead outside his Braeside (south-east Melbourne) home on

January 18, 1964, just two days after the shotgun death of Vincenzo Muratore.

JANUARY 19

THE BREAK-IN KILLING (1903)

Publican Theodore Trautwein, who ran the Royal Hotel in the Sydney suburb of Auburn, was awakened on the night of *January 19*, 1903, by what he thought was a shot from a revolver. He went to investigate and found police officer Samuel Long, who had entered the hotel to investigate strange noises, lying in a pool of blood on the bar floor. Constable Long, about 35 years of age, had been shot and died shortly later. Six days later, police arrested a man who had a loaded revolver by his bedside table and, eventually, charged tearaways Henry Jones and Digby Grand with murder. Both men were found guilty, but the jury foreman recommended mercy as no one was sure who had pulled the trigger and the jury also thought a third man had been involved in the crime.

When Judge Rogers sentenced Jones and Grand to death and said "may the Lord have mercy on your soul", Grand replied: "And the same to you." The two convicted police killers were executed at Darlinghurst Gaol on *July 7*, 1903. The *Age* newspaper reported that Jones died instantly, but Grand "was less fortunate". The newspaper noted: "For over three minutes, he (Grand) struggled convulsively, and life was then apparently extinct. But a minute later his arms and shoulders could be seen working. These struggles continued for only a few seconds, however. 'He's gone,' said a warder to the newspaper reporters as the final tremor passed through the hanging body, and apparently that was the end.

'MONSTROUS' (2006)

Motivated by jealousy, Guy Russell Gidgup unlocked a door and entered the home of former lover Tracee Dufall in the early hours of *January 19*, 2006. Dufall was asleep in a bedroom with the couple's eight-year-old daughter but, on entering the room, Gidgup and Dufall became involved in a heated argument. Dufall fled from the house, but Gidgup dragged her by the hair back inside the house, where he shot her in the chest. This shot killed 39-year-old Dufall, but Gidgup then pumped three more bullets into her. Dufall's 16-year-old daughter Chanel then fled with her eight-year-old half-sister, only for Gidgup to fire at them. One bullet hit Chanel in the thigh and, while the eight-year-old ran to a neighbour's for shelter, Gidgup aimed at Chanel and shot her dead. Gidgup was sentenced to life imprisonment and Justice McKechnie, in the Supreme Court of Western Australia, told him: "Killing Chanel as her life was about to blossom (she was about to celebrate her 17th birthday) was simply monstrous."

JANUARY 20

CAPTAIN MOONLIGHT (1880)

The man who eventually became known as Captain Moonlight was born in northern Ireland in 1842 and arrived in Australia, via New Zealand, in 1868. Andrew George Scott soon found a position as a Church of England lay preacher and moved around Victoria. One of his positions was in the mining town of Mt Egerton and it was there that the manager, Ludwig Bruun, of the London Chartered Bank was held at gunpoint and robbed of the bank's holdings. Bruun was forced to face a wall as the thief wrote a note, which was signed Captain Moonlight. Bruun thought he recognised Scott's voice and the Irishman was arrested, only for Scott to turn the tables on the bank manager and have him charged, along with local schoolteacher James Simpson. Both men were acquitted, while Scott headed for Fiji.

Scott ran up debts in Fiji and fled to Sydney, where he was arrested for writing bad cheques. He was sentenced to a year's jail and, from there, his life spiralled downwards. Scott eventually was sentenced to 10 years' jail after the Mt Egerton robbery case was re-opened. On release, he and an accomplice robbed another bank and eventually was bailed up by police in New South Wales late in 1879. Scott and his accomplices eventually held 30 hostages and, in a gunfight, Senior Constable Edward Mostyn Webb-Bowen was critically wounded to the neck. Scott surrendered, but the police officer, who was taken by wagon to Gundagai, died of his wound. The Irishman was charged with murder and, along with accomplices Tom Williams, Tom Rogan and Graham Bennett, was sentenced to death. Williams and Bennett were reprieved on appeal, but Scott – aka Captain Moonlight – and Rogan were hanged on *January 20*, 1880.

THE ABORIGINAL REBEL (1791)

Aboriginal rebel Pemulwuy was a hero to his people in the earliest days of Australian settlement. Angry with what he believed to be the white man's breaking of traditional tribal laws, Pemulwuy gathered a following believed to number more than 100. Most were Aborigines, but his group also included a handful of escaped Irish convicts. Pemulwuy's first victim was Governor Arthur Phillips' game shooter, John McIntyre, courtesy of a deadly spear-throw. McIntyre survived for a time but collapsed and died suddenly on *January 20*, 1791. Phillips declared Pemulwuy an outlaw and offered a reward for his capture or killing.

Pemulwuy and his group retaliated by raiding farms, ruining crops and stealing food and clothing. They attacked various outposts and, in 1797, Pemulwuy led his men in a pitched battle against the English. Pemulwuy was hit by seven bullets but, incredibly, recovered from his wounds and escaped custody. His Aboriginal supporters claimed he had changed himself into a bird, and so a legend was born. Free again, Pemulwuy continued to harass the settlement until, in 1802, was shot dead by two bounty-hunters. He was decapitated and his head sent to England as a gift for botanist Joseph Banks.

**

HANGED (1842): Aborigines Bob and Jack were hanged in public at Melbourne Gaol on *January 20*, 1842, for the murder of two whalers at Port Fairy.

JANUARY 21

BODIES UNDER THE HOME (2003)

After 43-year-old Karen Kramer killed her parents on *January 21*, 2003, she hid their bodies under the family home at

Ingleburn, New South Wales. They remained there for 18 months and, after being discovered, Kramer told police: "I kept looking out the window waiting for you. I'm glad it's all over. Kramer, a schizophrenic, stabbed parents Tudor and Della Jones, both in their late 70s, after they had caught her stealing $100 from them to support a drinking habit. She kept their bodies in the house for two days, but then dragged them outside before hiding them under the house. Kramer sealed windows and airvents with silicone to prevent odours from the decomposition of the bodies. Justice Buddin, in sentencing Kramer to 21 and a half year's jail, with a non-parole period ending late in 2019, told her she was "a deeply troubled woman", but added that her chances of rehabilitation were good, as long as she abstained from alcohol.

JANUARY 22

THE TRURO KILLER (1977)

William Thomas was in a paddock near Truro, 80 kilometres from Adelaide, on *April 25*, 1978, when he found human bones which later were identified as those of 18-year-old Veronica Knight, who had last been seen on *December 23*, 1976. Then, a year later bushwalkers found a skeleton less than a kilometre from where Knight's remains were discovered. The remains were of another Truro victim, 16-year-old Sylvia Pittman and police, understandably, believed they had a serial killer to track down. Their worst fears were realised when the remains of 16-year-old Connie Iordanides and 26-year-old Vicki Howell were discovered.

Police then took a call from a woman who told them she had heard a man named James Miller saying that motor accident fatality Christopher Worrell had boasted about killing girls". Miller, a youth with a long list of offences, was arrested on *May 23*, 1979, and questioned about the human remains at Truro. He showed police where three other bodies — of Deborah Lamb, Tania Kennedy and Juliet Mykyta — had been dumped. Miller also told police of how the girls had been killed and, in one chilling account, told of the death of Myktya, just 16 years of age.

He told police how he and Worrell had offered her a lift outside an Adelaide hotel late on the evening of *January 21*, 1977, and drove her to a dark spot near the Port Wakefield Road. Miller, a homosexual, said he saw Worrell tie the girls hands together and, when she managed to get out of the car, his companion held her down and strangled her very early on the morning of *January 22*. Worrell, a 23-year-old convicted rapist, killed his final victim, Lamb, on *February 12*, but died a week later in a car crash. Miller was charged on seven counts of murder, pleaded not guilty, but was found guilty on six of the charges. He was sentenced to life imprisonment and is not eligible for release until 2014.

JANUARY 23

THE HAUNTED HOTEL (1939)

The derelict Windsor Hotel in the old gold-mining town of Dunolly in central Victoria was the near-perfect "doss" house. Its walls might have been cracked, its timber flooring might have been uprooted in places and many of its windows broken, but it was home to a colony of tramps. In October, 1938, at least five men were living there, despite the lack of running water or anything resembling comforts. It was little more than a roof over the head and some Dunolly residents claimed the hotel, which was de-licensed in 1914, was haunted.

Those living at the derelict hotel included pensioners Frederick Douglas, Charles Bunney and Robert Gray, along with a younger man, Thomas Johnson. On Monday, *October 3*, 1938, 61-year-old Bunney (a World War I veteran) and 73-year-old Gray were seen alive for the last time. The following day, Douglas suggested to Johnson that "something has happened" to Bunney. They later made a search for him and found a trail of blood on a landing outside one of the rooms. However, the door to the room was padlocked so, in a state of near panic, Douglas ran to a young local to ask him to climb a wall to peep through the room's window.

The young man climbed up to the window and, peering through the dust and gloom, was able to see what appeared to be two men lying on the floor. He yelled to the men in the room. But there was not the slightest movement from them. Police were called immediately and when the door was broken down, found the bodies of Bunney and Gray. Both men had been bludgeoned to death with an axe, which was still in the corner of the room. The wounds were horrific, with both men having their skulls split wide open.

Police soon deduced that Bunney had been killed on the landing and had been dragged into the room where it was discovered. Bunney had taken one savage blow to the head and police found his bloodstained felt hat on the landing. He obviously had been wearing the hat when attacked as it had a long gash across its crown. Gray was killed in the room and had taken two heavy blows to the head. The axe, covered in blood, was the most obvious clue and suspicion fell first on its owner, fellow squatter Lancelot Cazneau. However, Cazneau told police he had lent the axe to Johnson and, further, that Johnson had tried to borrow money from several of the men. Suspicion therefore fell on Johnson, who had disappeared.

Police immediately launched a manhunt for Johnson, but were still in the process of distributing a description of him when he walked into a police station at Dandenong, on the other side of Melbourne, and confessed. He told police that he was asleep at the old hotel when Gray woke him by hammering at some floorboards. Johnson said he picked up the axe and smashed the old man over the head. Bunney, who went to investigate, copped the same vicious treatment.

Johnson, 40, stood trial at Ballarat before Justice Lowe and jury, and the court was packed as Johnson, wearing a dark brown suit, was led to the dock. Johnson's only explanation for attacking his fellow residents was that he had lost his temper, killed Gray and then attacked Bunney, who had witnessed Gray's killing. The jury found Johnson guilty of murder and he was sentenced to death. Although the case provoked considerable public debate and the Victorian government was urged to have Johnson undergo psychiatric examination in an effort to have the sentence commuted to one of life imprisonment, he was hanged at Pentridge early on the morning of *January 23*, 1939.

JANUARY 24

EXECUTED (1916)

John Jackson was hanged on *January 24*, 1916, for his role in the murder of Constable David McGrath at Melbourne's Trades Hall. Jackson, with two other men, Richard Buckley and Alexander Ward, broke into Trades Halls to rob a safe, but police were called and several shots were fired. Jackson was sentenced to death, while Buckley was sentenced to seven years' jail and Ward six years. Jackson wrongfully believed he would be given a last-minute reprieve.

JANUARY 25

THE BLACK NAPOLEON (1825)

Aboriginal bushranger Musquito, known as "The Black Napoleon" was transported from the mainland of Australia to Van Diemen's Land for the murder of his "lubra", or tribal wife. Then, with a band of other disgruntled Aborigines known as the Tame Mob, he embarked on a brief reign of terror. The gang attacked homesteads and rustled cattle before killing several stockmen at Grindstone Bay in 1823. The colony's Lieutenant Governor sent black trackers in pursuit of the gang and the men eventually were captured. Musquito was shot in the thigh and then was hanged at Hobart on *January 25*, 1825. He was reported to have said on his scaffold: "Hanging no good for black fella. All right for white fella, they used to it."

THE SHAMELESS KILLER (1830)

At around midday on *January 25*, 1830, a man named Michael Best was seen on the property of gentleman farmer Richard Garner at Lower Clyde, Tasmania. One of Garner's servant's Samuel Lee approached Best and was struck on the face and told that he would "serve me as he had served my master". Lee and another man then entered their master's house and found Garner dead, with blood under his right ear. When asked if he had anything to do with Garner's death, Best replied: "I am not ashamed of it." Garner had been stabbed three times in the neck and four times to the chest with a butcher's knife, with a surgeon later declaring that one of the slashes to the neck had proved fatal.

Another servant, William Smith, told the court at Best's trial that he had seen Best, wearing only boots, at the back of a hut. Best ran about 100 yards away, but Smith told him if he didn't stop he would shoot him. Best returned and was apprehended with the help of two constables. He also told the court that Best's hands were wet, as if he had been washing himself. Garner had accused Best of stealing sheep and this obviously was the motive for the frenzied attack on the 30-year-old gentleman farmer. Although evidence was given at Best's trial that he might have been insane, a jury took just 10 minutes to find him guilty of Garner's murder. Best was hanged at Hobart, on *February 11*, little more than a fortnight after he had killed Garner.

JANUARY 26

THE BEAUMONT CHILDREN (1966)

Australia Day, *January 26*, broke hot and dry in Adelaide in 1966 and the three children of Jim and Nancy Beaumont were allowed to go to the beach at Glenelg, not far from their suburban home of Somerton Park. The eldest Beaumont child was Jane and although only a shy nine-year-old, she was thought responsible enough to look after herself, seven-year-old sister Arnna and four-year-old brother Grant. The Beaumont children left home at 10.30 in the morning and took a five-minute bus ride to Glenelg. They were expected to return home by noon but, by 3.30pm, their mother was worried.

Police launched a search for the children and were told the Beaumonts had been seen in the company of a tall, blond man in his mid-30s. To worry police even further, a shopkeeper reported that Jane Beaumont had bought cake and a meat pie with a one-pound note, even though her mother had given her only coins for the bus fares and food. One witness, a postman the children knew, had seen the children walking towards home at about three o'clock. The children were never seen again and their disappearance remains a mystery. Public interest in the Beaumont children was phenomenal and all sorts of theories were put forward for their disappearance.

A clairvoyant, Gerard Croiset, was even brought out from Holland and, after examining areas where the children might have been taken, pointed out a site where he believed the Beaumonts had been buried. However, it was a building site and the owners were reluctant to allow excavation until public pressure forced their hand. The search proved fruitless, as have many other leads provided to police over almost 40 years. Many theories have been put forward and every suggestion creates headlines, but there has been no proof of where the Beaumont children might be or whether they are still alive.

✻✻

A POLICE KILLING (1865): Bushranger Johnny Dunn shot Constable Nelson dead at Collector, NSW, on **January 26,** 1865.

JANUARY 27

LONELY LEO'S FATAL FAVOUR (2004)

When lonely Leo Filippone opened his home to a friend in need, the last thing he expected was for the beneficiary of his generosity to become his murderer. A legally-blind father of a severely disabled boy who lived with his former partner, Filippone lived by himself and generally kept to himself. One of his few so-called friends was Mark Andrew Kuster, who provided some home handywork in return for advice on investment and property. It seemed a good arrangement – initially at least.

When Kuster's hot water unit broke down, Filippone was only too happy to let him, along with his defacto wife, Christina Krajina, and their seven-year-old son, Shayne, stay at his home in Newborough (near Moe, Victoria) for a few days until the problem was fixed. Kuster, 36, and Ms Krajina, a 38-year-old schizophrenic, had a fiery relationship and their short stay with Filippone was apparently true to form. After five days – on *January 27*, 2004 – Ms Krajina drove back to Melbourne with their son to resume work.

That night, seemingly inexplicably no motive was established, Kuster, a large man, viciously attacked his smaller, harmless 'mate', inflicting multiple stab wounds and bashing him repeatedly about the head with a heavy object, resulting in fatal injuries. The next night, Kuster set fire to Filippone,s house in an attempt to make his good Samaritan's death appear accidental. However, the autopsy on Filippone's extensively burnt corpse revealed the truth. Kuster, who was previously convicted for committing an indecent act on a three-year-old girl, was sentenced to 25 years' jail, with a minimum non-parole period of 17 years and six months.

THE BUNGLED HANGING (1847)

After Jeremiah Connell had been found guilty of the murder of Edward Martin at Buningyoong, Victoria, he was sentenced to death by hanging. On *January 27*, 1847, he was led on to the scaffold at Melbourne Gaol and proclaimed that he never intended killing Martin and that he begged God's mercy. The hangman pulled the bolt, the trapdoor opened, but Connell's body swayed and swayed and swayed. Connell struggled for life to the last and he dangled for 10 minutes before eventually succumbing to the rope. It later was dicovered that a priest had wrapped rosary beads around Connell's throat before the drop and this hampered a quick execution.

JANUARY 28

THE POISONOUS WIFE (1887)

Louisa and Charles Andrews lived with their seven children on Botany Bay at a desolate place named Fog Hollow. Louisa, 20 years younger than her husband, was a regular at the local pub and eventually had an affair with young labourer Michael Collins. Louisa Andrews fell in love with the younger man and wanted to marry him. She therefore set a plan into action, insuring her husband's life and collecting 200 pounds on the policy soon after he died of "acute gastritis" on *January 28*, 1887. Just three months later she married Collins and, seven months after the wedding, she bore him a son. However, the baby died at five months of age, with Collins to die in agony soon after.

This time there was suspicion, after a glass containing elements of arsenic was found in her kitchen, Louisa was arrested. Her first husband's body was exhumed, along with that of her dead infant, and traces of arsenic were found in both bodies. Louisa Collins faced trial, not once, but four times for murder. The first three juries could not reach a verdict, but the fourth found her guilty. Louisa Collins was hanged at Darlinghurst jail in January, 1889, and went to her death "as if she were performing an everyday function". The media of the day had focused enormous attention in the Collins case, but there was little sympathy for the poisonous wife.

THE SISTERS KILLINGS (2006)

When West Australian police officer Acting Sergeant Shane Gray pulled over a motor vehicle on a highway south of Karratha, in WA's remote Pilbara, he had no idea of what was to follow. The man driving the car had driven away from a service station without paying for fuel and when Sergeant Gray intercepted the Victorian registered car, an altercation erupted. The police officer, who had his nose broken, fired two shots and unwittingly ended a massive manhunt. The man driving the Victorian car was William John Watkins, 38, wanted in Melbourne for the stabbing deaths of sisters Colleen and Laura Irwin.

Colleen, 23, and Laura, 21, were murdered in their home in the western suburb of Altona North on *January 27*, 2006, and their bodies found the next day, *January 28*. One of the sisters tried to call 000 before dying, but the call lasted just five seconds. Her throat had been cut and it would have been impossible for her to be able to speak. Victoria Police issued a state-wide alert for the main suspect, a convicted rapist who had lived in the same street and was now missing. Watkins was on the run and headed west, not knowing that he would be run down and then killed.

The girls' father was furious that the convicted rapist was free to kill. Allen Irwin said: "All these clowns should have tattoos on their forehead for whatever they do. I'm talking about a cattle-brand tattoo." An uncle of the murdered girls, Hugh McGowan, called for mandatory minimum sentences for repeat violent offenders. He said the justice system had robbed his nieces of their lives and added: "He (Watkins) was a habitual criminal whose crimes got worse as he got older. He was clearly beyond rehabilitation yet was allowed to walk the streets because the judiciary either did not understand what kind of person he was, or misjudged what he was, or worse still, empathised with him because he showed no remorse."

JANUARY 29

HANGED (1918)

Convicted murderer Albert Edward Budd was hanged in Melbourne on *January 29*, 1918. He had been convicted of the murder of his foster sister, Annie Samson, at Port Melbourne on *October 19*, 1917.

JANUARY 30

COP KILLER? (1952)

The question mark in the title of this section of the book refers to the insistence by the man convicted of killing Constable Georhe Howell in the southern Melbourne suburb of Caulfield on *January 30*, 1952, that he was innocent and was not even at the scene of the crime. William John O'Meally, who always has claimed he was with his wife at the time of the killing, almost hanged for Constable Howell's death. The police officer was shot dead when he went to investigate someone tampering with a car near the Crystal Palace Theatre and died two days later. Howell, before he died, was able to give police a description of the man who had shot him and heard him use the word "walloper", an old-fashioned term for a policeman.

O'Meally was known to have used this expression and was arrested on little more than circumstantial evidence. He was found guilty of murder and sentenced to death. What's more, his papers were marked "never to be released". Regardless, he was released on *July 4*, 1979, after more than 27 years in jail and was the longest-serving prisoner in Victorian history. His years in jail were truly eventful as he escaped from Pentridge in 1955 and again two years later when a prison guard was shot in the leg by O'Meally's fellow escapee, Robert Henry Taylor. He then gained notoriety as the last man legally flogged in Victoria and spent more than a decade in solitary confinement. O'Meally was known as "the man they couldn't break". On release, O'Meally continued to protest his innocence over the death of Constable Howell and claimed that although four men were at the scene of the crime, he wasn't one of them.

JANUARY 31

BODY FOUND (1998)

The body of 16-year-old Heather Turner was found in a creek in Port Gawler, northern Adelaide, on *January 31*, 1998, and her murder remains a mystery. It is believed she spent the previous few days with a group of young Caucasians and Aborigines.

FEBRUARY

February can be Australia's hottest month and this applies to crime as well as climatic conditions. Australia is back at work after the summer holidays and newspapers are full of headlines about stabbings, slayings, court cases and executions. Crimes this month include:

THE RONALD RYAN HANGING.

THE PAEDOPHILE PRIEST

THE AXE MURDERER

THE LAST WOMAN HANGED

THE BRISBANE "RIPPER"

THE HEADLESS BODY

And much, much more.

FEBRUARY 1

THE HOARY-HEADED MONSTER (1841)

Elderly ex-convict George Saunders, a man with a long list of convictions, faced the Supreme Court of NSW on *February 1*, 1841, for allegedly violating a seven-year-old girl near Kiama the previous December. He was found not guilty of this charge, but was found guilty of a secondary charge of assault with intent to rape. He was sentenced to work, in leg irons, on the colony's roads for two years. Meanwhile, a 28th Regiment bandsman two weeks later was found guilty of a similar offence and was sentenced to two years' hard labour in Newcastle Gaol, with one week in each month to be spent in solitary confinement. A third man, John O'Heife, also was found guilty that day of assault with intent and Chief Justice Dowling told him: "You, a hoary-headed monster, for that is the proper term for you, with one foot in the grave, have dared, at your advanced years, to do your utmost to violate a young and innocent human being." He sentenced O'Heife to working on the road, in irons, for three years.

FEBRUARY 2

THE HOTEL SHOOTING (2002)

Vietnamese migrant Phuoc Giau Nguyen and two friends were at the Pavilion Hotel, in George St, Sydney, in the early hours of *February 2*, 2002, when they came across two other men, Khahn Thanh Nguyen and Tri Bihn Tran. At one stage someone flicked a cigarette butt at Tran, sparking an argument. Phuoc Giau Nguyen produced a handgun from his clothing and shot Khahn Thanh Nguyen twice, in the stomach and the lower back, before firing three shots into Tran, hitting him in the right shoulder, left hip and left thigh. The gunman fled, leaving Khahn mortally wounded.

An arrest was made seven weeks later, on *March 20*, but the accused man declined to be interviewed and then did not give evidence at his trial. The 24-year-old Phuoc Giau Nguyen, who had migrated to Australia with his mother and four siblings after completing his primary schooling in Vietnam, was sentenced to 12 years' jail for the wounding of Tran and 20 years for killing Khan Thanh Nguyen, with a non-parole period of 14 and a half years. The aggregate sentence imposed by Justice Hidden was 22 years, with a non-parole period of 16 and a half years. Phuoc Giau Nguyen will be eligible for parole in 2018.

**

AUSTRALIA'S WORST CRIME (1986)

Attractive nurse Anita Cobby, 26, was walking home from Blacktown train station at about 10pm on *February 2*, 1986, when she was abducted at knifepoint by a carload of five men. The one-time entrant in the Miss Australia quest, who stood only 175cms tall and was of a light build, was viciously and repeatedly beaten and gang-raped in the car, which travelled around Sydney's outer western suburbs. Ms Cobby was taken to an isolated back road and dragged through a barbed wire fence where the assaults continued.

The leader of the gang, mentally-disturbed teenage delinquent John Travers, enjoyed his reputation as a rapist among his mates. He was known, as a party trick, to have sex with a sheep and simultaneously slash its throat. He was also a "poofter-basher" who, despite reacting violently to suggestions he was gay, even raped a 17-year-old homosexual boy in front of his own mates. Travers had a teardrop tattooed under one of his eyes, but he was devoid of emotion. When finally tired of brutalising Ms Cobby, he matter-of-factly slit her throat and almost severed her head in the process.

Travers and his four associates – Michael Murdoch, and the Murphy brothers, Michael, Les and Gary – are serving life sentences in jail, their files marked: 'never to be released'.

FEBRUARY 3

RONALD RYAN'S EXECUTION (1967)

There have been few manhunts of such magnitude in Australian criminal history as the one that tracked down Pentridge escapees Ronald Ryan and Peter Walker over 17 days from *December 19*, 1965. The shooting and killing of prison guard George Hodson outraged Victorians and the media went into a frenzy over the chase for Australia's most wanted criminals. The case forever will hold a place in infamy as Ryan eventually was found guilty of the murder of Hodson and became the last man hanged in Australia. The execution was seen by hundreds of thousands of Australians as an outrage and by many close to the case as a travesty of justice and even a political exercise.

Ronald Joseph Ryan was born in Melbourne on *February 21*, 1925, into a working class family. He had three sisters — Violet, Irma and Gloria — and a half-brother, George Thompson (by his mother Cecilia's first husband). Father Jack

Ryan could not always find work and life was tough for the family. So much so that Cecilia Ryan could not cope and the Ryan children were put into homes, Ronald to the Salesian order's monastery at Sunbury and the girls to a convent in the inner Melbourne suburb of Abbotsford. Ryan apparently was a good student, but ran away from the orphanage when he was just 14 years of age and headed north where he found work as a rail-cutter and general hand. He worked hard and long and, in 1943, returned to Melbourne. By now he was 18 years of age and had money in his pockets.

Ryan took his sisters from the convent and, reunited with his mother, he became the family breadwinner. He led a steady life for several years and, in 1948, married Dorothy George and settled down to raise a family — daughters Janice, Wendy and Rhonda. However, rail-splitting and timber-cutting did not enable Ryan to earn enough money to provide for his family as well as he would have wished and he finally attracted police attention when he passed forged cheques. Ryan was 31 years of age when he was given a bond for these offences but, not long after, he again was caught passing bad cheques. Convicted, he as given a five-year bond and he again seemed to settle down.

However, Ryan three years later was arrested for theft but escaped from custody at the Melbourne City Watch House. Recaptured, he was sent to prison and, instead of settling down on release, drifted back to a life of crime and in 1964 was sent to Pentridge after a brief career as a safe-cracker. Dorothy Ryan divorced her husband and re-married, but Ryan refused to concede that he had lost his family and set about planning to escape from Pentridge.

After studying the sentry catwalks and measuring the thickness of the prison walls, Ryan decided that Sunday,

December 19, 1965, provided him with the perfect opportunity to escape. Ryan informed fellow prisoner Peter Walker of his plans and the 24-year-old agreed to join him in his bid for freedom. That Sunday was selected because it was the day of the prison guards' Christmas party and the pair knew there was a skeleton staff on duty. Ryan gave Walker the go-ahead early in the afternoon and they scaled a wall to reach a catwalk. Ryan, with a piece of water pipe as a weapon and Walker behind him, came across prison guard Helmut Lange and grabbed an M1 rifle from a rack. Lange, with the rifle pointed at him, opened a door to the outside while Ryan ejected a live round. Ryan demanded car keys from a passer-by and, when these weren't handed over, knocked the man down.

The alarm by now had been raised and Ryan and Walker ran into busy Sydney Road, Coburg. Ryan tried to hijack a passing car, but noticed that Walker was just about to be nabbed by guard Hodson. A shot rang out and Hodson fell dead on the tram tracks, while the escapees jumped into a car and fled from the scene. Melbourne was abuzz with the escape and killing and, as police scoured the city, Ryan and Walker holed up in the house of a sympathiser in the seaside suburb of Elwood. Emboldened by their escape and desperately needing funds, they then held up a bank in the southern suburb of Ormond. By now, the media was in a frenzy and headlines blared every police comment or reported sighting of the outlaws.

In fact, Ryan's mother at one stage appeared on television with an an appeal for her son to give himself up. Just five days after their escape, on *December 24*, their female sympathiser went to a party and brought home a companion, James Henderson. On meeting Ryan, the young man made the biggest mistake of his life in telling Walker that his companion looked like the escaped criminal Ronald Ryan. Walker shot Henderson dead in a public toilet in Albert Park and he and Ryan were forced to go on the run.

They travelled to Sydney and moved into a flat in the seaside suburb of Coogee. However, Walker could not resist the opposite sex and, after making arrangements for a date, he and Ryan were caught in a police trap after 17 days on the run. The pair were extradited to Melbourne and their trial opened on *March 15*, 1966, before Justice Starke. The prosecution case relied on numerous eye-witnesses, whereas defence counsel Philip Opas QC was able to point to numerous instances of conflicting evidence. For example, Opas used a leading mathematician to demonstrate that the shot which killed Hodson could not have been fired from ground level. Also, no fired bullet was ever found and, in fact, only one round was unaccounted for, yet Ryan had ejected that round. It begged the question of whether another weapon had been involved.

Opas argued that Hodson's wound was caused by a shot from the prison guard tower. Years later, in 1986 and well after Ryan's execution, a prison guard came forward to say that he might have accidentally fired the shot that killed Hodson and feared to say anything at the time in case he got into trouble. He also was convinced Ryan would never be hanged and that the death sentence would be commuted to life imprisonment.

Ryan denied he had killed Hodson and, despite fierce cross-examination, did not deviate from his account of what had happened, and there were many who believed he would be given the benefit of the doubt. However, the 12-man jury returned a "guilty" verdict and Justice Starke had no option but to pronounce the mandatory death sentence. Walker was sentenced to 12 years' imprisonment for manslaughter, with another 12 years for the killing of Henderson. He was released in 1983. However, no one — least of all some of the jurors — expected the death sentence to be carried out. After all, there had been 36 reprieves since the previous execution in 1951. An appeal to the Victorian Court of Criminal Appeal was dismissed and Victorian Premier Sir Henry Bolte announced that Ryan, indeed, would hang. At one stage Bolte, whose government was facing re-election, said: "There is no possibility of the decision to hang Ryan being reversed. It is quite definite and final." He was determined to make his point on law and order.

The Bolte government announced that the execution would take place on *January 9*, 1967, but this was rescheduled after an appeal to the Privy Council in London. This appeal also failed and a new election date was set, for *February 3*, 1967. At 10 o'clock the night before the scheduled execution, a special meeting of the State Executive Council rejected Ryan's last minute appeal for mercy. Ryan's solicitor, Mr Ralph Freadman, said: "We have just received a message from the Crown Solicitor, Mr Mornane, that the Queen, acting through the Governor-in-Council, has rejected the petition to exercise mercy. And that's the end of it."

Ryan wrote letters to his family on prison toilet paper and said: "With regard to my guilt I say only that I am innocent of intent and have a clear conscience on this matter." The day of the execution broke with the promise of heat as more that 3000 protestors, including Ryan's mother, stood outside Pentridge as Ryan was hanged at 8am. His last words to the hangman were: "God bless you, please make it quick." At the same time, Ryan's mother told television journalist Dan Webb: "He's a good boy, really." The remains of Ronald

Joseph Ryan were buried in quicksand within the grounds of Pentridge.

**

REPULSED BY HIS OWN PAST (2005)

Gregory Robert Webb's life was in a downward spiral. Although the 23-year-old from Melbourne had held a succession of jobs, he had a drug problem, was often unemployed and homeless, and had regularly been in trouble with the law.

Webb was so desperate to support his drug habit that he agreed to a homosexual relationship with 43-year-old Jason Michael King, whom he allowed to perform oral sex on him in exchange for money. However, the arrangement ended about 16 months later when Webb discovered King had video recorded some of their sexual encounters.

Webb appeared to clean up his act after being employed as a builder's labourer in a home renovation business run by a husband and wife team he looked up to.

But Webb had become increasingly repulsed and ashamed at the fact he had engaged in sexual acts with another man. He was also furious that King had recorded what were supposed to be secret liaisons.

On *February 3*, 2005, just four days after turning 25, Webb made the fateful decision to confront King.

After work, Webb consumed a few alcoholic drinks before driving to King's unit, where he drank more alcohol as they watched pornographic videos together. Webb led King to believe they could resume sexual relations and as King knelt before him, Webb started strangling him. In the struggle,

King pleaded with Webb to spare his life, but Webb strangled King for about 15 minutes – including about five minutes after King had stopped struggling, to ensure he was dead.

Webb dumped King's naked body in a roadside ditch before stealing some of his possessions, including CDs, a mobile phone, a video recorder and a DVD player he later pawned.

After his arrest, Webb made a full confession and expressed remorse for his actions. He was jailed for 15 years, with a minimum of 11 years.

**

JAIL RIOT (1974): Ten prisoners were shot and buildings burnt to the ground during 10 hours of rioting at Bathurst jail on *February 3*, 1974.

**

SENTENCED (1853): Bushranger Captain Melville was sentenced on *February 3*, 1853, to 32 years' jail for robbery under arms.

FEBRUARY 4

THE FRENCH GUNMAN (1903)

A group of French men and women descended on a vineyard at Guilford, Western Australia, on *February 4*, 1903, and at least one of them used a revolver for target practice before approaching Charles Lauffer about the purchase of some wine. Lauffer refused and an argument broke out, with the French party breaking through a fence and attacking the vintner. They used sticks and stones in the attack but one of the men, Fredrick Maillat, told them the stones they were throwing were not big enough. He then went up to Lauffer and shot him dead. Lauffer fell dead and his body rolled down a hill. The killing seemed senseless, as there were at least two witnesses other than members of the French party. Tricenne Lauffer said Maillat shot her husband, as did vineyard labourer Francseco Rocchiccioli.

Maillat was charged with murder, was found guilty and executed at Fremantle Gaol on *April 21*, 1903. Maillat, 24, landed in Australia in 1898 as a deserter from a French barque and worked as a fisherman and general hand. While awaiting trial, he tried to marry Frenchwoman Marie Renaud, but permission was refused. However, Renaud was given her lover's body after he had been executed and organised his funeral. Before his death, Maillat gave Renaud some small items of jewellery and instructions not to tell his mother in France of the circumstances of his death.

THE PAEDOPHILE PRIEST (1993)

Gerald Francis Ridsdale's conduct as a parish priest was nothing short of despicable. The skin-crawling Ridsdale used his position of trust in the Catholic Church to sexually abuse countless numbers of defenceless boys in Victoria's western district between 1970 and 1987. Ridsdale committed the vile crimes — numerous counts of indecent assault, gross indecency and buggery — mainly on altar boys, some as young as six, when he was parish priest in Warrnambool, Ballarat, Bacchus Marsh, Apollo Bay, Inglewood, Edenhope, Mortlake and Horsham.

Ridsdale often gained the trust of parents and then abused their children in confessionals, presbyteries and in his car, and these offences took place before and after Mass, Holy Communions, weddings and funerals. The abominable clergyman even abused children in his own family.

As a result of Ridsdale's depravity, his victims suffered a range of problems, including mental and marriage breakdowns, depression and drug abuse, leading to suicide attempts and possible suicides. Ridsdale, who was diagnosed with significant psycho-sexual dysfunction, warned his victims not to tell anyone about their "secret". He once threatened an 11-year-old boy that he wouldn't become an altar boy unless he did as he was told.

For almost two decades Ridsdale acted with virtual impunity under the cloak of the Catholic Church, which shuffled him around the countryside as allegations about his appalling conduct surfaced. Only too aware of Ridsdale's perversions, the church sent him to the United States in 1990 for a nine-month break and treatment at a home for sex offenders. On *February 4*, 1993, Ridsdale, then 59, was charged with numerous counts of paedophilia and was later sentenced to 18 years' jail, with a non-parole period of 15 years.

In 2006, after serving 12 years of his original jail term, he pleaded guilty to new child sex charges and received a new jail term of 13 years, with a minimum of seven years. On handing down the sentence on *August 11*, 2006, Justice Bill White said Ridsdale had betrayed and capitalised on the "blind trust" of Catholic families to perpetrate his "degrading conduct".

"Having regard to your position of trust, the attitude of Catholic families at the time of placing priests on a pedestal, the power you were able to exercise over those families and children, and your vocation as a priest, there is no doubt your conduct plummets to the depths of evil hypocricy," Justice White told him. "Your conduct has given rise to disastrous, catastrophic and, at times, tragic results."

Justice White also criticised the Catholic Church for its handling of such serious allegatiuons against one of its own. "The Catholic Church cannot escape criticism … of its lack of action on complaints being made as to your conduct, the constant moving of you from parish to parish, providing more opportunities for your predatory conduct, and its failure to show adequate compassion for a number of your victims," he said.

While Ridsdale stood motionless, and emotionless, in the dock, a victim screamed: "You could have said 'sorry' you bastard!" Outside the court, another victim summed up the feelings of anguish when he said: "What Ridsdale did to me and what he did to many other children is a crime worse than murder." Ridsdale will be eligible for parole in August, 2013, when he will be 79 years of age.

FEBRUARY 5

NOT A BLOODY WORD (1833)

John Butcher, holder of a ticket-of-leave, was cleaning wheat at the Upper Minto property of Murdoch Campbell around dusk on *January 15*, 1833, when he heard a commotion and someone yell out "stop thief". He saw Campbell's servant hand him a blunderbuss and then watched as his boss confronted a man who was trespassing on his land. When Campbell lowered his weapon, the man shot him dead.

Butcher told the Supreme Court of New South Wales: "Mr Campbell never stirred after; he was wounded in the head just above the left eye; the blood flowed freely and he was quite dead." Butcher bravely confronted the trespasser, who pulled out two pistols before another of Campbell's workers fired two shots.

The killer fled, but Butcher spotted him two days later at Liverpool and constables arrested James Lockhard, who was wanted for bushranging. A witness, Thomas Eccles, told the court the man known as Lockhard had dropped a bundle after the slaying of Campbell; it contained two small loaves of bread, the skirts of a coat and a small amount of sugar. Lockhard, who earlier had robbed a man of one pound, nineteen shillings and sixpence, had nothing to say in defence of the murder of Campbell.

Meanwhile, Dr William Kenney told the court: "I was on the spot shortly after Mr Campbell was shot … he was quite dead, a large gunshot wound had been inflicted in the head, over the left eye, that was the cause of death. It was a wound of great depth; I think there must have been more than one shot, or the musket was of a large calibre. The wound had penetrated the brain and would cause instant death." Lockhard was found guilty of murder and was executed on *February 5*, 1833. The trial had been held on the Friday and the hanging took place the following Monday. This was customary at that time to give the condemned a Sabbath in preparation for death. Under the 1752 statute, An Act for Better Preventing the Horrid Crime of Murder, judges were empowered to order that a murderer's body be hanged in chains. Otherwise, the Act required that the body be dissected by surgeons before burial.

THE AXE MURDERER (1838)

Station overseer John Nagle, who was known as a troublemaker, would tease dairyman Bryan Flannigan that he would "have" his garden, ducks and fowls. Flannigan must have taken this to heart as, on the morning of *February 5*, 1838, he walked into a hut near Mudgee and told a man named John Sheering: "I have put an end to all three", at a hut across the Mudgee River. Flannigan then produced a pair of blood-stained trousers, so Sheering and a shepherd named Martin went to the hut across the river and came across the gruesome sight of three people who had been savaged by an axe. The dead were Nagle and his wife, and a man named Riley.

Flannigan seemed to rejoice in what had happened and said he "had put three bad members away". Surgeon Mr F. Hawthorn told the Supreme Court of New South Wales: "I saw the bodies of Nagle and his wife, and Riley. Nagle's body had five or six wounds on it; the top of the head was almost cut off; the left hand was severed at the wrist joint almost completely; there was a deep wound about five inches in length on the shoulder and a wound on the right side of the thigh near the knee; the wound on the head was sufficient to cause death; a large portion of the brain had fallen out; they (the wounds) must have been inflicted with a heavy sharp instrument. Nagle's wife and Riley had apparently been killed by the same means; the woman was pregnant, and there was a slight degree of warmth at the abdomen; I should think she had advanced to the seventh month of pregnancy. Riley had one very extensive would in the head, so large that I could put my hand in it; the skull was laid completely open; all the bodies were undressed as if they had been in bed."

Police could not find the murder weapon, despite a two-day search, including aborigines diving into the Mudgee River. Although Flannigan seemed pleased with himself when the bodies were discovered, he later denied all knowledge of the crime and pleaded not guilty. However, he was found guilty of the murder of Nagle and sentenced to death.

THE ICE-CREAM WAR (2002)

Widow Laura Giunta wept as she told the Supreme Court of Victoria in 2004 of the death of her 26-year-old husband two years earlier. She told the court that she awoke in her Williamstown (bayside Melbourne) home on *February 5*, 2002, on hearing her husband, Dennis Timothy Giunta, screaming. She saw a masked man with a sword attacking her husband, who was trying to protect himself. "He was screaming and I was screaming — there was blood everywhere," Mrs Giunta told the court. Afraid for her life and on her husband's insistence, she raced to a first-floor balcony and jumped onto the house's garage roof. The impact broke her leg, but she bravely dragged herself to a neighbour's house to raise the alarm.

Dennis Giunta was stabbed 55 times in the frenzied attack and died of his wounds. His cousin, Franceso Mangione, was charged with his murder and the court was told there was bad blood between the two over territory for selling ice-cream from vans. The Crown suggested Magione had "developed and nurtured an intense hatred" for Giunta, but pleaded not guilty at his trial. However, DNA blood samples from a glove at the scene matched Mangione's DNA. Also, police found a home-made sword near the scene of the murder. Mangione was found guilty of murder and Justice Harper described the crime as a "cold-blooded, planned assassination". He sentenced Mangione, 47, to 22 years' jail, with a non-parole period of 18 years.

FEBRUARY 6

THE TAXI MURDER MYSTERY (1943)

Francis John Phelan was a driver with Red Top taxis and knew the ropes well. In fact, it was rumoured that Phelan had contacts in the black market and sly-grog rackets. Phelan, a former wharf labourer, was 32 and married with four children when he went on duty on *February 6*, 1943.

He seemed to be doing well early that evening and had been seen driving two American serviceman and at least one woman at about 8.30pm. Phelan's cab later was seen in St Edmund's Road, Prahran, an inner Melbourne suburb. The cab was stationary when shots were fired, with local residents reporting "loud bangs". The taxi sped off but stopped in Izett Street, Prahran, where Phelan's body was dumped. The car then stopped at the corner of Commercial and Punt Roads, a distance of about half a mile. The cab then was abandoned and a solid man was seen getting out.

Phelan had been shot three times from behind. One shot went through his left shoulder, while the other two shots went through his chest, one passing through his heart. A newspaper report said: "Phelan's body was first seen at 9.30pm by a passer-by who told Prahran police that a drunken man was lying in the street. When two constables went to Izett Street they lifted the body and found Phelan's clothing saturated with blood and the corpse still warm. There was no sign of a struggle and nothing to indicate that Phelan had been shot where his body was found."

Police found empty shells on the front floor of the cab and were struck by one incredible coincidence. The sign "L.Phelan" had been painted in white on a front fence opposite to where Phelan's body had been discovered. However, the sign proved to be nothing more than a macabre coincidence, having nothing to do with the killing. Police were baffled, especially as they found 11 pounds, 15 shillings and sixpence in one of the dead man's pockets.

However, there was one significant clue – an American service cap found in the back of the murder vehicle. Police even had two names to work on as the cap bore two names, of Sergeant Robert Willard French and Sergeant John Freeman Martin, who were both at Camp Murphy, Melbourne. French told police he had sold the cap to Martin in 1941, while Martin said he had lost the cap in America. Both Americans had alibis and police were forced to abandon that line of investigation.

Phelan's widow, Mrs Joyce Phelan, told the City Coroner, Mr Tingate, that her husband did not carry a gun and did not own one. She also said that her husband sometimes had trouble with his customers and, in such cases, did not hesitate in going to the police. Mr Tingate found that Phelan had been willfully and maliciously murdered by some person unknown. The taxi murder mystery has never been solved.

THE LONELY HEARTS TOMB (1992)

Veronica Dienhoff, known to her friends as Ronnie, was a slim, attractive 45-year-old who lived in a neat-as-a-pin flat in the inner eastern Melbourne suburb of Armadale. She worked

as a secretary and, to help with the mortgage payments, also had a part-time job as a restaurant waitress. Life seemed full for Ronnie Deinhoff, except that she was lonely; so lonely, in fact, that she contacted a Melbourne dating agency in an effort to find a partner. Ronnie had been married three times – the first at just 16 years of age – and had four grown-up children. All three marriages had failed, but Ronnie seemed determined to find Mr Right. And why not? Ronnie, who had been born in Czechoslovakia had migrated to Australia as a child, had succeeded in every other regard and had even won a brave fight with breast cancer.

Wolfgang Hindenberg, a 30-year-old who worked at a Dandenong engineering firm, also was seeking happiness and had contacted the same club. They were "paired", but Ronnie was never told that her new friend had a history of violent behaviour and, in fact, had once been charged with the attempted murder of a policeman.

Ronnie started dating Hindenberg in 1985, but soon became aware of his violent nature. She became terrified of him and avoided his company at all costs, even changing her telephone number to avoid his calls. Then, on *November 28*, 1985, Ronnie failed to keep a luncheon date with a friend. Police were called but Ronnie had disappeared. Ominously, Hindenberg had left his employment on *November 22* and had never returned. Police issued a description of Hindenberg's car, a white four-wheel vehicle which once had been used as an ambulance, but it too had vanished.

Then, on *February 6*, 1992, the distinctive white vehicle was found entangled in bush off a country track near Rubicon, 130 kilometres east of Melbourne. The badly decomposed bodies of Hindenberg and Ronnie Dienhoff were found on a mattress in the back of the vehicle, which had

been used as a bush tomb for more than six years. A hose had been connected to the exhaust pipe.

THE PROSTITUTE WHO KNEW TOO MUCH

On *February 6*, 1986, 31-year-old prostitute and police informant Ms Sallie-Ann Huckstepp was strangled and drowned in a lake in Centennial Park in Sydney. Ms Huckstepp was the lover of Warren Lanfranchi, who was later shot dead by corrupt detective Roger Rogerson, who, in turn, was strongly linked with underworld heavyweight Arthur "Neddy" Smith.

Smith, a convicted killer, was charged with Ms Huckstepp's murder. The Crown case depended largely on secret tape-recordings of Smith telling a cellmate how he had disposed of Ms Huckstepp. At one point, Smith said it was "the most satisfying thing I ever did in my life."

On the tapes, Smith revealed he had attacked Ms Huckstepp from behind and had punched her, lifted her off the ground by the throat and strangled her for about six minutes, before dragging her into a 60cm-deep pool and standing on her back for a several more minutes to finish the job.

However, Smith's barrister claimed his client had told outrageous lies on the tapes and that he had been in Newcastle with his wife on the night of the murder. The jury believed him and acquitted Smith.

Smith is serving two life sentences for murders he committed in 1983 and 1987.

FEBRUARY 7

THE ROBIN HOOD ASSAULT (1832)

Police Constable William Crisp was traveling along the Campbelltown Road, near Lower Minto, on *December 25, 1832*, when he heard cries of "murder". When he investigated near the Robin Hood public inn, he found Phillip Cunningham on top of an intoxicated woman, Eliza Besford. When tackled about what he was doing, Cunningham replied that it was the way he would treat any female caught entering his master's property. Cunningham was charged with rape but, at his trial in the Supreme Court of NSW on *February 7*, 1833,Besford was too drunk to give evidence. Cunningham was then indicted on another charge, of assault. He was found guilty and was sentenced to two years' hard labour in irons on the public roads.

**

RELEASED (1986): Lindy Chamberlain released on *February 7*, 1986, following the discovery of forensic evidence that proved she did not kill her baby, Azaria.

**

UNDERWORLD HIT: Disbarred-lawyer-turned-underworld-heavyweight Mario Condello, 53, became another victim of Melbourne's vicious gangland wars when he was shot dead in the driveway of his Brighton home at about 10pm on *February 6*, 2006. Condello, who had previous convictions for fraud, arson and drug offences, was due to make an appearance in court on charges of incitement to murder the next day. He was a close associate of Mick Gatto, who was found not guilty of the murder of Andrew "Benji" Veniamin.

FEBRUARY 8

THE RAPE CONSPIRACY (1840)

After a man named John Doyle was charged with raping 13-year-old Mary McMahon at Wollongong in July, 1839, several of his friends rallied around him and tried to pervert the course of justice. Siblings Edward, Michael and Ann Wholohan and Francis Darling told the girl that she would be rewarded if she left the area and remained in hiding during Doyle's trial. When this failed, they threatened her with violence, but this was reported to a Justice of the Peace and all three were brought to trail to face charges of conspiracy. The Wholohans and Darling claimed that they only interfered in the matter because they were trying to get Doyle to keep a promise to marry the 13-year-old. However, they were found guilty and, on *February 8*, 1840, were handed separate sentences. Ann Wholahan was ordered to be confined in a factory for two years, her brothers were sentenced to two years' jail and Darling was ordered to work in irons for two years.

FEBRUARY 9

THE "LIFE" RAPIST (1995)

After Jeffrey John Hornsby had been sentenced to life imprisonment in 1996 in relation to a number of offences, including rape, he appealed to the Queensland Court of Appeal for a reduction of sentence. However, the Court of Appeal not only rejected the application but, in its judgment stated: "In the very distant future a parole board might consider this man for parole. Any suggestion that he should be paroled should cause the authorities to think long and hard before recommending his release." Hornsby had been sentenced in relation to seven rapes, three offences of abduction, five of assault occasioning actual bodily harm, one of indecent assault with a circumstance of aggravation, one of common assault, one of administering a stupefying drug, two of robbery, one of indecent treatment of a child under 16 years, one of indecent assault and one of stealing.

Hornsby's offences were committed against three women, one aged 15 and another 67. The first of the complainants was 18 years of age when, on *February 9*, 1995, the 44-year-old Hornsby asked her if she would like to travel with him to Russell Island to see his de facto wife. The young woman agreed but, once on the island, he drove her to a secluded area, punched her and pushed her to the ground before placing a hood over her head and inserting two fingers into her vagina. Hornsby threatened her with a knife before forcing her to take a sedative and then raping her four times. In fact, he held her prisoner for 12 hours and, on releasing her, forced her to withdraw $1000 from her bank account and to hand the money to him.

The second complainant, a 15-year-old girl, also was invited to Russell Island less than a fortnight later, on *February 20*. Hornsby took her to a house, knocked her down and tied her wrists behind her back. He threatened to kill her before he twice had intercourse with her. Then, on *March 10*, the grandmother of the first complainant received a telephone call from Hornsby to say that the 18-year-old was on Russell Island and wanted to see her. Hornsby drove the 67-year-old widow to the island but, on arrival at a house, punched her and knocked her to the ground. The woman suffered a compressed fracture of the spine, but Hornsby added to her pain when he falsely claimed he had killed the woman's granddaughter. He pinched her breast, threatened her with a knife and raped her with her hands tied behind her back.

FEBRUARY 10

THE PICNIC PARTY KILLER (1924)

It was a perfect summer's day, ideal for a bush picnic. Sunday, *February 10*, 1924, dawned hot and still and Mr and Mrs Charles McGrath made early preparation for a picnic they would hold on the banks of the Jingellic Creek, a small tributary of the Murray River. A group of country neighbours had been invited to the picnic, just 200 yards from the McGrath homestead and guests were asked to assemble from about 1 o'clock.

Dairy farmer Charles Barber and his wife Ruth were the first to arrive, followed by Mr and Mrs McGrath, tobacco grower Richard King, butter factory manager David Shephard and his wife and child, farmer Charles Gainer and his wife and eight-year-old George Pointz. The group ate a lazy luncheon under the willows draping the creek, unaware that someone on the opposite bank had been watching every mouthful, every gesture, every movement.

Barber decided at 2.30pm that it was time for the men to go for a walk, but moved only 100 yards from the women and children when they heard a loud cracking noise from the opposite bank. King fell to the ground, seriously wounded in the chest. The men looked up and saw a man in a black hat taking aim for a second shot. Barber immediately recognised the man as his farmhand, Claude Valentine Batson, regarded as one of the best shots in New South Wales. The men were sitting ducks as Batson fired the second shot, which hit Gainer in the right knee. Shephard then took a bullet through the body as Barber shouted to the women and children to take cover.

Barber, showing great courage, ran to a horse and rode off, while former army major McGrath decided Batson had to be shot down. He made a dash for his homestead but was hit by four bullets. Although critically wounded, McGrath managed to scramble back to the creek bank with a gun in his hand. Meanwhile, Barber's daring ride alerted the entire region and a massive manhunt was launched in search of the gunman.

Shephard died in hospital the next day and the search party became more determined than ever to apprehend Batson, a 23-year-old who had spent his entire life in the bush and knew every source of food and shelter in the area. On the second day of the search, Batson was confronted by two police officers at an orchard near Lankeys Creek. Shots were exchanged, but Batson managed to escape and he later left a note at a farm which said he had taken cyanide. However, police knew this was a ruse as cyanide killed instantly and Batson would not have been able to write a note.

Finally, on *February 15*, Batson walked up to two men on a dairy farm just outside Jingellic and, when farmhands Robert Emerson and William Hore asked him about the shootings, he replied: "I was driven to it. I hope they put me on trial. I will tell them something." Batson then was arrested by two police officers who had been called to the farmhouse.

Batson was committed for trial on one charge of murder and three charges of felonious wounding with intent to murder. However, he never stood trial as he was committed to a mental institution. Batson obviously had had a mental breakdown and no one now will ever know why he shot at innocent picnickers.

THE EASEY STREET MURDERS (1977)

The house at number 147 Easey Street in the inner Melbourne suburb of Collingwood became infamous because of the events of *February 10*, 1977. Two women, Suzanne Armstrong, 28, and Susan Bartlett, 27, were stabbed to death and their bodies discovered three days later when neighbours heard Armstrong's 16-month son Gregory whimpering and crying. Armstrong had been stabbed 29 times, while Bartlett's body had 55 separate stab wounds. In August 1999, the eight prime suspects for the murders were subjected to DNA tests. All eight were cleared.

FEBRUARY 11

'MR STINKY' – THE MADILL-HEYWOOD KILLER (1966)

When police arrested a man for masturbating in his car outside a department store in Albury, onlookers merely viewed it with a mix of disgust and mild amusement. Soon they would feel horror, disbelief and, finally, relief that one of

Australia's most wanted double-murderers was at last off the streets.

However, when police initially made the arrest – about noon on Saturday *March 16*, 1985 – they had no idea what they had, by chance, stumbled upon.

As was mandatory police procedure in New South Wales, the man, 41-year-old Raymond Edmunds, was fingerprinted. The sobering, sickening irony is that if he had been caught committing a similar offence just a few kilometres away in Victoria, Edmunds could have refused to be fingerprinted – this law has since been changed – and would have been free to go about his evil ways.

Edmunds' prints matched those left by the killer of two Victorian teenagers in an unsolved double-homicide 19 years earlier.

On Thursday *February 10*, 1966, Garry Heywood, 18, and Abina Madill, 16, were among hundreds of teenagers who attended a concert at Shepparton Civic Centre.

Madill later agreed to go for a drive in Heywood's green FJ Holden, his pride and joy, and the couple weren't seen alive again.

The bodies of Madill and Heywood were discovered 16 days later, on *February 26*, in bush in Murchison East. Madill, naked from the waist down, had died after being severely beaten about the head. Heywood had been fatally shot through the temple. They had been killed about midnight, or shortly after, on *February 11*.

Heywood's car was found dumped by the side of a road, with two bloodied fingerprints above the driver's door. In the early 1980s, those prints were matched with prints recovered from numerous rape scenes around Melbourne where a calculating individual, brandishing a large butcher's knife had staked out houses for weeks in order to attack women when they were on their own and their children were often present. Edmunds got his nickname, 'Mr Stinky', from the testimony of several victims who described the rapist's strange odour.

Edmunds pleaded guilty to the murders and was jailed for life.

Adding to the tragedy of the Madill-Heywood case was the suspicion that fell upon certain individuals who were close to the murdered teenagers, in particular, Abina's boyfriend, Ian Urquhart, who had been the chief suspect and the subject of malicious gossip. Urquhart died tragically in a car crash, almost six years to the day after the murders, at the age of just 24, without ever being publicly exonerated.

Andrew Rule's book *Cuckoo* is a brilliant account of Edmonds' sordid life and the Madill-Heywood murders.

FEBRUARY 12

THE CHURCH-GOER WHO KILLED (1901)

Charles Beckman, a 35-year-old with a passion for fossicking around the Bowen district in Queensland, asked his best friend Alfred Anderson to accompany him on a trip in search of gold. The two set off on *November 12*, 1900, and, after spending a night at Gypsy Creek, Beckman arrived at the Ida Creek Hotel five days later on his own. He then moved on to visit friends at the Upper Euri Creek and stayed almost two weeks, and with each passing day, the Anderson family fretted more and more, especially as Beckman was seen with Anderson's horse and various goods. Finally, brother Henry set off in search of Alfred, with police later joining in the search for the missing man.

Beckman was arrested on *February 1*, 1901 and was driven into the bush in a search for Anderson's body. A police officer noted that at one stage Beckman started staring at a particular rock. Suspicious, the police officer lifted the rock and discovered Anderson's body. His skull had been smashed to pieces and Beckman was charged with his friend's murder. The trail opened on *February 12* and it did not take long for Beckman to be found guilty of murder and subsequently sentenced to death. Beckman was hanged at Brisbane's Boggo Road Gaol on *May 13*, 1901. A newspaper report suggested: "Charles Beckman met his death with unflinching courage, and made a last statement affirming he was innocent. Beckman to his final minute insisted Anderson had fallen to his death.

THE HEROIN HIT (2001)

Heroin addicts David Attard, 24, Dennis Yannopoulos, 29, and Sacha Oakley, 21, were desperate for a hit of their filthy drug of choice.

On the morning of *February 12*, 2001, Attard pawned some car wheels which fetched only $220, which wasn't enough to buy the half-a-gram of heroin the trio so desperately wanted. But Attard decided he would get it one way or another. Yannopoulos had bought the handgun just days earlier, so a plan was formulated whereby Attard would rob his regular drug-dealer, Quang Minh Vo, at gunpoint, in broad daylight.

About 12.30pm, Attard arranged to meet Vo outside disused shops in Douglas Avenue, St Albans – their usual exchange point. Attard, who had sold drugs for Vo just months earlier and knew him to be a married father of young children, went with Ms Oakley and Yannopoulos to the meeting place, the other two agreeing to keep their distance in Oakley's car until the deal was done.

Vo soon arrived on a motorbike. The robbery didn't go to plan. Attard shot the unarmed drug-dealer several times and was hurriedly picked up by his friends and they left the scene.

Attard claimed self-defence and that he reacted to provocation from Vo – claims that were rejected by Justice Teague, who said: "You had the gun as part of a contingency plan. You too readily fell back on that plan. But then you over-reacted. You not only produced the gun. You fired it at the deceased. You did so not just once but several times at an unarmed man."

Attard was found guilty of murder and sentenced to 18 years' jail with a minimum of 13 years, while Oakley and Yannopoulos were both convicted of manslaughter and sentenced to three years with a minimum of one year, and five years with a minimum of three years, respectively.

FEBRUARY 13

DEATH AT THE CRICKET (1952)

It would be impossible to describe a more typical Australian summer scene. It was Wednesday, *February 13*, 1952. The sun was shining, cicadas were singing in chorus and the flannelled fools were at their game of cricket. The match was between the South-East and Upper-North at the Railway, Oval, 10 minutes from the city streets of Adelaide, as part of

South Australia's Country Week. South-East batsman George Kay was about to play a shot from the bowling of Les Patroney when the handful of spectators noticed that the fieldsman at point, Captain Arthur Francis Henderson, 31, had fallen to ground.

They at first thought Henderson, who had served in the Middle East and New Guinea in World War II, was skylarking. However, they soon noticed blood from a wound over his heart, Captain Henderson was dead. Almost immediately spectators heard the crack of a rifle and another fieldsman, 22-year-old builder Ron Reed, fell with a severe wound to an arm. A bullet had severed an artery.

Cricketers made a dash for the pavilion as further shots whistled through the air from the tree-lined eastern end of the ground. Witnesses saw a small dark-haired man running in a crouched position from one tree to another and then watched in horror as the gunman held the rifle in a firing position and aimed a shot at a pedestrian. Incredibly, the pedestrian seemed unaware of what was happening, even after the shot had been fired. A bullet thudded into the ground just in front of him, setting alight long grass.

Meanwhile, one of the spectators had telephoned the police, who were at the oval within minutes from Thebarton station. One of the officers, Detective Brian Giles, showing remarkable courage, decided to confront the gunman. He abandoned his crouched position and walked straight up to the gunman – 100 yards, 90 yards, 80 yards, 70 yards – he kept walking until he was within 60 metres of the gunman and the barrel of a .303 rifle. The gunman lifted the rifle and aimed it at Giles' heart, but not even this deterred the detective. Finally, with the rifle still pointed at Giles, a police officer moved from behind the gunman to disarm him.

The arrested man was 24-year-old Lebanese migrant Elias Gaha, a former patient at two Melbourne mental institutions. Gaha appeared to have an inferiority complex and was convinced that Australians looked down on him. Doctors said he was suffering from a mental disorder known as paraphrenia. Gaha had moved to Adelaide and got a job as a railway cleaner, with workmates describing him as a quiet and apparently inoffensive young man. However, he bought the rifle just days before the tragedy and it seemed obvious he wanted to avenge some perceived grudge.

Gaha was charged with the murder of Captain Henderson, the father of three young children, but did not stand trial. He was sent for medical examination at the Parkside Mental Hospital, where doctors certified him as insane. He later was deported to Lebanon, with Detective Giles as one of his escorts. Detective Giles was awarded the George Medal for his courage and the wounded man, Reed, made a full recovery.

**

BOMBING (1978): Two garbagemen and a policeman were killed when a bomb exploded in a rubbish bin outside Sydney's Hilton Hotel at 12.40am on *February 13*, 1978, during a regional prime ministers' meeting. Just who planted the bomb, and why, remains a mystery.

FEBRUARY 14

THE VALENTINE KILLING (2000)

When Andrew Stephen Doherty and his wife Vivienne were experiencing marriage difficulties in 2000, she approached a minister of the Church of Christ, in the eastern Melbourne suburb of Mitcham, to ask him to convince her husband the marriage was over. The minister passed on the message to Doherty, whose engineering business was struggling, but there did not appear to be an immediate reaction.

Then, on *February 14* (St Valentine's Day), 2000, Mrs Doherty took her two young sons (she also had 21-year-old twin sons from a previous marriage) to school and stayed talking to other mothers before returning to the family home at Donvale. She then was attacked in the home, suffering severe head injuries caused by blows from an iron bar. An autopsy revealed that she had taken seven blows to the head, some fracturing her skull. The house had been "turned over", with cupboards and drawers open, as if an intruder had entered the house.

Doherty, meanwhile, had prepared documents to help him account for his movements on the morning of the murder. However, he was charged with his wife's murder and Justice Bongiorno told him that his attempt to create a false alibi had suggested "a degree of premeditation". The judge also described the killing of Mrs Doherty, 46, as "horrendous". He told Doherty: "Whilst no amount of punishment can rectify the wicked wrong which you have committed, the community demands that your sentences reflect the punishment for that wickedness." He sentenced Doherty to 21 years' jail, with a minimum term of 16 years.

FEBRUARY 15

BLACK CAESAR (1796)

The First Fleet, which arrived at Botany Bay in January, 1788, included at least one coloured man — John Caesar — who apparently had been a slave who had escaped from the West Indies to England, was arrested for a minor crime and transported. Caesar, a huge man, was known as "Black Caesar". He found it extremely difficult to settle at Botany Bay, especially as the food rations weren't sufficient enough for a man of his size to comfortably survive on. So, with likeminded convicts, he escaped to try to forage a living in the bush. He was recaptured but ran away several more times, never being at large for too long.

Finally, Caesar had a price placed on his head and a man named Wimbow was given the task of hunting him down. Wimbow and another settler tracked Caesar for several days and, on the evening of *February 15*, 1796, caught up with the gentle giant. Without warning and without Caesar even knowing he had been hunted down, Wimbow shot him dead.

FEBRUARY 16

THE KORP-HERMAN LOVE TRIANGLE (2005)

Few cases have created as much public interest as that involving Joe and Maria Korp and Tania Herman in early 2005. The drama started on *February 9*, when Joe Korp reported wife Maria as missing. He told police he had last seen her at their outer suburban Melbourne home of Mickleham at approximately 6.20am two days earlier. However, Maria Korp was found unconscious and barely alive in the boot of a car and taken to the Alfred Hospital. Joe Korp and his mistress Herman were arrested on *February 16*, and charged with attempted murder. Herman admitted that on *February 9* she had choked Mrs Korp until unconscious in the garage of the Korps' Mickleman home.

Maria Korp was able to cling to life for months and, meanwhile, the 38-year-old Herman pleaded guilty to the attempted murder of Mrs Korp and, on *July 1*, was sentenced to 12 years' jail, with a non-parole period of nine years. Joe Korp on *August 3* pleaded not guilty to charges of attempted murder, conspiracy to murder and intentionally causing serious harm. A few days earlier, on *July 26,* Public Advocate ruled that Mrs Korp's feeding tube should be removed as there was no hope of recovery. Mrs Korp died in hospital early in the morning on *August 5* and was cremated a week later. Joe Korp than hanged himself on the night of the cremation.

FEBRUARY 17

'SICK KILLER'S' TRIAL (1936)

Arnold Kark Sodeman, "the Sick Killer" goes on trial for murder on *February 17*, 1936. He is executed at Pentridge on *June 1*, 1936.

FEBRUARY 18

THE REFORMED BUSHRANGER

Tasmanian bushranger Martin Cash, the leader of the famed gang known as "Cash & Co.", was released on a ticket-of-leave on *February 18*, 1854, following the closure of the brutal Norfolk Island penal station. Cash was one of the few well-known bushrangers to denounce his fast life of crime, genuinely reform and live a tranquil life into relative old age.

The young Cash was wild. On *Boxing Day* 1842, while serving a prison sentence for cattle stealing, Cash, along with Lawrence Kavenagh and George Jones, staged a dramatic escape from the Port Arthur penal settlement, and even braved a treacherous swim, in darkness. While on the run, the trio robbed mainly wealthy landowners. When police caught up with them on *August 29*, 1843, a vicious brawl ensued in Brisbane Street, Hobart, and Cash shot and mortally wounded Constable Peter Winstanley. Cash and Kavenagh were captured and sentenced to death, but both gained a reprieve an hour before their intended executions.

After his release, Cash married and became an overseer of gardeners. He died peacefully in his own bed on *August 27*, 1877 at the age of 69.

FEBRUARY 19

THE LAST WOMAN HANGED (1951)

Attractive Jean Lee was not alone in the murder of old, overweight starting-price bookmaker Bill Kent in Carlton, an inner Melbourne suburb, on *November 7*, 1949. Robert Clayton, her lover, and another accomplice, Norman Andrews, were also found guilty of murdering Kent. But Lee's name stands out because she was the last woman hanged in Victoria. In fact, Lee believed her sex would save her from the gallows. However, the murder of Kent was so brutal that even the Victorian State Cabinet turned down a mercy plea and she was hanged on *February 19*, 1951, only 15 months after Kent was tortured to death.

Lee's early life was to give little hint of the life of crime she was to lead after leaving school in Sydney aged 16. She was brought up with a regard for law and order but knew what she wanted – and that was the good life. She married when aged 18 and that temporarily ended her life as one of Sydney's Depression butterflies. She had a daughter, but drifted away from her family into prostitution during World War II.

It was during her "busy" days entertaining American and Australian troops that Lee met Clayton, who was to become her pimp. Lee and Clayton worked a racket in which Lee was found by Clayton in a compromising position with "another man". Clayton then would threaten violence if the "other man" did not compensate for luring his "wife" into sex. This racket worked so successfully over several years that Lee and Clayton decided to branch out in Victoria and headed south in quest of even more suckers. That was in 1949 and, about that time, they met up with Andrews. The three hit it off almost immediately and they worked their racket in Melbourne, with the bigger Andrews now threatening the violence, usually as Lee's "husband" or Clayton's "brother".

Pickings were good but not as good as when the unholy trio came across old Bill Kent in a Lygon Street, Carlton, hotel. Kent, well known throughout Carlton, had a fistful of notes and Lee, Clayton and Andrews devised a plan to get that bankroll, with Lee as the attractive bait. She sidled up to Kent and plied him with drinks before she, her two friends and Kent headed off to Old Bill's home in nearby Dorritt Street. Lee told her two friends she would "entertain" Kent, so the others headed off temporarily. However, Kent, as drunk as he was, was certainly no fool. He had his money tucked into his fob pocket and Lee, no matter how hard she tried, could not get it.

When Andrews and Clayton returned she gave them the bad news and declared that she would have to get the old SP to take his trousers down. But this only made Kent more aware of Lee's real passion, and that was when it got violent. Lee smashed Kent over the head with a bottle, battered him with a piece of wood and then tied him up with sheet strippings. The terrible trio then cut Kent's fob pocket from his trousers, but were convinced the bookie had much more money hidden. They bashed, cut and jabbed at Kent with several weapons, including the broken bottle, and left him for dead.

Kent's body was found within an hour when a neighbour grew suspicious about "the quietness of the party". Police were called immediately and it did not take them long to track down the three killers. The gang was celebrating when police fronted them at 4am at their Spencer Street hotel, less than 12 hours after the brutal slaying of Kent. On *March 25*, 1950, all three were sentenced to death after being convicted of murder. Lee broke down and had to be helped from court. On appeal to the Court of Criminal Appeal two months later, a new trial was ordered, but that did not save Kent's killers. The Australian High Court reversed that decision and the Privy Council in England turned down a further appeal. All three were hanged on that morning of *February 19*, 1951.

THE REDFERN RIOTS (2004)

As 17-year-old aborigine Thomas Hickey, known as "TJ", was riding his bicycle home on *February 14*, 2004, after visiting his girlfriend, he saw a police car and assumed he was being chased because of an outstanding warrant. Hickey lost control of his bicycle as he turned a corner and was killed when he was impaled on a spiked fence. As friends gathered, there was talk that the police had caused Hickey's death and aboriginal youths started rioting. Bottles, bricks and even Molotov cocktails were thrown as police tried to restore order. The riot continued into the next morning and, by the time it was broken up, more than 30 police had been injured. A subsequent inquest into Hickey's death found that police had not been pursuing Hickey and no action was taken. A memorial service was held in Sydney for Hickey on *February 19* and another in his home town of Walgett on *February 22*.

**

EXECUTED (1863): Thomas McGee was executed at Melbourne Gaol on *February 29*, 1863, after being found guilty of the murder of a fellow miner at Sandhurst, Victoria. It was alleged that McGee hit his victim, a man named Brown, over the head with a length of wood filled with lead.

FEBRUARY 20

THE FOUR-BABY KILLER (1989)

The name Kathleen Folbigg is synonymous with the death of children — her own. To all intents and purposes, she seemed to be a devoted wife and mother. She had married steel worker

Craig Folbigg and settled in Newcastle, where their first child was born. However, Caleb was just 20 days old when Mrs Folbigg woke early on *February 20*, 1989, and realised he was not breathing. The death was recorded as Sudden Infant Death Syndrome (SIDS), but the Folbiggs had another son in June 1990. The boy was named Patrick and, at four months of age, on *October 20*, Mrs Folbigg woke early and noticed her son appeared to have had an epileptic fit. The boy survived but, *on February 13*, Mrs Folbigg again reported that her son had had a fit and the child was rushed to hospital. However, he was dead on arrival and the death was put down to natural causes.

Daughter Sarah was born to the Folbiggs in October, 1992, but she died at 11 months of age, with the death recorded as due to SIDS. A second daughter, Laura, was born in August, 1997, but she died 19 months later, on *March 1*, 1999. There now were suspicions over all four infant deaths and police launched an investigation. Then, in April 2001, Kathleen Folbigg was arrested. A jury took just hours to find her guilty of the murder of her four children and she was sentenced to 40 years' jail, with a minimum of 30 years. On appeal, the 40-year sentence was reduced to 30 years and her miniumum term by five years. At the time of publication, it is believed another appeal is pending.

FEBRUARY 21

THE "PISSED OFF" KILLER (2004)

Mark John Oswell, a 26-year-old fencing contractor, and Rachael Lorraine Lawton, 19 years of age, were drinking at a

Cranbourne (east of Melbourne) hotel on the evening of *February 20*, 2004, but there was no pre-existing relationship between them. As staff prepared to close the bar for the night at around 1am on *February 21*, Oswell drove Lawton to his parents' home, where the couple kissed and cuddled. Oswell wanted sex, but Lawton refused and asked to be driven home to the bayside suburb of Frankston. Oswell, who felt that he had been used only to provide Lawton with transport, grabbed her by the throat and blocked her nose and throat because he was "pissed off with her". She said to him when she regained consciousness: "I suppose you are going to rape me", and he replied "yes, just for the hell of it".

Oswell then raped Lawton while she was semi-conscious and, when she tried to get up, he again subdued her because he feared she would go to the police. Then, while Lawton was unconscious, he carried her to his car and drove towards Cannons Creek. However, Lawton regained consciousness and started screaming. When Oswell reached the boat launching ramp at Cannons Creek, Lawton jumped from the car and ran away — only to reach the water's edge. Oswell produced a knife, grabbed her from behind and cut her throat. The young woman tried desperately to free herself and, at one stage, bit Oswell on the thumb. He then stabbed her repeatedly in the stomach and chest before pushing her body in the water.

When arrested on *February 24*, Oswell at first denied any involvement in Lawton's death, but eventually made a full admission. He pleaded guilty to murder and rape and, in the Supreme Court of Victoria, Justice Osborn told him: "The life that you took was young and vibrant. You acted in a totally self-centred and brutal fashion and subjected Ms Lawton successively to a violent rape and vicious murder. You first debased and humiliated her and then, after a period of considered conduct, overpowered and savagely stabbed her. The circumstances in which she died could scarcely have been more terrifying or sickening … You have violated the sanctity of human life and the common humanity we all share." Justice Osborn sentenced Oswell to a total of 23 years, with a fixed non-parole period of 18 years.

FEBRUARY 22

MEETING (1989): Underworld identity Gary Abdallah and his solicitor met with police on *February 22*, 1989, over the Walsh Street police killings in Melbourne.

FEBRUARY 23

THE SERVANT RAPIST (1836)

Servant James Crook was charged with raping Mrs Charlotte Denniseall at Campbell Field, Sydney, on *February 23*, 1836, and the Supreme Court of New South Wales was told that he grabbed the woman from behind and dragged her into the back room of where he lived. Mrs Denniseall eventually broke free and ran to tell police what had happened. He was found guilty of rape and broke down and cried when sentenced to death.

THE MOTORCYCLE SHOOTING (1929)

Three Adelaide detectives were called to check on a disturbance on the night of *February 23*, 1929, when they came across a motor-cycle left in Grenfell Street, in the city. The trio, in attending the disturbance, asked if anyone knew who owned the motor-cycle. No one seemed to know, so the police officers decided that because it was late at night they would move it so that the owner could claim it later. Two of the policemen rode off slowly, but were approached by a man who thought they were stealing it. Constable John Holman started explaining that they were police officers when the man, who claimed it was his bike, fired a shot which hit Constable Holman. Although severely wounded, Holman tried to chase the gunman. More shots were fired and, finally, the gunman went to ground after being hit in the leg by shots fired by another police officer.

Constable Holman later died in hospital and the gunman, John McGrath was charged with murder. He pleaded not guilty at his trial, claiming he did not know Constable Holman was a policeman. He also claimed that he earlier had been in a row and that he thought someone was out to get him. McGrath also told the court that he always carried a pistol as he was a wharf labourer and needed the firearm for self-defence. McGrath was found guilty and although sentenced to death this later was commuted to life imprisonment.

THE BRISBANE RIPPER (2003)

Francis Michael Fahey led a blameless life and, for 28 years, worked as an ambulance driver in and around Brisbane. However, he was diagnosed with post-traumatic stress disorder in 2002 and was prescribed an anti-depressant drug. The man described by his wife and mother of his three children, Beth Fahey, as "a loving, caring husband", said his personality seemed to change from a gentle and respected member of the community to a monster.

Fahey in September, 2005, was found guilty of the murder of two sex workers and later was sentenced to life imprisonment, with Supreme Court of Queensland's Justice Margaret White ordering a minimum 25 years in prison. This means Fahey, 53 years of age when sentenced early in 2006, will be 78 years of age when eligible for release. Fahey had pleaded not guilty to the murder of both Jasmin Crathern and Julie McColl.

The jury at his trial heard that Fahey stabbed Crathern 14 times in August, 2002, after she had performed a sex act on him in his car at Hendra, in Brisbane's north. He had killed her with a bayonet he kept under the front seat of his car and, on *February 23*, 2003, McColl became his second victim. He told her he wanted to engage in bondage sex and, four days later, McColl's naked body was found bound by ropes "bondage style" at Deep Water Bend, again in Brisbane's north. McColl had been stabbed 24 times and prosecutor Peter Feeney told the court the murders were "chilling" as they involved careful planning. He described Fahey as a "calculated murderer and a predator". However, Mrs Fahey said before her husband was sentenced: "It is important to me that they (the public) realise he is not the monster that people are making him out to be."

KILLED OVER MANGOES (1997)

Following the breakdown of his marriage, David Laxalle went to live with his mother at Berala, New South Wales. On the night of *February 23*, 1997, Laxalle saw a group of teenagers stealing mangoes from a tree in his mother's back garden. He pursued and caught one of the four teenagers and became involved in a fight with 18-year-old Choi Kia Tang.

Tang admitted that he punched and kicked Laxalle, but indicated that he also was punched. As the two fought, Laxalle was stabbed seven times to the body and left arm. He staggered inside his mother's house and although she called for immediate help, her son died in hospital the following morning.

Tang, who arrived in Australia from Cambodia with his mother and siblings after his father had been killed in the Pol Pot regime, was found guilty of Laxalle's murder and Justice Hidden told Tang the public had an abhorrence of young men carrying knives and sentenced him to a total of 15 years' jail.

'PSYCHO AND SCHITZ' (1999)

Mohamed Heblos, who arrived with his family from Lebanon when he was two years of age, was employed as a tyre fitter at Sam's Tyres, in the inner northern Melbourne suburb of Brunswick. In 1998, Heblos stole $3500 from his employer, Samuel Borenstein, but was caught out and was asked to return the money. Despite this, Borenstein continued to employ the teenager – until Heblos slashed a number of tyres. Then, when Heblos was in debt in early 1999, he formulated a plan to rob Borenstein. On *February 23*, 1999, he watched the Sam's Tyres premises from a bus shelter and then entered the premises between 7 and 8pm. Heblos hid in a storeroom before confronting his former employer. He hit Borenstein eight times over the head with a jack handle and threw a car battery at him, inflicting terrible head injuries. Heblos then ran away with $9000 and buried the cash in several locations around Sydenham.

Interviewed by police four days later, Heblos gave a false alibi but later, in a long recorded interview, admitted he was responsible for Borenstein's death. Heblos, 18 at the time of the killing, pleaded guilty to manslaughter at his trial in April, 2000, but was found guilty of murder. Mr Justice Hempel then told him: "In light of the number and nature of the blows inflicted which caused death, and your admissions to the police, it is, I think, not surprising that you were convicted of murder." However, the judge added: "Despite your behaviour after killing Mr Borenstein, I think that your admissions in the record of interview overall show that you intended to co-operate with the police ... your behaviour and efforts in custody over a year also help me to conclude that, at your age and with your supportive family, you have reasonable prospects of rehabilitation." He then sentenced Heblos to 15 years' jail, with a fixed period of 10 years.

FEBRUARY 24

THREE LITTLE ANGELS (1924)

Few Australian cases have been as sad as the slaying of three innocent little girls in Sydney in 1924. The case shocked, revolted and saddened the nation and when the bodies were discovered there was an enormous outcry. The killings occurred in the Sydney suburb of Paddington, which was then a slum suburb. Edward Williams, a 52-year-old piano teacher, struggled to raise his three daughters, Rosalie (five), Mary (three) and Cecilia (two) by himself. His wife was an inmate at the Callan Park asylum and Williams and his three girls visited her there almost every weekend. It was a tough, difficult life for Williams and he eventually cracked under the strain. On the night of *February 24*, 1924, he told Rosalie, the eldest of his innocents, that he would help her get to heaven. Rosalie had earlier told her father that she would like to go to heaven and this was one of the contributing factors to his actions. He cut the throats of his daughters with a razor, bundled their bodies on top of their double bed and placed newspapers under the bed to catch and mop up the dripping blood.

He then left Sydney, but not before arranging to sell some furniture. When the dealer arrived to collect the furniture, he failed to discover the bodies of the three little angels. The gruesome discovery was made by landlady Mrs Florence Mahon, who was horrified. Meanwhile, Williams handed himself in to police at Newcastle and he was charged with murder. The piano teacher, at Sydney Central Court, made a pathetic figure as he tried to explain his actions and described the killings as "acts of love" and wanted to save his girls from their mother's fate.

On the night of the killings, he believed he saw his wife's crooked eyes in one of Rosalie's and therefore decided to kill her. Then, with twisted logic, he decided that if he killed one he would have to kill all three daughters. He also said: "I seek neither favour nor mercy. I only ask for justice. I am entitled to a fair trial, and I know I shall receive it from you. If I am to be hanged, then let me be hanged. Take no notice of the plea of insanity. I myself do not raise it. As for it being temporary insanity, I can't say myself." As a Catholic, Williams would not resort to suicide to appease his conscience, but little to save himself from the hangman's noose. He was found guilty of murder and was hanged on *April 29*, 1924, just two months after he killed his little girls.

FEBRUARY 25

THE BATTERING OF BABY JORDAN (2000)

Little Jordan Anderson-Smith was just seven months of age when he died on *February 25*, 2000, at Wagga, NSW. Jordan choked on his own vomit after being beaten and tortured. His injuries included a lacerated liver, a torn lip, facial abrasions, broken ribs and crush injuries to the toes caused by a clamp. Christopher Hoerler, the defacto husband of Jordan's mother, Louise Anderson, was charged with murder. However, halfway through his trial, he pleaded guilty to the lesser charge of manslaughter. He was sentenced to 11 years' jail, with a minimum of eight years and three months. The NSW Director of Public Prosecutions appealed the sentence, arguing it was inadequate, and the NSW Court of Criminal Appeal applied a sentence of 14 years and four months, with a minimum of 10 years and nine months.

Hoerler, 26 at the time, had walked a friend home in the early hours of *February 25*, 2000, after a party at the home he shared with Ms Anderson. He was affected by alcohol and cannabis, but at that time Jordan was asleep in the lounge room. Some time later, Hoerler tugged at Ms Anderson's shirt to tell her that Jordan had fallen out of his pram and was not breathing. When she found Jordan on the rug she started calling out for help and an ambulance rushed the baby to hospital. Hoerler told police when they arrived at 3.30am that he had found Jordan frothing at the mouth and on the floor.

An autopsy report indicated that the baby had died of "multiple injuries" and forensic evidence indicated that there were blood spatter patterns on Hoerler's shorts consistent with projection of blood from little Jordan. A paediatric physician also gave evidence that vomit had entered the baby's lungs and that death followed this inhalation of vomit. Hoerler did not give evidence at the sentencing stage but, in a statement, said he struck the child twice to stop him crying. He said he hit the baby with an open hand and then left the room, shocked at what he had done.

Justice Miles told Hoerler: "I conclude, and am satisfied beyond reasonable doubt, that the extent of the child's injuries was much greater than what could have been caused by striking the head twice with an open hand. The injury which pushed the lower teeth into the roof of the mouth must have involved considerable force delivered by a punch. Similarly, the injury or injuries to the abdominal area must have involved considerable force also delivered by at least one punch. There is a possibility that the rib fractures were caused by squeezing or hugging of the baby, but it is unlikely. The injury to the frenulum (part of the lip) was caused either by the severe blow which caused the injury to the palate or by a separate blow of less severity. Overall, there must have been several and not only two blows."

FEBRUARY 26

A FAMILY TRAGEDY (1929)

A farmer on *February 26*, 1929, noticed smoke coming from the home of the Archer family in the tiny township of Don, near Devonport, Tasmania. It was early morning and the flames had already turned the timber house into an inferno. Neighbours stood helpless as the flames devoured the building and its contents. Later, after the flames had died to an ember, it was discovered that the entire Archer family of husband, wife and five children had died in the flames. Seven charred bodies were found in the ruins of the homestead.

Andrew Thomas Archer, 49, had shot himself in the head and his body was found on the floor, resting on a shotgun. Olive Archer, also 49, had died in her bed, along with her 10-month-old daughter Nilma. The bodies of the other children, Lexie (11), Phyliss (eight), Murray (six) and Trevor (five) were found in another bedroom. All bodies were charred beyond recognition, but it was presumed that Andrew Archer had shot his family dead before setting the house on fire and then turning the gun on himself. A note found outside the house in a leather bag was final proof. It was written by Archer, known as Tom, and said simply: "The bag and contents is from Tom. Goodbye." The word "goodbye" trailed off and was unfinished. It later was learned that Archer had visited a doctor two years earlier about fears he would have "mental troubles".

THE HEADLESS BODY (1964)

The condemned and abandoned cottage in Greeves Street, Fitzroy, was the perfect hiding place for 10-year-old Edward Irvine, who was playing "cowboys and Indians" with his friends from the George Street State School on *February 26*, 1964. The grey building, which had no front garden, had its windows covered by corrugated iron for several months. However, Edward discovered a way to enter the cottage – to his eventual horror. Little Edward stared wide-eyed at what he saw and rushed to tell his friend, nine-year-old Terry Karvalis, who immediately rushed to have a look at Edward's discovery.

The boys, who both lived in nearby Napier Street, went to tell their parents that they had seen parts of a man's body. However, their parents chastised the boys for returning home late from school. The boys, not wanting to get into deeper trouble, kept their secret to themselves until the following morning when they met a teacher on the way to school. They blurted out the details of what they had seen and the teacher sensibly contacted the police. Detective Sergeant Tom White and two uniformed constables went to the boarded-up cottage and took only seconds to confirm what the boys had been saying.

The head of the Homicide Squad, Detective Inspector Jack Matthews was called in to investigate a discovery that had Melbourne buzzing for days. The two schoolboys had made one of the grisliest discoveries in years as the body was in two parts – the chest and shoulders, and the pelvic part of the torso. The middle part of the torso was missing, as were the limbs and head.

Then, just 24 hours later, 14-year-old John Garoni and 15-year-old Terry Kennedy were riding their bikes around a lot in nearby Gore Street when Kennedy hit a bump and fell off his bike. He reached out and was horrified. He literally had stumbled on two arms (one with a watch on the wrist), thigh sections and part of an abdomen. The human jigsaw was being locked together, but with no head.

The major breakthrough came when a reader of the Melbourne *Herald* responded to information that the name "Molack" had been found on the pocket of trousers found at the cottage. Police finally deducted that the dead man was 32-year-old process worker Imre "Jimmy" Mallach, who had not turned up for work for several days. The dead man's head and right arm finally were found in a reserve off Alfred Crescent, North Fitzroy.

Mallach, a naturalised Australian, had been born in Hungary and had migrated to Australia in 1957. On *February 29*, 1964, police charged 37-year-old Mrs Vilma Broda with the murder of her estranged de facto husband. The Criminal Court was told that Mallach had turned up at her home drunk and demanded money. They fought and Broda hit him over the head with a hammer before dissecting the body. The jury found Broda not guilty of both murder and manslaughter and she walked away a free woman.

**

BODIES FOUND: The bodies of murdered teenagers Garry Heywood and Abina Madill were found in a paddock in Murchison East, Victoria, on *February 26*, 1966. They had been killed by Raymond 'Mr Stinky' Edmunds. (Refer to *February 11*.)

FEBRUARY 27

A PRESENT OF BULLETS (1904)

To use a common euphemism of the nineteenth century, Florrie Eugenia Horton had "a peculiar disease of long standing". Being infected with a venereal disease angered 24-year-old Thomas Horton as, apart from anything else, he was unable to "fulfil his duties". The two had separated, but Mrs Horton was worried that the man known as "Cranky Tom" or "Silly Tom" might do her some harm and therefore wrote a letter to a friend stating she was convinced her husband would kill her. Mrs Horton was walking down Rundle Street, Adelaide, on the evening of *February 27,* 1904, when she bumped into her husband, who invited her into an alleyway to give her a present. She replied: "Yes, I know, a present of bullets."

Horton followed her and the other women and shot his wife three times in the back, killing her almost instantly. Two of the bullets pierced the right lung and the other passed through the heart. Horton fled from the scene, but was arrested the following day by a mounted constable between Bridgewater and Ambleside in the Lofty Ranges. He had been walking along a railway line and, when confronted, said: "All right, sir, I have been driven to it." Horton had a loaded revolver and a number of cartridges when arrested.

Facing trial in the Criminal Court the following April, Horton pleaded not guilty on the basis of insanity. Evidence was given that his father had died in an asylum and that the young man himself suffered from convulsions and once had fallen on his head from a height of 13 feet. However, a Dr Ramsay Smith gave evidence that he believed Horton was sane and was shamming loss of memory. The jury returned a guilty verdict and Horton was sentenced to death.

**

EXECUTED (1902): Harry Harbord "Breaker" Morant, 37, was executed in South Africa on *February 27,* 1902, after being found guilty of murdering enemy prisoners in the Boer War. Debate continues to rage over whether he was actually guilty.

FEBRUARY 28

THE SHOOTING RAMPAGE (1986)

Gunman Andrew Mark Norrie, 23, went on such a wild shooting spree from *February 28*, 1986, that he terrorised residents of three states — Queensland, New South Wales and Victoria. With two automatic rifles and thousands of rounds of ammunition, he dressed himself in army camouflage, picked up 16-year-old companion Scott Wayne Thompson and drove south through Queensland. On *March 1*, the pair fired shots at a family driving along the Pacific Highway and two days later shot at another family, this time in NSW.

Although no deaths had been reported so far, that changed when they shot dead fisherman Ian Breust at Narooma before executing hitchhiker Mark Lynch. Police quickly realised the killings were the work of the same men and launched a massive manhunt. Thompson was captured in Mt Gambier, South Australia, but Norrie avoided capture and led police on a chase through the bush. However, he was arrested on *March 7* and later was jailed for life while Thompson was sentenced to eight years in a juvenile institution.

FEBRUARY 29

MAD OR BAD? (1912)

For some inexplicable reason, 32-year-old butcher Joseph Victor Pfeiffer went to his sister-in-law's home in the Melbourne bayside suburb of Albert Park one night in November, 1911, and shot her dead. Pfeiffer admitted he was infatuated with Florence Whiteley, 23, but told police when he was apprehended that there no reason for killing her and there had been no quarrel between them. The police thought otherwise and reasoned that Whiteley had rejected Pfeiffer's advances, promoting him to kill her.

Pfeiffer was charged with murder and, at his trial, said he could not remember shooting Miss Whiteley and that insanity ran on both sides of his family. He told of a brother who also had memory problems and of two other family members who had committed suicide. Incredibly, Pfeiffer did not call on expert testimony to back his claims of insanity and he was found guilty of murder. He was executed at the Melbourne Gaol on *February 29*, 1912.

THE WOMAN BUTCHER

An abattoir became the first woman in Australia to be jailed for life when the NSW Court of Criminal Appeal on *September 11*, 2006, dismissed her appeal on sentence. Katherine Knight had been found guilty and sentenced for the murder of her partner, John Price, on *February 29*, 2000. Knight, 50, appealed against her life sentence, claiming the killing was not in the worst category. However, her tale of extraordinary circumstances and included the skinning of her former partner and then hanging his hide in a lounge room in the home they shared at Aberdeen, in the Hunter Valley. Justice McClennan, who originally sentenced Knight, said: "This was an appalling crime, almost beyond contemplation in a civilised society."

Knight and Price had a row on the night of *February 29* and the former abattoir worker stabbed her partner at least 37 times in various parts of the front and back of his body. The

Supreme Court was told that many of the wounds were deep and extended into vital organs, resulting in a great loss of blood. Then, after Price has been dead for some time, his body was dragged from the hallway into the lounge room, where the skin from his head, face, torso, nose, ears, genitals and legs was removed to form one pelt. Knight then put the pelt on a meat hook on the architrave of the door of the lounge room.

The head and neck were removed and parts of the dead man's buttocks were sliced off. The head was placed in a large pot, together with some vegetables and stewed, while the buttock slices were baked in an oven with other vegetables before being placed on plates ready for a meal (not eaten) for the dead man's son and daughter. Another piece was thrown on the back lawn, presumably for the family dog. As Justice McClennan said: "Objectively the circumstances mark the killing and its accompanying incidents as being of the most gruesome kind, the murder as being in the most serious category of crime."

**

KILLED (1916): A taxi-driver was killed in Bulleen Road, Melbourne, on *February 29*, 1916, and notorious gangster Leslie "Squizzy" Taylor and John Williamson were later acquitted of his murder amid rumours of witness intimidation and jury-rigging.

**

EXECUTED (1863): Alexander Davis was executed at Melbourne Gaol on *February 29*, 1863, for killing a man named George Sims at Smythesdale, Victoria, on *May 31*, 1863. Davis, in robbing Sims of a one-pound note, struck his victim over the head with a length of wood.

MARCH

The heat of summer and early autumn has dragged on, and so has the crime rate. Murders continue unabated, the culprits punished with execution or long sentences and there are cases of arson, rape and robbery. March generally might be a quiet month but, for the police, it is as busy as usual. Crimes this month include:

THE HANDSOME BUSHRANGER

THE WHISKEY AU GO GO FIRE

A TAXI KILLING

THE ROYAL SHOOTING

THE SPEAR-GUN MONSTER

THE LIMBS IN THE YARRA

And much, much more.

MARCH 1

THE RACETRACK ROBBERY (1858)

Racegoer Andrew Burke made the mistake of having too much to drink at a race meeting at Ararat early in 1858. He went behind a grandstand to sleep off the effects of alcohol, but was robbed at gunpoint late in the night. Police arrested two young men, Edward Brown and Williams Jones, who were charged with robbery with violence — a capital offence at that time. Both were sentenced to death and were executed at Ballarat on *March 1*, 1858

∗∗

'JUSTICE FOR JAMIE' (1999)

In October 1991, Francis Barry Arnoldt was found dead outside a public toilet block in the inner Melbourne suburb of Brunswick. The 60-year-old had suffered numerous stab wounds and had clearly been attacked in a wild frenzy. Arnoldt's trousers were down and his wallet had not been stolen, ruling out robbery as a motive, leading police to categorise the murder as a gay sex crime. However, with no forensic evidence to prove that sex had taken place or, if it had, the identity of the other participant, police investigations fell flat. It wasn't until five-and-a-half years later that the case took a sensational twist.

In April 1997, Jamie Martorana informed police that a friend of his, Jamie Koeleman, had revealed he had killed a man in Brunswick in 1991. Martorana claimed Koeleman – a homosexual with no history of violence – said he had met a man in a park in Victoria Street and, while having oral sex with him, had stabbed him to death. Koeleman said he had kept the murder weapon but that it was later stolen.

Martorana agreed to introduce an undercover police officer, Mark Dolan, to Koeleman. In conversations between the trio, which were secretly taped, Koeleman again confessed to the murder, and also took Dolan to the park and re-enacted the crime. When the sting was revealed, Koeleman claimed he had simply made it all up. It took three trials before he was convicted of murder on *March 1*, 1999, and he was sentenced to 19 years' jail with a minimum of 15 years.

Koeleman's case sparked outrage among sections of Melbourne's gay community, who instigated the 'Justice for Jamie' campaign. According to the figureheads of the campaign, Koeleman was a "bullshit artist", not a murderer. However, the jury believed Koeleman's intimate knowledge of the crime placed him at the scene.

MARCH 2

THE BOMBING OF A POLICEMAN (1994)

An unprecedented terrorist attack on the Adelaide office of the National Crime Authority (NCA) – one of the worst of its kind in Australia – claimed the life of Western Australian Detective Sergeant Geoffrey Bowen on *March 2*, 1994.

Shortly after 9am, an Express Post package neatly marked 'NCA, Geofrey Bowen' arrived at the Waymouth St office and passed through a scanner completely undetected before being directed to its intended recipient. Bowen briefly inspected the parcel and, with cruel irony, joked: "It might be a bomb." Further examination prompted more humour: "Well, there's no wires." He then removed the cardboard box from within the plastic pack and, using scissors, sliced open the seal. According to NCA lawyer Peter Wallis, who was in the room with Bowen, what followed was "a loud crack, like a rifle shot ...and I remember Geoff letting out a strangled-type cry, a yell, and falling sideways ...There was an enormous buffeting of ...wind ...and an enormous sound that I can only describe as very, very loud static ... I was immediately blinded. That was the last thing I saw."

Wallis lost an eye and suffered damage to the other and was also severely burnt. Bowen, a 36-year-old father of two young boys, wasn't so lucky. Despite the valiant attempts of ambulance workers to revive him, Bowen was pronounced dead at 9.39am. A post-mortem examination revealed he had died as a result of "haemorrhage due to blast injuries to the upper and lower limbs".

In 1999, coroner Wayne Chivell found convicted criminal Dominic Perre responsible for sending the evil parcel. Perre had been arrested by Bowen six months before the bombing as part of a probe into organised crime. At the time of the bombing, Bowen had been preparing to prosecute Perre in court the next day. "In my opinion," cornoner Chivell said, "the only reasonable inference to be drawn from the evidence is that Dominic Perre was responsible, in the sense that he constructed the bomb, and either posted it or arranged for someone else to post it on his behalf to Detective Sergeant Bowen. (But) from all the evidence, I am unable to find whether Perre acted alone or in concert with another person or persons."

Perre was charged with the police officer's murder nine days after the bombing but the charges were subsequently dropped. Despite this and the offer of a $500,000 reward, no one has ever been brought to justice for the bombing.

MARCH 3

DEATH OF A STANDOVER MAN (1995)

Stuart Pink was known in the seaside Melbourne suburb of St Kilda as a pimp and standover man who mingled with drug dealers. On *March 3*, 1995, he attacked a man named Tom Juricic, who had to be treated for a cut hand. Pink had stolen heroin and cash from Juricic and, eight days later, Juricic and associate Mende Georgiev saw Pink, prompting Georgiev to return home "to get something". That "something" was a gun and Georgiev then returned to where he had spotted Pink, near Fitzroy Street, St Kilda. When Georgiev returned home at about 10.30pm, he told girlfriend Joanne Guziak that he had "got him". Pink had been shot dead and Georgiev even returned to the scene of the killing to make sure Pink really was dead. Georgiev also said he disposed of the gun somewhere in the western suburb of Sydenham.

Justice Hampel, in the Supreme Court of Victoria, told the jury it had to be satisfied beyond reasonable doubt of Georgiev's confession to his girlfriend. He also pointed out that there was other evidence and although Georgiev's counsel challenged Guziak's evidence, Georgiev did not give evidence at his trial. In sentencing Georgiev to a term of 20 years, with a fixed 16-year period, the judge said: "It (the murder) can be seen as nothing but a premeditated revenge execution style killing in the context of the heroin trade ... the sentence must reflect the tragedy which you caused and the very serious crime you committed."

MARCH 4

I JUST ENJOY KILLING PEOPLE' (1986)

When Andrew Mark Norrie decided to take a long drive south from Queensland to Victoria in March 1986, sightseeing was the last thing on his mind. In fact, Norrie, 24, was obsessed with waging what his sentencing judge later described as a "campaign of indiscriminate, murderous violence". The first intended victims of his premeditated bloodlust were a couple and their two infant children, who occupied a van at Ballina, on the north coast of New South Wales. Norrie opened fire on the van but luckily no one was injured. Unfortunately, his aim would improve.

On *March 3* at Meroo, on the south coast of New South Wales, Norrie shot 46-year-old fisherman Ian Breust seven times. The unsuspecting Breust never stood a chance. The next day, *March 4*, Norrie, who was later diagnosed as a psychopath, shot dead hitchhiker Mark Lynch in East Gippsland, in eastern Victoria. After his capture, he shocked police when he revealed: "I just enjoy killing people."

MARCH 5

THE HANDSOME BUSHRANGER (1826)

Matthew Brady's popularity among the lower classes in Tasmania in the early 19th century was perhaps the equivalent of a modern-day pop star. Handsome, daring and possessing great charisma and charm, he was the kind of man women wanted to woo and other men wanted to be.

Born in Manchester, England, in 1799, the ever rebellious Brady was found guilty of forgery in April 1820 and was sentenced to seven years' transportation to Van Diemen's Land. Forever plotting to escape, Brady finally achieved his goal in June 1824 when he and 13 fellow convicts fled the hell-hole of Macquarie Harbour after stealing a whale-boat. For the next two years, he and his gang of thieves evaded police and revelled in their notoriety.

An example of their mocking disdain of authority came on *April 20*, 1825, when Brady responded to Lieutenant-Governor Sir George Arthur's reward of 20 gallons of rum for his capture by riding to the Royal Oak Hotel at Crossmarch and attaching the following declaration to its front door: 'It has caused Matthew Brady much concern that such a person known as Sir George Arthur is at large. Twenty Gallons of Rum will be given to any persons that will deliver this person to me. I also caution John Priest that I will hang him for his ill-treatment of Mrs Blackwell, at Newtown.'

Brady's worst crime followed an act of betrayal by a confederate named Thomas Kenton, who led him into a police trap which resulted in his capture. Brady promptly escaped and, on Sunday *March 5*, 1826, took his revenge on Kenton, whom he shot dead in cold-blood after a brief conversation in the Cocked Hat Inn. It was the only killing known to have been committed by Brady.

Still hobbling after being wounded in the leg in a skirmish with soldiers, Brady finally succumbed to the superb tracking skills of bounty hunter John Batman, who later founded Melbourne. Tired of being hunted like an animal, Brady lamented: "A bushranger's life is wretched and miserable. There is constant fear of capture and the least noise in the bush is startling. There is no peace day or night." Brady was hanged on *May 4*, 1826.

MARCH 6

CHARGED (1944): Frank Agostini on *March 6*, 1944, was charged with the murder of his wife Linda, in the infamous the Pyjama Girl case.

MARCH 7

DEATH OF AN ANTIQUES COLLECTOR (2003)

Alan Barker was a retired businessman who lived alone in his apartment in the inner Melbourne suburb of South Yarra. A keen antiques collector, he had run a precision instruments business and had even introduced speed cameras and radar guns to Australia. As a widower, he employed a housekeeper and, on *March 7*, 2003, when Mary Scott went about her daily duties, Barker told her he had had a surprise telephone call from his 66-year-old cousin, Bernard Saw. Ms Scott left Barker at about midday and when she called him that night there was no reply. She then went to the apartment the next morning, at around 11.30, and found the security door to the apartment ajar. Inside, she discovered Barker's body, just inside the door. He had been smashed over the head with a French figurine which usually was on a table just inside the doorway. There was blood everywhere and it was obvious there had been a theft.

An autopsy revealed that Barker had 28 injuries to the head and neck, with multiple fractures to the head and face. He had been hit to the back, front and left side of the head, with other injuries to both arms. Security footage showed Barker's cousin Saw, carrying a suitcase, walking towards the apartment at 2.30pm and leaving five hours later. Also, Saw's DNA was found on a door handle near the lift, on the lift button and on a wall inside Barker's apartment. After killing his cousin, Saw spent several hours collecting antiques and a Pro Hart painting. When police arrested him on *March 10*, 2003, his suitcase was packed with many of his cousin's antiques, with a collective value of $21,000.

Justice Redlich told Saw: "I am satisfied that at the time you killed Mr Barker you were showing little insight or judgment as to your conduct. You were not reasoning in a sound manner. You went to Mr Barker's apartment with the intention to steal. That is not in dispute. Usually a thief or rover who wishes to avoid detection will seek to conceal his identity from the victim and anyone else who might place them at the crime scene. You had made an appointment to see Mr Barker and informed the building supervisor of your intention to visit the deceased." The judge added that he accepted Saw did not visit Barker with the intention of killing him. It was, the court was told, "a crazy scheme to get money".

Saw, who pleaded guilty was sentenced to fourteen and a half years' jail, with a fixed ten and a half years period.

MARCH 8

THE WHISKEY AU GO GO FIRE (1973)

The Whiskey Au Go Go was one of Brisbane's most popular nightclubs and attracted a varied clientele. In Valley, the nightclub was well patronized on the morning of *March 8*, 1973, when two fire bombs exploded downstairs. Within minutes, the nightclub was well ablaze as poisonous fumes made their way upstairs where more than 100 patrons were drinking and enjoying the party atmosphere. The blaze left 10 people dead and another 46 injured in one of Australia's greatest criminal tragedies. Yet, another nightclub — the Torino — had been set ablaze, with no casualties, just two weeks earler. Even more sinister was a phone call Whiskey Au Go Go owner Brian Little had taken a few weeks earlier. The caller told him the nightclub would be torched.

Brisbane was outraged and the Queensland government quickly offered a $50,000 reward for information leading to the conviction of whoever had set the nightclub ablaze, and therefore killing 10 people. Within a few days, police had arrested two men — John Stuart and Englishman James Finch. Stuart had walked into a police station to tell officers he had previously warned them of a possible blaze. The lead-up to their trail created enormous interest as both went on hunger strikes and swallowed foreign objects. Finally, however, both were sentenced to life imprisonment. Stuart died in Brisbane Gaol on *January 1*, 1979, from heart disease caused by a virus, and Finch was paroled in 1988. Stuart and Finch had always denied their involvement in the fire but, when Finch returned to England, he admitted his part in the torching of the nightclub. He recanted when it was pointed out to him that he could be taken back to Australia to face further charges.

THE JEALOUS HUSBAND (2003)

Vasily and Tina Karageorges, from the northern Melbourne suburb of Diamond Creek, had been happily married for 29 years and, to all intents and purposes, were a devoted couple. However, Vasily Karageorges, 53, was prone to fits of jealousy and, on *March 8*, 2003, accused his wife of being unfaithful after finding bruises on her legs. Tina, 47, eventually felt overwhelmed by his obsession and made a false confession to affairs. Her husband, in a red mist of rage, went berserk. He stabbed his wife 27 times and, after killing her blacked out and, when he woke, found his wife on the ground with a knife in her stomach; he then dialled 000.

After a jury had found Karageorges guilty, Victorian Supreme Court Justice Stephen Kaye sentenced him to 18 years' jail, with a minimum parole term of 14 years. He told Karageorges: "You stabbed to death your faithful wife of almost 30 years, and you did so with repeated brutal and merciless blows from a sharp knife. The violence which you inflicted on the woman you loved so much was of considerable magnitude. Whatever your feelings of anger, indeed, rage, they provided no excuse or justification for you inflicting violence on her, let alone repeatedly stabbing her as she desperately fought to protect herself." The judge said there was "unanimous and overwhelming" evidence that

Karageorges' wife had been a "loving, faithful and devoted wife and mother".

MARCH 9

ARRESTED (1895): Frederick Deeming, Melbourne's "Body Under the Hearth" killer arrested in Western Australia on *March 9*, 1892.

MARCH 10

'TIGHTEN THE ROPE' (1866)

When Chinese-born Long Poy was executed at Melbourne Gaol on *March 10*, 1866, he begged the hangman not to let him drop too quickly and to "tighten the rope". The hangman pulled the lever, but Long Poy convulsed for several minutes before dying. He had been found guilty of the shooting death of another Chinese immigrant, Ah Poy, following an argument.

MARCH 11

A TAXI KILLING (2004)

Taxi driver Benu Ahikari was a pillar of the community and did not deserve to die as the victim of a stabbing in his own cab. Born in Nepal, he was a university graduate who drove cabs part-time to support his mother, wife and two sons. A former president of the Nepalese Association of Australia, he picked up a fare on *March 11*, 2004, and drove to his own death. A 19-year-old youth, Omar Khoder had hailed Ahikari's cab in Sydney Road, Coburg, and asked him to drive a short distance to a block of flats in Garnet Street, Brunswick.

Khoder got out of the cab and explained that he was getting the $9 fare. Meanwhile, the taxi driver spoke by mobile telephone to one of his sons. Khoder then got back into the cab and, instead of paying the driver, stabbed him repeatedly. He then climbed a fence into the home of his parents and placed the knife in a pot plant. It was a brutal and callous crime and Khoder merely walked from the scene.

A heroin addict for four years, Khoder several days before the murder of the taxi driver had talked of suicide and, even on the morning of the murder, had spoken of suicide while attending the Emergency Department at the Royal Melbourne Hospital. After the killing, he went to the flat of a friend, a woman described in court as Ms J. She left briefly and, when she returned, she found Khoder with a needle in his arm. He told her of the killing of the taxi driver and called for an ambulance and police.

At a committal hearing in February, 2005, Ms J gave evidence and, as she walked past Khoder, he shouted to her that she was "finished" and that he would cut off her head. Khoder, at his trial, was found guilty of murder and of threatening to kill a witness. Justice Teague told him: "You viciously stabbed to death a vulnerable taxi driver sitting in his taxi, waiting for his fare of a few dollars. I accept that it was not a planned attack, and that you acted spontaneously when adversely affected by drugs. Nevertheless, he sentenced Khoder to 19 years' jail for murder and two years for threatening to kill, the sentences to be served concurrently. The judge fixed a non-parole period of 15 years.

**

HANGED (1857): Chinese immigrant Chu-aluk hanged in Melbourne on *March 11*, 1857, for the murder of friend Ah Pud at Campbell's Creek following a row over 10 shillings. Chu stabbed his friend and fled to Ballarat, where he was arrested.

**

EXECUTED (1873): Samuel Wright executed at Melbourne Gaol on *March 11*, 1873, after being found guilty of assaulting a woman and a companion who went to her assistance. Wright threatened to hit the woman with a pick-axe if she resisted his sexual approaches and, when she refused, he struck her and a man who went to her help.

MARCH 12

THE ROYAL SHOOTING (1868)

The Australian colonies were honoured and delighted when Prince Alfred, the second son of Queen Victoria, made the first royal tour in 1968. There was enormous pride in this visit, but all this self-esteem was shattered by a gunshot on *March 12*, 1868. While Prince Alfred was on a picnic at Clontarf beach, Sydney, Irish patriot Henry James O'Farrell fired a revolver into his back. Although Prince Alfred was not critically injured, the attempted assassination horrified the colonies. In fact, there was disbelief when the news first broke, and then anger. O'Farrell, long a protagonist for the Irish case, became the subject of scorn and deep-seated hatred among the colonies' Protestant population. The news of the attempted assassination was devastating and, apart from women sobbing when they heard the news, O'Farrell was attacked by a mob and only narrowly survived lynching.

The shooting, naturally, was the subject of intense debate and speculation. O'Farrell at first claimed he was acting on behalf of the Fenian movement, but later denied this. On the other hand, the Orange movement railed against what they believed was a "diabolical Fenian plot". O'Farrell, a Melbourne resident who had just been released from a mental institution, was found guilty of the attempted assassination of Prince Alfred and was hanged on *April 21*, just six weeks after committing the crime that shocked the Australian colonies. Prince Alfred made a full recovery and sailed for Britain on the HMS Galatea a fortnight before O'Farrell was hanged.

MARCH 13

SEX OFFENDER (1997): Phillip Harold Bell sentenced on *March 13*, 1997, to 14 years' jail for sex offences against boys aged between 12 and 15 years between 1978 and 1981. Bell died of natural causes in Sydney's Long Bay Jail on *September 9*, 2005.

MARCH 14

THE WIFE MURDERER (1877)

Police did not waste much time when William Hastings' wife was reported as missing. They arrested Hastings and charged him with the murder of his wife and of the sexual interference of his daughter. When Hastings was found guilty and sentenced to death, he claimed that he was to face the hangman only because his wife's family had given evidence against him. He was hanged at Melbourne Gaol on *March 14*, 1877.

MARCH 15

HUNTED (1817): A military patrol under the leadership of Ensign Mahon hunted down and killed two bushrangers in Tasmania on *March 15*, 1817.

MARCH 16

DEATH BY RAZOR (1891)

When John Phelan argued with girlfriend Ada Hatton in a house off Chapel Street, South Yarra, he produced a razor and slashed her across the throat. He then tried to slash his own throat, but was prevented by a neighbour who ran into the house after hearing Miss Hatton's screams. Phelan, when told his girlfriend had died, mumbled "poor girl". He was excuted at Melbourne Gaol on *March 16*, 1891.

**

ARRESTED (1985): Ray Edmunds, known as "Mr Stinky" was arrested while masturbating in his car on *March 16*, 1985, for the murder of Abina Madill and Garry Heywood at Shepparton. (Refer to *February 11*)

MARCH 17

HANGED (1821): Two unnamed Aborigines hanged in Sydney in Sydney on *March 17*, 1821, apparently for rape and robbery.

MARCH 18

THE EXECUTION MYSTERY (1889)

When timbercutter William Harrison was executed at Bendigo, Victoria, on *March 18*, 1889, he left behind a mystery. Firstly, was he guilty of the murder of farm labourer John Duggan on *May 30*, 1888, and secondly, had he committed another murder several years earlier? Harrison was convicted of Duggan's murder mainly on circumstantial evidence after a jury earlier failed to reach a decision. Although Harrison protested he did not kill Duggan, he had gone from being broke to having money almost overnight with no explanation. Then, when about to be executed, he was asked of the other murder, in Deniliquin, NSW. Harrison cryptically said the wrong man had been excuted for this murder, but refused to say he was the killer.

MARCH 19

THE JOCKEY BUSHRANGER (1866)

If young John Dunn had stuck to his original ambition of being a top jockey, he would not have been hanged as an outlaw bushranger. Dunn, born near Yass, NSW, in 1846, rode at bush meetings in and around his home town as a young teenager, but fell in with thieves and criminals at just 18 years of age and joined up with Ben Hall and John Gilbert. On *January 26*, 1865, a group including Dunn, Hall and Gilbert raided a store at Collector. Dunn was the "cockatoo" (look-out) when he saw a police officer run in the direction of the store. Dunn fired at Constable Nelson and shot the father of eight children. Not content with severely wounding the police officer to the stomach, Dunn pumped two more bullets into him to finish him off.

Hall and Gilbert were horrified as Dunn had involved them in murder and were declared outlaws. Dunn went on the run and managed to avoid the law for more than eight months as he moved around NSW earning a living in any way he could, but mainly as a horsebreaker. Finally, on *December 24*, 1865, he was cornered and shot in the foot and in the back in a gun battle. Dunn then was taken to Dubbo Gaol, but escaped on *January 14*, 1866, before being recaptured the following day and then being escorted to Sydney, where he was went on trial for Constable Nelson's murder. He was found guilty and was hanged on *March 19*, 1866, despite being in agony because of his back wound.

**

HANGED (1866): James Jones executed at Melbourne Gaol on *March 19*, 1866, after being found guilty of the murder of Dr Julius Saener at Scarsdale, Victoria. There seemed no motive for the killing, with Jones pumping three bullets into Saener.

MARCH 20

GANG-RAPED (1824): A woman was raped by three young men in The Rocks area of Sydney on the evening of *March 20*, 1824, and although there was outrage in the colony, no one was charged.

MARCH 21

CONVICTED (2006): Melbourne criminal Tony Mokbel is convicted and sentenced to 12 years' jail on *March 21*, 2006, but goes on the run.

MARCH 22

'GOODBYE CHUMMY' (1840)

The ship *Susan* was on the high seas near Jarvis Bay on *March 22*, 1840, when Malay sailor Gregory Tabee went below to the berth of his friend Peter Anderson and, as he said "goodbye chummy", stabbed him in the stomach. Anderson died of his wound 17 hours later, but Tabee denied any knowledge of the murder of his shipmate. Instead, he claimed, he was acting in a dream. Tabee even joked about the incident, even though some on board the *Susan* wanted to throw him overboard. Tabee eventually was tried in the Supreme Court of New South Wales because the crime had been committed on a British ship and the victim was a British subject. The only real problem for the prosecution was that there did not seem to be any motive for the killing. Witnesses also gave evidence at Tabee's trial that he was awake for at least five minutes before plunging the knife into Anderson's stomach and therefore could not have killed "in a dream". The jury, without even leaving the box, found Tabee guilty of murder and he was sentenced to death.

MARCH 23

THE SPEAR-GUN MONSTER (2004)

Melbourne television viewers were saddened in May, 2004, as a tearful John Myles Sharpe begged for his missing wife Anna and daughter Gracie to return home. Sharpe had claimed Anna had left him for another man and had taken Gracie with her. However, police had their doubts and kept a watch on the moody and socially-inept Sharpe, and eventually arrested him on *June 22*. During an 11-hour interview, he eventually confessed to two horrific killings. Sharpe, feeling that his wife was controlling his life, shot her dead with a spear-gun on *March 23* and buried her body in a shallow grave at their Mornington home on Melbourne's outer south-east.

Then, five days later, he turned the spear-gun on little Gracie's head to help him maintain his story about the

41-year-old Anna leaving him for another man. The 38-year-old Sharpe then dug up his wife's body, dismembered it with a chainsaw and dumped it and Gracie's at a tip. The Victorian community was horrified and there were no tears for Sharpe when, after pleading guilty to two counts of murder, Justice Bernard Bongiorno sentenced him to life imprisonment, with a parole period of no less than 33 years.

The judge said the murders were barbaric and unspeakably horrific. He said: "Killing your wife was an act of desperation." Describing Gracie as "a defenceless child", Justice Bongiorno added: "Whatever your motive for killing Anna might have been, in Gracie's case it was simply so that your first crime would not be discovered." Sharpe will not be released until after he turns 70.

**

THROAT CUT (1891): Tram conductor John Wilson executed at Melbourne Gaol on *March 23*, 1891, after being found guilty of murdering his girlfriend Stella Marks by slashing her throat in a fit of jealousy. Wilson accused his girlfriend of seeing another man "on the side" and slashed her throat while they argued in a public park in the inner northern Melbourne suburb of Clifton Hill. Miss Marks died in hospital of her wound and Wilson turned himself into police.

MARCH 24

HANGED (1853): Miner Aaron Durrant robbed a man named Wright on the Bendigo goldfields on *March 24*, 1853. In association with another miner, John Windsor, Durrant pistol-whipped Wright and beat him to death while Windsor kept watch outside the victim's tent. Durrant was captured, found guilty of robbery with violence and sentenced to death. He was hanged in Melbourne on *July 11*, 1853, but Windsor was found not guilty.

MARCH 25

SENTENCED (1950): Jean Lee, Norman Andrews and Robert Clayton on *March 25*, 1950, were sentenced to death for the murder of bookmaker Wiliam Kent in Melbourne. The Melbourne *Herald* that evening reported that Lee and Clayton stood arm-in-arm in the dock as the sentence was passed by Justice Gavan Duffy. All three were later executed.

MARCH 26

THE BANK FRAUDSTER (1970)

Peter Geoffrey Huxley, former secretary of the Rural Bank of NSW, was one of Australia's most notorious fraudsters and admitted his guilt on 129 charges of misappropriation and forgery involving $5.3 million. And where did the money go? According to Huxley, it was largely spent on a gambling habit, although more than $1 million was never recovered. Huxley had resigned from his position with the bank in 1969, but bank officials were suspicious of his lifestyle and conducted an audit. The 43-year-old did not wait for the police to tap him on the shoulder and, on *January 19*, 1970, admitted his guilt to a bank solicitor.

Huxley was arrested and, in the Sydney Quarter Sessions, Judge Head described the crimes as "callous, cunningly conceived and elaborately executed with the skill of a master criminal." The judge added: "I believe Huxley's conduct should not only stand condemned but should be held in utter abhorrence by all ordinary men and women." In sentencing Huxley on *March 26*, 1970, to 20 years jail, Judge Head said victims of the disgraced banker included friends and colleagues. Huxley was released in 1978.

KILLED FOR HIS KINDNESS (1999)

Samuel Macumber, fast approaching his 60s, was known for his kindness, generosity and unsuspecting nature. He lived in the south-east Melbourne suburb of Clayton and was always willing to help anyone in need. A man named Stephen Morison borrowed from him and told a friend, Lorenzo Lavata, that Macumber did not always keep an eye on his cash or possessions. He introduced Lavata to Macumber on *March 26*, 1999, and the 31-year-old Lavata returned two nights later with overalls, an old pair of boots, gloves, a balaclava and a small crowbar.

He brazenly knocked on Macumber's front door and, when the middle-aged man opened the door, Lavata demanded to know where he kept his money. Macumber then made the fatal mistake of telling the burglar he recognised his voice. Lavata hit him with the crowbar and stabbed him before searching for cash. After stealing several thousands of dollars, Lavata drove off in a stolen car. He later abandoned the car and left the boots, gloves, balaclava and crowbar at a local tip. When questioned by police, Lavata said he had been in bed with his wife at the time of the killing and she

supported the claim. However, in a police "sting" two years later, Lavata admitted in a recorded account that he had killed Macumber.

Justice Teague, in sentencing Lavata to 21 years' jail (with a minimum of 16 years), said: "You acted totally out of self-interest. You went to his (Macumber's) home with a premeditated plan to commit a very serious crime. You intended to rob him because you wanted his money. You preyed on his vulnerability. Although you had not planned to kill him, you were quick to do so when you saw a risk of your being caught out ... once you made the decision to kill him, you did so with particular savagery."

**

EXECUTED (1900): William Robert Jones executed at Pentridge, Melbourne, on *March 26*, 1900, after being found guilty of murdering eight-year-old Olive Jones (no relation). The partly-burned girl's body was found behind a butcher's shop where Jones worked in the country town of Broadford.

MARCH 27

THE LESBIAN KILLING (2005)

Joanne Stenhouse and Anne Maher had known each other for 16 years and had been sharing an on-off relationship for several years before the lesbian lovers had a series of rows in March, 2005. The first was over the trivial matter of a dog's toy, but both women were affected by drink and, for one reason or another, the rows continued for more than a week. Stenhouse took offence at a number of sharp comments

Maher made about her and, on Easter Sunday *(March 27)*, 2005, she snapped. She went to the kitchen at the house they shared in the northern Melbourne suburb of Reservoir and stabbed Maher in the chest with a carving knife. The knife penetrated the sack surrounding the heart and Maher died within a few minutes.

Attempts were made to revive the mortally wounded woman, but Maher was dead by the time an ambulance arrived. Stenhouse was taken to the Preston police station and denied she intended to kill her lover. She pleaded not guilty of murder at her trial, but a Supreme Court of Victoria jury found her guilty of manslaughter. Justice Nettle told Stenhouse: "The insults delivered during the course of Easter Sunday afternoon were, it was said, the straw that broke the camel's back and sent you over the edge into a frenzy of rage and passion." He sentenced her to eight years' jail, with a non-parole period of five years

MARCH 28

THE LOCK-UP AXINGS (1903)

The *Sydney Morning Herald* of *March 30*, 1903, reported what it described as "a horrible murder" in the lock-up yard at MacKay jail on *March 28*. Kanaka labourer Sow Too Low, who was awaiting trial for the murder of Alice Gunning, was exercising with several prisoners when he went berserk with an axe. Prisoner John Martin was hanging washing on a line when Sow Too Low struck him in the head with the axe. Martin died instantly, but Sow Too Low's rampage was far from finished. Another prisoner ran to get help and when a warder named Johnson rushed to see what had happened, Sow Too Low smashed him over the head with the axe, killing him instantly. The kanaka rushed to a cell, only to be shot in the thigh by a warder who climbed a mango tree overlooking the yard. Other prison officers rushed Sow Too Low, who was captured after a fierce struggle.

Sow Too Low was hanged at Brisbane Gaol on *June 22*, 1903. The Melbourne *Age* of *June 23* reported that the condemned man ate a last meal of fruit and then was attended by an Anglican clergyman. The *Age* report said: "When he walked onto the drop he scarcely appeared to realise his position and looked around him in a somewhat dazed manner. Death was apparently almost instantaneous."

MARCH 29

THE LIMBS IN THE YARRA (1937)

It was described in a Melbourne newspaper headline of the time as a "Ghastly Discovery". It was *March 29*, 1937, and Melbourne buzzed with excitement for several weeks after the finding of a woman's severed arms and legs in the Yarra River. Two boys were playing on the banks of the river near the Morell Bridge, Richmond, when they noticed something floating in the water near a stormwater drain. The boys investigated and were horrified when they noticed a human leg protruding from a sugar sack. They ran screaming for help and hailed down passing motorist Mr Elvin Heyre, who took one look at the decomposing contents of the sack and drove to the city, where he stopped traffic policeman Constable J.

Wardle, who later pulled the sack and its grisly contents from the water.

The sack contained two arms and two legs, and an immediate inspection revealed that the dismemberment had been expertly done with a sharp instrument. The arms had been amputated at the shoulder joints and the two legs at the knees. Police took the limbs to the city morgue, where they were examined by the government pathologist, Dr R.J. Wright-Smith. Police had no idea of whether they would find the head or the torso, and this made their task of identification almost entirely reliant on Dr Wright-Smith's work. His preliminary investigation revealed that the limbs were from a woman aged between 30 and 40. Dr Wright-Smith also concluded that she was well nourished and had four vaccination marks at the top of her right arm. The pathologist told detectives working on the case that the woman had been dead about three weeks and that the body had been dismembered about a week after death. Dr Wright-Smith also told police that the body had been drained of blood and this in itself made his task extremely difficult. However, the doctor was able to remove a "glove" of skin from the right hand for fingerprinting, although the left hand was too badly decomposed for prints.

Police dragged the Yarra but hauled in only the corpses of cats, dogs and rats. The case eventually was referred to the Melbourne City Coroner, Mr Tingate PM, who gave the police as much time as possible to solve the mystery. However, an inquest finally was held on *June 3*, 1937, and although police evidence was presented, it was impossible to identify the body or cause of death. It also was the first time in Victorian legal history that an inquest was held without either

the head or torso being "viewed" by the coroner. The inquest was adjourned indefinitely and the mystery remains.

THE INSCRUTABLE ORIENTAL (1947)

Melbourne newspaper reporters had never seen anyone like Chang Gook Kong in court before. Chang, a Chinese seaman from the docked British freighter Fort Abitibi, was charged with the murder of 23-year-old labourer Douglas Vivian Alcock outside a hotel in the inner Melbourne suburb of Fitzroy on *March 29*, 1947. Chang, who did not speak much English, sat almost motionless throughout his trial two months later and reporters were treated to the near-perfect example of the inscrutable Oriental. Chang appeared to have little idea about the proceedings of the court and spoke only rarely, through an interpreter. Even when the Criminal Court jury gave its verdict Chang showed little or no sign of emotion.

He had found himself in court as a result of an incident outside the Perseverance Hotel, Brunswick Street. Alcock was stabbed twice in the stomach, with medical evidence stating that either wound would have been fatal. He died an hour later in the nearby St Vincent's Hospital. Chang claimed, through his interpreter, that he was attacked and knocked down by three men, including Alcock. He defended himself with his knife, which had a spring-blade operated by a brass stud, striking one of the men (Alcock) as they closed in on him.

Chang said he believed the men were going to rob him and told police: "These men fight me, knock me down. I didn't want fight. I say, 'I do not want fight'. I have knife, I kill." Chang then ran away from the fight scene. The jury obviously

believed his claim of self-defence and Chang was acquitted of both murder and manslaughter. Chang walked from the dock as inscrutable as ever, a free man.

MARCH 30

KILLINGS (1993): Religious fanatic Leonard Leabetter and two others killed five people in Queensland and New South Wales before holing up in Cangai, sparking a farmhouse siege.

MARCH 31

FLAMBOYANT FLANIGAN (1869)

Irishman Michael Flanigan was desperate to join the Victoria Police after migrating to the colony in 1859 and, after making a successful application, was sent to various postings in western Victoria. However, he had an appalling disciplinary record and several times was rebuked for drunkenness and misbehaviour. In one instance, he attended a race meeting when he was supposed to be on duty. It was all too much for Thomas Hull, the Station Sergeant at Hamilton. He reported Flanigan for a various breaches of discipline and the Irishman was dismissed from the force.

Because he had had been drummed out of the force, Flanigan was told to return his uniform. Then, when he handed it in, Sergeant Hull complained that the sidearm was dirty and ordered Flanigan to clean it. As the sergeant turned to leave the room, Flaingan fired a number of shots and Hull fell dead. Flanigan was charged with murder, found guilty and sentenced to death. Incredibly, he sought permission to wear his police uniform at his execution on *March 31*, 1869. Permission was granted and Flanigan was hanged at the Melbourne Gaol in uniform.

**

EXECUTED FOR ROBBERY (1868): Irishman Joseph Whelan was executed at Melbourne Gaol on *March 31*, 1868, for the robbery with violence of hawker Thomas Bramley on *August 31*, 1867. Whelan waylaid Bramley at Rokewood, Victoria, and repeatedly hit his victim over the head with a revolver. Bramley recovered and identitified Whelan as his attacker. He had two reprieves before finally being executed.

APRIL

Easter usually falls in April, but death and mayhem takes no holiday for Christianity's most solemn period. In fact, April crime rates usually are extremely high and, in colonial times, bushranger activities seemed to peak over this period. A number of sensational murders have been committed in April, along with many other ghastly offences. Crimes this month include:

> THE RAILWAYS MAN-HUNT
> THE SOCIETY MURDERS
> AXED AND ROASTED
> MR CRUEL
> THE MUTILATING MONSTER
> THE GREAT BOOKIE ROBBERY
> And, much, much more.

APRIL 1

THE TAB SHOOTING (1967)

An alarm at the Victorian Totalisator Agency Board's Melbourne headquarters on the night of *April 1*, 1967, showed there was a hold-up at the agency's Mont Albert branch. Police immediately rushed to the quiet eastern suburb, hoping they would still be in time to nab the bandit. Police had no idea that their call for help was about to lead to a murder investigation. When police arrived at the Mont Albert TAB, manager Miss Margaret Pavarno was already dead, shot through the chest with a bullet from a .25 revolver.

Miss Pavarno, an attractive 35-year-old, was an experienced small business operator and seemed to love her involvement with the TAB. She was just about to close the agency shortly before 9pm on *April 1* when the bandit struck, obviously waiting to be alone without interference from customers. Significantly, all betting on that night's Melbourne Showgrounds trots meeting had closed only a minute before the bandit entered the agency. The bandit was about 5ft 6in, was stocky, wore dark clothes and had a stocking over his face as a mask. Police knew this because there was a witness to the hold-up. A local identity, who was not named at the coroner's inquest into Miss Pavarno's death, walked into the agency soon after the bandit. He saw the bandit and Miss Pavarno near the office safe and told police that the bandit ordered the manager to open the safe, which she refused to do. The witness than made a bolt for the door to raise the alarm. He just managed to escape, but almost immediately heard a shot from the TAB and rushed back to the agency.

The witness was horrified. Miss Pavarno was lying in a pool of blood, mortally wounded. The bandit escaped with $166, a paltry amount for such a horrible crime. However, an armoured escort service had picked up the agency's takings shortly before the hold-up, the bandit obviously unaware of this procedure. Police reasoned that Miss Pavarno died because of her bravery in refusing to open the safe, especially as it was empty. She must have managed to ring the alarm to TAB headquarters before being shot but her steadfast refusal to open the safe obviously angered the bandit, who fired into Miss Pavarno's chest almost from point-blank range. It was a cold-blooded killing but the man who shot Miss Pavarno so callously avoided capture.

APRIL 2

THE RAILWAYS MAN-HUNT (1936)

Herbert Kopit, a half-Egyptian petty thief, specialised in breaking into hotel rooms and stealing anything he could find. In March, 1936, he went on a robbery spree through northern Queensland and, in Cairns, he stole a railways pass which enabled him to travel south to Brisbane.

The dark and swarthy Kopit eventually boarded a Brisbane-bound train at Gympie and the conductor, Thomas Boys, ushered him into a compartment he would share with two other men, who were both asleep at the time. Boys later checked to see if all passengers were comfortable and, when he reached the compartment in which Kopit was ushered into, he saw the late arrival pilfering the other men's clothes.

Kopit was caught red-handed and his reaction was to bash Boys over the head with an iron-bar he had wrapped in a newspaper before boarding the train. When the train pulled into Brisbane early on the morning of *April 2*, 1936, railway officials found the body of one man and the bloodied and barely living Boys and the other traveller. The dead man was identified as Post Master General employee Harold Steering, while the other badly injured man was commercial traveller Frank Costello, who later died from his horrific head injuries.

Police inspecting the scene noted that the killer had washed himself in a basin, but who was he? Their first lead was the report of a man carrying a gold-embossed PMG bag had been spotted at the Wooloowin station. From there, police tracked the man to South Brisbane and then to Southport. The chase was on and police then learned that the man they wanted to interview had caught a train to Sydney and then to Melbourne.

Meanwhile, the killer had bought himself a complete women's outfit — skirt, stockings, underwear and even high heel shoes. This "woman" then checked into a Melbourne hotel under the name "Miss S. Williams". However, the receptionist was suspicious as this "woman" had a six-o'clock shadow and large hands. She reported her suspicions to her manager, who then contacted police, who had no idea at that time that they were on the scent of Australia's most wanted man.

When they questioned the "woman", they were told there was a mistake and that the person dressed in women's clothing really was a man and that it was all part of a practical joke. Then, when the two Melbourne detectives asked the "woman" to accompany them to police headquarters, Kopit identified himself. He later admitted in a statement that he had attacked the railway conductor after being caught going through the pockets of Steering and Costello. Kopit said he then attacked Steering, who was about to get out of his sleeping berth, and then Costello, who was about to pull the stop cord.

Kopit, who had thrown the tyre lever from the train, changed his story at his trial in Brisbane as Boys was unable to give evidence against him. Sadly, the blows Boys had taken to the head had left him with brain damage and a loss of memory. Kopit said he was framed for the multiple attacks, but a jury took little time to convict him of the murder of Steering. There was no needed to charge him with Costello's murder and he was sentenced to life imprisonment, his papers marked "never to be released". Boys never recovered from his injuries and died an invalid in July, 1950. The brutal Kopit died in jail just nine months later.

APRIL 3

THE 'JEW-BOY' GANG (1839)

The *Sydney Gazette* of *April 3*, 1839, carried this report of bushganger activity: "The country between Patrick's Plains and Maitland has been the scene of numerous outrages by bushrangers. A party of runaway convicts, armed and mounted, have been scouring the roads in all directions. In one week they robbed no less than seven teams on the Wollombi Road, taking away everything portable. They also went to Mr Nicholas' house and carried away a great quantity of property after destroying a great many articles which they did not want. Mr Macdougall, late Chief Constable of Maitland, and a party of volunteers set out in pursuit."

The gang was led by convict Edward Davis, who was known as "Jew-Boy", Naturally, this nickname was given to his gang, most of whom were young and reckless. Davis and his men not only held up coaches, but also robbed stores and homesteads. After shooting a store-keeper dead at Scone late in 1840, a troop of volunteers hunted down Davis and his gang. The volunteers eventually caught up with them and surrounded and captured them. They were hanged in Sydney on *March 16*, 1841.

APRIL 4

THE SOCIETY MURDERS (2002)

Although Melbourne newspapers, particularly the *Herald Sun*, tagged the slaying of Margaret Wales-King and husband Paul King 'The Society Murders', it was a misleading label and, in fact, had nothing to do with cocktail parties, opening nights or even champagne. Rather, it earned this slightly misleading tag because Mrs Wales-King was a wealthy woman who was worth more than $5 million and drove a Mercedes Benz. Also, the slain couple lived in the expensive and leafy eastern Melbourne suburb of Armadale.

Yet Mrs Wales-King and her second husband led quiet, exemplary lives. Indeed, Paul King had had two strokes and their daily lives were far from boisterous or glamorous. Family events took precedence as they settled into their golden years. It was at one of these family gatherings that they were killed, by Mrs Wales-King's youngest son, Matthew. To all intents and purposes, it was just a normal family dinner, with

Matthew and his wife Maritza as hosts at their townhouse in Glen Iris.

The evening meal was a simple affair — a first course of vegetable soup and a main course of risotto. However, there was a special ingredient, provided by Matthew Wales. He had crushed powerful painkiller and blood pressure tablets to make his guests feel drowsy.

Then, as they left the townhouse, he bludgeoned his mother and stepfather to death with a piece of pine. It was alleged at his trial that Wales first hit his mother over the back of the head and then struck his stepfather. Supreme Court Justice Coldrey told Wales: 'You followed them out the front door. Paul King was walking in front of your mother. You switched off the veranda downlight, picked up a length of wood and, wielding it with both hands, you struck your mother on the back of the neck. She was immediately rendered unconscious and fell forward onto the paved concrete surface. You then struck Paul King on the back of the neck because you knew it would be quick. Your purpose was to break their necks and your intention was to kill each of them.'

The motive? Dissatisfaction over what Wales perceived to be her dominance in financial matters and the proposed sale of a Surfers Paradise unit. Mrs Wales-King, who owned her Armadale home, the Mercedes Benz, antiques and jewellery, and also had substantial superannuation and shareholdings, also had made a will — with her five children (Sally, Damian, Emma, Prudence and Matthew) and husband Paul getting one-sixth each on her death. Paul King was the elegant Margaret Wales-King's second husband.

Born in 1933, Margaret Lord, had married airline pilot Brian Wales and bore him five children before moving in with

King. Matthew Wales, born in 1968, and his mother long had had rows over financial matters and it all came to a head in the lead-up to that fatal dinner on *April 4,* 2002.

However, it all went pear-shaped for Wales as soon as he wielded that one-metre length of pine. He might have planned the killings, but his movements from there were clumsy at best. Although the Chile-born Maritza Wales had no involvement whatsoever in the deaths of her in-laws, she saw her husband drag the bodies across the front lawn and cover them with their two-year-old son Dominik's deflated plastic pool.

That seemed to be the extent of Wales' planning and the disposal of the bodies was both ad hoc and poorly enacted, starting with the disposal of his mother's Mercedes. Wales drove the car to the seaside suburb of Middle Park, locked it and then caught a taxi. To help cover his tracks, he dropped the car keys down a drain. But what to do with the bodies? First, he used sheets to cover his victims' faces, so he could not see their seemingly accusing expressions, placed the pool cover back over the bodies and generally made everything look like a pile of rubbish ready for removal.

On the Friday after the killings, Wales put his body disposal plan into action, starting with the rental of a motor trailer. He hitched the trailer to the back of his own vehicle and drove home. There, he wrapped each of the bodies in a doona and then bought a mattock and ordered mulch for his garden. The following morning he loaded the doona-wrapped bodies into the trailer and headed through Melbourne's outer eastern suburbs towards the picturesque mountain resort of Marysville. Wales drove on to a track more than 20 kilometres past Marysville and started his gruesome task of burying the bodies. He dug a grave no more than a metre deep about 20 metres away from the track, and placed his mother's body face down and his step-father's body on top. Wales then drove back to Melbourne, more hopeful than convinced the secret grave would never be discovered.

Wales, in fact, was so concerned that he returned to the grave the following Monday and not only bought and then placed rocks on the site, but added soil and the newly-delivered mulch. It was a desperate but futile attempt to prevent the grave being detected. Then, on the way back home, he pulled into a car wash and thoroughly cleaned the trailer before returning it to the hire company. Meanwhile, other family members had tried to contact Mrs Wales-King and were becoming increasingly concerned. Wales' sister Emma on *April 8* reported to police that Mrs Wales-King and her husband missing.

The disappearance of the wealthy couple made the television news and, within the hour, Mrs Wales-King's missing Mercedes was found where Matthew Wales had left it. The mystery deepened, but police already were suspicious of Wales, especially after they noticed a distinct odour of cleaning fluid at his Glen Iris home. Also, they found traces of blood on the garage floor. The bodies finally were discovered on *April 29*, almost four weeks after the killings. Bush rangers had noticed that a vehicle had been driven in a protected area and that there was a mysterious mound — the hastily-dug grave.

Police that night recovered the bodies and an autopsy revealed that both the dead had been asphyxiated and that Mrs Wales-King had suffered facial injuries. Police recovered the trailer used in the disposal of the bodies, but no charges were laid by *May 8* when Wales wept at a private funeral service in Toorak, at the church where his mother had worshipped.

The public memorial service was held the following day and Wales offered prayers on behalf of the mourners. Finally, on Sunday, *May 11*, Wales was arrested and taken for interview by the Homicide Squad in St Kilda Road. Wales soon after confessed to the killings and was charged with murder. Wife Maritza, meanwhile, was charged with attempting to pervert the course of justice by making a false statement. Wales was sentenced to 30 years' jail, with a minimum of 24 years. Wife Maritza was handed a two-year, wholly-suspended sentence.

APRIL 5

A BURNING RAGE (1840)

A drinking session on the evening of *April 5*, 1840, resulted in tragedy over what seemed to be a relatively trivial incident. Convict Catherine Phillips, her husband and Catharine Wapshaw were drinking in front of a fire at Patrick's Plains when Phillips struck one of Wapshaw's three children. Phillips flew into a rage and struck Wapshaw, who, in turn, pushed her attacker into a fire. Phillips' dress caught fire but, when she tried to escape the flames, Wapshaw pushed her back into the fire. Phillips eventually was able to make it to a tub of water and plunged into it to douse the flames. However, she suffered terrible burns and died on *April 18*.

The Supreme Court of New South Wales was told that the dead woman's torso was "one burned mass", while she also had burns on the face, arms, chest, back and shoulders. Wapshaw's defence counsel claimed that because she was drunk at the time, she was not responsible for her actions and that she merely had pushed Phillips away. Wapshaw, in fact, claimed Phillips had fallen into the fire and her death was an accident. The jury retired for just 10 minutes before returning a verdict of guilty. She was sentenced to three years of hard labour at what was known as "the female factory" at Parramatta, an institution for women prisoners.

Chief Justice James Dowling told Wapshaw: "The bare mention of such a death when arising merely from accident, fills the mind with anguish; but when it is the result of criminal design, the heart sickens with horror. It may be you possess the form and feature of woman – but no more! The soul that dictated such an act could never have been intended for so chosen a vessel. Nothing but the Temper of Hell could prompt your mind to such an enormity."

APRIL 6

TORTURED (1989): Dimitrios Nanos was bashed, tortured and killed on *April 6*, 1989 after being given a heroin "hot shot and later buried in the front yard of his home in the outer western Melbourne suburb of Hopper's Crossing.

APRIL 7

EXECUTED (1843): An Aboriginal youth known as Sultia was executed by hanging near Port Lincoln, South Australia, on *April 7*, 1843, after being found guilty of murder.

APRIL 8

THE BLACK NEGLIGEE (1959)

Eileen Joan Moriarty, a 23-year-old nurse, was not the typical Australian woman of the 1950s. She had had a child in Western Australia before moving to Sydney and then to Tasmania to seek a new life for herself and, during this time, she had at least a couple of lovers. Miss Moriarty's daughter was eight months old in 1959 and was boarded out in Hobart while her mother lived at Wingfield House, part of the Royal Hobart Hospital complex. It was in the Apple Isle that Miss Moriarty met a most unusual man.

Graham Alan Stewart, a 24-year-old Tasmanian, was an amateur hypnotist whose hobby was the occult. Stewart, a dark, slim man with a goatee beard, carried business cards which suggested he specialised in the hypnotic treatment of nervous disorders. He also performed in nightclubs and decorated his flat with occult signs and symbols. His flat, in north Hobart, had an attic which had a mysterious black circle, with accompanying symbols, painted on the floor. A red light, which blinked on and off, was rigged to the ceiling to highlight the circle and symbols. It was suggested that Stewart regularly held midnight black magic sessions.

Stewart met the pretty, dark-haired Miss Moriarty in 1958 and soon fell in love with her. However, this love was not entirely reciprocated, despite Stewart's best endeavours. He made many approaches but although Miss Moriarty "liked" Stewart, she was wary of his unusual appearance and pursuits. Finally, on *April 8*, 1959, Stewart proposed marriage and – strangely – Miss Moriarty accepted. Stewart therefore prepared a marriage application, which Miss Moriarty signed.

The couple was to have been married the following day but, for some unknown reason, she changed her mind and fixed another wedding date – *April 23*. Stewart made preparations for the wedding, but was left at the altar. Miss Moriarty had returned to a former lover.

Stewart, infuriated, went on a shopping spree. He bought himself a black-handled stiletto and a black negligee before renting a luxury apartment at the seaside suburb of Sandy Bay. He contacted Miss Moriarty, who then failed to turn up for work at the hospital. The police were contacted three days later and an officer from the Hobart Missing Persons Bureau investigated the girl's disappearance. After learning that Stewart had hired an apartment, they went there and, after entering through an unlocked window, found Stewart and Miss Moriarty dead in a huge pool of blood on a double bed. The dead woman's body was covered only by the black negligee Stewart had bought. The stiletto he had bought was by his side and police determined that Stewart had stabbed Miss Moriarty a number of times in the chest and then thrust the knife deep into his own heart after she rejected him yet again.

APRIL 9

THE ABDALLAH SHOOTING (1989)

Victorian police regarded Gary Abdallah as a suspect in the murder of police officers Damian Eyre and Steven Tynan in Walsh Street, South Yarra, on *October 12*, 1988, and therefore planted a listening device in his flat in the inner Melbourne suburb of Carlton. Then, on *April 9*, 1989, the 24-year-old

Abdallah was searched by police officers Clifford Lockwood and Dermott Avan before being taken back to his flat. Abdallah then was said to have produced an imitation pistol and was shot in self-defence.

**

SHOT DEAD (1865): Notoriously bloodthirsty bushranger "Mad" Dan Morgan, whose real name was William John Owen, shot dead on *April 9*, 1865, in a hold-up at Peechelba Station. His body was taken to Wangaratta, where an inquest into his death was held. The verdict was "justifiable homicide".

APRIL 10

CONVICTED (1999): John Gregory Adams convicted in the District Court, Ipswich, Queensland, on *April 10*, 1997, on three counts of rape, one count of assault with intent to commit rape and one count of indecent dealing. In each case, the complainant was his stepdaughter, who was 10 years of age on the first count and between 14 and 15 years of age on the other counts. Adams was sentenced to 10 years' jail on the rape charges and three years on the other charges. He appealed both the conviction and the sentence, but these appeals were dismissed by the Supreme Court of Queensland Court of Appeal.

APRIL 11

AXED AND ROASTED (1825)

After sawyer Edmond Bates, his wife Julia and several others had been drinking heavily on *December 24*, 1824, an argument broke out the next day between husband and wife before Bates ran to a neighbour's home to say he had killed his wife and had "burnt her". The neighbour found Julia Bates' body near a fireplace and noted a strange remark by Bates, who said: "If I had killed her I would have put her where you could not have found her, no, not for six months." A surgeon examined the body and noted: "A contusion on the forehead, near the bridge of the nose; nearly all the ribs on the right side fractured and rent from their articulation with the spine, which could have been affected by an axe … a compound fracture near the ankle of the left leg and burns on the buttocks and right leg."

Bates was arrested and although he admitted he had killed his wife, added: "If I killed her I did it when I was drunk." Bates admitted that he threw a heavy kettle at his wife and inflicted other injuries, leading to her death. However, the neighbour told a jury that Bates was not drunk, but merely tipsy. It clearly was evident that Bates had killed his wife and, after the jury found him guilty, he was hanged on *April 11*, 1825.

APRIL 12

THE RAMPAGING RUMANIAN (1953)

Zora Kusic had the face of a woman who had seen the seamier side of life. She was, in fact, a slut. Zora Kusic frequented Adelaide's darker salons and bars, selling her body virtually to anyone who would buy her a day's drinking. She lived with a Bulgarian named Ivan Nankintseff in a tiny shanty behind a house in North Parade, Torrensville, and sometimes took men to this hut. On the night of *December 5*, 1952, Nankintseff returned to the hut after a drinking session and found Kusic on their bed. He did not realise it at first, but his companion was dead. In fact, she had been killed in the most revolting of circumstances and Nankintseff soon realised he had come across a dead and mutilated body. He fled in terror and police immediately launched a murder investigation.

Zora Kusic's throat had been cut almost from ear to ear and her stomach had been ripped open. Her chest was slashed and there was blood everywhere in the little tin shanty. In fact, there was a dish containing blood-stained water, while a knife was found on the floor. Nankintseff had last seen Kusic alive at seven o'clock that morning when he left for work and although he arranged to meet her at 4pm, she did not turn up. Nankintseff discovered the body at 6.30pm, police estimating Kusic had been dead for two to three hours. Police were convinced she had been killed by a psychopath and no stone was left unturned in the search for the killer. Because Kusic frequented New Australian clubs and bars, police called in a team of translators to help them and hundred of migrants were interviewed in clubs around Adelaide.

The prime suspect was a 28-year-old Rumanian immigrant who had been seen with Kusic shortly before her death. However, the man denied he had been with her and police were told their suspect led a quiet, respectable life. Then, however, discrepancies appeared in the man's statements and police finally charged John (real name Joan, pronounced Jo-anne) Balaban with the murder of Kusic.

However, the charge was dismissed in sensational circumstances after a five-day hearing in the Adelaide City Court when it was argued that suspicion was not enough and that there was not enough evidence against Balaban, an industrial chemist with qualifications from a Rumanian university. Balaban admitted that he had been drinking with Kusac, but was not involved in her death. Although this seemed the end of the matter, the Balaban saga was in its infancy as he soon went on a rampage and destruction for about an hour soon after 1.30pm on *April 12*, 1953.

Passers-by heard screams from Balaban's Sunshine Café in Gouger Street, Adelaide, but could not have guessed the horror that had erupted upstairs in the unfashionable café and snack bar. They then saw a woman fall 20 feet from an upper café window. The woman, Verna Manie, a waitress at the club, was critically injured, suffering back and head injuries. She later lapsed into unconsciousness, although she recovered in hospital. Meanwhile, police forced their way into the café and discovered one of the most blood-curdling sights in South Australian criminal history.

Balaban's wife Thelma, 30, was dead in her bed, her face smashed to pulp. Her mother, 66-year-old Mrs Susan Ackland, was critically injured in another bedroom, but later died in hospital. Even more tragically, police disovered the mortally wounded six-year-old son of Mrs Balaban by a previous marriage. Little Phillip Cadd died 11 days later in hospital. Police were stunned as it was one of Adelaide's worst murder cases. The search therefore was on for Balaban, who had been discharged only three months earlier. The rampaging Rumanian finally was found outside the café and was charged with the murder of his wife – and Kusic.

Balaban stood trial at the Criminal Court in July, 1953, and pleaded insanity. The most interesting part of his trial was that he was charged with the murder of a woman (Kusic) for which he already had been in the dock. His trial was a sensation from start to finish, but the most incredible was Balaban's statement, made in a halting voice, in which he admitted to FIVE killings, including one in Paris. Of this killing he said:

On February 10 (1947) I met a woman called Iva Kwas in a subway tram. She worked at a chemistry laboratory. We were talking and I walked home with her. We sat up so late talking that I missed the last tram. She showed me a couch to sleep on. I went to her bedroom and made love to her. After about an hour I became furious with her. I felt very powerful and strong. I put my hands around her neck and strangled her. I did not have any intention of killing her but I had a feeling I had to. I had not been drinking beforehand. I stayed in her room until about five o'clock in the morning and then I decided to come to Australia.

Of killing Kusic, he said that after the woman asked for a payment of five pounds, he looked at her and saw how common and dirty she was. He said:

I became very disgusted and angry with her and put my hand on her neck and started to strangle her. She struggled for a minute and then lay still. I continued to strangle her. I then took a knife off the dressing table and cut her throat. I then cut her up and down the body and across her chest … I did not feel sorry for

Kusic. *I thought I was quite justified for doing so because anybody could tell she was a low woman and deserved to die.*

Of the other killings, he said he decided "instantly" he would kill his wife when he returned to the Sunshine Café after he had hit a man with an iron bar after seeing him making love with a woman on the banks of the Torrens river. He said:

I went into her bedroom. I did not switch on the light. I hit her on the head. I don't know how many times. Then I thought I would kill Mrs Ackland. Mrs Ackland had made my wife's first husband, Mr Cadd, unhappy and I thought she would also make us unhappy. Phillip sat up and cried and I hit him. I thought it better that he die too. I would like to die, too, myself. I went out to the sleepout where Verna Manie slept. I went out to kill her because she had been stealing money from the shop, and she had been siding with my wife against me. She had been insolent. I hit her on the head and told Verna that I wanted her, and put her on the bed. I had intercourse with her. I went back and had a look at the bodies and hit them again and then came back to the sleepout and saw that Verna was on the ground. I took some money and climbed over the roofs into Thomas Street. I only killed the people from the Sunshine Café because they deserved to die.

Balaban, who pleaded insanity, was unmoved when the jury foreman announced the verdict of guilty. Balaban turned to Justice Abbott and said: "According to the law, I want to obey the law, and I think I am not guilty. The judge then sentenced him to death and an appeal to the South Australian Full Court failed. Balaban spent his last few days playing chess and cards and was executed on *August 26*, 1953.

APRIL 13

MR CRUEL (1991)

Thirteen-year-old Karmein Chan was babysitting sisters Karly (nine) and Karen (seven) at the family home in the northern Melbourne suburb of Templestowe on the evening of *April 13*, 1991, while their parents were working at their Chinese restaurant. The girls were watching television when Karmein and Karly were confronted by a man wearing a mask and wielding a knife. The third sister, Karen, walked in on the scene and was forced into a cupboard with Karly. He pushed a bed against the cupboard to prevent them getting out and disappeared into the night with Karmein, who was dressed only in a nightie.

Karly and Karen took about 10 minutes to escape from the cupboard and immediately phoned their parents to tell them what had happened. The abductor had sprayed an anti-Asian message on Mrs Chan's car, but this was merely to throw the police off-track. The abduction was the work of a man police knew as Mr Cruel, who had been responsible for a number of attacks on children. For example, he had broken into a home in Lower Plenty on *August 22*, 1987, and attacked an 11-year-old girl. On *December 27*, 1988, he broke into a Ringwood home and kidnapped a 10-year-old girl, releasing her 18 hours later. He abducted and molested another girl for 50 hours before releasing her and, police believed, was responsible for more than a dozen sexual attacks.

Mr Cruel obviously was aware of forensic techniques as he not only thoroughly washed himself after his attacks, but also made his victims wash themselves. He went to great deal to eliminate evidence and although police were horrified by the

Karmein Chan abduction, they hoped Mr Cruel would return her alive. As days, weeks and months passed, grave fears were held for Karmein's safety. Then, on *April 9*, 1992, a man walking his dog spotted what looked like a human skull in a land-fill area at Edgars Creek, Thomastown. A body eventually was recovered and dental records eventually established that it was that of Karmein Chan. She had been shot three times in the back of the head and police assumed she had been killed because she had seen Mr Cruel's face and therefore could identify him. Police interviewed 27,000 suspects in relation to the Mr Cruelty attacks and believe they know his identity. However, they do not have the evidence to charge him with any offence, let alone Karmein's murder. There is a $300,000 reward for information leading to his conviction.

APRIL 14

A BIRTHDAY IN COURT (1969)

Young Michael Anthony Curran, just 15, was so unhappy at home that he wanted to join the navy. The boy had had frequent rows with his policeman father, sometimes suffering physically for his trouble. Michael's father, 38-year-old Clifford James Curran, wanted his son to stay at school. They argued about the boy's career on the night of *April 14*, 1969, also arguing about the boy eating his food too fast. It was all too much for Michael, who later went to his parents' bedroom, stabbed his father with a kitchen knife and later slashed his mother with the same knife. Clifford Curran died in the kitchen of the police house in the Launceston,

Tasmania, suburb of Mayfield. Mrs Doris Curran was found with stab wounds to the throat and face, was rushed to Launceston General Hospital and recovered from her wounds.

Michael Curran was charged with the murder of his father and stood trial at the Supreme Court in July, 1969. Michael, who turned 16 on the second day of his trial, admitted stabbing both his father and mother, although he made an original statement to police claiming his mother had stabbed his father. A second alleged statement, read to the court by Detective Sergeant B.J. Morgan, said Curran intended killing his father. Curran allegedly wrote: "He was always hitting me and growling at me. And often hit Mum, too." Mrs Curran told the court her son and his father "did not get on". She said her late husband kicked or punched Michael almost every day and also was violent to daughter Julie, 13.

Michael Curran, who pleaded not guilty, told the court his father several times a year threatened to kill him. He also said that at the night of his father's death, his father had held a bread knife to his throat and threatened to kill him if he did not do well in examinations. He said the look on his father's face convinced him he would carry out the threat.

Justice Neasey told the jury it had three alternatives – guilty, not guilty or not guilty but insane. The jury retired for almost four hours and then returned the verdict – not guilty on the grounds of insanity. Justice Neasey told Michael Curran: "Having regard to the jury's verdict and the provisions of the criminal code, I order that you be kept in strict custody in Her Majesty's jail at Risdon until Her Majesty's pleasure be known." Michael Curran embraced his mother as he was led away.

**

CLAIM OF INNOCENCE (1902): When Albert Edward McNamara was hanged at Pentridge, Melbourne, on *April 14*, 1902, he claimed his innocence right to the time the rope was placed around his neck. He had been found guilty of killing his four-year-old son in a fire he deliberately lit. To his dying moments, McNamara claimed it was his wife who had set fire to their home

APRIL 15

DOUBLE MURDER (1918): English-born Arthur Oldring, whose real name was George Blunderfield, was executed at Pentridge, Melbourne, on *April 15*, 1918, for the murder of Margaret Taylor and her daughter at Trawool on *November 11*, 1917. He confessed to his crimes just before he was hanged.

APRIL 16

THE PONG SU HAUL (2003)

As the North Korean vessel Pong Su sailed through Australian waters, it was being observed by an Australian Special Operations Command group. The ship, registered in Tuvalu but North Korean-owned, moved close to shore off the Victorian coast near the surf resort of Lorne on *April 26*, 2003, and Australian officials tracked two men as they made their way to a local hotel. The two men finally were apprehended in possession of 50kg of heroin, but the real drama occurred when the body of a North Korean was found on a beach near Boggaley Creek. They surmised that a dinghy was overturned while bringing the heroin ashore and that the North Korean had drowned as a result. Police also apprehended another North Korean and a Chinese drug trafficking suspect.

The Pong Su was ordered into harbour, but the ship's captain decided to make a run for it. A sea-hunt was launched and, four days later, the ship was stormed in a helicopter landing and brought back to Sydney. The crew and captain were charged with drug traficking and four — Choe Dong-song, Song Man-seon (the ship's captain), Lee Jin-man and Lee-Jon-ju faced court. However, they all were found not guilty.

**

AXE KILLING (1878): Bushman Hugh Fagan hanged at Adelaide Gaol on *April 16*, 1878, for the axe killing of his mate, Patrick Bannon at Saltia, on *November 26*, 1877.

APRIL 17

THE FENIAN ESCAPE (1876)

The Fenian movement, popular in the Australian colonies over the second half of the nineteenth century, was a republican movement founded in Ireland with a large number of members in the Australian colonies. One of them was John Boyle O'Reilly, who originally had been sentenced to death for a rebellion in Ireland, with this sentence commuted to transportation for 20 years. He arrived in Western Australia in 1868, but managed to escape to the United States aboard a whaling vessel. From there, he made plans to rescue a number of Fenian supporters held in Western Australia.

O'Reilly raised enough funds to buy a cargo ship, the *Catalpa*, but converted it to a whaling vessel and sailed for the south seas. From there, he headed for Western Australia and berthed at Bunbury on *March 29*, 1876. From there, O'Reilly made contact with eight Fenians held at Fremantle Gaol and devised a complicated plot to set them free. Two of the eight Fenians were unable to join the escape attempt as they were confined to cells and therefore unable to join outside work parties. The escape was planned for *April 17*, 1876, and after a number of adventures, the six Fenians were taken aboard the *Catalpa* and reached the United States in August that year.

THE KILLER CHIMNEY SWEEP (1939)

Soon after the bodies of Annie Wiseman and her niece Phyliss Wiseman were found in their home in the north-west Melbourne suburb of Glenroy on *November 13*, 1938, police had a suspect. They found a scrap of paper under one of the body's and were told it had come from a chimney-sweep, George Green, who had been given the paper from a woman for him to call on for work. There also was considerable circumstantial evidence pointing to the fact that Green had strangled the two women. His footprints were found around the murder house and robbery seemed the likely motive. Green was charged with murder, found guilty and sentenced to death. He claimed he knew nothing of the two murders and claimed that, at the time, he was drunk and could not recollect his whereabouts. He was hanged at Pentridge on *April 17*, 1939.

APRIL 18

THE PARENT KILLER (1998)

When Guiseppe Russo was convicted the second time for the murder of parents Gaetano and Maria Russo, he kept protesting his innocence and insisted that DNA eventually would clear him. Russo's parents were bashed to death with a walking stick at their Altona North home on *April 18*, 1998. Their injuries were severe, with Russo's father being beaten with 18 blows, while Mrs Russo was unrecognisable after her head was pounded on concrete steps.

Russo insisted after his second trial that DNA found on the walking stick would prove his innocence, yet expert testimony at this trial stated that the evidence would have been left on the stick by a cough or a sneeze by an unidentified person. The jury had taken two days to find Russo guilty of murder, more than two years after he was found guilty at an earlier trial. That verdict, at a trial conducted by Justice Redlich, was overturned on appeal on legal grounds, but it really was little more than a stay of fate as, at the second trial, Justice Bell imposed the same sentence of 28 years' imprisonment, with a 23-year non-parole period.

Justice Bell told him: "The nature and the gravity of the crimes are of the most serious kind and deserve the strongest denunciation. You and other people must be deterred from committing such crimes in the future. The most precious human right your parents possessed was the right to life itself. Respect for the sanctity of human life, especially for the lives of those who have given *us* life, is our most fundamental moral and legal obligation."

The near penniless Russo was an only child and the sole beneficiary of his parents' $200,000 estate. His parents doted on him and he repaid their devotion with death. Justice Bell told him: "You were retrenched and then dissipated your own modest savings. Under pressure of money, you called on your parents' generosity, as you had done so often in the past. When they refused, you exploded into a murderous rage and bashed them to death."

APRIL 19

THE MUTILATING MONSTER (1999)

Peter Norris Dupas was just 15 years of age when he first came to the attention of the Victoria Police. Dressed in his school uniform, he visited a neighbour and asked to borrow a knife. He then started slashing her before breaking down in tears and then explaining to police that he did not know what he was doing. Dupas was put on probation but, despite being given psychiatric treatment, he was found guilty of rape in 1973 and sentenced to nine years' jail. However, he was released after five years, only to almost immediately re-offend and was sentenced to a further five years' jail.

Although a report in his file noted that Dupas was a 'disturbed, immature and dangerous man' he was freed again in 1985. Then, just a month later, he raped a 21-year-old woman at a Rye beach. This time he was jailed for 12 years, with a 10-year minimum. Released in 1992, he held a woman at knifepoint in a toilet block at Lake Eppalock and was sentenced to a further two years and nine months in jail.

A serial sexual offender, he was convicted in 2000 of the murder of 28-year-old psychotherapist Nicole Patterson, whose mutilated body was found at her Northcote home on *April 19*, 1999. Both Miss Patterson's breasts had been removed, but never found. She had been stabbed 27 times Dupas was sentenced to life imprisonment, with no possibility of parole for this murder, but then faced another charge of murder, of 40-year-old prostitute Margaret Maher, whose mutilated body was found by fossickers in long grass at Somerton on *October 3*, 1997. Significantly, her left breast had been removed and stuffed into her mouth.

Police believed that the body of Maher, who had plied her trade along the Hume Highway just north of Melbourne, had been dumped after her death elsewhere. A black glove was found near the body and evidence was given at Dupas' trial for the murder of Maher that it could be linked to him. Forensic scientist Dr Henry Roberts told the Victorian Supreme Court there was strong evidence that DNA taken from the woolen glove came from Dupas and at least one other person. He also said that a DNA test revealed that the glove was more than 450,000 times more likely to have come from Dupas and another person than from two other randomly selected Caucasian people in the state of Victoria.

Dr Roberts added in the trial before Justice Stephen Kaye: 'In my opinion it (the test) provides very strong evidence the DNA came from Dupas and at least one other unknown person.' Dupas, 52, pleaded not guilty, but the jury took less than a day to announce its verdict. As the guilty verdict was announced, a relative of Dupas' other victim, Nicole Patterson, shouted 'yeah'. Dupas, however, described his trial as a 'kangaroo court'.

Meanwhile, police said they would review at least two other unsolved cases in which they believe Dupas was involved, one being the murder of 25-year-old Mersina Halvagis, who was killed in the Fawkner Cemetery in November, 1997, when she was visiting her grandmother's grave. Halvagis, a quiet, reserved young woman who was very close to her family, was stabbed to death. Police also believe Dupas could be connected to the death of 95-year-old Kathleen Downes in a Brunswick nursing home in December, 1997. Mrs Downes was stabbed to death and, significantly, the murders of Maher, Halvagis and Downes all occurred in Melbourne's northern suburbs, where Dupas lived (in Pascoe Vale) over just three months. Dupas, short, bespectacled and podgy, was sentenced to a second term of life imprisonment. Australians therefore can be thankful the Mutilating Monster will never be released.

DEATH AT SEA (1924)

Murders have been committed in every imaginable situation and place, in pubs, alleys, theatres and even at sea. There have been several cases of murder at sea involving ships plying coastal Australia and at least one documented case aboard an Australian Navy vessel. It was the sad case of two naval ratings who quarrelled aboard HMAS Brisbane in 1924. The vessel was anchored off Garden Island, Sydney, on *April 19* when the body of 17-year-old seaman David Rich, from the western Melbourne suburb of Yarraville, was found in his hammock. His head had been hammered in and his throat had been slashed.

Police were called immediately and, meanwhile, the ship's officers called for a muster. All hands were accounted for, except one. The missing seaman was an assistant cook, George

Brown, from Brisbane. A search for Brown resulted in the discovery of a second death aboard HMAS Brisbane as his body was found hanging in a refrigerator chamber. Brown obviously had killed Rich before suiciding, but police were unable to determine a precise motive, although ratings did tell police and naval officers that Brown often had quarrelled with his shipmates.

Brown had bashed in Rich's forehead with a hammer, which later was found under the 17-year-old's hammock. Rich had joined the navy in search of adventure, but was killed by a shipmate in a cruel and vicious attack barely months after embarking on his chosen career at sea.

APRIL 20

VICTIM DIES (1986): Police Constable Angela Taylor died on *April 20*, 1986, from wounds suffered in Melbourne's Russell Street bombing.

APRIL 21

THE GREAT BOOKIE ROBBERY (1976)

It was one of the most brazen robberies in Australian criminal history and quickly became known as "the Great Bookie Robbery". It took place in Melbourne on *April 21*, 1976, and the thieves got away with $1.3 million. Around noon on *April 21*, a "tradesman" walked into the Victoria Turf Club's headquarters in Queen Street and made his way to the second floor and then to the "settling room", where Mayne Nickless guards had just deposited more than $1 million for the settling of debts.

From there, the "tradesman" went to a disused lift and let five accomplices onto the floor. Carrying a range of weapons, they disarmed the guards, although one was struck over the head with a gun when he tried to tackle one of the masked bandits. Bookmakers in the settling room were warned they would risk having their heads blown off if they interfered as the gunmen quickly emptied the cash into bags. The operation was well planned and, despite massive police efforts, the perpetrators have never been brought to justice.

APRIL 22

KILLED FOR CLOTHES (1835)

James Hamilton kissed his wife goodbye as he left his home for a race meeting three miles out of Sydney on *April 22*, 1835; she never saw him alive again. Hamilton met up with convict Patrick Kilmartin at the races and the two were seen having drinks together. Hamilton's naked body was discovered two days later. There were strangulation marks around the neck, there was a long cut on the abdomen and a slash across the penis. Kilpatrick was arrested wearing what appeared to be Hamilton's clothing and, on the inside of a hat, the name J.S. Hamilton was written on the lining. Hamilton's wife Sarah also identified the clothing as her husband's and noted that they were a tight fit on Kilpatrick.

Surgeon James Stewart told the Supreme Court of New South Wales that when he examined Hamilton's body he noted an injury to the left side of the neck, wound to the abdomen and "an injury to the private member, apparently as if an attempt was made to sever it from the body". He said: "I am of the opinion that strangulation was the cause of death, and that the wounds were inflicted before vitality had ceased. I did not open the head to examine the brain as I consider the injury on the neck quite sufficient to cause strangulation. The pressure on the neck caused respiration to be intercepted; the knife produced (in court) would inflict such wounds as I saw on the deceased." Kilmartin, in his defence, claimed he had "the misfortune" to find the clothes and tied them up in a bundle before wearing them. He was found guilty of murder and hanged on *May 11*, 1835.

APRIL 23

THE BONES MYSTERY (1939)

In May,1939, drover Charles Carpenter came across drifter Albert Andrew Moss near Narromine on the western plains of New South Wales and noted a chestnut horse in Moss' possession. Carpenter immediately recognised the horse as one belonging to a friend of his, local identity Tom Robinson. Carpenter tackled Robinson about the horse, sparking a row as Moss claimed he had raised the horse from a foal while Carpenter insisted the horse belonged to his friend Robinson.

Carpenter did a little snooping and discovered that Robinson had not touched his pension since January and therefore went to the police. Two police officers went to the Moss camp, but there was no sign of the drifter. He obviously had done a moonlight flit but, even worse, the police were told he had been seen in Robinson's company several months earlier. Before setting out after Moss, police decided to investigate his background and discovered he had been in and out of asylums and had been in trouble with the law, including convictions for forgery and attempted rape.

Police got their first lead in the case through sheer luck when they came across a piece of blotting paper among Moss' possessions and held it to a mirror to reveal the name T. O'Shea. However, there was no trace of another local identity, Tim O'Shea, and police now were worried about the safety of two men. Finally, there was another missing man – William Bartley - and police launched a massive search, raking over every camp fire they could find.

They eventually made a discovery on *April 23*, 1940, when they found fragments of bone at an old fire site three miles north of Narromine. Moss was charged with the murders of Robinson, O'Shea and Bartley but was tried before Justice Owen and jury only on the charge of having murdered O'Shea. The trial was sensational, apart from being one of murder without the discovery of a full body.

Moss earlier had attempted to convince police that he was mad and would pick thistles and pretend they were lettuces. The jury, however, took just 45 minutes to reach its verdict – guilty. The judge then sentenced Moss to death before praising police officers in charge of the investigation, saying their efforts had been responsible for having a daring criminal brought to justice. Moss' sentence was commuted to one of life imprisonment and he died in Long Bay jail in January, 1958.

APRIL 24

KILLED OVER A BREATH TEST (2005)

Senior Constable Tony Clarke was on patrol near Launching Place along Victoria's Warburton Highway on the night of *April 24*, 2005, when he pulled over a car driven by 27-year-old Mark Bailey, a man with a history of mental illness. It seems Clarke wanted to test Bailey for alcohol consumption and there was a struggle. Bailey threw the breath-testing unit away and then somehow managed to get hold of the police officer's service revolver from its holster and fired a shot as Clarke tried to take cover.

Bailey then confronted Clarke and forced him to lie on the ground, where the policeman was shot execution-style to the back of the head. Bailey then rang his mother to tell her of what he had done, then drove off and shot himself dead. The killing of Senior Constable Clarke sparked outrage among the police community, especially as he had left behind a widow and a six-year-old son.

APRIL 25

THE BURNING BODY (1854)

Former naval rating David McGee was executed on *April 25*, 1854, for a crime he insisted he did not commit. The crime was horrific in the extreme as residents at Avoca, Victoria, heard terrible screams and later discovered a man's body in a fire. McGee was arrested for murder, but it was never discovered whether the victim, a man named McCarthy, was killed before his body was placed on the fire as none of those who heard the screams could tell whether it was because of the flames. McGee, who had been transported to Australia in 1829, was hanged publicly in Melbourne.

**

EXECUTED (1892): An aborigine known only as Donald executed in Brisbane on *April 25*, 1892, after being found guilty of rape.

APRIL 26

HANGED (1944): Harold James Box hanged at Adelaide Gaol on *April 26*, 1944, for the murder of Lance Brown.

**

BUSHRANGERS (1826): Four bushrangers, named Brown, Goodwin, Hodgetts and Tilley, were hanged in Hobart on *April 26*, 1826.

APRIL 27

THE SINGING, DANCING KILLER (2005)

Roof tiler David Copland had had an extremely stormy relationship with his partner of more than two years, 19-year-old Christie-Lea Danskin, the mother of his two children. In fact, the relationship had deteriorated so badly that Ms Danskin not only had complained to police about his behaviour, but had taken out intervention orders. One, made on *March 7*, 2005, stipulated that the 23-year-old Copland was not to assault, harass, molest, threaten or intimidate Ms Danskin or even approach, telephone or contact her without the company of a police officer.

Copland then took steps to rehabilitate himself by agreeing to undertake an anger management course and to attend a drug and alcohol clinic. However, his good intentions lapsed and, on *February 1*, Ms Danskin contacted police to tell them that Copland again had intimidated her at her home. Ten days later, Copland visited Ms Danskin at her home in Melbourne's western suburbs and, when she told him to leave, he told her he would serve 25 years for murder rather two years for breaking an intervention order.

Then, on *February 26*, Copland approached Ms Danskin, her mother Janine Gray and a friend while they were shopping at Melton. He told his girlfriend that if she did not return to him he would kill himself. Mrs Gray intervened and Copland told her to "shut the fuck up" and threatened her. A bystander telephoned police and Copland told them he did not care about the intervention order and "I don't give a fuck what you coppers do". Copland later went to his parents' home and, because of his angry and drunken behaviour, they told him to leave. In fact, his mother was so concerned that she rang police to tell them her son had threatened to go to Ms Danskin's home and "smash her head in". Mrs Copland then heard her son shout: "I'll just stab her in the fuckin' head."

Copland then went to the Crown Casino, where he consumed alcohol and bought some ecstasy tablets. The following morning, on *April 27*, he caught a train back to the western suburbs and returned to his parents' home. He took his mother's car without her permission and, armed with a knife, drove to Ms Danskin's home. His mother rang police to say her son was "as drunk as anything". Copland, meanwhile, threw a rock through the kitchen window of Ms Danskin's home and told his estranged girlfriend, her mother and a friend: "I' going to kill youse all." Ms Danskin and the friend fled from the kitchen, but the 39-year-old Mrs Gray tried to telephone police. Copland grabbed her, stabbed her in the chest and then said he was going to slit her throat. Copland carried out his threat, but Mrs Gray already had been mortally wounded. Copland then danced as he sang "die, die, die — I have just cut her throat. I have killed the bitch."

Copland, who had been born in Scotland and had arrived in Australia as a four-year-old, told police he was very intoxicated at the time of killing Mrs Gray and "not thinking straight". He pleaded guilty to murder and Justice Eames told him: "I do not consider you have shown any genuine remorse for the death of Mrs Gray. In my opinion, your statements to the effect that you wish you could take time back represent concern as to your predicament, rather than acknowledgement of the appalling nature of your crime." He sentenced Copland to 17 years' jail, with a non-parole period of 13 years.

THE SON WHO 'SNAPPED' (2003)

Robert Isles Hewitt, 53, looked after his 87-year-old mother Ivy Jean Hewitt at their home in the bayside Melbourne suburb of Hampton. Hewitt led a relatively lonely life but there was no doubt he was a loving and dutiful son – until one evening after he had been drinking at a football match.

On *April 27*, 2003, Hewitt walked down to the local shopping centre and bought himself some beer before going to watch his local football team, Sandringham. He watched the senior team play and, after drinking the contents of his six-pack, also consumed another 10 pots of beer. Then, when he returned home, his mother told him off for drinking so much and asked him why he made a fool of himself.

Hewitt went to his own room and "snapped". He grabbed a tie from a cupboard, went back into the kitchen where his mother was standing at a sink and tried to strangle her. Ivy Hewitt fell to the floor, her son then stomping on her upper body and neck. A post-mortem revealed that Mrs Hewitt suffered injuries to the neck, chest and head and that she died as a result of the force used in her son stomping on her.

Hewitt then rang a relative to tell her not to visit his mother the following day as she was ill. He then drove to a hotel and drank more beer before returning home at around 4am, with his mother dead on the kitchen floor. She remained there for a week, until Hewitt presented himself at the local police station and confessed to killing his mother. Hewitt pleaded guilty and Justice Kellam noted that there was "full, frank and open honesty" about the killing. The judge sentenced Hewitt to 13 years' jail, with a minimum of 10 years.

APRIL 28

DEATH OF AN INSPECTOR (1857)

The killing of Victoria's Inspector General of Prisons, John Price, at Williamstown shocked the colony. Several prisoners approached Price about the horrendous conditions under which they worked and lived and, when he ignored their complaints, they attacked him. The men, using their work tools of picks and shovels, bludgeoned him to death. Although 15 convicts were arrested, only seven paid the extreme penalty. Henry Smith, Thomas Maloney and Thomas Williams were hanged on *April 28*, 1857, while Thomas Brannigan, William Brown and Richard Bryant were hanged the following day. The seventh man, John Chesley, was hanged on *April 30*.

THE PORT ARTHUR MASSACRE (1996)

It seemed like just a normal day at the Port Arthur tourism attraction in Tasmania. The former convict station attracted thousands of tourists each year but *April 28*, 1996, was to become a day in infamy. It was the day of the Port Arthur Massacre in which 35 people were killed and another 37 wounded by a crazed gunman.

David and Sally Martin were shot in their guesthouse near the tourist site and the killer, Martin Bryant, then drove to the ruin and opened fire on tourists. At the completion of his shooting spree, he returned to the guesthouse, where police believed the Martins were still alive and being held hostage. Finally, 18 hours later, Martin set fire to the guesthouse and attempted to escape. However, he was captured and taken to the Royal Hobart Hospital with burns to his body.

Bryant pleaded guilty to murder and was sentenced to life imprisonment. In fact, he was ordered to be detained to his death. Bryant, born in 1967, was described in 1984 as having a personality disorder, while some reports suggested he had tortured animals as a child. One report suggested the killing spree might have been sparked by a refusal when he was nine years of age of selling trinkets outside a Port Arthur café.

APRIL 29

GUILTY, BUT NO BODY (2002)

Jeffrey Kevin Mitchell, 47, had been in a relationship with Leanne Brown for a number of years and had two sons, aged 11 and nine, when a younger rival, 23-year-old Andrew Preston came along. Preston struck up a relationship with Brown and the couple moved to a caravan park at Lilydale, on the outskirts of Melbourne. Then, on *April 29*, 2002, Mitchell and Brown's brother Gavin went to the caravan park and accompanied Preston to a four-wheel drive vehicle. Preston was never seen again but, after about a year, Gavin Brown started co-operating with police and searches were made for Preston's body. These searches proved unsuccessful and police believed this was because of roadworks in the area several months earlier.

Then, shortly before Mitchell's arrest, he made admissions to Leanne Brown in conversations taped by the police. At Mitchell's trial in February, 2005, Gavin Brown said he and Mitchell had driven Preston to a remote location near the timber township Powelltown, where Mitchell stabbed and killed the young man. Mitchell, who was worried about the possibility of losing custody of his sons, and Brown then pushed the body into the bush. Mitchell, who pleaded not guilty, said he only took Preston away to "warn him off". However, the jury was not convinced and Mitchell was found guilty of murder. Judge Whelan told him: "The offence of which you have been found guilty is clearly a most grave and serious one. Andrew Preston was a drug user, and the evidence in your trial suggested that he encouraged drug use in your partner, Leanne Brown. I accept, as your counsel submitted in your plea, that the circumstances of the relationship between Leanne Brown and Andrew Preston were such as to make any father concerned. That matter, however, does not detract from the gravity or the seriousness of the offence of which you have been found guilty and for which you are responsible.

The judge added: "On any view of the facts, Andrew Preston went through a terrifying ordeal prior to his death. He was forcibly taken at night from the caravan and driven to an isolated spot. I have no doubt that he was terrified before he was murdered by you." He sentenced Mitchell to 18 years' imprisonment, with a non-parole period of 14 years. Gavin Brown, who had successfully applied for a separate trial and pleaded guilty, gave an undertaking to give evidence against Mitchell. He was given a suspended sentence.

APRIL 30

SPIRIT VOICES (1934)

Anyone walking past the Turner home in the quiet suburb of Glen Iris in the east of Melbourne would have rated it one of the prettiest in the neighbourhood. A white weatherboard cottage with a neat picket fence, it could have been a setting for domestic bliss. Instead, the home in Tooronga Road became a slaughterhouse on *April 30*, 1934.

Boilermaker David Turner left for work early that morning, leaving his wife May at home with their two children. When Turner returned home just after 6pm, the house was in total darkness and the key was missing from its usual hiding place. Turner sensed something was wrong, and on eventually entering the house, saw his wife on the floor in a pool of blood. He ran to a neighbour's to get help but, when he returned, found his daughters Martha (10) and Eliza (eight) with serious head wounds. The two girls, who had been bashed with an axe, died from their wounds and their 35-year-old mother had an extremely deep wound to the throat and slashed wrists.

Mrs Turner was rushed to the Alfred Hospital, but also died of her wounds. At an inquest into the Glen Iris tragedy the following month, the Alfred Hospital's Dr Eric Langley told the coroner, Mr McLean PM, that he had asked Mrs Turner who had attacked her. The dying woman, whose vocal cords had been severed, was unable to answer but wrote a note for the doctor. Mr McLean was handed this note, but refused to release its contents.

Later, Constanble M. Murphy told the inquest he had found an exercise book in the Turner home and one entry read: "After being followed all day I wish to die with my children." Another entry said "spirit voices" had been speaking to Mrs Turner every day. Turner told the inquest that he and his wife had migrated to Australia from Scotland eight years earlier and that his wife's mother had died in a mental institution. He also said his wife had become increasingly morbid and fascinated with spiritualism. The coroner found that Martha and Eliza Turner had died of injuries inflicted by their mother "while of unsound mind" and that Mrs Turner had died as a result of self-inflicted wounds.

THE KINGSGROVE SLASHER (1956)

When a young woman was slashed across the chest by a night-stalker in the Sydney suburb of Kingsgrove on the night of *March 8*, 1956, police at first thought it probably was a random attack. However, there were more and more attacks and, finally, residents in and around Kingsgrove were terrified. Some women refused to go out at night and husbands and fathers padlocked doors and windows. The attacks continued for more than three years and police came under enormous pressure to make an arrest. They tried every trick and ruse in the book to try and nab "the Kingsville Slasher", but came up empty every time.

Finally, on the night of *April 30*, 1959, Sydney's most wanted man slashed two women in separate attacks. However, one of the women was awakened and alerted police, who arrested the attacker as he flew towards a railway station to escape. The man known as "the Kingsgrove Slasher" confessed almost immediately, much to police relief. He was 29-year-old married man David Joseph Scanlon, who even had installed locks at his own home to "protect" his wife. Scanlon told police he committed his frightening crimes simply for thrills. He said: "I did all those things so people would chase me." He was charged with 18 offences and eventually was sentenced to a total of 104 years' jail, to be served concurrently and with a minimum term of 18 years.

MAY

The nights are starting to get chilly and it is time to read of murder and mayhem only in company. The merry month of May has seen some of Australia's most horrific crimes, including several truly notorious murders. From bushranger days to the criminal elements of Sydney's turbulent 1930s, this month has seen police both baffled and triumphant. Crimes this month include:

SLAVE TERROR

BOLD BEN HALL

THE SHARK ARM CASE

BUTCHERED!

THE COCAINE DEALER

And much, much more!

MAY 1

THE SEXUAL ASSAULT FINE (1824)

Although former convict John Cable was acquitted of raping married woman Martha Harris in Sydney on *May 1*, 1824, he was found guilty of the perpetration of "a gross and violent assault upon her" with intent to rape her. The Supreme Court of New South Wales jailed him for 14 days and fined him 20 pounds; he also was ordered to keep the peace for 12 months.

KILLED IN JAIL (1994)

It appeared to be just another day at the Cessnock Correctional Centre, New South Wales, on *May 1*, 1994. Two inmates, Ahamid Ibrahim and Clarence English had just completed kitchen duties in preparation for lunch and were playing cards when Ibrahim, who had been jailed for armed robbery, suggested English was a "screw lover". English reacted by punching Ibrahim in the face and knocking him to the ground before kicking him in the back. Ibrahim, who lost a tooth during the attack, appeared upset but worked with his attacker during the serving of lunch. He then went back to his cell and produced a knife he had sharpened into a dagger. Ibraham then went into English's cell and stabbed him with the knife, which had a 10 centimetre blade. English had sustained five separate wounds and died of blood loss before he could be taken to hospital.

Ibrahim hid the knife under the seat of a toilet bowl in his cell and denied killing English, insisting another prisoner was the attacker. Ibraham was charged with murder and in a written application at his trial referred to being attacked in a severe beating in which he was kicked while on the ground. Ibrahim was sentenced to a cumulative jail sentence of 23 years, with an 18-year minimum.

RENE RIVKIN (2005)

Rene Rivkin was one of Australia's most high-prolife stockbrokers. He published the *Rivkin Report* and led a flamboyant lifestyle, often seen smoking a cigar. Following an investigation by the Australian Securities and Investments Commission, he was found guilty in April, 2003, of insider trading. Rivkin had bought 50,000 Qantas shares, resulting in a meagre $346 profit. However, he was sentenced to nine months' weekend detention. Then, after two days in Sydney's Silverwater facility, he collapsed and was rushed to hospital. Apparently depressed, Rivkin was found dead at his Point Piper home on *May 1*, 2005, believed to be from an overdose of prescription pills.

MAY 2

KELLY ARREST (1870): Ned Kelly was arrested for the first time on *May 2*, 1870, and charged with assisting charismatic middle-aged bushranger Harry Power in committing highway robbery. Kelly, who held the horses in the background while Power relieved travellers of their finery, was acquitted despite his guilt being widely recognised.

MAY 3

COOKED IN A WOK (1977)

Kyung Bup Lee was a Korean national who arrived in Australia from Japan in 1974 seeking a better life. He spent about three years in Queensland before he contacted a service organisation and moved into a South Melbourne warehouse on *May 3*, 1977. The following day the 43-year-old was stabbed to death.

Police were not aware of any crime until a woman found a severed penis in the women's toilet at the Flinders Street railway station. The gruesome discovery sparked a prompt and efficient investigation and, soon after, a woman found a scrotum on tram lines in South Melbourne. Police were set a puzzle but a breakthrough came when the New Zealand Customs Department notified the Victoria Police it had intercepted an intriguing letter in which someone had boasted of killing a Korean, with full details.

Police went to a South Melbourne warehouse to question the writer of the letter and walked straight into a chamber of horrors. The man they wanted to question had dismembered a human body. Police found pieces of flesh in a cooking wok, a pile of bones and burnt pieces of body under railway sleepers. They also found numerous weapons, including a blood-stained hunting knife and a rod with a screwdriver attached to it.

New Zealander David William Philip, 32, was remanded in custody and a committal hearing at the Hawthorn Magistrates' Court was told that he had killed Lee and then had cut off the Korean's genitals. The court also was told that

Philip had stripped parts of Lee's thighs before cooking the meat in a wok and then eating some of it.

Philip stood trial at the Supreme Court of Victoria and the jury was told he had stabbed Lee in the stomach before cutting his victim's throat. Philip allegedly had told police he had killed Lee because he was "getting slacked off about this lopsided world where the Asians have everything". The jury took just 20 minutes to announce its verdict – not guilty on the grounds of insanity. Justice O'Bryan ordered that Philips be detained at the Arandale Hospital, Ararat.

MAY 4

KNIFED TO DEATH (1865)

Englishman Joseph Brown was drinking in the Whittington Tavern, Bourke St, Melbourne, on *March 22*, 1865, when Emmenual Jacobs was stabbed the death. The innkeeper told police that Brown was the killer but, although Brown had a knife in his possession, he claimed it was only for cutting tobacco and insisted he was innocent. Brown maintained through his trial that he was a mere bystander and had nothing to do with Jacobs' death. However, he was found guilty of murder and hanged on *May 4*, 1865. Brown, a 43-year-old labourer, even insisted on the gallows that he was innocent.

MAY 5

THE KILLER LAW STUDENT (1997)

Post-graduate law student Michael Erik Gonzalez Leonboyer met his girlfriend Sandra Morales at the Victorian Supreme Court Library on *May 5*, 1997, and, together, went to St Kilda where they agreed to lease an apartment. They seemed a happy and devoted young couple, both with South American backgrounds. Leonboyer, 25, was born in Columbia and arrived in Australia with his family when he was two and a half years of age, while Ms Morales, 19, had arrived with her family from Chile at 15 years of age. The couple had been engaged, but Ms Morales broke off the relationship because she felt that Leonboyer was trying to dominate her. They reconciled and, after agreeing to rent the apartment in St Kilda, went to his family's house in Carlton.

It seemed to be just another normal life in a normal household. While Leonboyer and his family watched television, Ms Morales went to bed. Then, early in the morning of *May 6*, the family heard screams from a bedroom. Leonboyer had stabbed his girlfriend 25 times, with nine stab wounds to the head, 12 to the centre of the back and others to an upper arm and left elbow. Ms Morales was conscious when members of the family entered the bedroom and although the young woman was rushed to the nearby St Vincent's Hospital, she died of her wounds the next day.

Evidence was given at Leonboyer's trial that he had had intercourse with Ms Morales on the night of *May 3*, but during an autopsy on the woman's body, there was presence of semen from another man. Leonboyer claimed that Ms

Morales had told him she had been seeing another man and, in Spanish, said she could fuck anyone she wanted to fuck. Leonboyer gave evidence that he then could not remember anything after that. Justice Cummins, in the Supreme Court of Victoria, said: "On the evidence the jury found proved beyond reasonable doubt that your actions in fatally stabbing Ms Morales were voluntary and conscious."

Justice Cummins added: "When, on that fateful night she told you that she had had an affair, you in a rage killed her because she had exercised her independence in a way you would never accept. There is no lawful excuse for your deadly conduct … The most fundamental right is the right to life. The law does not excuse from liability the murderous conduct of a man who in anger cuts down a woman because he is told of her infidelity." He sentenced Leonboyer to 18 years' jail, with a minimum term of 14 years.

MAY 6

AMBUSH IN A PUBLIC STREET (2001)

Andrew Abou Chabake and Romeo Nasr knew each other and shared several mutual friends in their Lebanese community in the Sydney suburb of Campsie. But whatever hopes either had of becoming true friends were ruined by a disagreement that was to have fatal consequences. At about 5pm on *May 6*, 2001, Nasr received a telephone call from Chabake, after which he decided they should resolve their problems in person.

Nasr drove to a house in Frederick Street where Chabake, a 26-year-old pool hall operator, and his wife lived with his parents. As Nasr walked up the driveway, Chabake attacked him without warning. Both men went at each other wildly and just when Nasr started getting the upper-hand, the fight was broken up by Bek Hadid, a friend of both men, and Chabake's father. Nasr was threatened with a handgun and ordered to leave the property. As he did so, an understandably angry Nasr, who received a black eye and a swollen cheek in the fight, warned Chabake that he had not heard the last of it.

Nasr wanted to settle the score, so that night, through a mutual friend, he challenged Chabake to a "fair fight". Chabake declined, telling friends he feared Nasr would stab him. Nasr went to the house of his uncle, Fadi Nasr, a young man not much older than him, to watch a football match on TV. When the match finished just before 10pm, Nasr was still distracted by his late afternoon fight with Chabake, so he decided to find Chabake and confront him. Nasr's uncle, who had some status among the young men in the community, went with him to ensure a fair fight.

They stopped outside Chabake's darkened house. Nasr called out: "Come out you dog and f—-ing finish what you started!" There was no response, so they drove to a friend's house nearby. On finding no one awake, they turned the corner into Frederick Street and were surprised when Chabake approached the car, raised a pistol and fired seven shots, one of which grazed Nasr's left leg, another inflicting fatal injuries as it pierced his back and penetrated his heart and right lung.

Nasr died within minutes in the arms of his distraught uncle. No weapon of any sort was found in Nasr's car. In sentencing Chabake to 20 years' jail with a non-parole period of 15 years, Justice Howie said: "I find it difficult, if not impossible, to understand how a young man...could possibly have laid in wait for (Nasr) in effect to ambush and kill just to avoid the consequences of a fistfight. Yet on the available evidence this is what the offender did. He decided to take that course while completely sober and apparently rational...I acknowledge that there was a degree of provocation in the challenge issued by (Nasr) and his promise to return, but I find it impossible to understand how (Chabake) could have reacted to that provocation by forming the view that he should arm himself, await (Nasr's) return in a public street, and, without any warning, shoot at him with the intention of killing him."

COLD DESIRE (1997)

Successful businessman Bernard Whelan had helped his one-time friend Bruce Allan Burrell out of the odd tight spot when he was down on his luck. Although their friendship went cold, Mr Whelan could never have predicted that Burrell would one day use his success against him in the vilest possible manner.

Mr Whelan was the managing director in Australia of Crown Equipment, an international corporation with headquarters in the United States. In the 1980s, he met Burrell, an advertising manager for a firm that did business with Crown Equipment (in Smithfield, NSW). The pair soon became friends who shared a passion for sporting shooting. Mr Whelan and his wife, Kerry, 20 years his junior, attended Burrell's wedding in 1985, and the Burrells visited the Whelans on their farm in the country. When Burrell's employer became bankrupt in 1987, Mr Whelan arranged for Burrell to join Crown Equipment.

In 1988, the Burrells and Mrs Burrell's parents bought a 470-acre property called 'Hillydale' near Bungonia, in the Goulburn district. The Burrells soon discovered that the property was not prime farmland and was too small to support a single person, much less a couple.

Burrell worked for Crown Equipment until December 1990 when the recession hit and he was one of about 30 staff the company had to lay off. Significantly, Mr Whelan was forced to deliver the bad news. After a series of temporary contract jobs, work became scarce for Burrell.

Following the uncomfortable retrenchment, there was still some contact – both professional and social – between Burrell and Mr Whelan. But Mr Whelan severed all contact after a couple of disturbing incidents. The first involved Burrell agreeing to agist some of Mr Whelan's prized pedigree cattle on Hillydale, but somehow the cattle escaped from an unfenced section of the property and were lost in the adjoining bushland. The final straw was when Burrell borrowed one of Mr Whelan's rifles – a .44 magnum semi-automatic rifle – and soon claimed the rifle had been stolen from his car.

Compounding matters for Burrell was the ill health of his wife. But in 1995, her health problems behind her, Mrs Burrell formed a successful business. By this stage, Burrell was spending most of his time at Hillydale and was almost entirely reliant on his wife's income for support.

The Burrells separated in mid-1996 and in December came to a financial settlement, which required each to buy out Mrs Burrell's parents, share in Hillydale. Burrell got a bank loan of $125,000 which had interest payments of more than $1000 a month. By April 1997, Burrell's finances were in dire trouble. He had resorted to selling his possessions, and borrowed a further $30,000 from his father. The downward spiral could not continue. Something had to give, or he would lose everything.

Burrell, 44, hatched a plan to kidnap someone and demand a ransom. He made handwritten notes in point form setting out his evil scheme, using seemingly harmless words as "collection" and "advisement". He soon identified Mrs Whelan, a 39-year-old mother-of-three, as his target.

On *April 7*, 1997, Mr Whelan was surprised to receive a phone call from Burrell, as it had been about four years since they had spoken. He was even more surprised when Burrell didn't ask for a job or a loan. But unbeknown to Mr Whelan, Burrell was simply trying to ascertain his movements, and Mr Whelan revealed he would visit Crown Equipment's premises in Adelaide on April 16. Burrell earmarked that date for Mrs Whelan's kidnapping.

When the day came, Burrell went unannounced to the Whelan's house at Kurrajong. The front gates were locked and could only be opened by entering a secret code that he didn't know. Rather than use his mobile phone to call the house, which he knew would be tracked back to him, he drove about 10km to Richmond to make the call from a public telephone.

To Burrell's disappointment, Mrs Whelan was not home alone – with her was one of her three children, who was ill, and Ms Minton-Taylor, an employee of the family. Burrell's phone call was answered by Ms Minton-Taylor, who, after consulting Mrs Whelan, agreed to let him in. Once inside, Burrell and Mrs Whelan spoke privately for some time. When Burrell left, Mrs Whelan asked Ms Minton-Taylor not to tell anyone that he had been there, and reassured her that she would explain everything soon, suffice to say that nothing improper was going on between her and Burrell.

Whatever Burrell had told Mrs Whelan had surprised and embarrassed her, and he somehow persuaded her to meet him in Parramatta at 9:30am on *May 6*. On that particular morning, a security camera at Parramatta's Park Royal Hotel captured footage of Mrs Whelan parking her car and walking into Phillip Street at 9:38am. Shortly after, Burrell tricked Mrs Whelan to get into his car.

"At first the journey had all the appearance of normality to Mrs Whelan," Justice Graham Barr said at Burrell's trial in August 2006. "(But) at some point on the journey...(Burrell) detained her. At some time afterwards, in a place it is not possible to identify...(he) killed Mrs Whelan...(and) disposed of her body."

The kidnapping accomplished, Burrell posted a ransom letter to Mr Whelan. Claiming to have been written by a foreign consortium experienced in kidnapping and extorting, the menacing letter read:

There will be no second chances. Follow all instructions or your wife will die.

By the time you receive (sic) this letter she will be safely in our keeping. To ensure her safe return you must at no time bring in the police the press any authorities or outside assistance. We will know if you do so. The consequences of breaching tis (sic) rule will be dire for your wife.

You are not our first Australian target there (sic) have been others. You have not heard of this in the past because they have implicitly followed all instructions and been reunited with there (sic) loved ones. Do not underestimate our capabilities.

We will know if you breach any condition at any time and you and your family will not see her again. This is our only guarantee (sic).

The ransom for her return is one million US dollars. The rate of exchange means you will pay one million two hundred fifty thousand Australian dollars to be paid in one hundred dollar Australian notes. Ensure only the new plastic ones are used. No paper currency. No consecutively numbered noted, the money is to be delivered in a heavy duty green plastic garbage bag.

The money is not to be photo copied. No remote transmitting devices. No radioactive dusts. No dyes. No means of tracing the money is to be used.

We are able to scan and test for all such devices and any other method you may use. Do not be tempted for if anything is used to trace the money it will not be collected and your wife will die. No further contact will be made.

You have seven days. When the money is ready you are to put an advertisement in the public notice section of the Sydney Daily Telegraph newspaper saying: Anyone who witnessed a white Volkswagon beetle parked beside the eastern gates of the Sydney Olympic site at 10.30pm on Tuesday 8.4.97 please call .... then put you (sic) telephone number at the end of the advertisement.

After the advertisement has been in the newspaper we will be in contact within the next three days at your home to tell you the next step. Be ready to leave with the money at any time.

The money is to be delivered by you and nobody else. Do not substitute yourself for the delivery. You must be alone. Have no wires on yourself or in the car you use. We will know if you try to use them. Do not use the car radio

Any sign of outside involvement or interference and your wife will die. We will be aware of everything you do. Take cae (sic). This is your only means of ever seeing her alive again.

Mr Whelan didn't receive the ransom note until the day after his wife went missing, by which time he had already contacted the police.

On *May 23*, Burrell, whose home had first been searched by police two days earlier, left a message for Mr Whelan at work, saying he was "the man with the white Volkswagen", that Mrs Whelan was OK and warning Mr Whelan to call off the police and the media. He said he would be in touch again within a fortnight.

Burrell told police that on the day of Mrs Whelan's disappearance he had been at home, incapacitated with debilitating back pain – the result of falling onto a hay-baling hook many years earlier. This explanation appeared flimsy when it was found that he had not sought medical treatment for his back ailment during his time in the district. Further suspicion fell on him when, around neighbours, he claimed his pain rendered him unable to sit down for any period, yet he was able to drive seemingly unhindered.

With police failing to find Mrs Whelan's body, despite intensive searches, the Crown case against Burrell was entirely circumstantial. Burrell was originally charged with murder in 1999 but it took a further seven years, a coronial inquest and two trials – the first of which resulted in a hung jury – for Burrell to be found guilty.

"(Burrell) must have devised a plan to carry Mrs Whelan, unsuspecting, to a secluded place and there to overpower her," Justice Barr said. "He must have taken care not to leave any trace of her in his vehicle. He hid her body carefully, probably in a place he had in mind before the abduction, and concealed it well enough to defeat a series of thorough police searches ... In my opinion the offender's detailed planning, his persistence, the precautions he took to avoid detection, his motive, namely the cold desire to extort a large sum of money, and the intent he harboured...to kill Mrs Whelan, comprehend a level of culpability that is...extreme."

Burrell, who showed no remorse for his crimes, was sentenced to life imprisonment. Outside the court, Mr Whelan said: "It was a premeditated and carefully planned execution and I think Mr Burrell has been given what he deserves...We're not happy. We will never be happy, because we lost Kerry. But at least our faith in the criminal justice system has been justified."

Mr Whelan's voice quivered with emotion when he spoke of the importance of finding his wife's body. "We hope one day that my children and I will be able to lay her to rest," he said.

MAY 7

SLAVE TERROR (2004)

Those in the County Court in the Victorian goldfields city of Ballarat in 2004 had heard nothing like it before. Businessman Graeme Slattery had been charged with 69 offences relating to cruelty and sexual assault, with many of these charges involving a woman he treated like a slave at the Warnambool home he shared with his wife and six children. The woman, referred to in court as "Robin" was beaten almost daily over a long period in a garage with no heating, cooking or toilet facilities. The woman used a bucket as a toilet and was hosed down on a lawn every few days. She also told the court of how she was forced to drink motor oil and eat snails.

However, "Robin" was not Slattery's only victim as he also mistreated other men and women, including two men who worked for him at a boat factory in Warrnambool. One, a 19-year-old referred to as "Stephen" was physically, sexually and psychologically abused from November, 2000 until early in 2001. He slept on the factory's concrete floor and also was hosed down twice a week. Another worker, 32-year-old invalid pensioner "Bruce" also was humiliated and, at one stage, was ordered to punch "Stephen's" nose until it broke. "Stephen" and "Bruce" also were ordered to expose themselves to factory visitors, and to perform indecent acts on each other.

Finally, however, "Bruce's" relatives raised concerns about conditions at the Warrnambool factory and Slattery was arrested on *June 26*, 2001. Slattery on *May 7*, 2004, was sentenced to 14 years' jail, with an 11 and a half year's non-parole period. "Robin" thanked the court for restoring her faith in people and said: "You live with a mad man for three years, then you find out there are people who really care for you."

MAY 8

UNDERWORLD EXECUTION (2000): Underworld identity Frank Benvenuto was shot dead while at the wheel of his car outside his home in the Melbourne suburb of Beaumaris on *May 8*, 2000.

MAY 9

THE DEADLY DELUSION (1997)

Solomon Bannon was a promising apprentice jockey under the tutelage of his stepfather Michael Bannon in Melbourne. However, the youngster had weight problems and then developed a mental disorder in his late teens. He lost touch with reality and was bordering on schizophrenia when he convinced himself that his parents were dead and that his mother Raewyn and Michael Bannon were conspiring to rob him of a multi-million dollar inheritance. This preyed on the young man's mind and, while he was living in Brisbane, came into possession of a .22 rifle.

He returned to Melbourne on *May 9*, 1997, and was so broke that his mother had to pay the taxi-driver who had taken him to her house. However, she would not let him sleep there and Bannon therefore got some rest in a car parked in the garage before he unlocked the back door of the house at Five Ways. He waited until his stepfather went to the stables and then demanded that his mother tell him all about the supposed inheritance. Then, when she called out to her husband, her son shot her in the head, killing her almost instantly.

Bannon at first blamed his stepfather for her death, but later claimed the shooting was an accident. Bannon was charged with murder but Justice Vincent, in the Supreme Court of Victoria, told him "there can be little doubt that you were suffering from a severe mental disorder at the time at which you caused your mother's death." The judge, who said Bannon required treatment for his mental illness, ordered the 23-year-old to be admitted to and detained in an approved Mental Health Service for 11 years, with a fixed non-parole period of seven years.

MAY 10

THE MARKET BOMBING (1983)

Police believed for many years from the early 1960s that dapper little Italian-born Liborio Benvenuto was a Mafia godfather and was involved in the gangland battle for control of the fruit and vegetable market in Melbourne. However, Benvenuto always claimed he was just a quiet family man with no enemies and could not explain to police why his car was blown up outside the Victoria Market on *May 10*, 1983. The 55-year-old Benvenuto told them: "I have no enemies, only friends at the market. I don't know why anyone would do this. I have never done anybody harm."

However, just one year later, the tortured bodies of two close market associates, Rocco Medici and Guiseppe Furina, were found in the Murrumbidgee River and police were convinced the slayings had something to do with the market bombing. Benvenuto died of natural causes on *June 10*, 1988, but his son Frank was shot dead in a car outside his bayside Beaumaris home on *May 8*, 2000, and the killer(s) has never been brought to justice.

MAY 11

LURED BY LOLLIES (1891)

Convicted child molester John Wilson, who once had been sentenced to 10 years' imprisonment and a whipping for sexually molesting a child, offered a six-year-old girl a bag of lollies before assaulting her. Men gave chase and, after Wilson was arrested, police found lollies in his possession. He was charged with criminal assault and was executed in Ballarat, Victoria, on *May 11*, 1891.

MAY 12

EXECUTED (1904): Thomas Horton executed by hanging at Adelaide Gaol on *May 12*, 1904, after being convicted of the murder of his wife Eugena on *February 27*, 1904.

MAY 13

BOLD BEN HALL (1865)

Although both Ben Hall's parents were released convicts, it seemed he was destined for a quiet and ordinary life until events overtook him as a young man. Born at Breeza, NSW, in 1837, he led an honest hard-working life on the land and, after taking over a run (the Sandy Creek Station), married Bridget Walsh in 1856. Life seemed sweet for Hall but, in 1862, after being arrested for involvement in a local robbery, returned home to find that his wife had taken up with another man. To make matters worse, Hall's rival in love was a former police constable named Taylor. Hall had been acquitted of the robbery charge, but his wife's betrayal, with his homestead in ashes and his cattle dead of hunger and thirst, he took to the road with bushrangers who roamed the district.

Hall was involved in a number of robberies and hold-ups and quickly became one of the most wanted men in NSW. He was known as sometimes kind-hearted robber who had the demeanour of a gentleman. He was tall, handsome and not afraid to take risks in his holding up mail coaches and stealing horses. On *October 24*, 1863, Hall and his men raided the home of Gold Commissioner Henry Keightley at Dunn's Plain, only for Keightley to fire at the raiders and kill one of them, a man named Bourke. Hall continued his criminal spree until he was betrayed by an old friend. Blacktrackers led police to a hideout in scrub at Billabong Creek on *May 13*, 1865. Hall was known to be dangerous and when tracker Billy Dargin spotted him and shot the bushranger twice to the body. Police then finished the job.

THE POISONOUS GRANNIE (1953)

The poison thallium became a popular rat killer in Australia in the first half of the nineteenth century and was supposed to be undetectable in the human body. It therefore became popular with those who wanted to kill without detection. Caroline Grills had a rat problem at the Goulburn home she shared with her husband and the poison Thall-rat solved the problem. Then, when the Grills moved into the Sydney suburb of Gladesville, there were more rats. However, Grills did not stop with killing rodents and used thallium to kill her 87-year-old stepmother Christina Mickelson and then 84-year-old Angelina Thomas. In both cases, Grills benefited from estates, coming into possession of two houses.

The next victim was her husband Richard's brother-in-law John Lundberg, who died in October, 1948. Then followed Grills' dead brother's wife Mary Mickelson. In 1951, her husband's sister, Eveline Lundberg (widow of John), took seriously ill, with the woman known as Aunt Carrie looking after her. However, on *May 13*, 1953, daughter-in-law

Chrissie Downey made Eveline Lundberg a cup of tea, which Grills offered to take out to the sick woman sitting on a verandah. Downey's husband John then saw Grills take something from a pocket. He switched the cups of tea and, on the pretext of wanting more water, poured the contents into a jar; the tea contained thallium. Two bodies were exhumed and found to contain traces of thallium, while two other bodies had been cremated.

Grills was charged with four counts of murder and three attempted murders. Traces of thallium were found in the pocket of a dress she was wearing when she tried to poison Eveline Lundberg and Senior Crown Prosecutor Michael Rooney QC suggested that Grills was "a killer who poisoned for sport, for fun, for the kicks she got out of it, for the hell of it, for the thrill that she alone in the world knew the cause of the victim's suffering". That "suffering" included severe gastric pain, heavy legs, delirium, blindness and, eventually, death. The jury took just 12 minutes to find Grills guilty and she was sentenced to death. However, that sentence was commuted to life imprisonment and she died in 1960 in a Sydney hospital of a ruptured gastric ulcer. Ironically, she must have experienced pain similar to that experienced by her victims.

MAY 14

THE EAST BRIGHTON STRANGLING (1950)

It seemed just another Sunday morning for plasterer Richard Hall as he hopped into his truck to go to a job. However, Sunday, *May 14*, 1950, was to prove no ordinary day. Hall, as he drove down Glencairn Avenue, East Brighton, a fashionable bayside Melbourne suburb, noticed a pair of shoes protruding from long grass. Hall stopped to investigate and saw the body of a young woman with a neatly folded newspaper covering the back of her head.

Several Glencairn Avenue residents failed to identify the girl, who had been beaten about the face and strangled, Even Hall could not recognise the girl, although he later realised he knew her well. A description of the girl was broadcast on a Melbourne radio station and Mr Roy Walters, who lived with his wife, daughter and two sons in Glencairn Avenue, heard the special broadcast and thought they knew the identity of the dead girl. However, Mr Walters could not identify the body as he had been blinded while serving with the RAAF in World War II, so sent his brother-in-law to identify the body. The dead girl was Mr Walters' daughter Carmen, just 19. She had not returned home on the Saturday night, but Mr and Mrs Walters had assumed their daughter was spending the night with friends.

Carmen, a quiet, steady girl who worked as a porter at the nearby Hampton rail station, was seen on a bus on the Saturday night with a tall, thin young man and, naturally, police wanted to interview him. In particular, they wanted to interview Carmen's former fiancé, Morris Sutton Ramsden Brewer, 24, of the northern Melbourne suburb of Reservoir. Finally, on *May 17*, Brewer gave himself up three days after Carmen's death and was charged with murder. In a statement to police, Brewer said he was trying to patch up his relationship with Carmen, but she had told him she blamed his parents for what had happened between them. He took exception to this and "everything seemed to clog up in my mind". He strangled her, walked away, caught a taxi to Oakeligh and then hitch-hiked to Gippsland.

Brewer pleaded not guilty on the grounds of insanity at his trial at the Melbourne Central Criminal Court in September, 1950, and much of the court's time was taken up with hearing evidence from medical experts. The jury took five and a half hours to hand down its verdict – not guilty on the ground of insanity. Justice Barry ordered Brewer to be detained "at the Governor's pleasure". Barry was released from Pentridge on *November 27*, 1957.

MAY 15

THE BATTERED BRIDE (1925)

Pretty Mona Beacher was radiant as she prepared for her "marriage" to James Turner. Unwittingly, she was also preparing for her death at the hands of her young "husband", who used the wedding ceremony as the first step in an elaborate plan to free himself of the entanglements of love.

The young couple were married at the Catholic church in the Newcastle suburb of Tighes Hill on the afternoon of Friday, *May 15*, 1925. Mona and Jim told everyone, including the bride's parents, they would be honeymooning in Melbourne. In reality, they headed straight for their newly rented home at Lake Macquarie, an extremely popular honeymoon destination between the two world wars. Jim convinced Mona that this would give them even greater privacy and would also help them settle into married life not far from where he worked in Newcastle.

Mona booked the cottage on a six-month rental agreement through an advertisement in a Newcastle newspaper. The cottage owners, Mrs and Mrs Arthur Williams, lived in Newcastle but used the cottage as a holiday home and were delighted to rent it to the young couple. Although Mona made the initial inspection and agreement, Jim Turner made a follow-up inspection and was delighted with his fiancee's choice. Mr Williams, keen to see how his tenants had settled in, made calls on the honeymooners but, although bread, milk and newspapers had been delivered, there was no answer. He therefore prised open a window and saw the blood-splattered body of Mona Beacher, who had given Williams the name of Miss Anderson. An autopsy later revealed she had been battered around the head and had been slashed across the throat.

Every effort had been made to hide the body's identity as clothes had been burned and a broom handle even had been used to shove underclothes up a narrow chimney. Police, however, discovered fragments of rosary beads in ash from under the stove and started making enquiries at Catholic churches. Also, police found a brooch with the name "Mona" engraved on the back. Police therefore were able to contact Mona Beacher's parents in Newcastle, but were told Mona was on her honeymoon in Melbourne. Also, Mr and Mrs Beacher told police Mona had not married a man named James Turner, but her long-standing boyfriend Arthur Oakes, a warehouse worker.

Oakes immediately became a wanted man and eventually was apprehended on the evening of *May 24* at his home at Tighes Hill. Both he and his wife were preparing to go to bed. Oakes at first denied any knowledge of Mona Beacher, but the evidence was so overwhelming he was charged with the young woman's murder. Oakes told the jury at his trial before Chief Justice Sir Philip Street that Mona knew he was married, but insisted on a wedding ceremony even though she knew it was bigamous. He also said he went to bed on the night of *May 16* and woke up with Mona dead beside him. He panicked and tried to hide any identification of the body. Oakes was found guilty of murder and sentenced to death. However, this sentence was commuted to one of life imprisonment.

MAY 16

SHOT DEAD (2000): Enforcer and underworld identity Richard Mladenich shot dead in the Esquire Motel, Acland St, St Kilda, on *May 16*, 2000. The 37-year-old Mladenich was an immensely powerful man feared by many. However, he was sitting in a chair in the motel room when gunned down by a man wearing a jacket with a hood pulled over his head. The Homicide Squad has not been able to identify his killer.

MAY 17

THE SHARK ARM CASE (1935)

Brothers Ron and Bert Hobson wanted a star attraction for their aquarium at the seaside Sydney suburb of Coogee and decided that what they needed was a shark – a big shark. They therefore set up lines off Maroubra on *April 17*, 1935, and waited. Within 14 hours they had hooked a monster of the seas – a four-metre tiger shark, so big that it had to be lifted out of the sea by block and tackle.

The shark went on display at the Hobson aquarium but, a week later, a young man named Narcisse Young was watching the huge shark become distressed and making what appeared to be coughing movements. The shark then shuddered hugely and disgorged an object and considerable brownish liquid. The shark had vomited up a human arm.

The arm, severed from the shoulder, had a rope knotted with a clove hitch around its wrists. The arm was tattooed, with the figures of two boxers outlined in red and blue and this tattoo convinced police that identification would be relatively easy. But, just to make sure, police scientists took a "human glove" from the hand. The fingerprints from this "glove" proved beyond doubt that the arm was from well-known criminal James Smith. The problem for police was whether Smith was dead or alive as the arm was not conclusive proof of his death.

Police eventually learned that Smith had been holidaying near Port Hacking with a man named Patrick Brady, a shearer and noted forger. They were convinced Smith, who ran an SP book in Sydney, had been involved in criminal activites and had been "silenced". A boat-builder named Reginald Holmes told police Smith had had a row with Brady over a forged cheque and that Brady had said "I have done for him". When Holmes asked Brady about the body, he replied: "They won't get that. I dumped him in a tin trunk outside Port Hacking."

Brady, on *May 17*, 1935, was charged with Smith's murder, but three days later there was another sensation when police were asked to intercept a motor launch which had been running out of control on Sydney Harbour. They investigated, boarded the boat and found Holmes at the helm with a bullet wound to his head. However, the wound was not serious and Holmes later told police that he had tried to commit suicide.

An inquest was held into the shark arm case and Holmes' evidence would have been critical – except that he was shot dead in a car near the Sydney Harbour Bridge less than 12 hours before the opening of the inquest on *June 12*. He had been shot three times in a circle around his heart. Two men were charged with his murder, but both were acquitted in the great side-show of the Shark Arm Case.

The inquest was conducted by the Sydney City Coroner, Mr Oram, and evidence was given that the arm had not been amputated by a surgeon, but done roughly. Following the inquest, Brady was sent for trial. However, Justice Jordan said a conviction on the evidence presented could never be allowed to stand and directed an acquittal. Brady died in 1965 at 71 years of age, still insisting he did not kill Smith. The most logical explanation is that someone killed Brady and stuffed his body into a sea trunk, with not enough room for the entire body. The left arm therefore was hacked off, tied to the chest and thrown into the sea. The huge tiger shark then gobbled up the arm with glee, ripping it from the trunk. It certainly was a one in a million chance that the shark even was captured, let alone vomit up the arm of a murdered man. The gruesome mystery remains.

MAY 18

THE CROW ON THE CORPSE (1826)

Thomas Stanley was a servant on a property at Port Stephens, New South Wales, on *May 18*, 1826, when he and others decided they would do some kangaroo hunting. Stanley and a man named Chips decided to get into a boat, along with a 12-year-old aborigine known as Tommy. They planned to travel along the coast and meet up with others who had decided to walk through bushland. Stanley and Chips promised to take care of the aboriginal boy but, when the two parties met up about an hour later, Tommy was missing. A witness, Joseph Pennington, told the NSW Supreme Court that Stanley had told Chips: "Don't tell them anything about it."

Pennington's suspicions were aroused, especially when the boy was found 10 days later – with a huge crow sitting on the corpse. Pennington immediately ordered the body to be buried, while Stanley suggested the boy had fallen from a tree and then drowned. Although no cause of death was given, a jury found Stanley guilty of murder at his trial on *March 1*, 1827. Stanley was sentenced to be hanged, but this was commuted and he eventually was sentenced to hard labour for life in chains on Norfolk Island.

MAY 19

A TODDLER'S MURDER (1968)

Three-year-old Simon Brook was last seen alive in the back garden of the family's Sydney home on *May 19*, 1968. The toddler's body was found in bushes and an autopsy revealed that he had newspapers rammed down his throat. The boy died of suffocation and, at an inquest into his death, the coroner said: "It would be almost impossible to find words to express the revulsion felt at the fiendish crime perpetrated on this child." The NSW government offered a reward for the arrest and conviction of the killer and police interviewed more than 300 suspects. Of these, one stood out, but has never faced trial for the killing of little Simon.

MAY 20

A FINAL TREMOR (1903)

Publican Theodore Trautwein, who ran the Royal Hotel in the Sydney suburb of Auburn, was awakened on the night of *January 19*, 1903, by what he thought was a revolver shot. He rushed to the bar room and heard someone jump on and over the bar counter before heading for the front door. When Trautwein eventually reached the bar room he found a police officer lying on his side in a pool of blood. Constable Samuel Long, about 35 years of age, had been shot while investigating noises and never regained consciousness. Trautwein ran across the road to the local police station and Long died just as colleagues reached him. Police spotted marks by hob-nail boots on the bar and a black tracker showed how footmarks had led to a horse and sulky which had been tried to a tree in a paddock opposite the hotel. Police six days later arrested a man who was trying to get away with boots in his hand; he also left a loaded revolver on a dressing table.

Two tearaways named Henry Jones and Digby Grand were eventually charged with murder and faced trial in the Criminal Court. The trial was a sensation and crowds waited outside the court while the jury deliberated on *May 20*. Finally, after five and a half hours, the jury announced it had found both men guilty of murder, with a recommendation of mercy. When Judge Rogers asked why they had added this rider, the jury foreman replied that they were not sure which one had pulled the trigger and, besides, they thought a third man might have been involved. Then, when asked if he had anything to say, Grand replied to the judge: "I have to tell Your Honour to your face that you have conducted the case more like a Crown prosecutor than a judge … I will meet you before our God, and then you will see whether I am innocent or guilty." Jones told the judge: "You have been prejudiced from the first."

When Grand and Jones were sentenced to death and the judge said "may the Lord have mercy on your soul", Grand replied: "Same to you." The two convicted police killers were executed at Darlinghurst Gaol on *July 7*. The *Age* reported that Jones died instantly, but Grand "was less fortunate". The newspaper noted: "For over three minutes he (Grand) struggled convulsively, and life was then apparently extinct. But a minute later his arms and shoulders could be seen working. These struggles continued for only a few seconds, however. 'He's gone,' said a warder to the newspaper reporters as the final tremor passed through the hanging body, and apparently that was the end."

MAY 21

THE ART VANDAL (1972)

The world was shocked on *May 21*, 1972, when a young man apparently studying Michelangelo's Pieta statue in St Peter's, Rome, started vandalising the masterpiece depicting the Virgin Mary with the dying Jesus Christ. Wielding a hammer, he shouted: "I am Jesus Christ, risen from the dead." The vandal was Hungarian-born Australian geologist Lazlo Toth, 32, who obviously was unbalanced as he severely damaged the statue. His attack knocked the arm off the Virgin Mary's statue and removed part of her nose and one of her eyelids. Toth was never charged but, on *January 29*, 1973, was committed to a psychiatric hospital in Italy. He was released two years later and deported to Australia.

MAY 22

THE REVENGE KILLING (2005)

In June, 2003, David Neil Pyke was bashed by two men outside the Gippsland town of Morwell and suffered a fractured skull and some brain damage, also losing the hearing in one ear. He believed one of his assailants was a man named Mark Logan.

Then, on *May 22*, 2005, Pyke drank heavily from a cask of wine and smoked marijuana before leaving his home at about 6pm armed with a shotgun and cartridges. He took a car, a Ford, belonging to a friend of his mother and drove to Logan's home. After knocking on the front door and inviting Logan outside, he fired a shot at the man he believed had attacked him two years earlier. Logan, shot in the left arm and chest, slumped to his lounge-room floor, where he was attended by his fiancée. Pyke got back into the car, then did a U-turn before returning to Logan's house. He then shot Logan a second time, this time at point-blank range in the abdomen, killing him.

Police caught up with Pyke several hours later and he fully co-operated in their investigation of Logan's death, even telling them he had intended to kill. Justice Teague, in the Supreme Court of Victoria, told Teague: "The sentence must recognize that your execution of Mark Logan was premeditated and cold-blooded. It was fuelled by the ingestion of alcohol and marijuana. There was planning in the preparation of the shotgun, and the stealing of the Ford. The shooting was inside a family home. The second shot was especially cold-blooded given that it was fired after you returned to the house and in the immediate presence of a loved one." Justice Teague sentenced Pyke to 27 years' jail, with a non-parole period of 22 years.

MAY 23

BUTCHERED! (1837)

A butcher named Wholaghan was slaughtering a beast behind his shop at Maitland on *May 23*, 1837, when assistant Michael Cagney chastised him over a minor matter. Then, when Wholaghan asked Cagney what right he had to question his master, the assistant picked up one of the slaughtered animal's feet and struck Wholaghan over the head with it. Although Wholaghan was dazed, he continued to butcher the slaughtered beast and, with the assistance of three other men, carted the beef to the shop. The 20-year-old Cagney was waiting for them and wanted to continue the argument with his master. Then, after a few minutes, he picked up a heavy paling and struck one of the men, Edward Hughes, across the head. Hughes was pole-axed and fell dead at the entrance to the shop.

Cagney ran away, but was arrested the following day and charged with murder. A surgeon testified in the Supreme Court of New South Wales that the cause of death was so obvious "it was quite unnecessary to open's the deceased's head". Mr Justice Burton explained to the jury the distinction of murder and manslaughter but, after just a few minutes' deliberation, Cagney was found guilty of murder. He was sentenced to death.

THE BODY UNDER THE HEARTH (1892)

When the owner of a house in Andrew Street, Windsor (an inner Melbourne suburb) checked on a strong and offensive odour reported by a would-be tenant, he called in the police. A hearthstone was removed and, underneath, was the decomposing body of a woman. Police immediately launched an investigation and a post mortem revealed that the woman's throat had been cut. The previous tenant, a Mr Druin, had paid a month's rent in advance, but then disappeared. However, police soon were led to believe that Druin really was a man named Albert Williams, who had arrived in Australia from England with his wife in 1891.

The body under the hearth was believed to be that of his wife, Emily Williams and, soon after her funeral, police in Western Australia arrested the man known as Williams. Meanwhile, police had learned that his real name was Frederick Bayley Deeming and that he and his family had lived at Rainhill, near Liverpool, England. Police from Liverpool went to Deeming's old address at Rainhill and discovered five bodies — of a woman and four children. A nine-year-old girl had been strangled, but the others had had their throats cut. The bodies were identified as those of Deeming's first wife, Marie, and their children.

There was outrage, both in Australia and England, with calls to "lynch the bastard". Deeming was extradited by ship from Perth to Melbourne where an inquest was held into the death of the woman now known as Emily Mather, who had "married" Deeming in England on *September 22*, 1891. Deeming was sent for trial at the Victorian Supreme Court and his defence lawyers, including future Australian Prime Minister Alfred Deakin, raised the question of insanity. However, the jury returned a verdict of "guilty" of the murder of Emily Mather and Deeming was executed at Melbourne Gaol on the morning of *May 23*, 1892.

MAY 24

PARDON ME, GUV (1817): On *May 24*, 1817, Governor Macquarie promised to seek a pardon for bushranger Michael Howe, who was released on parole and told to wait in Hobart. However, Howe broke parole and to resume his bushranging career and was declared an outlaw. He was finally cornered in October 1818, and was bashed to death in a ferocious fight with three men, a kangaroo hunter, a sailor and a soldier.

MAY 25

SHOT DEAD (1870): Bushranger Captain Thunderbolt shot dead by Constable Alexander Walker at Kentucky Creen, near Uralla, NSW, on *May 25*, 1870.

MAY 26

FINDING (1927): A Royal Commission found police responsible for the murder of seven Aborigines in the Northern Territory on *May 26*, 1927.

MAY 27

EXPOSED (1982): The 'Bottom of the Harbour' tax avoidance scheme was exposed in Melbourne on *May 27*, 1982.

MAY 28

THE SEALED ROOM MURDER (1916)

Young Salvatore Tabone left his home in Malta in 1916, determined to make a fortune in Australia. Tabone, who later changed his name to Borg, did not make a fortune but he did build up a profitable business after years of hard work. Sam Borg worked in Queensland's cane fields after arriving in Australia but later built up a café business in Melbourne's Little Lonsdale Street. It was not a fancy café but Borg seemed reasonably happy with his lot. He made a small amount of money and was able to indulge in his favourite pastime – card gambling.

Borg was hooked on cards and often played with migrant friends in Maltese clubs. He also made money by renting a room in his café for gambling purposes. Card games were everything to Borg and he was able to build up substantial bank rolls through his gambling activities. In fact, Borg was regarded as an expert gambler and the only problem was that, like many people his age, he did not trust banks. Instead, he preferred to hide his money in his bedroom. It was a dangerous habit as Borg eventually was killed, with robbery the probably motive.

Borg, 67, was seen flashing 1000 pounds in notes shortly before he was murdered in May, 1960. That was most unlike Borg, who usually was smart enough to keep his winnings to himself, and the last anyone saw of him was when he was leaving a Maltese club in North Melbourne on the night of Saturday, *May 28*. His body was discovered the following Monday night.

Police were called to Borg's café when a local Maltese identity told them had not seen Borg for a couple of days. Police immediately went to the café and had to smash in the front door. Borg's battered and bloodied body was found in a bedroom but, incredibly, the door to that bedroom had been nailed – from the inside. Melbourne newspapers immediately tagged the case the "Sealed Room Murder".

Police, in reconstructing the crime, reasoned that Borg had been battered to death with the leg of a heavy wooden table, the body then dragged into a spare bedroom where it was pushed under a bed. The killer, or killers, then climbed out of the room through a skylight which adjoined another room. The killer(s) then left the building by the front door. Borg's pyjama-clad body was wrapped shroud-like in sheets and blankets and bound by strips of rag. Despite claims that Borg had been seen with 1000 pounds, 450 pounds was found in the bedroom and café.

More than 400 people were interviewed over Borg's death and police believed they had an excellent lead when it was reported that a man wearing a dark overcoat had been seen lurking outside Borg's café on the Saturday night. However, the mysterious man never came forward to answer police questions. Members of the Homicide Squad later interviewed two men in Queanbeyan and Sydney but were satisfied they had nothing to do with the murder. The police investigation ran into a dead end and the mystery remains.

MAY 29

THE RESTAURANT KILLING (1951)

Zigfield's restaurant in King St, Sydney, was the place to be seen – except on the night of *May 29*, 1951. That was the night well-known criminal John Frederick "Chow" Hayes confronted another gangland identity Bobby Lee over the death of Hayes' nephew Danny Symons. Hayes, who had spent a large proportion of his life behind bars and was as dangerous as a cobra, walked over to Lee and told him he was going to kill him. Hayes produced a .45 revolver, but Lee was convinced there were far too many witnesses present for Hayes to pull the trigger and virtually dared him to shoot. Hayes obliged, pumping six bullets into Lee and killing him.

One of Sydney's most feared criminals, Hayes walked away from the restaurant but was soon arrested. Lee had been right — there were far too many witnesses. Found guilty of murder, he was sentenced to death and even spent time on death row before his sentence was commuted to one of life imprisonment. Hayes, who had a lengthy police record dating back to 1928, spent 15 years in jail, being paroled in 1967. However, he could not stay out of trouble and was jailed again after assaulting another criminal with a broken beer glass. He was released on *February 14*, 1977 and, by that time, he was all but a broken man and died just months later of lung cancer.

THE COCAINE DEALER (1923)

There were reports in Australian newspapers in May 1923, that police in Melbourne had charged a man with being in possession of a "deleterious drug". That drug was cocaine and the arrest on *May 29*, 1923, marked a watershed in Australian criminal history. The man, Henry McEwan was believed to be one of the first to import this drug into Australia. McEwan admitted selling the cocaine for two shillings a packet.

The Melbourne City Court was told this of the effects of cocaine: "They (purcashers of cocaine) sniff it up the nose. Instead of putting the coacaine under skins (with syringes), victims place it on a surface so that it will be absorbed. They get the same effect as if it were injected. It is a very dangerous drug if injected. It has been used for dental purposes. In recent years, during the war, owing to the shortage of morphia, people have taken to the cocaine habit."

A plainclothes Police Constable told the court: "Many times when we go into the slums we see women who are victims of this habit. They are excitable, and are often laughing loudly. At other times, when the effects of the cocaine have died away, they are remorseful and are dejected." McEwan was sentenced to just six months' jail.

MAY 30

RELEASED TO KILL AGAIN (1934)

When wharf labourer George Bromell found the bodies of an entire family in a small, weatherboard shack in the inner Melbourne suburb of Richmond on *May 30*, 1934, he could hardly have suspected he would be unlocking the door to one of the greatest controversies of the era. Bromell had not seen his workmate and neighbour Frank O'Brien for several days and decided to enlist the help of another neighbour to break into the house in Bosisto Street. Bromell feared the worst as O'Brien had been severely depressed and had told his wife that he did not have enough money to buy food for her and their three small children. However, Bromell was not prepared for the ghastly scenes he saw in O'Brien's house. O'Brien, 59, his wife Rose, 39, and their children were all dead – their throats slashed.

All the bodies were found in the tiny bedroom at the front of the house. The bodies of O'Brien and his wife were fully dressed in their double bed and the bodies of the three tiny children – Owen (three), Joan (two) and Marie (nine months) – were found in their bloodstained cots. The scene was heart-rending. O'Brien obviously had wiped out his entire family in desperation over his fear that he was not able to support them and left a suicide note in which he feared he soon would not be able to work.

Melburnians were still trying to come to terms with the tragedy when the Melbourne *Herald* on *June 1* broke the news that O'Brien appeared to be the same man who had killed his wife 10 years earlier. The newspaper suggested that a photograph of O'Brien's body had been taken at the city morgue and that officials from the Mont Park Mental Home had "expressed the belief that he was identical" to the man who had killed his wife.

Fingerprints were taken of the dead man and these later matched those on police files. O'Brien therefore was the man who had killed his wife 10 years earlier, and the slaying of his family and his subsequent suicide opened a very nasty can of worms for Victorian government officials. The Inspector General for the Insane, Dr W.E. Jones, admitted that O'Brien had been charged with murder in 1924 and had been committed to an asylum (Mont Park) during the Governor's pleasure. O'Brien had been found to be suffering from "transitory confusional insanity". He was a highly educated man and, according to reports, his mental and physical conditions improved dramatically at Mont Park.

O'Brien, in fact, had been a school teacher who was found not guilty of the murder of his wife at Mildura in 1924 because of insanity. He was released from Mont Park three years and eight months after being committed on the approval of the Attorney-General, the condition being that he reported monthly to Dr Jones.

At the inquest into the deaths of the O'Briens, the Coroner (Mr McLean PM) was told that Rose O'Brien herself had been a patient at Mont Park, but was "perfectly normal" after her marriage to O'Brien. However, the sensation of the inquest was when the medical superintendent of Mont Park, Dr John Catarinich, said he made a report on O'Brien in 1924 which read: "Under no circumstances would I suggest O'Brien ever again live with his children (from his first marriage), nor do I consider it safe to give O'Brien his liberty, even with restrictions."

Yet O'Brien was released, only to kill again in horrific circumstances and the coroner said: "In my opinion, the public is entitled to expect that when a person has been found not guilty of murder on the grounds of insanity, and has been committed to custody during the Governor's pleasure, ample precaution is taken to guard against any repetition of the homicidal act."

MAY 31

EXECUTED (1880): A man named Jimmy Ah Sue executed in Queensland on *May 31*, 1880.

JUNE

Winter has arrived and, with it, crime to turn the stomach. They include shootings, knifings and torture and mutilation. They all have been part of the start of Australian winters and society has been shocked by the horror in their midst. Gruesome and nauseating, June's crimes rank among Australia's worst and include:

THE WALKING CORPSE
THE PLANE HIJACK
THE ANITA COBBY CASE
THE HEAD IN THE SINK
DEATH AT THE VICARAGE
THE SUNDOWN MURDERS
And much, much more!

JUNE 1

HANGED (1886): Thomas John Griffin hanged in Queensland on *June 1*, 1868.

JUNE 2

A GREEK TRAGEDY (1998)

Melbourne man George Karalis, 28, was holidaying in Greece when he and 30-year-old cousin George Loizos hired a boat near Athens and set out to sea on *June 2*, 1998. They did not return to shore that night and a fisherman made an horrific discovery early the next morning when he came across two bodies in the drifting boat. Karalis' body was hanging from a rope at the stern of the boat, while Loizos' body was bound and pressed against the boat's propeller. Amazingly, Greek authorities quickly decided that there were no suspicious circumstances and declared that the two men had been lovers who had quarrelled. They therefore announced the tragedy was a murder-suicide, with Karalis killing his cousin and then hanging himself.

Greek coroners even declared there was no third party involved, even though Karalis' neck injury was deeply suspicious. There were ligament marks or burns at the back of the neck, not at the front of the neck, which would be normal in suicide hangings. An independent autopsy on Karalis' body was performed in Melbourne and Deputy Coroner Iain West on *July* 28, 2004, found that Karalis was murdered and was not involved in a murder-suicide. The Coroners Court was told that there were suspicions the two men were killed after they stumbled across some form of smuggling, involving either drugs or tobacco.

JUNE 3

MULTIPLE KILLER (1960): Mass murderer William MacDonald kills his first victim on *June 3*, 1960.

JUNE 4

THE WALKING CORPSE (1961)

There have been few more shocking murders than the ones committed by a man known initially as 'The Mutilator' and then as 'The Walking Corpse'. William MacDonald's gruesome crimes horrified Australia yet, incredibly, his blood-saturated spree could have continued indefinitely if he had not panicked after killing his final victim. Born Allan Ginsberg in England in 1924, he served in the British army before changing his name to William MacDonald and migrating to Canada and then to Australia. Unable to hold down a job for any length of time, he moved from city to city before settling in Sydney.

Then, just before midnight on *June 3*, 1961, the lonely MacDonald started a conversation with vagrant Alfred Greenfield as they sat on a bench in a Darlinghurst park. MacDonald, who was working as a letter sorter with the Post Master General (now Australia Post), suggested to Greenfield that they move on to a more secluded spot to drink some beer. Then, after a walk to a spot near the Domain Baths,

MacDonald repeatedly stabbed his unsuspecting victim. It was a frenzied and premeditated attack as MacDonald had slipped into a plastic raincoat before he slashed and slashed Greenfield, severing the arteries in the vagrant's neck.

But there was worse to follow. MacDonald, just after midnight on *June 4*, removed Greenfield's trousers and sliced off the dead man's penis and testicles. The Mutilator had struck. Yet the man whose deeds shocked the nation walked calmly away. MacDonald slipped his blood-stained knife into a plastic bag and threw Greenfield's genitals into Sydney Harbour. The discovery of Greenfield's body created uproar. The horrific murder, naturally, was splashed all over the front pages of Sydney's newspapers, with the term 'The Mutilator' used for the first time to describe the killer.

The police, despite every effort, were baffled and the NSW government eventually offered a reward of 1000 pounds ($2000) for any information leading to the arrest of the mutilation killer. Every police inquiry led to a dead-end and, six months later, MacDonald struck again. The body of Ernest William Cobbin was found in a blood-splattered public toilet in Moore Park. MacDonald again had used the lure of drinking beer together. The Mutilator slashed Cobbin to the neck, severed his jugular vein and inflicted many other wounds. He then sliced off his victim's penis and testicles. The seemingly cool, calm and collected MacDonald washed himself on the way home and again threw his victim's genitals into the harbour.

The media again referred to 'The Mutilator' and the police, despite staking out public toilets in the area and issuing warnings, again were baffled. Another five months passed and, with the police fearing The Mutilator could strike again at any time, MacDonald made their worst nightmares come true. He struck again in Darlinghurst after striking up a conversation with a man named Frank McLean. Again, MacDonald invited his intended victim for a drink but, for the first time, ran into difficulties in carrying out his murderous intention. McLean resisted after being stabbed in the neck and tried to fend off MacDonald's thrusts with the sheath-knife. Despite being much taller than his attacker, McLean was unable to ward off the many blows and was stabbed in the neck, chest and face. MacDonald then cut off McLean's penis and testicles.

However, the mutilation killer was far from cool, calm and collected this time and almost panicked. He fled the scene as quickly as he could and not long after his frenzied attack, McLean's body was discovered. Although police were on the scene almost immediately, MacDonald had made it safely home. Sydney, of course, was in a frenzy over The Mutilator's killing.

Police formed a special task force and the State government increased its offer of a reward to 5000 pounds ($10,000). Meanwhile, MacDonald, who had been working at the PMG under the alias of Allan Brennan, had decided in a change of career and took over a mixed business in the Sydney suburb of Burwood. However, the urge to kill remained and, on the night of *June 2*, 1962, The Mutilator struck again.

MacDonald's next victim was Irish derelict Patrick Hackett, who has just been released from jail for a minor offence. This time MacDonald took his victim back to his own home and, when Hackett, had passed out from drinking too much, The Mutilator stabbed him in the neck. The Irishman quickly came to his senses and shielded himself from the blows MacDonald rained on him with his knife. In the process, MacDonald slashed his own hand. Finally, however, the multiple killer stabbed Hackett in the heart. MacDonald tried to remove Hackett's genitals, but the knife by now was too blunt for the task. Exhausted, the killer fell asleep, but next morning took himself to hospital to have stitches inserted in his wounded hand. He then set about cleaning up his shop, wiping away pools of blood and tearing up the linoleum on the floor. His final task was to drag Hackett's body under the shop.

Realising he would find it almost impossible to dispose of the body, MacDonald decided to flee the scene. He caught a train to Brisbane and prayed he could change his identity and melt into the background. Although MacDonald daily expected to read headlines about the discovery of Hackett's body, there was no mention in any newspaper or on any radio news service.

Then, several weeks after Hackett's murder, neighbours noticed a terrible odour from MacDonald's shop on Burwood Road. Police discovered Hackett's body, but it was so decomposed that identification was impossible. In fact, police believed the body was that of MacDonald and it was buried under MacDonald's assumed name of Allan Brennan. Coroner F.E. Cox, who returned an open verdict, was not convinced it was the body of the man known as Brennan and said: 'It seems extraordinary that the body of Mr Brennan should have been found in the position and the condition in which it was found.

According to the evidence, the deceased had neither his trousers on, nor his boots or shoes, or singlet. He was clad only in his socks, with his coat and trousers alongside him. 'Nothing was found to indicate to any degree of certainty that the deceased had taken his own life, even if it were his intention to do so. It seems to me an extraordinary thing that the deceased should have gone under the house to commit an act that would result in his death.'

The astute coroner then added that the dead man could have been 'the victim of foul play'. Although he stressed that he had no evidence of this, he noted: 'I cannot exclude that possibility.' MacDonald breathed easier in the belief that he was a dead man walking. No one knew he was still alive and he believed the police would never be able to charge him with even one of the murders he had committed. However, he had not counted on fate, in the form of a former workmate.

MacDonald was walking down a Sydney street one day when he bumped into an old work mate who expressed great surprise that 'Allan Brennan' was still alive. The work mate, who even had attended the funeral service, could not believe his eyes. The stunned MacDonald fled down the street and almost immediately caught a train to Melbourne. The work mate contacted a Sydney crime reporter with his remarkable near-collision with a ghost and the following day the *Mirror* newspaper ran Morris' account under the headline CASE OF THE WALKING CORPSE.

Police, stunned by the report, re-examined the case of the body under the shop and finally realised they had made a mistake and, in fact, that the body was that of Irishman Hackett. The body was exhumed and this time stab and cut marks were found on the body's genitals. The police believed they finally were onto the trail of The Mutilator, albeit almost by accident. The police released an identikit description of MacDonald, and it paid dividends when workers at Melbourne's Spencer Street railway station thought the portrait resembled a new work mate.

They notified the Victoria Police and arrested the man who had moved from Sydney as The Mutilator. MacDonald confessed to his crimes and was brought to trial in Sydney in September, 1963. However, he pleaded not guilty on the grounds of insanity. After all, what sane man would kill for the thrill of it and then remove his victim's genitals? Yet the jury did not see it that way and found MacDonald guilty on four count of murder. He was sentenced to life imprisonment. However, after bashing an inmate at Long Bay jail, he was removed to the Morriset Pyschiatric Centre for the criminally insane before eventually being returned to protective custody.

JUNE 5

TRACKED DOWN (1938)

When the body of 12-year-old schoolgirl Elizabeth Mary Nielson was found in scrub at Monash, South Australia, on *June 5*, 1938, there was enormous public outrage. The body had been pushed into a sack after the girl had been sexually assaulted and strangled. Police investigated every possible angle, but without result – until they called in a back-tracker Jimmy James.

The black-tracker had almost immediate success, being able to trace 27-year-old labourer James Mark Watherston to his home. The police hunt and investigation was over as Watherston confessed to killing Elizabeth Nielson and was sent to trial for murder.

The young labourer was found guilty and sentenced to death. He was hanged at the Adelaide Gaol at 9am on *August 11*, 1938, and the Adelaide *Advertiser* reported: "As is usual when an execution takes place, there were a few morbid sightseers outside the gaol … they comprised men and youths, and a young woman who had arrived there on a bicycle and was chatting to two mounted constables on duty about 100 yards from the gaol gates."

JUNE 6

EXECUTED (1882): South-sea islander Jimmy Towater executed in Queensland on *June 6*, 1882.

∗∗

HANGED (1961): Convicted murderer Mervyn Fallows hanged at Fremantle Gaol on *June 6*, 1961.

JUNE 7

DEATH OF A PROSTITUTE (1934)

The bludgeoning death of pretty, vivacious prostitute Jean McKenzie in her flat in the bayside Melbourne suburb of St Kilda in 1934 almost certainly will never be solved. McKenzie, 24 years of age and elegantly slim and well dressed, was not your average prostitute. She loved the good life and appeared to live in a fantasy world in which princes came to the rescue of fair young maidens. McKenzie was waiting for her prince to arrive on a white stallion one dark wintry Melbourne night when she was killed in the most brutal of circumstances.

She was at home in her flat on the night of *June 7*, 1934, when there was a knock at the door. Her landlord, Henry Bloom, later heard McKenzie arguing with a man for more than an hour, but could not catch the words. Earlier, a tall, fair-haired man in an overcoat had been seen entering McKenzie's ground-floor bed-sit. The row died and Bloom saw the tall man leave McKenzie's flat and walk through the front garden. He thought no more of the row until the next morning when there was no sign of McKenzie. Bloom's wife investigated and, when she opened the door to McKenzie's flat, found the young woman dead in the hallway.

McKenzie's head had been battered with a huge piece of wood taken from the fireplace. It was an horrific sight, with McKenzie dressed only in a white singlet. There was blood everywhere and it was obvious McKenzie had struggled with her killer. Furniture had been knocked over and clothing was strewn around the room. Police also disclosed that the killer had washed his hands before leaving the flat. He obviously was a cool customer and the nature of the crime suggested to police that McKenzie had been executed.

Police learned that McKenzie had used a number of aliases in her career as a prostitute, but also suggested she might have used these aliases to hide her real identity in fear of someone and was trying to lose herself in the seedier parts of St Kilda. One theory was that McKenzie had been bashed to death by a pimp, but police were unable to prove this. An inquest was held at the Coroner's Court five months after McKenzie's death, but police were forced to admit they did not have enough evidence to identify the killer. The coroner had no alternative but to return a finding of murder against "a person unknown". It now is likely McKenzie's killer has gone to the grave with his secret.

JUNE 8

THE PLANE HIJACK (1979)

When a TAA DC-9 jet liner took to the air from the Queensland resort of Coolangatta headed for Brisbane just before 9pm on *June 8*, 1979, the 41 passengers aboard did not know they would be the centre of one of Australia's most dramatic in-flight incidents. A hijacker burst into the cockpit and held a sawn-off shotgun to the pilot's head. Captain Grahame Mackelmann held his nerve, even though the plane was within a minute or so of crashing to earth, and managed to land safely. The 41 passengers were released as police cordoned off the runway, but the gunman held the pilot, co-pilot and four hostesses as hostages. Finally, after half an hour, the gunman was distracted and a hostess knocked him off his feet, disarming him.

The gunman was Irishman Phillip Sillery, who had smuggled the shotgun on board the plane by hiding it under a shirt. Sillery had marital problems and wanted to be reunited with his wife and two children. He demanded during the hijack that they be brought to the plane but, instead, landed himself a life sentence under recently introduced hijacking laws. His sentence later was reduced to 10 years.

**

ARSON (1991): The Central Fruit Market in the Melbourne bayside suburb of Bentleigh was set alight with kerosene on *June 8*, 1991.

JUNE 9

THE SEX SLAVES (2006)

Brothel owner Wei Tang on *June 9*, 2006, became the first person in Australia to be found guilty of slavery. She was convicted in Melbourne by a County Court jury of possessing and using five women as sex slaves in 2002 and 2003. The women were required to work in Tang's sex club in the inner suburb of Fitzroy. The five women had been smuggled into Australia from Thailand and 44-year-old Tang took their passports from them and threatened they would be deported if they did not service clients. Each had $45,000 "contracts" and, to pay off these massive debts, they were forced to satisfy hundreds of clients. Although they were provided with accommodation, they were penniless, friendless and unable to escape their "slave" environment.

Tang, an Australian citizen who was born in China, charged customers $110 for her slaves' services and, of this, $50 went to paying the massive debts. The women worked six days a week and the only way they could earn money for themselves was to work seven days a week and earn $50 per client on what would have been their day off. Judge Michael McInerny, in sentencing Tang to 10 years' jail (with a non-parole period of six years) said that although the door to the apartment where the women lived was not locked, it did not mean the women were free to leave as they feared Tang and the threat of deportation.

JUNE 10

THE MAN-WOMAN (1938)

Eugenia Falleni was born in Florence in 1875, but migrated to New Zealand with her parents as a small girl. At around 16 years of age, Falleni started dressing as a boy and, after running away to sea, she worked as a deck hand on ships plying the Pacific islands. Despite her obvious sexual leanings, she gave birth to a daughter, Josephine, in Newcastle in 1899. Falleni, who adopted the name Henry Crawford, took the baby to a childless couple in Sydney's Double Bay and told them that because the mother had died they could raise the little girl. Falleni often visited her daughter and continued to live and dress as a man, working at various jobs in and around Sydney.

Then, in 1914, she "married" widow Annie Birkett after a two-year courtship. Birkett believed Falleni was a man and, incredibly, did not discover her "husband's" real gender for three years. This was in September,1917, and, on discovery, Falleni suggested she and Birkett discuss the problem during a stroll to a lonely bush spot in the Lane Cove River park. Falleni bashed his "wife" to death and then burned her body in a bonfire. The man-woman told everyone that "his" wife had left him and although Falleni at first appeared to have escaped detection, the charred remains of Birkett were found by two boys playing in scrubland. Although police at first could not identity the body, a dentist later confirmed it as Birkett.

Falleni disappeared but eventually was tracked down to a house at Canterbury where she was living after "marrying" a woman named Lizzie Allison. She was arrested for the murder of Birkett, found guilty after the jury deliberated for just two hours and sentenced to death. However, that sentence was commuted to life imprisonment following a plea to the New South Wales Executive Council and, after serving 11 years at Long Bay Gaol, was released in 1931 under the strict condition she live as a woman. Falleni was killed when struck by a motor vehicle on *June 10*, 1938, living under the name of Jean Ford.

THE ANITA COBBY CASE (1982)

Anita Cobby was a beauty queen who had the world at her feet. The attractive 26-year-old was a nurse at the Sydney Hospital and could have had her pick of suitors. She had married John Cobby in March, 1982, but the marriage failed and Anita went back to live with her parents Garry and Grace Lynch in the Sydney suburb of Blacktown. She had regular habits, was considerate and worked hard. In fact, whenever she worked late, she would always telephone her parents to stop them worrying.

Anita did not ring her parents immediately after work late on the afternoon of *February 2*, 1986, as she went to a restaurant with two of her nursing friends. These friends dropped Anita off at the Central Railway station and that was the last anyone saw of her alive. When Anita did not turn up for work the next day, a sister called the Lynch's, who assumed their daughter was with friends. However, Mr Lynch eventually decided to call police, who organised a search for the missing woman.

Then, two days after Anita disappeared, farmer John Reen rang police to tell them he had made a gruesome discovery on his farm at Boiler Paddock. Police rushed to the scene and were horrified by what they saw. The body fitted the description they had been given of Anita and it was a sickening sight as the beautiful young woman had been raped and bashed and had her throat slashed. The wounds were terrible and it was obvious Anita had been tortured. Also, a post-mortem revealed that the woman's throat had been slashed twice and that the head was almost severed from the body. She also had been sodomised and it later transpired that she was forced into oral sex. Bashed, kicked and slashed, the naked Anita was left for dead.

Police set up a task force and the first public reports started pouring in, with several people reporting they had seen a woman being dragged into a car at the Blacktown railway station. The car was described as a white Holden Kingswood, but there was little else for the police to work on in their massive hunt for the killer(s). Public interest was phenomenal as the killing was one of the most brutal ever committed in Sydney and, finally, police got the call to put them on the right track. The man who called police said they should be looking for a man named John Travers who had stolen a car a couple of days before Anita's killing.

Travers had a shocking reputation and police, believing he could help with their enquiries, made a dawn raid on a property at Wentworthville and found a bloodstained knife. They also found Travers and another man, Mick Murdoch, in bed together and believed they finally were getting somewhere, especially as they also picked up a man named Les Murphy at a house in Doonside. Police then charged Murphy and Murdoch with car theft and released them, hoping they would lead them to vital evidence.

Meanwhile, police set up a "sting" operation to nab Travers, using a woman he had confided in over a rape charge. The police set up a meeting and were confident of success. That confidence was justified as Travers admitted abducting

Anita and how he and his pack of animals raped, tortured and killed her. Police then arrested Murphy and Murdoch, while Travers confessed to police, implicating two others, Gary and Mick Murphy, brothers of Les. Police eventually captured Gary and Mick Murphy at the Sydney suburb of Glenfield, and the entire gang now had been apprehended. Travers and his gang eventually faced trial and those in court were disgusted with what they heard of the killing of Anita Cobby.

The gang had been drinking on the day of the abduction on *February 2*, 1986, and decided on the spot to grab Anita. Travers and Murdoch started undressing her and punching her in the face as she struggled in the back of the stolen car. Travers and Mick Murphy raped her at knifepoint while she was still in the back of the car, while Travers and Gary and Les Murphy raped her after she had been thrown into a ditch. The animals then dragged her through a barbed wire fence and she was forced to have oral sex with Mick Murphy and was sodomised by Les Murphy. Finally, Mick and Les Murphy kicked her in the head and left her for dead. It was then that Travers went back to her and slit her throat so that she could never tell anyone of what had happened and who had done it.

The jury returned its verdicts on *June 10*, 1987, after a 54-day trial in which every detail sickened the Australian public. The five men – John Travers (18), Michael Murdoch (18), Les (24), Gary (29) and Michael Murphy (33) - were found guilty and Justice Maxwell sentenced them all to life imprisonment, with their files marked "never to be released". The judge told them: "There is no doubt that apart from the humiliation, the degradation and terror inflicted upon this young woman, she was the victim of a prolonged and sadistic physical and sexual assault including repeated sexual assaults – anally, orally and vaginally." The judge compared their behaviour with wild animals and said it was the most horrifying case of sexual assault he had encountered in his 40 years of law.

JUNE 11

FOUR DAYS OF TORTURE (2003)

In the early hours of Wednesday, *June 11*, 2003, an emergency 000 phone call was made by a man who said his partner needed medical attention after being assaulted by an unknown attacker. When police and an ambulance arrived at the house in David Avenue, Cranbourne (a satellite suburb of Melbourne), they were shocked by what they found. Mother-of-one Jennifer Lorraine Brodhurst, 29, was dead on the floor. Police soon ascertained that the story told by her 30-year-old de facto husband, Robert Clifford Barrett, was a mere cover for the appalling truth — that he had subjected Ms Brodhurst to four successive days of vicious beatings and torture that culminated in her agonising death.

Ms Brodhurst' list of injuries make for difficult reading: cuts and bruises from head to toe, two broken rubs, a broken finger, several human bite marks and, worst of all, numerous lacerations to her head. She had been attacked at various times with a knife and a stick that had broken after wielded with tremendous force. Some of Ms Brodhurst's injuries were up to three days old, while others had been inflicted only a few hours before her death. Around Ms Brodhurst's body were "splatter" bloodstains, which indicated that the much bigger and stronger Barrett had continued to hit her directly on freely bleeding wounds.

Attempts had been made to clean up the house, but there were bloodstains in the main bedroom and en suite, the hallway, and even in the bedroom of their nine-year-old son, who thankfully wasn't home to witness the prolonged killing of his mother. Ms Brodhurst's death was a sad finale to a stormy 12-year relationship in which she suffered many severe beatings and injuries which required medical treatment and occasional hospitilisation.

Barrett could not contain what a psychiatrist later described as a "morbid jealousy" — he always had the deluded idea that Ms Brodhurst was cheating on him. Although he recognised this mental illness became worse when he used amphetamines, he refused to quit drugs. In 2001, his paranoia led him to attack a man and earn himself a short jail term. But Barrett didn't learn his lesson behind bars and, upon release, continued to beat Ms Brodhurst, who, in the 12 months before her death, sought crisis accommodation nine times and also obtained an interim intervention order against Barrett.

In sentencing Barrett, Justice Whelan said: "Your attack on a person whom you claim to have loved was not only fatal, it was vicious, repeated and cruel. Over several days you bashed your partner to death. When she was already injured you resumed your attacks on her ... If you had got the deceased the medical treatment she so obviously and desperately needed she probably would not have died from the injuries you had inflicted upon her." Barrett, who had five previous convictions for drug offences and violence, was sentenced to 25 years' jail, with a non-parole period of 20 years.

JUNE 12

DEATH AMONG THE TOMBSTONES (1946)

Joan Norris, 11 years of age, was a charming, pleasant girl who liked to help her mother with the household chores. Early on the evening of *June 12*, 1946, Joan's mother asked her to go down the street to buy some bread for her stepfather's breakfast the next morning. Joan skipped out of the house on the simplest of errands and her mother never saw her alive again.

As Joan was a punctual girl, her mother contacted police as soon as she realised her daughter was missing, and one of the biggest Sydney searches for years was launched in an effort to find Joan. Police nightmares turned to reality early the next morning when Joan's mutilated body was found among mossy old tombstones at a disused Camperdown cemetery. Joan was lying on her back, with a piece of her own singlet knotted around her throat. Police were horrified and described the attack as one of the most brutal they had seen.

The cemetery, badly overgrown and dotted with rotting tombstones was – strangely enough – a favourite playground for local children. However, children were terrified of going anywhere near the cemetery at night and police suspected that Joan had been taken into the cemetery through one of may holes in the surrounding fence as her body was found about 50 metres from the cemetery entrance. There was no lighting where the body was discovered.

An examination by the government medical officer revealed that Joan had been dead for about 10 hours when her body was found. She had been strangled and there were marks on the body that were so severe that the killer was described as "a degenerate of the worst type". Meanwhile, police retraced Joan's movements from the time she left her home in Enmore Road, Newtown. Apart from trying to buy the bread her mother had wanted, Joan had called in to the home of her second cousin, Mrs Hazel Geary, in King Street, Newtown. Mrs Geary directed her to a local milk bar, but also told the girl to get home as soon as possible because it was getting dark.

Joan also was seen in a hamburger shop and there were reports she had been seen in a telephone box with a man wearing a military greatcoat. He was described as being 27 or 28 years of age, of medium height and build and wearing a light-coloured open neck shirt and grey trousers. The phone booth was outside the cemetery and police believed this lead was vital. They inspected the booth and found that its light had recently been smashed, with glass scattered around the floor. Police now worked on the theory that the killer had taken Joan to the phone booth and knocked her unconscious before killing her at the cemetery.

The inquest into Joan's death was held in November, 1946, and Detective-Sergeant Denis Hughes told the coroner that police believed the dead girl must have known her killer. Mrs Norris, who broke down during the inquest, said she did not believe her daughter would approach anyone she did not know. Joan's killer has never been identified and her murder remains a mystery.

THE WOMAN-HATING KILLER (1993)

Triple murderer Paul Charles Denyer added insult to injury for Victorians in 2004 when he announced that he wanted to change his sex to become a woman and was seeking details on government policy. Earlier, Denyer had been refused permission to wear make-up at the Barwon prison, where he was serving a life sentence, with a minimum of 30 years. Yet Denyer, when asked to explain why he killed three women in Melbourne's bayside suburbs in 1993, had replied: 'I just hate them'. When pressed by a police interviewer as to whether he hated his particular victims or women in general, Denyer said chillingly 'general'. Denyer had gone on a murder frenzy over seven weeks from June to July, 1993, stabbing and slashing three women, with another just managing to escape with her life at the hands of the monster.

Denyer was born in 1972 in Sydney, but moved to Melbourne with his family when he was just nine years of age. A lazy, indolent boy, he had few interests and, on leaving school, drifted from job to job with long periods of unemployment. However, he struck up a relationship with a girl named Sharon Johnson and moved in with her at her Frankston flat in 1992.

Then, on *June 12*, 1993, Denyer struck for the first time, killing 18-year-old student Elizabeth Stevens, whose body was found in Lloyd Park, Langwarrin. Her throat had been cut, she had been stabbed several times in the chest and her torso slashed. Significantly, however, she had not been sexually assaulted.

Police launched a massive hunt for the killer but, less than four weeks later, on *July 8*, their attention turned to two attacks, one in which the victim survived and the other not so fortunate. The first attack occurred after bank clerk Roszsa Toth stepped from a train at Seaford. Dragged into bushes by a man she believed was carrying a gun, she eventually managed to fight off her assailant and then called police.

However, that very night another woman was attacked, with fatal consequences. Young mother Debbie Fream, 22, had driven to a store in Seaford to buy some milk but never returned home. Her body was found four days later in a paddock at Carrum. She had been stabbed 24 times but, again, there had been no sexual assault. Then, 12 days later (on *July 30*), the killer struck in broad daylight after carefully planning his third murder. Denyer, after cutting wire alone a fence at a reserve, waited for a victim to drag her through the gap and into bushes.

Schoolgirl Natalie Russell, just 17, was Denyer's third victim. She was riding her bike home from school when the monster struck and her body later was found in bushland. She had been stabbed and her throat cut. However, police soon were onto their man as they discovered a piece of skin on the neck of the dead girl. Also, a policeman had taken down the registration number of a yellow motor vehicle sighted near the bike track earlier in the day.

Police soon discovered that the car was registered to Denyer. Police called at the flat where he lived with Johnson, but Denyer was not home. Police told Johnson that they merely were making 'routine inquiries' and asked if her partner could call them when he returned home. Johnson called them two hours later and police returned to the flat, where they noticed Denyer had cuts on his hand. He explained these had been caused by trying to fix a motor fan, but the police knew they had their man. Denyer was taken to the Frankston police station where he confessed after intitially pleading his innocence.

After asking about what DNA tests would prove, he blurted out: 'OK, I killed all three of them.' In his statement, Denyer said of killing his first victim, Stevens, that he followed her and then grabbed her from behind before marching her into Lloyd Park. He then said he reached a particular area and then started strangling her. The statement said: 'She passed out after a while. You know, the oxygen got cut off to her head and she just stopped breathing.' Denyer then stabbed her repeatedly and admitted 'I stuck my foot over her neck to finish her off'. Asked why he had killed the teenage student, Denyer callously replied: 'I just wanted ... just wanted to kill. Just wanted to take a life because I felt my life had been taken many time.' Denyer admitted attacking Toth and said he was 'gunna drag her in the park and kill her'.

When Toth escaped, Denyer went in search of another victim and saw Fream get out of a car outside a milk bar. He then let himself into the back of the car and waited for his intended victim to return. He said in his statement: 'I startled her ... and she kept going into the wall of the milk bar, which caused a dent in the bonnet. I told her to, you know, shut up, or I'd blow her head off and all that shit.' Debbie Fream drove herself to her death and, after Denyer told her to stop the car, pulled out a length of cord and started strangling her. Then, just as she was passing out, he stabbed her repeatedly before dragging her body into bushes and then covering it with branches.

When police asked why he had killed the young mother, who had given birth to a son less than a fortnight earlier, Denyer said: 'Same reason I killed Elizabeth Stevens. I just wanted to.' Of the killing of schoolgirl Russell, Denyer said in his statement that he grabbed her from behind and held a knife to her throat. Russell, obviously fearing for her life, offered Denyer sex in exchange for letting her go, but he kept telling her to 'shut up'. In the most appalling part of his statement, he said: 'I cut a small cut (in her throat) at first and then she was bleeding. And then I stuck my fingers into her throat ... and grabbed her cords and twisted them.'

When police asked him why he did this, he replied: 'Stop hear from breathing … so she sort of started to faint and then, when she was weak, a bit weaker, I grabbed the opportunity of throwing her head back and one big large cut which sort of cut almost her whole head off. And then she slowly died.' But, to make sure his victim was dead, the callous killer kicked the body before slashing Russell's face. Denyer pleaded guilty to the murders of Stevens, Fream and Russell and the attempted murder of Toth.

His trial opened at the Supreme Court of Victoria before Justice Frank Vincent on *December 15*, 1993. Just five days later, Justice Vincent sentenced Denyer to three terms of life imprisonment with no fixed non-parole period. Denyer appealed to the Full Court of the Supreme Court against the severity of the sentence and subsequently was granted a 30-year non-parole period. This outraged the victims' families and, of course, there was further outrage a decade later when the woman-hating killer declared he wanted to become a woman.

THE AGGRESSIVE NEIGHBOUR (2002)

Peter John Howard was a 70-year-old recluse who lived in the eastern Melbourne suburb of Boronia. Described as an "aggressively friendly" neighbour, he sometimes was in dispute with those who lived near him. For example, he had told Olive Martha Maas, who lived opposite him that he did not like cars parked outside his house and she, in turn, told friends to comply with this wish.

Some time in the middle of 2001, a house in the street was vandalised and another neighbour asked Ms Maas if she would keep an eye on it. Howard therefore seemed to take a close interest whenever Ms Maas and the property owner, who also was Howard's landlady, met in the street. Then, in the early hours of *June 12*, 2002, Howard put a murderous plan into operation.

He prepared a long carving knife as a murder weapon by wrapping the handle in the sleeve of a rubber glove and securing this with a black tape. He then broke into Ms Maas' home through a laundry window and confronted his victim, dressed in her nightgown. Screams were heard from the Maas house some time just after 5am and there was considerable banging and shouting for 30 seconds, then silence. Ms Maas' body was not discovered for a week, but she had been the subject of a vicious attack and a knife was protruding from her left side. She had been stabbed up to 57 times, with one wound penetrating the right eye and entering her skull. Ms Maas, 59 years of age, also had cut wounds on her hands, indicating she had fought her attacker.

Howard, who had a criminal record for armed robbery and kidnapping, was arrested, charged with murder and was found guilty. Justice Williams, in the Supreme Court of Victoria, told him: "Your crime involved planning and preparation. You made an apparently unprovoked brutal attack on a woman living alone, in what should have been the safety of her own home, in the early hours of the morning." The Judge, in noting Howard did not appear to show any remorse, said that, despite the offender's age, the sentence had to reflect the need for community protection. He sentenced Howard to 20 years' jail, with a minimum term of 15 years.

JUNE 13

EXECUTED (1910): Convicted murderer Alexander Joseph Bradshaw executed in Brisbane on *June 13*, 1910.

✳✳

HANGED (1932): Convicted murderer John T. Smith hanged at Fremantle Gaol on *June 13*, 1932.

JUNE 14

THE VOYEURISTIC WIFE-KILLER (1999)

George Burleigh and his wife Mary had what appeared to be a normal 27-year marriage. But behind closed doors, the parents of three adult children were secretly indulging in a scandalous sex life. Burleigh satisfied his voyeuristic fantasies by watching his wife have sex with other men.

But although Mrs Burleigh had been a willing participant in the risque liaisons for 16 years, a sense of embarrassment and shame had built inside her. On *June 2*, 1999, following another of these sessions, she resolved that it would be their last. On *June 11*, Mrs Burleigh, 48, mustered the courage to tell her 55-year-old husband she would no longer submit herself for his gratification. But bigger bombshells were to come. Mrs Burleigh also announced she was leaving the marriage and, furthermore, would inform their children of their unconventional sexual activities.

Burleigh was devastated. In the previous three years, he'd lost his job with Warragul Shire Council, his parents had died and cancer had claimed a brother. His wife's revelations, and the thought of the inevitable humiliation that would follow, tipped him over the edge. He threatened to commit suicide if his wife left him.

On *June 13*, they attended a family function to celebrate the wedding anniversary of Mrs Burleigh's parents and although Burleigh held out hope that his wife would return to him, Burleigh felt she had been frosty toward him.

The next morning, *June 14*, the Burleigh's youngest child, a 20-year-old son, left the family farm at Ellinbank in Gippsland (Victoria) about 11.35am. Burleigh was so distressed that he remained sobbing in bed until almost noon when his wife arrived, intending to install a light in the piggery.

About 2pm, Darnum-Ellinbank Fire Brigade received a call from Burleigh, who said, in a calm tone of voice, that the house was on fire. A passer-by noticed flames coming from the house and on closer inspection saw the couple on fire just outside the back verandah. He desperately tried to extinguish the flames but his efforts were in vain. Mrs Burleigh was already dead. Her husband wished he was too. Burleigh's simple explanation to an ambulance paramedic was: "My wife wanted to leave me so I decided to burn the house."

In an outside toilet, Burleigh had left a suicide note which read: "Michelle, Belynda and Jason go to solicitors...for super money. Dad." It was signed "A.G. Burleigh", under which were the words: "Belynda have the car," relating to a vehicle owned by Mrs Burleigh. It was clear that Burleigh had planned a murder-suicide.

Burleigh had attacked his wife with a hammer, rendering her helpless, and deliberately set fire to the house using petrol. A post-mortem examination of Mrs Burleigh's body revealed extensive burns to her face and upper limbs and six head injuries consistent with forceful blows from a hammer, the most severe being on her forehead, which had an underlying skull fracture. She also suffered injuries to her left hand and right elbow as she tried to shield her head from her husband's vicious attack. Mrs Burleigh died from a combination of burns, smoke inhalation and head trauma. Burleigh suffered burns to 45 percent of his body, including both legs and arms, his buttocks and lower back, with 30-35 percent being full-thickness burns.

Mrs Burleigh was a much-loved member of the local community, as evidenced by the large gathering of mourners who attended her funeral.

Her husband, who played club cricket until he was 48, badminton until he was 50 and even officiated as a local football boundary umpire, was sentenced to 18 years' jail with a minimum of 13 years.

THE HEAD IN THE SINK (1998)

When New South Wales police went to a townhouse in Albion Park on *June 14*, 1998, they could hardly believe the scene of utter horror. They had had reports that a mutilated body had been found in the flat, but could not possibly have been prepared for what encountered in this house of horrors.

David John O'Hearn, 59, had been the victim of one of the most vicious, most sickening attacks in Australian criminal history. Among other gross wounds, he had been decapitated and his head found in the kitchen sink. The left hand had been severed and there were deep wounds to the abdomen. On medical examination, it was revealed that there were five intersecting and parallel cut wounds to the lower chest and the wounding of the abdomen showed the shaft of a hammer had been rammed up the anus. The dead man's penis had been mutilated and parts of intestine were found on a breakfast bar. Naturally, police had never seen anything like it.

Police also found a number of knives and implements used to mutilate the body and these included a saw, four knives, a razor blade and a corkscrew. The word Satan had been written in blood on a mirror and the severed hand was resting just above that word, with a pentagram (star-shaped figure with five points, often used in the occult) also written in blood.

The post mortem revealed that mutilation of O'Hearn's body had taken place after trauma blows to the head had caused death. There were numerous injuries to the head and, in fact, the left eyeball had been punctured by a sharp object and there were gross lacerations to the brain. It was estimated that there had been at least 10 top 12 blows to the head, delivered with extreme force.

Police were still recovering from the shock of the O'Hearn death when another body was discovered two weeks later, on *June 27*. This time the victim was 68-year-old Francis Neville Arkell, a former mayor of Wollongong. His mutilated body was found in a granny flat adjoining his weatherboard house and, once again, the scene was sickening. The body, dressed in tracksuit pants and a white singlet, was on its back with legs outstretched. The head had been bashed in and three tie pins had been pushed through various places, one in the left cheek, one in the corner of the left eye and another in the right eyelid. Arkell also had an electrical cord around his neck and some timber embedded in his neck; it also was obvious he had been bashed with a heavy glass ash-tray. The post mortem revealed that there were no less than 34 head injuries, with numerous deep lacerations and fractured teeth. The hyoid bone (in the neck region) was broken and the left jugular was punctured.

Then, three months after the discovery of Arkell's body, a 19-year-old walked into the Wollongong police station and admitted to killing both Arkell and O'Hearn. Mark Mala Valera told police his surrender "seemed the right thing to do". He told them he went to O'Hearn's home because he felt he "could kill someone". After O'Hearn admitted him to the townhouse, Valera struck him over the head with a decanter. He also described to police how he mutilated the body.

Valera said he killed Arkell – "a very, very horrible man" – after he went to the former mayor's home and "pretended to be gay" and attacked him a couple of minutes after being admitted to the home. Valera said he did not like Arkell because of "all the nasty things he has done to kids – read about him". He admitted to strangling him, with a cord and kicked him in the face. However, when on trial, Valera said he had no intention of killing either man and pleaded not guilty to murder but guilty to manslaughter, pleas rejected by the Crown.

During Valera's trial, the court was told he had been sexually abused by his father from a young age. However, after Valera had been found guilty of murder, Justice Studdert said: "There are, in my opinion, features of these crimes of very great heinousness ... David O'Hearn was subjected to a most savage attack, and I am satisfied beyond reasonable doubt that the prisoner acted in such attack with intent to kill and that it was a random and utterly senseless killing. The way in which the prisoner mutilated the body of his victim showed his utter contempt for his victim and so too did his use of the severed hand and the writings on the wall and on the mirror. Indeed, this first crime exuded evil of the prisoner's making. Francis Arkell was likewise subjected to a most brutal attack, and again I am satisfied beyond reasonable doubt that the prisoner conducted the attack with intent to kill. The prisoner sought to explain, and indeed to justify, his attack upon an adverse judgement he had formed of the second victim. Once again he demonstrated his utter contempt for his victim after inflicting the savage injuries which inevitably would have led to death by inserting into the head of the body three tie pins he found." The judge added that there were no mitigating circumstances and sentenced Valera to two terms of life imprisonment, with no non-parole period.

JUNE 15

GUNNED DOWN (2000): Melbourne underworld identity Mark Moran gunned down while sitting outside his home in Essendon on *June 15*, 2000.

JUNE 16

LASHED (1840): Convict Thomas Walsh lashed for attempting to escape from Cockatoo Island, in Sydney Harbour, on *June 16*, 1840. He attempted to steal a boat and, after the lashing, was sent to Port Arthur, Tasmania.

JUNE 17

GUILTY (1987): Beauty queen Anita Cobby's killers found guilty of murder on *June 17*, 1987. (Refer to *June 10*).

JUNE 18

THE AMOROUS BARBER (1962)

Gregario Marazita, widely respected in Melbourne's Italian community, and his brothers ran a flourishing licensed grocery business opposite the Victoria Market. Marazita had a number of friends in the area and these included Salvatore Manusco, who worked as a barber in Victoria Street, North Melbourne, opposite Marazita's grocery shop.

Marazita, 37, treated Manusco, 25, like a brother and the two got on well together. Marazita even took Manusco to his home in West Brunswick, where Manusco used to cut the children's hair. Manusco and Marazita had been friends for about four years in 1962, when the friendship started cooling, after Marazita had heard that Manusco had tried to kiss his wife. The situation exploded into violence on the night of *June 18*, 1962, after Marazita left the grocery shop and started walking to his car parked nearby. However, Marazita tangled with Manusco and a scuffle developed. Shots were heard and Marazita was found badly wounded. He was rushed to the nearby Royal Melbourne Hospital with bullet wounds, but died soon after arrival.

Manusco later walked in the Swan Hill police station in northern Victoria and later was charged with murder and committed for trial. The Crown alleged at Manusco's trial in the Criminal Court that Manusco fired four shots from a revolver at Marazita in Little Cobden Street, North Melbourne, at about 5,40pm on *June 18*. The Crown also claimed that the shooting followed adverse advances by Manusco's towards Marazita's wife. Mrs Rita Marazita told the court that Manusco had repeatedly tried to kiss her and that only five weeks before the shooting her husband had slapped Manusco to the face. She said that her husband had told Manusco over the tea table in West Brunswick: "I have treated you like a brother and you are trying to upset my home."

The court was told that there originally had been three shots, but a witness, Stephen Chiodo, said he then saw Manusco run up behind Marazita, lift a revolver and fire and fourth and fatal shot into Marazita's back. However, Manusco claimed he had never tried to kiss his friend's wife and had not made advances to her. He admitted he walked up to Marazita on the night of the killing, but said Marazita grabbed him by the coat with one hand and punched him with the other. He said that as they struggled, Marazita pulled out a revolver and the gun went off. The jury took an hour and a quarter to find Manusco guilty of murder. He stood motionless as Justice O'Bryan sentenced him to death, that sentence commuted to one of 40 years' jail.

JUNE 19

THE 'DISGUSTING' MONSTER (1980)

Theresa Crowe, to say the least, had a most unusual lifestyle. And, tragically, this led to a most unusual death. The twenty-two-year-old former student teacher was a regular on the Melbourne disco scene and lived almost hermit-like in a tiny room measuring no more than four metres by three metres. This room, which was really a loft above and behind a boat building factory, was off Chapel Street, Prahran, an inner Melbourne suburb.

Crowe's meagre possessions were crammed into this minute living area, jostling for space with a swing seat which hung from the rafters. Crowe would climb into her room from a staircase and enter through a trapdoor. It might have been ever so humble, but it was home, sweet home to Theresa Crowe. Few people ever received an invitation. Theresa, who had attended Strathmore High School and Toorak Teachers' College before accepting, and abandoning a number of jobs, loved the nightlife and was a regular at Chaser's Nightclub, not far from her 'home'. In fact, she was there six nights a week and was such a familiar face there that she was a gold pass member, giving her free admittance.

She almost always wore black and, because of this and her surname, her nickname was 'Blackbird'. If Theresa was not at Chaser's there usually was a good reason, and that was why her friends started asking questions after they had not seen her for several days from *June 19*, 1980.

Theresa's 'disappearance' was still the subject of discussion at Chaser's when, on *June 25*, two Prahran men, Simon Greig and Hugo Ottoway, went to her room and made an horrific discovery. They found Theresa's naked body wrapped in a blanket. Police later said that Theresa had been dead several days and that her body had been mutilated. There were numerous cuts on her face and a sharp instrument had been used to slash her body from throat to vagina. Although the initial post-mortem failed to disclose the cause of death, there were bruise marks on Theresa's neck and it was later proven that she had died of asphyxiation. Police were mystified at first and even suggested that Theresa might have been held captive for several days before being killed. They also considered the possibility that the unfortunate young woman had been killed in some weird satanic rite. They based this theory on the fact that medical evidence pointed to Theresa being killed on *June 24*, which was a beltan — one of four Sabbaths on the Satanists calendar.

However, police later indicated they had a suspect, but not enough evidence to press charges. The Blackbird Case, as it was dubbed by the Melbourne media, faded from the headlines for three years. Police then charged Malcolm Joseph Thomas Clarke, a twenty-eight-year-old assistant projectionist from the inner western suburb of Brunswick, with manslaughter. Clarke had seen Theresa Crowe at Chester's on the night of her death three years earlier and had later walked with her to her loft. She went upstairs and Clarke left, only to return later. By this time Theresa had stripped for sleep, and when she rejected his overtures, Clarke got angry. However, Clarke insisted that Theresa's death had been accidental and that she had died of asphyxiation when her neck pressed against a rope on her swinging chair. Medical evidence suggested that this could well have been the case. On the other hand, government pathologist Dr James McNamara told the Criminal Court that he had found a bite mark on Theresa's back, apart from the throat-to-vagina mutilation.

Clarke was found guilty of manslaughter and Mr Justice Nathan, in passing sentence of fifteen years' imprisonment, said a "joyful and pleasant" young woman had died because of Clarke's motive of "sexual gratification". He added: "You committed this crime in the most horrific and depraved circumstances because not only did you cause her death, but after death you defiled her body ... in the most disgusting of all defilements."

Clarke was ordered to serve twelve years before being eligible for parole but, two years before he was jailed, he had committed a far worse crime, the killing of six-year-old Bonny

Clarke (no relation) at her home in the inner Melbourne suburb of Northcote. Clarke, who was released from jail in 1994 for Theresa Crowe's death and the stabbing and raping of a woman at Brunswick in August, 1983, boarded with Bonnie's mother Marion for eight months at the Westbourne Grove house in 1982.

Bonnie Melissa Clarke was asphyxiated and stabbed on the night of *December 21*, 1982, but, despite an inquest and intensive police efforts, the crime remained unsolved for 22 years. However, when police re-examined the case in 2001, Clarke eventually became the chief suspect. In a video-taped interview he said the little girl woke when he sexually abused her. He then put a pillow over her face to quieten her. He said: "I was extraordinarily drunk ... and when I come to my senses (after pressing a pillow to the girl's face), I realised that Bonnie was deceased. When I took the pillow off ... she didn't struggle. I just held it down with one hand 'cause she had one hand up. 'She was lying down and one hand came up when I put it over her face. Her hand came up, then it just dropped. It just dropped. It was like, lifeless. I gave her a bit of a shake, whatever, I realised there was something wrong and I maybe, as I said, in panic did it with the knife."

The Supreme Court of Victoria jury in June, 2004, took just seven hours to find Clarke guilty of murdering little Bonnie. Clarke burst into tears, but others in the court cheered the verdict.

JUNE 20

BODY DUMPED (1998): Paul Joseph Harris, 47, was bashed to death in Queanbeyan, ACT, on *June 20*, 1998, and his body dumped in the bush. Pieter Egbert Helmhout and Mark William Hemlhout sentened to 13 and a half years' jail.

JUNE 21

THE ARTHUR CALWELL SHOOTING (1966)

Arthur Calwell was leader of the Australian Labor Party in 1966 when he became the first Australian political leader to be the target of an assassination attempt. Calwell, who had been Immigration Minister from 1944-49, had just addressed an anti-conscription rally at the Mosman Town Hall, Sydney, on the evening of *June 21*, 1966, when he entered his chauffeur-driver car. Before the car could take off, a young man rushed forward and fired a rifle shot through a window. Calwell, 70 years of age, was not hit by the bullet, but suffered cuts to the face and neck from the splintered glass. He was rushed to the North Shore hospital and a photograph of him being placed in an ambulance was featured in newspapers all around Australia. Australian Prime Minister Sir Robert Menzies described the assassination attempt as "a monstrous happening" and "un-Australian".

The gunman ran away, but was soon apprehended. He was 19-year-old Peter Raymond Kocan, who had set out from his Moore Park flat that morning with a .22 rifle and murder in mind. And the reason why he made this ill-planned assassination attempt? He explained lamely at his trial: "Unless I did something out of the ordinary I would remain a nobody all my life." Kocan was found guilty of wounding and attempted murder and sentenced to life imprisonment. However, he later was transferred to a high security mental institution after being declared mentally ill. He was released about 10 years later, while Calwell died of natural causes in 1973.

**

DOUBLE SHOOTING (2003): Melbourne underworld figures Jason Moran and Pasquale Barbaro were gunned to death while watching a junior football clinic in Pascoe Vale on *June 21*, 2003.

JUNE 22

DEATH AT THE VICARAGE (1936)

Parishioners at St Saviour's Anglican Church, Collingwood, loved their vicar, the Reverend Harold Cecil. He truly was a man of the people and worked tirelessly for the many poor in his parish. The quietly-spoken, bespectacled Reverend Cecil tended his flock like the best of shepherds and even went without to help the more unfortunate. He lived an extremely modest life at the vicarage facing Smith Street, in one of Melbourne's toughest neighbourhoods. However, there had been persistent rumours that the Rev. Cecil was a very wealthy man and that he had a fortune hidden at the vicarage.

The rumours were only partly true as although the Rev. Cecil had invested wisely in a farming venture in the 1920s, there was very little money at the vicarage, let alone a fortune in hidden gold. However, every petty criminal in the neighbourhood in 1935 knew that the Rev. Cecil was making his annual Christmas appeal and that there had been a number of donations.

Of course, the Collingwood parish was a poor one and the donations amounted to no more than 35 pounds in cash and cheques. But they were desperate times and the Rev. Cecil should have been more careful when he opened his door to a stranger on *December 12*, 1935. The Rev. Cecil's body was discovered by church officials the next day.

The vicar had been bashed over the head with a heavy object. The autopsy revealed 17 separate wounds to the head, with a number of other cuts and abrasions to the body. Robbery was the obvious motive as the vicar's wallet was missing, the pockets had been torn from his trousers and two watches (on chains) and a gold chain were missing. One of the watches had an unusual design and police reasoned that if the murderer tried to "hock" it they would make an early arrest. The only significant clue at the ransacked vicarage was a signed notice-of-marriage certificate dated *December 12*. It was almost certain that the killer had used the notification of marriage to get into the vicarage, and it had been signed Francis Edward Loyne or Layne.

Police next day found a blood-splattered spanner wedged between the brick chimney and the weatherboards at the old vicarage. A pattern on the spanner matched perfectly with the Rev. Cecil's head wounds. The murder weapon and the marriage certificate were to become vital clues in the apprehension of the killer. However, police investigations ran into a dead-end, even though the signature on the certificate was photographed and printed in Melbourne newspapers. Police even checked with signatures at Pentridge in the hope they would be able to match one with the one on the certificate.

The investigation stalled for several weeks, until a detective recalled that a petty criminal once signed the Pentridge record as Frank Lane. Police therefore kept a close eye on 29-year-old Edward Cornelius, who often used the name Frank Lane as an alias. Besides, a South Yarra jeweller had bought the Rev. Cecil's missing gold chain from a young man whose description fitted that of Cornelius. More importantly, the handwriting on the receipt book was similar to the signature on the wedding certificate at the vicarage.

Cornelius was arrested at his home in East Melbourne on *February 12*, 1936. He had been released from Pentridge only a short time before the vicarage murder after serving three years for housebreaking. Cornelius broke down under police questioning and confessed to the murder of the Rev. Cecil. He told police he went to the vicarage to ask about a wedding certificate purely as an excuse to prepare for a future housebreaking but, after walking away, remembered that the vicar had not closed the front door. Cornelius returned and was rifling through doors when the vicar confronted him. The pretty criminal said there was a struggle and he hit the vicar several times with a spanner.

Cornelius was found guilty of murder and sentenced to death. Although he appealed the sentence, he was hanged at Pentridge on *June 22*, 1936. He spent much of his time at Pentridge in the exercise yard with serial killer Arnold Karl Sodeman.

JUNE 23

KILLED IN FRONT OF HIS SONS (2001)

Just after midnight on Saturday, *June 23*, 2001, middle-aged Sami Sarraf was at his Guildford (west Sydney) home with his children and a visiting nephew from Lebanon when there was a knock at the front door. Wondering who could possibly be calling at such a late hour, Sarraf answered the door and was confronted by Joseph Melhem Azar, 41, who swiftly produced a pistol. Sarraf back-pedalled frantically into the house, but was followed by Azar, who fired seven shots from close range, three of which struck Sarraf, including a fatal shot through the forehead that passed through his brain.

Sarraf's oldest child, his 15-year-old son John, bravely grappled with Azar, who soon broke free and fled into the street. The courageous youth pursued his father's killer and tackled him to the ground, disarming him and beating him over the head repeatedly with the murder weapon — causing injuries that later required hospitalisation — until subdued by his cousins. Neighbours dialled 000 and police took control of the situation minutes later.

Azar claimed his crime was not murder but manslaughter, suggesting he suffered an abnormality of the mind at the time of the shooting. He claimed that when he was six or seven, the then 14-year-old Sarraf had sexually assaulted him when both boys were living in their native Lebanon. Azar, a heroin addict with a previous prison record for receiving stolen goods, alleged his ultimate decision to kill Sarraf was sparked that night when he grimaced through graphic scenes depicting child abuse in the movies *Sleepers*. The jury was not persuaded and Azar was sentenced to 17 years' jail, with a non-parole period of 12 years.

THE FATHER KILLER (2004)

Cristian Emil Simionescu migrated to Australia from Rumania with his parents and sister around 1989, but later developed a paranoid nature and a pre-occupation with knives and other cutting instruments. He believed he needed these weapons for his own protection, but his conduct took its toll on his family as police occasionally were called to their Sydney suburban home of Roselands because of Cristian's behaviour. He eventually shifted to his own unit in Wiley Park but, despite being largely estranged from his parents, sometimes visited the family home. In fact, he visited his parents on the night of *June 21*, 2004, and his mother noted that Cristian seemed agitated and stressed.

Then, in the early evening of **June 23**, Cristian stabbed his father Emil to death, decapitated the head, wrapped it in a plastic bag and placed it on the roof of the family garage. Forensic evidence also revealed that the father's face had been mutilated and the only question for Justice Peter Hidden, sitting without jury, was to determine whether Simionescu was mentally ill. In law, the issue is whether, at the time of the offence, the accused was labouring under such a defect of reason, from disease of mind, as to not know that what he was doing was wrong.

Evidence was heard that Simionescu, who had a history of drug abuse, had heard voices telling him that his parents intended killing him and selling his body organs. He also heard voices telling him that his parents wanted to hospitalise him. Justice Hidden determined that Simionescu, 27, was entitled to the special verdict of not guilty by reason of mental illness. As such, he ruled that Simionescu would not be released into the community except by order of the Governor on the recommendation of the Mental Health Review Tribunal. He will only be released if he is not considered a danger to himself or others.

JUNE 24

THE SUNDOWN MURDERS (1958)

Raymond John Bailey was executed at Adelaide Gaol on *June 24*, 1958, after being found guilty of the murder of Mrs Thyra Bowman at Sundown Station, in outback South Australia on *December 5*, 1957. The bodies of Mrs Bowman, her daughter Wendy and family friend Thomas Whelan were found on *December 13*. Mrs Bowman, Wendy and Whelan had travelled from the Glen Helen station with Mr Hubert Bowman and another daughter, Marion, on *December 3*. However, Mr Bowman was in ill-health and he and Marion decided to take a plane from Alice Springs to Adelaide while the others drove through the outback in their Vanguard car.

When they failed to arrive in Adelaide, Mr Bowman notified police and it later was reported that the group last had been seen at the Kulgara cattle station. An air search was launched and Mr Bowman even offered a 1000-pound reward but no sight of the missing group was made until *December 13* when a pilot in a low-flying RAAF plane spotted the missing car in scrub, well off the beaten track. Police rushed to the scene and found the murdered group. They had been shot dead while taking an evening meal and their bodies driven by another car to where they were dumped.

Robbery seemed the most likely motive, especially as Mrs Bowman's diamond ring and about 30 pounds in cash was missing. Travellers in the outback had to account for their movements and police finally tracked down Bailey, who had collected a De Soto motor vehicle under false pretences. Police tracked him from the opal town of Cooper Pedy to Alice Springs and finally, to Mt Isa. Queensland police interviewed him and although he denied he even owned a firearm, a .32 calibre revolver was hidden in his car. Bailey then said he was walking through the scrub when he shot at what he thought was a dog. He had killed Whelan and decided he had to kill the woman and her daughter to "cover up". However, forensic evidence at his trial showed he had bashed his victims before killing them.

JUNE 25

THE POISONED BABY (1864)

Suzanne Maree Marshall was born blind, but her parents Robert and Rosalind always hoped their daughter's condition could be cured. They therefore agreed to admit little Suzanne to Sydney's Royal Alexandria Hospital in the hope that a specialist could give the two-year-old sight for the first time. Suzanne entered the hospital on *June 18,* 1964, and placed in a ward with other infants. She died on the evening of *June 25* and doctors were puzzled as there seemed no obvious cause of death. Because it was regarded as an unexplained and sudden death, Suzanne's tiny body was the subject of a post-mortem and a government analyst examined several organs, including the liver and kidneys. Meanwhile, the two-year-old was buried with love and dignity at the Field of Mars Cemetery, Ryde.

However, tests performed by the government analyst, Mr E.S. Ogg, revealed the little girl had been poisoned by cyanide. The baby's body therefore was exhumed and this, of course, created enormous attention in Sydney. The two-year-old had been murdered, with someone slipping cyanide into her mouth while she slept. Police believed someone might have killed the little girl to save her a life of blindness, while some members of the public believed a maniac was at large, a child killer who had a heart as cold as the grave. Police, despite an exhaustive investigation, were never able to identity the killer and Mr and Mrs Marshall were left to grieve over the death of their baby daughter. They had tried to give Suzanne the chance of a normal, sighted life, but someone had stolen that life and never faced the consequences. Saddest of all, tests revealed that Suzanne would always have been blind.

JUNE 26

KILLED (1880): Ned Kelly's best mate and lieutenant of the Kelly Gang, Joe Byrne, shot dead his childhood mate Aaron Sherritt for perceived treachery in Beechworth, in Victoria's north-east, on *June 26*, 1880. Sherritt's murder was part of an elaborate plan to lure a special police train from Melbourne to its destruction in Glenrowan where the railway track had been ripped up. Instead, it resulted in the destruction of the gang. (Refer to *June 28* and *November 11*.)

JUNE 27

THE RUTHLESS WIFE AND THE HITMAN (1998)

David Cox was very ill. A sufferer of diabetes for 20 years, his condition had again flared, as it was occasionally prone to, requiring treatment in hospital. But Cox's wife Eileen was nowhere to be seen. Rather than supporting her husband at his bedside, Mrs Cox was trying to hire someone to kill him.

Although the Coxes had been together for 26 years and they had two sons, Mrs Cox had been discontented for several years. In conversations with a local bus-driver, whom she barely knew, she referred to her husband in a most derogatory manner, even describing him as a jealous person, despite the fact he had good reason – she had engaged in at least one adulterous relationship during their marriage.

However, when friends asked her: "Why don't you leave?" Mrs Cox explained that she wouldn't get anything if she did so.

A woman of relatively low intelligence, she was doing a fine job herself of frittering away the couple's funds. Cox's illness rendered him unable to work, which placed the couple under financial pressure. At such times, Cox was understandably annoyed by his wife's insistence on playing bingo, which only compounded their money problems.

By April 1998, Mrs Cox was seriously thinking about ending her marriage in the most drastic manner possible. About three months later, on *June 27*, married father-of-two Richard Alexander Bradley – the man Mrs Cox paid to murder her sick husband – succeeded in his sordid commission.

Although the exact circumstances of the murder are unknown, Mr Cox was found dead in his bathtub with his head partially under water. Lengths of material were wrapped around his throat, indicating that attempts had been made to strangle him, and he also suffered a bullet wound to his head caused by a sawn-off rifle. Police combing the Cox family house at Wyndhamvale in Melbourne's outer-western suburbs also found a cushion that had been damaged by a gunshot.

Although Cox was ill, it was clear he had still managed to put up a strong fight and did not die easily.

At their trial in December 1999, Justice Vincent described Mrs Cox – who had tried to implicate her own sons in their father's murder – as "a ruthless individual". Justice Vincent found Mrs Cox, 51, and Bradley, 44, equally responsible for Cox's death, and sentenced both to 17 years' jail, with a minimum of 13 years.

JUNE 28

HANGED (1842): Three bushrangers — Charles Ellis, Martin Fogarty and Daniel Gepps — hanged in Melbourne on *June 28*, 1842, following a gunfight with troopers.

**

NED KELLY'S LAST STAND (1880): The Kelly Gang and police waged arguably the most famous gunfight in Australian criminal history at Glenrowan on *June 28*, 1880. In a battle that lasted hours, Ned Kelly received 28 gunshot wounds and bravely took on the might of a police cordon, only to be brought down and captured. His three mates, brother Dan, Joe Byrne and Steve Hart died in the battle. (Refer to *November 11*.)

JUNE 29

MICHAEL McAULIFFE'S HANGING (1985)

Sydney barman Michael McAuliffe was arrested at the Penang International Airport, Malaysia, on *June 29*, 1985, and charged with allegedly carrying 141 grams of heroin packed in condoms in his money belt. However, McAuliffe vigorously pleaded his innocence and told the Malaysian High Court at his trial that after he had taken a Thai dancer home for sex, she produced an aphrodisiac she described as "bang bang powder". McAuliffe rubbed some of the white powder on his tongue and then asked her if he could buy some of it. He claimed he only put the powder in the condoms to save himself embarrassment if anyone discovered it.

The 38-year-old, who was born in Queensland and led an unsavoury life haunting bars in south-east Asia, was convicted on *August 17*, 1991, and sentenced to death. McAuliffe was convinced he would be hanged, but desperately sought a way to extend his life. He studied an Asian form of meditation in which he hoped his mind would escape from his body and allow him to escape from his cell. However, he was hanged on *June 19*, 1993.

THE WHEELIE BIN MURDER (2003)

Belgian Youssef Tecle Imentu found himself involved in murder when he helped flatmate Basheeruddin Mohamed, known as "Ben" eradicate a $20,000 debt. "Ben" allegedly owed $20,000 he had borrowed for a bridging visa. But, in the inner Sydney suburb of Redfern on *June 29*, 2003, the pair force-fed Mohamed heroin and hit him over the head with a baseball bat before strangling him. They then dumped his body in a wheelie bin and left outside an apartment block. Closed circuit television showed "Ben" and Imentu return from a sports store with a sleeping bag and a baseball bat on the day of the murder. On the same footage, the couple is shown several hours later pushing a wheelie bin, with Mohamed's feet protruding from it. They pushed the bin through the apartment block and into the street.

Although Supreme Court Acting Justice Peter Newman said he accepted that "Ben" had been the ringleader in the crime: "What is not clear from the evidence is who it was who administered the heroin to the deceased, struck him with a baseball bat and who it was that strangled him. However, I have no doubt that they were committed by the prisoner and "Ben" acting in concert." He sentenced Imentu to jail for a minimum of 20 years and a maximum of 26 years. "Ben" had been deported for being in breach of his student visa before his involvement in the murder was known and his whereabouts were unknown when this edition went to press.

JUNE 30

"SMUTTY JACK" (1830)

Two men, William Thomas and John Warne, who was known as "Smutty Jack" were seen together leaving Launceston on *April 14*, 1829, when a shot rang out. Several men ran up to a place known as Magpie Hill and came across Thomas, who had blood on his coat pocket. They also came across a cart to which the body of "Smutty Jack" was tied, along with a butchered calf. A constable found silver and blood-stained money in Thomas' pocket and he was arrested for murder. However, Thomas said he and the dead man had been attacked by bushrangers and had had nothing to do with "Smutty Jack's" death. Thomas also claimed at his trial that he had no motive to kill Warne as the dead man had promised to sell him all his property for 300 pounds. In his defence, Thomas also claimed that the blood on his pocket and money came from the dead calf. The jury refused to believe his story and took just 10-15 minutes to find him guilty of murder. Thomas was sentenced to be executed and his body then handed over to surgeons to be anatomised. He was hanged on *June 30*, 1830.

JULY

July might represent the heart of Australian winters, but crime generally blooms in this month, raising its ugly head in many forms, from killings to rape. Bodies and even parts of human remains have been discovered in horrific circumstances and even Australians apprehended overseas have captured national attention. Crimes this month include:

BARLOW AND CHAMBERS

DEATH AT THE ABORTION CLINIC

RAPED AT KNIFEPOINT

BURIED UNDER CONCRETE

THE SOUTHGATE RAPE

AUSTRALIA'S GREATEST CONMAN

And much, much more!

JULY 1

'THE FREE THINKER' (1895)

Arthur Buck thought of himself as a "free thinker", but apparently did not relish the thought of the women in his life following this philosophy and was a deeply jealous man. He lived with a woman named Catherine Norton in NSW in the 1880s and, following a separation of about five years, asked her to return to him. Norton, who was living with another man in Melbourne, refused. Buck pressed his claim and, after meeting Norton in South Melbourne, he drew a razor and slashed her throat. Norton later died in hospital and although Buck pleaded manslaughter, he was found guilty of murder and executed on *July 1*, 1895.

JULY 2

HANGED (1841): Two aborigines, Mullan and Ningavil, hanged in Brisbane on *July 2*, 1841, for murder.

JULY 3

BODY FOUND (1998): The body of Mustapha el Ahmad, 31, found in scrub beside the Princes Highway near the Drouin overpass, Victoria, on *July 3*, 1998. He had been savagely beaten around the head.

JULY 4

THE NAB TRADERS (2006)

Two National Australia Bank (NAB) traders, the final players in a $650 million foreign exchange scandal, were handed jail sentences on *July 4*, 2006. David Bullen, a senior trader, was sentenced to three years and eight months (with a non-parole period of two and a half years, while junior trader Vincent Ficarra was sentenced to two years and four months (with a minimum of 15 months). Bullen had been found guilty of 17 of 19 charges of gaining financial advantage for himself and others, along with one count of gaining financial advantage by deception. Ficarra was found guilty of 12 counts of gaining financial advantage for himself and one of gaining a bonus dishonestly. Earlier, Luke Duffy pleaded guilty to three counts of dishonestly using his position as an employee to gain financial advantage and was sentenced to two years and five months' jail, with a minimum of 16 months. Also, London trader Gianni Gray pleaded guilty to dishonestly using his position as an employee to gain advantages for himself and others and was sentenced to 16 months' jail, with a non-parole period of eight months.

JULY 5

PRISON FIRE (1984) : Fire broke out at Melbourne's Pentridge jail on *July 5*, 1984. Convicted murderer Barry Robert Quinn died in hospital hours after being set alight inside the notorious Jika Jika maximum security facility.

JULY 6

MURDER AT THE MILL (1946)

Paddy O'Leary was a tough customer, and he knew it. Charles Patrick O'Leary had spent time in the merchant navy and the army during World War II and took a job as a sawmill hand after the war. In 1946, O'Leary was working at a government forest at Nangwarry in south-east South Australia. It was a tough life and the men who worked with O'Leary liked a drink, with a weekend spree eventually leading to the death of 59-year-old Walter Edward Ballard on *July 6*, 1946.

O'Leary and some of his workmates went on a drinking spree on the Saturday morning, their drinking lasting until well into the night. O'Leary, 34, was involved in a number of scuffles but no one could have guessed that the night would end in death for the inoffensive Ballard. O'Leary, well after Ballard had gone "merry" to bed, bashed and killed him, according to the Crown at O'Leary's trial at the Mt Gambier Criminal Circuit Court. The Crown Prosecutor, Mr R.R. Chamberlain, alleged that O'Leary visited a cubicle occupied by Ballard, bashed him, dumped him on a bunk, poured kerosene over him and set light to him. Ballard died two hours later in hospital.

Medical evidence was given at O'Leary's trial that Ballard had been bashed eight times across the head with a beer bottle and that the broken end of this bottle was smashed into his face. Although Ballard was still alive when he was pulled from his bunk, O'Leary was heard to say: "Give me an axe and I'll put the poor man out of his misery – let me finish him off." O'Leary, in a sworn statement, denied killing Ballard and, in fact, did all in his power to ease his suffering. However,

O'Leary was found guilty of murder and was sentenced to death. Several appeals failed and O'Leary was hanged at the Adelaide Goal on *November 14*, 1946.

JULY 7

BARLOW AND CHAMBERS (1986)

Australians long will remember Kevin Barlow and Geoffrey Chambers. They were executed in Malaysia after being found guilty of drug trafficking. Barlow and Chambers knew the risks they were taking as the death penalty for drug trafficking in Malaysia was mandatory. However, they both thought the risk of making big money was worth it and Chambers was assigned to collect heroin and deliver it to Barlow's hotel room in Penang, an island resort in Malaysia. Following a routine search, they were arrested at the Bayan Lepas International airport on *November 9*, 1983.

They at first accused each other of owning the 410 grams of heroin after a search of their luggage revealed 13 plastic bags of the drug. In desperation, both Barlow and Chambers then claimed they had no knowledge of the drugs or how they were found in the luggage. They claimed the heroin had been planted, but this was ridiculed in court and, on *August 1*, they were sentenced to death. Despite appeals and a plea for clemency by Australian Prime Minister Bob Hawke (who described hanging as "barbaric"), Barlow and Chambers were executed at Pudu Prison at 8am on *July 7*, 1986. Wearing white calico prison uniforms, blindfolded and their legs roped together, they went to their death to the prayers of more than 300 outside the prison gates.

JULY 8

VICTIM (1993): Multiple murderer Paul Denyer claims his second Frankston victim on *July 8*, 1993.

JULY 9

SENTENCED (1993): The killer of Ebony Simpson, Andrew Garforth, sentenced to life imprisonment on *July 9*, 1993.

JULY 10

THE GRIEVING SON (2001)

To all intents and purposes, Sef Gonzales was the epitome of a heartbroken young man dealing with a tragedy of monumental proportions. The fresh-faced Gonzales gave an emotional eulogy at the funeral of his parents and sister in singing pop hit 'One Sweet Day' made famous by Mariah Carey and Boys II Men. It went:

Sorry I never told you
All I wanted to say
Now it's too late to hold you
'Cause you've flown away, so far away ...
And I know you're shining down from me from heaven
Like so many friends I have lost along the way.
And I know eventually we'll be together –

One Sweet Day

Gonzales was the ultimate hypocrite because he had killed parents Teddy and Mary-Loiva and 18-year-old sister Clodine at the family's home in the quiet north-west Sydney suburb of North Ryde on *July 10*, 2001. The Gonzales family had migrated to Australia from the Philippines after an earthquake had destroyed a hotel the family had built. Sef, just 10 years of age, was trapped by debris on a staircase, but father Ted pulled him to safety.

Despite having his life saved by his father, Sef resented the strict discipline imposed on him and, besides, there was the question of $1 million he would inherit if his parents died. The 21-year-old Sef Gonzales therefore tried to poison his family with seeds he had bought on the internet. His mother was admitted to hospital, but recovered, so Sef waited just two weeks before setting in motion another plan. This time he stabbed his family to death and blamed it on a mystery intruder. Sef Gonzales even painted the words 'f… off Asians' on a kitchen wall to divert attention from himself. Police were suspicious from the start, but Gonzales appeared to have the perfect alibi as he told police he was having dinner with friends at the time his family had been slaughtered. Gonzales after making out that he had found the bodies of his three family members, called police and told them: 'Somebody shot my parents, I think. They're all bleeding; they're on the floor.'

Police: 'What suburb are you in?'

Gonzales: 'They're not breathing. What do I do?'

Police: 'What suburb are you in?'

Gonzales: 'North Ryde?'

Police at a press conference later said: 'Young Sef and his family have cooperated with the investigators at this stage, and we're satisfied with the explanation so far.' Then, when the dinner alibi turned out to be a lie, Gonzales said he was having sex at a brothel at the time and had made up the story about having dinner because his mother would have been horrified at the thought of him going to a brothel.

Police then broke through his tissue of lies bit by bit, starting with disproving Gonzales' claim that he had been to the brothel. It turned out that the particular prostitute Gonzales referred to was not at the brothel at the time he suggested. Police dogs were unable to pick up the scent of any intruder and traces of the paint used to daub the wall were found on one of Gonzales' jumpers. Also, he claimed to have hugged members of his family after he had found their bodies, but no trace of these signs of affection could be found on his clothes.

Meanwhile, Gonzales visited his father's accountant just three days after the family tragedy and then paid deposits on luxury motor vehicles. He moved into an apartment, sold his parents' car and generally lived it up. Gonzales was charged with three counts of murder 11 months after the slayings and he eventually pleaded not guilty before a six-week trial in the Supreme Court of NSW. Crown prosecutor Mark Tedeschi told the jury: 'Feeling his life unravel, Sef set in train a plan to murder his parents and his sister.' The court was told that when police seized Gonzales' computer they found reference to internet sites such as 'How to Kill' and 'White Man Killer'.

The jury took just four and a half hours to find Gonzales guilty and, as the decision was announced, his aunt, Annia Paraan, broke down and muttered 'thank you'. She said later: 'I think justice has been done, but it would have been easier to accept if it were another person. It's just so hard to accept.'

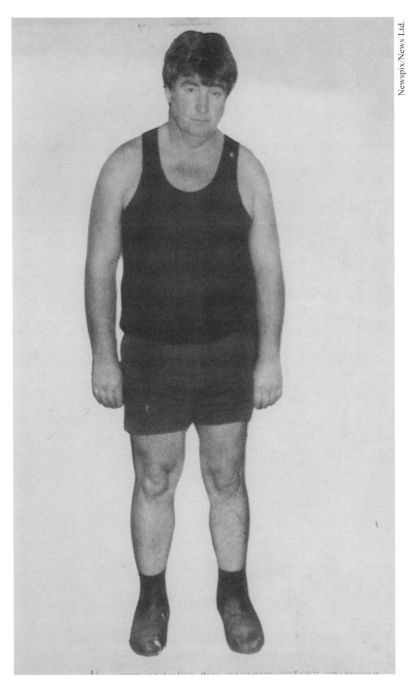

Raymond "Mr Stinky" Edmunds.

Melbourne gangster Leslie "Squizzy" Taylor interviewed by detectives after he gave himself up in 1922.

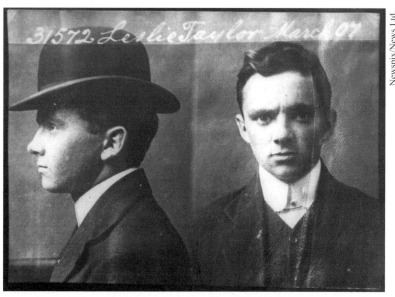

Mugshot of Leslie 'Squizzy' Taylor.

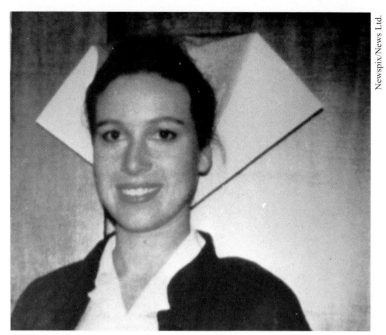

Murder victim Anita Cobby, in nurse's uniform, was abducted, raped and murdered by five men while walking home from Blacktown railway station.

Murder victim Nicole Patterson with her niece after competing in Lorne's Pier to Pub swim. She was murdered by Peter Dupas.

*Greg Domaszewicz was babysitting Jaidyn Leskie (14 months)
when the boy was allegedly abducted.*

*The last picture ever taken of Jaidyn Leskie on
April 30th, 1997, with Greg Domaszewicz's dog, Jack.*

*Valmae Faye Beck escorted by police detectives – on trial for
the murder of Sian Kingi on November 27, 1987 at Noosa.
Barrie John Watts was also charged as the main offender.*

Murder victim Gladys Hosking – one of three women strangled by US soldier Edward Leonski while he was stationed in Melbourne during World War Two.

A motorist lies dead at the wheel of his car after being shot during a massacre in Hoddle Street, Clifton Hill, by gunman Julian Knight (19), who shot dead 7 people & wounded 19.

Hoddle Street gunman Julian Knight leaves the Coroners Court in Melbourne under police guard.

Matthew Wales King, the son of Margaret Wales King and stepson of Paul King was convicted of drugging then murdering the couple on April 4, 2002. He was sentenced to 30 years in jail.

JULY 11

EXECUTED (1861): Henry Cooley executed in Melbourne on *July 11*, 1861, for the axe killing of his wife at McIvor on *March 16*, 1861. Cooley dumped the body in the bush and left it there for two weeks before returning and setting it alight.

**

ACCUSED (1988): Career criminal Raymond Denning tells an inquest on *July* 11, 1988, that Jason Moran was involved in an armed robbery at the Coles warehouse in the Melbourne suburb of Brunswick in which a security guard was killed.

**

BODY FOUND (2000): The body of 43-year-old Andrew James Munro, who was stabbed to death, found in his home in the Perth suburb of Gosnells on *July 11*, 2000.

JULY 12

HANGED (1859): William Armstrong and George Chamberlain hanged in Melbourne on *July 12*, 1859, for the shooting death and axe mutilation of a Constable Green near Bairnsdale.

**

SHOT DEAD (1999): Vicki Jacobs shot dead at her home near Bendigo, Victoria, on *July 12*, 1999, as she slept on a settee with six-year-old son Ben. Police believed the killing was related to Jacobs giving evidence in a murder trial in South Australia, but no one has been charged with her murder.

JULY 13

BURIED (1944): The body of the "Pyjama Girl", Linda Agostini, buried at the Coburg Cemetery, Melbourne, on *July 13*, 1944, almost 10 years after her death.

JULY 14

MURDER: Englishman Peter Falconio murdered by Bradley John Murdoch in the Outback on *July 14*, 2001.

JULY 15

THE CHILD BRIDE (1951)

Orma and Donald Warner were married as teenagers, with pretty dark-haired Orma little more than a child bride. She was just 17 years of age when she married 19-year-old timber mill worker Donald in early 1951. Neither was to know they would be married for just five months. Farmer Athol Lyon was driving past the Warners' weatherboard and fibro house near Casino, on the north coast of New South Wales, at about 9.45pm on *July 15*, 1951, when he noticed the house was ablaze. There was nothing he could do as the flames already had taken hold.

Police were called and shocked to find two charred bodies in the ashes left by the huge blaze. Even more horrifying, police also found the remains of a couple of rifles, a revolver and two shotgun cartridges. They immediately sensed that the newlyweds had been shot to death and the house then torched. A post-mortem quickly revealed that both Orma and Donald Warner had shotgun wounds to the body. There were numerous pellets in both bodies and, as proof that the house had been torched, police found the charred remains of three kerosene tins. Police did not have to question too many locals as there were persistent rumours that Orma had been nervous of a local stock inspector. However, 29-year-old William Henry Abbott, married with two children, had had an impeccable record during World War II and had even been awarded the Distinguished Conduct Medal for his bravery.

Police then learned that Donald Warner had complained to Abbott about "pestering" his young wife and that the newlywed husband had spoken about getting Abbott shifted from the district in his job. This was just three days before the deaths of Donald and Orma Warner and police, naturally, were now suspicious of the stock inspector. Abbott was unable to provide an alibi and when detectives found a shotgun at his home they knew they were close to breaking the case. Ballistic tests proved that the shotgun found in the Abbott home had been used to shoot the Warners.

Finally, police found bloodstained clothes at Abbott's home and although he at first insisted that the blood was from cattle, police suspected otherwise. He was charged with murder and, at his trial, claimed police had threatened to bash him to get a confession. However, he was found guilty and sentenced to death, this sentence later commuted to one of life imprisonment.

JULY 16

DEATH AT THE ABORTION CLINIC (2001)

Peter James Knight, 47, was something of a loner, a recluse who at one stage lived in a humpy in a forest in New South Wales. In 2000, he became interested in the anti-abortion movement and attended rallies and protests. The following year he moved to Melbourne and took more than a passing interest in the Fertility Control Clinic in Wellington Parade, East Melbourne. Finally, on *July 16*, 2001, Knight put a murderous plan into action.

He went to the clinic at about 10.20am, holding two bags, one of which contained a well-concealed rifle. Knight was intent on mayhem and entered the reception area by the main door. However, his plan of a massacre ran into trouble almost immediately as security guard Steven Rogers walked in from a different door. Near the end of his shift, Rogers moved towards Knight, who told him he had a gun. Knight then pointed the rifle at the security guard and pulled the trigger. Rogers fell mortally wounded to the floor and, after Knight reloaded the rifle, he pointed it at the stomach of a pregnant woman. The woman's male friend, Sandro De Maria, grabbed the gun to wrest it from Knight and it went off, firing a shot into the ceiling. However, Knight eventually was overpowered and arrested.

At his trial in Melbourne, Justice Teague told Knight: "The murder of Steven Rogers was a very serious crime. It is to be treated more seriously because of the context in which you carried out the murder. You were a loner on a personal crusade when you went to the clinic. Your crusade was to effect social change. Steven Rogers was just doing his duty. He got in the way of your crusade. He was one of those who was characterised by you as being in 'the abortion racket'."

He also said: "In July, 2001, you were able to put together a collection of items that had the potential to result in the death of dozens of people who were going about their normal lives in the East Melbourne clinic. You engaged in detailed panning and preparation. Your planning included having noted the usual timing of the departure from the clinic of Steven Rogers. Your entry to the clinic was at a time shortly after he would have been expected to have departed … You have not shown any remorse, in the sense of showing any sincere repentance or regret that Steven Rogers was killed. The closest you have come to that has been to argue that his death was just bad luck." Justice Teague then sentenced Knight to life imprisonment, with a non-parole period of 23 years.

JULY 17

RAPED AT KNIFEPOINT (2003)

When a 16-year-old girl was raped in her Newington (NSW) home during a violent robbery on *July 17*, 2003, she thought she was going to die at the hands of her attackers, who were armed with at least one knife. The girl survived her ordeal, but had to spend three days in hospital because of the brutal assault. Her father, who was tied up by the group of four attackers, told a NSW District Court: "My daughter never really cried." The girl's mother, who also had been bound, said: "When we were free I hugged my daughter and this is when I asked her if she was OK and she said they actually raped her."

The gang had targeted the first-floor apartment because they believed they would get away with jewellery and cash. Police later arrested four men and Dudley Mark Aslett, who was named as the ring-leader, was sentenced to 40 years' jail. He appealed on the grounds that this sentence was too severe and it was reduced to 30 years' imprisonment, with a non-parole period of 22 and a half years. A second gang member, Christopher Bonham was sentenced to 15 years' jail, while Aslett's nephew, Steven James Aslett, had his sentence reduced from 24 years to 20 on appeal. The fourth accused, who was 17 at the time, was sentenced to five years' jail.

Justice Barr noted that the offences "came into the worst category" and noted that Aslett held a knife to his victim's cheek as he raped her and threatened to "poke out" her eyes. The judge said that the girl, who had endured an ordeal which "amounted to torture", suffered physical and lasting emotional harm. "She was imprisoned, degraded and humiliated," he said.

JULY 18

HANGED (1825): Three Aborigines, whose names were not officially recorded, but were known as Billy, Jack and Ebony, were hanged in Sydney on *July 18*, 1825, for the murder of two white settlers eight miles (about 13 kilometres) west of Parramatta.

JULY 19

THE KILLER POET (1927)

Mabel Elizabeth James was an attractive young woman with curly blonde hair. She was a country girl living in Melbourne and, like many country girls of the 1920s, was shy and reserved. She had left her home in Maryborough to look for work in the city and secured a position as a housemaid at the St Ive's Guest House, Toorak Road, South Yarra. Poor Mabel James, just 20 years of age when she accepted the position, was not to know that her job would lead to her death at the hands of a crazed suitor.

One of her workmates was Cecil Ronald Leet, who had spent several years in the navy. He was a houseman at the guest house and fell instantly and hopelessly in love with Mabel. His infatuation was so intense that he drove Mabel to despair. He peppered her with declarations of love and wrote her passionate poems and letters. This situation lasted more than two years, until Leet resigned his position and went looking for work in rural New South Wales. Although he got a job as a boundary rider, he continued to bombard Mabel with letters and poems, even though she did her best to dampen his passion. However, Mabel made a fatal mistake in writing back to Leet and signing the letter with the words "your sincere friend". Leet rushed back to Melbourne in the belief he finally could win over young Mabel James.

Leet met up with Mabel in a Melbourne street on *July 19*, 1927, but the country girl again rejected his overtures. Next evening, Mabel was returning to her room at the back of the guest house when Leet jumped out at her. He was carrying a rifle and, after struggle, Mabel was shot in the leg. Then, as she struggled to break free, Leet fired a shot into her head before turning the gun on himself. Leet, well-educated and the son of an Edinburgh University graduate, had bought the gun only the previous day. When police went through his pockets, they found the following poem he had written:

Remember him thou leav'st behind,
Whose heart is warmly bound to thee;
Close as the ten'rest link can bind
A heart as warm as heart could be.

A letter police found read: "The sound of your voice today sent a longing thrill through my feelings … You cannot conceive how deep my regard of you is and so I have your whole interests at heart. My whole thoughts are centred in you. I think of you everlastingly, day and night, until the tears will in my eyes." Leet signed off this undelivered letter to Mabel "God bless you, Chere Ange, Fraternally, Ron". Melbourne coroner Mr Berriman later found that Cecil "Ron" Leet was of "unsound mind" when he killed Mabel James and then himself.

JULY 20

THE BODY ON DISPLAY (1853)

It was too good an opportunity for Victoria's most notorious bushrangers to miss. On *July 20*, 1853, a Melbourne Gold Escort Company dray, driven by Thomas Fookes and escorted by an armed guard, left McIvor carrying more than 200 ounces of gold and 700 pounds in notes. It was a king's ransom and the huge delivery to Melbourne was honey to the likes of bushrangers George Melville, Williams Atkins, George Wilson and others.

The dray and escort had travelled just 20 miles when the path was blocked by a large log pushed across the road. Shots rang out and, after Fookes was shot dead, the escort fled. The bushrangers might have been able to plunder the gold and bank notes, but they soon were hunted down. Melville, Atkins and Wilson were arrested and charged with the murder of Fookes.

All three were found guilty and sentenced to death. They were executed in Melbourne on *October 3*, 1858, and the bodies handed over to their respective relatives. However, Melville's wife placed his body in a coffin and put it on display in a shop window in busy Bourke Street. It remained there for several days before authorities insisted on a burial.

JULY 21

SHOT DEAD (2003): Melbourne underworld identity Willy Thompson shot dead in his car in the south-east Melbourne suburb of Chadstone on **July 21**, 2003.

JULY 22

I WANT TO GO TO HEAVEN (1971)

The death of a child is tragic, and the murder of a child is even more tragic. However, there can be few deaths as tragic as that of little Charles Benedek, just six years of age. Charles died because of an overwhelming love and trust of his father and the desire to go to heaven. His father, Edward Tobor Benedek, was the boys' killer but like the pathetic Edward Williams in *The Three Little Angels (1924)* deserved a great deal of pity, despite the nature of the killing.

Edward Benedek was a deserted father who struggled to make ends meet in the years before 1971. Born in Hungary in 1927, Benedek fled to Australia as a result of the infamous Hungarian uprising of 1956, settled down, worked mainly as a painter and married in 1964. Unfortunately, his wife later spent periods in mental institutions and finally left him. The Hungarian became father and mother to his two children, Charles and Susan. He struggled for three years to raise the children the best way he could, but it was difficult, with jobs hard to come by and money usually stretched to the limit.

Benedek finally made one of the most tragic suicide pacts in Australian history. He took Charles and Susan, four and a half, for a drive along Victoria's scenic Great Ocean Road on *July 22*, 1971. He previously had spoken to the children about heaven, little Charles reacting because of lessons taught at school. Benedek finally asked the children if they would like to go to heaven with him or live in a police home. Charles, showing unbelievable faith in his father, said he would like to go to heaven, Susan saying that she would prefer to live in a police home.

The distraught father later shot the boy dead and twice tried to take his own life with the same rifle. The girl was taken by a passing bus driver to the safety of a police station. Benedek was treated at hospitals in Geelong and Melbourne, spending several days in a psychiatric ward. "Susan didn't want to go to heaven with me and Charles, and I said to both Susan and Charles to wait in the car until a car or a truck comes by and ask the man to take them to the nearest police station, "Benedek said. "With that I missed Susan and Charles and I started walking away from the car towards the rear with my rifle in my hand. Charles ran after me and said, 'I want to go with you, Daddy', and he pointed to his chest and he said, 'shoot me there, Daddy'.

"I fired a shot towards his chest but it couldn't have been vital because he said, 'it hurts Daddy'. With that I put him back on the front seat of the car, covered him up with a blanket, told him to go top sleep, and when he closed his eyes, I fired a second shot in his chest, the one that must have been the fatal shot. Then I kissed Susan once again, told Susan to kiss Charles as well and told her to stay in the car until a car or a truck comes by, then she could go with them to the nearest police station. I walked away about 12 feet from the rear of the car to a grass edge on the road. I leaned over the rifle and fired a shot into my chest where I thought my heart was.

"I became very thirsty and very dizzy as I was sitting in the grass bleeding under the shirt and I asked Susan to bring me the water container so I could have a drink. She did give me the container, then I told her to go back to the back seat of the car, and with that I leaned over the rifle once again and fired a shot into my chest."

Benedek said that the morning before the tragic shooting he told the children about heaven. He said: "I explained to the children about heaven and, to my amazement, Charlie seemed to know a lot about it. I didn't know they taught that in the first grade at school. He asked me if we have any friends in heaven. I said yes and named a few people he knew who had passed away."

Benedek, 44, was found not guilty to murder because of insanity when he stood trial at the Geelong Criminal Court.

Justice Menhennit ordered him to be held in the strictest custody at the Governor's pleasure.

JULY 23

BURIED UNDER CONCRETE (1931)

Mary Edson was a tall, extremely attractive young woman with dark brown bobbed hair in the fashion of the 1930s. She was 22 years of age, had a 16-month-old daughter and lived in the Adelaide suburb of Knoxville when she disappeared without trace on *May 18*, 1931. Next-door neighbour Mrs Grace Lindsay was deeply puzzled and repeatedly asked the young woman's husband about the disappearance. Lawrence Edson (known to his friends as Lawrie), a 28-year-old tram conductor, at first told Mrs Lindsay that his wife had run off with another man and that he had been left to care for their daughter, June. Mrs Lindsay thought this strange, although she knew that the Edsons had quarrelled many times over the previous months and that Mary Edson had adopted a "beaten dog" attitude.

Other neighbours started gossiping but Edson merely changed his story and told everyone that his wife had died. After all, he even had a letter which Mrs Edson's sister Dorothy Malycha was alleged to have received from an H. Wilson in Melbourne telling her of her sister's "death" on *June 19*, 1931. He showed this letter to anyone who cared to read it as "proof" that his wife had died. However, the writer of the letter indicated it was not known at which cemetery Mary Edson was buried.

If neighbours had been suspicious before, they now were determined to get to the bottom of Mrs Edson's mysterious disappearance. They reported the matter to police, who went to Edson's home on *July 23* to investigate. Edson, a former police officer, showed police the letter (another two supposedly from Melbourne had been burned, he told them) and then made a statement at the City Watchhouse about how his wife had left him in May and then had died in Melbourne. Police were far from convinced and told Edson they would detain him until officers had had the opportunity to search his home and dig through his garden in Lestrange Street. Edson immediately stepped out of the room in which he was being questioned and on to a landing where he pulled an automatic pistol from his suit pocket and shot himself in the head. He died in hospital two days later without regaining consciousness. Police therefore were left with a riddle, but they knew that the thought of digging up Edson's garden had terrified him.

Naturally, police were convinced that Edson had buried his wife in the garden at their Knoxville home and rushed there to put their theory to the test. Neighbours had told them they had seen Edson working feverishly in the tiny shed at the back of the garden. Edson, who once had kept a pet wallaby in the shed, had been seen taking grapevine cuttings there. They were still there when police investigated, but when they swept them aside they discovered freshly laid concrete. Police used a pick to dig up the thin layer of concrete and found part of a woman's robe. They dug a little further and found a woman's body in a grave just a few inches deep. The body, after preliminary examination, was taken to the Adelaide morgue for identification. This horrendous responsibility fell on Mrs

Edson's other sister, Miss Rose Malycha, who made a positive identification.

Police continued their investigations and discovered that at least the first half of the letter allegedly sent from Melbourne had been written by 14-year-old John McMahon, who had identified Edson from a newspaper photograph. McMahon told police that Edson had asked him to write a letter and had provided him with a fountain pen for the task. However, the boy said he stopped writing halfway through the letter as he had become suspicious. Police were unable to determine who wrote the rest of the latter.

Meanwhile, Adelaide newspapers had a major sensation on their hands and pumped it for all their worth and reporters even tracked down Edson's first wife, even though few people suspected he had been married twice. The first Mrs Edson gave birth to a son in 1922 and Edson used to visit her to pay maintenance money after their divorce in 1928.

An inquest into the deaths of Edson and his wife was held in Adelaide from *July 29*, 1931. The acting coroner, Mr F.C. Siekman, presided over a case which held South Australia spellbound and, naturally, everyone wanted to know the cause of Mrs Edson's death. There had been reports that Edson had bashed her to death, but although there was some bruising to the body, Mrs Edson had been strangled, possibly with a pyjama coat which appeared to be wrapped around the neck. But why did Edson strangle his wife? No one will ever know, although an Adelaide newspaper reported at the time of his death that he recently had given a young woman an engagement ring and had promised to marry her. The newspaper reported that detectives had interviewed a woman at Reynella, but there was no mention of this at the inquest and the mystery remains in one of Adelaide's most infamous murder-suicide cases.

JULY 24

HANGED (1877): Dutchman Charles Streitman, a father of three, hanged in Adelaide on *July 24*, 1877, after being found guilty of the stabbing murder of a bailiff at Wallaroo on *April 18* that year.

**

STABBED (1987): Amed Hammouda, 27, stabbed outside his Housing Commission flat in the inner Melbourne suburb of Carlton on *July 24*, 1987.

JULY 25

THE VICTORIA MARKET MURDER (1916)

The execution of Antonio Picconi (sometimes spelt as Piccone or Piconi) at the Melbourne Gaol on *September 18*, 1916, hardly caused as ripple and, in fact, rated just two paragraphs on an inside page of the *Age* newspaper the following day. Naturally, the Great War hogged all public interest and the *Age* merely reported that Picone (as it referred to the executed man) was attended by a priest, the Rev. Father O'Donovan, as he was led to the scaffold and that death was instantaneous. Piccone, an Italian immigrant, was hanged for the murder of another Italian, Joseph Lauricella, at Melbourne's Victoria Market on the morning of *July 25*, 1916. Lauricella was playing cards with another man when Piccone walked up behind him and shot him twice. Then, when Lauricella fell, Piccone pumped another bullet into him.

Piccone fled from the scene, but was caught by a witness and then handed to the police. When asked why he had killed Lauricella, Piccone said the dead man had caused his family financial grief through business transactions gone wrong. Piccone was examined for any possible mental illness, but was passed fit to stand trial. The *Age,* in its brief report of Piccone's death, said: "His request that a small photo in his possession and a lock of hair should be buried with him was granted." Asked if he had any last words, Piccone mumbled a few inaudible words.

JULY 26

THE BODIES IN THE BUSH (1991)

On the morning of *July 26*, 1991, Alan Leahy walked into the Atherton police station to report that his wife Julie-Anne, 26, was missing. He told them that she and her friend Vicki Arnold, 28, had made a late decision the previous night to go fishing at the nearby Tinaroo Dam, even though it was close to freezing that night. When police discovered that a rifle Arnold recently had bought also was missing, they launched a massive police and emergency services search for the women.

Fifteen days later, trail-bike riders discovered a white four-wheel drive in a secluded clearing at Cheery Tree Creek, in the opposite direction to the Tinaroo Dam. Inside, they found the decomposing remains of the two missing women. Leahy's body was found in the driving seat with two bullet wounds in the side of her head. She also had other wounds as it appeared she had been struck on the head with a rock. Arnold had been shot three times, one fired at close range to the head from underneath her chin. Significantly, the weapon found in Arnold's hand was a cut-down .22 rifle altered to negate automatic reload; it could only be manually cocked before each shot.

An inquest returned a verdict of murder/suicide and the theory went that, for some unknown reason, Arnold launched an attack on Leahy and shot and wounded her through the cheek. She then bashed her with a rock, slashed her throat with a knife and finally killed her with the shot to the head. It also was theorised that she then turned the gun on herself. The case attracted enormous attention and controversy in Queensland, with many refusing to believe the murder-suicide theory. Yet, over two police investigations, a ministerial inquiry and two inquests, the mystery remains.

JULY 27

THE SOUTHBANK RAPE (2002)

Christopher William Empey attended a function at the Carlton Crest Hotel, in Queens Road, Melbourne, on the evening of *July 26*, 2002, and drank and danced with a woman from an adjoining table. They were last seen at around 1.30 the following morning, *July 27*, and both apparently had a considerable amount to drink. The next anyone can remember seeing them was outside an apartment at Southbank. Noises were heard outside the apartment and Empey was seen raping the woman and punching her in the vagina. He then was seen, from the apartment window, walking away. However, he returned and stomped on the head of his victim and kicked her.

Police quickly arrived on the scene, with Empey kneeling over the woman. He at first told police that he was trying to help her, but then ran off. When confronted a little later, he told police he had a gun and warned them to back off. There was no gun and Empey was subdued and taken to a police station, where he warned officers that he would harm himself. Then, at Homicide Squad offices, he broke a fluorescent light and cut his neck, with considerable blood loss.

Empey's wound was serious, but nothing compared to those of the woman he had attacked. Her injuries, which were life-threatening, included facial fractures, a torn ear and internal wounds. Empey pleaded guilty to rape and intentionally causing serious injuries and, in sentencing him on *November 6*, 2003, Justice Teague told him: "Although I have allowed for many mitigating factors, the fact is that your crimes were horrendous. They were the acts of a monster. Only a very long prison sentence is appropriate given the applicable sentencing considerations." He sentenced Empey to 14 years for rape and 10 years for intentionally causing serious injury, concurrent for eight years. This meant a term of 16 years, with a non-parole period of 12 years.

AUSTRALIA'S GREATEST CONMAN (1991)

John Friedrich might have had an aura of respectability for most of his life, but eventually was regarded as Australia's greatest conman. Born in Germany, he established a reputation as a sound and reliable businessman as managing director of the National Safety Council of Australia during the

1980s. However, it then became apparent that vast sums of money were missing from the accounts and, on *April 6*, 1989, Friedrich was arrested. It soon was revealed that he had forged his qualifications and, in fact, was living in Australia under a false passport. Friedrich faced 91 charges of fraud and, on *July 23*, 1991, he appeared in court over the disappearance of $244 million. However, Friedrich never faced the charges as he was found with a single gunshot wound to the head on his farm at Sale, Victoria, on *July 27*, 1991. His death was ruled as suicide.

JULY 28

MURDERED (1987): In what appeared to be a drug-related crime, 39-year-old Ray Abbey and his wife Dorothy, 38, were murdered in their Heidleberg Heights home on *July 28*, 1987.

JULY 29

A FIERY DEATH (1824)

Sawyer Thomas Brown was working with Irish convict John Donovan felling trees at the Emu Plains settlement in 1824, when he chastised the Irishman for not working hard enough. He told the convict he would report him and be punished for his laziness. Then, at four the next morning (*July 29*), Brown was thrown into a fire and suffered severe burns from feet to chest. He was taken by cart to a Dr West, a surgeon at Windsor, and temporarily treated. Brown then told Dr West an extraordinary story of Donovan and another man grabbing him and throwing him between two burning logs. Brown said he screamed and struggled, with Donovan and the unnamed man then running away.

The sawyer died of his burns four days later and, when Donovan was arrested, it was noted that his trousers had been singed and that he had marks on his face. Donovan insisted Brown had fallen onto the fire during the fight and also complained that the sawyer had called him "a Munster stork", a derogatory term suggesting a lazy attitude from that particular part of Ireland. He said Brown's death was an accident and that no third party was involved. The principal overseer of the settlement, Joseph Peters said at Donovan's trial that he had examined the ashes and that they were pressed flat as if someone had been lying in a fire. Donovan was found guilty of murder and hanged on *August 24*, 1824.

JULY 30

VICTIM (1993): The Frankston monster, Paul Denyer, killed his third victim on *July 30*, 1993.

JULY 31

HANGED (1867): William Terry hanged at Castlemaine, Victoria, on *July 31*, 1867, for the murder of Peter Reddick at Taradale five years earlier.

**

NOT GUILTY (1997): Dean Waters found not guilty on *July 31*, 1997, of the murder of his mother's lover, Alan Hall, in 1988. The court found that the real killer was Dean's deceased father Cec Walters.

AUGUST

Australia has had more than its share of sex offenders, perverts and paedophiles. Many such crimes have been committed in the late winter month of August, along with a number of truly horrific murders. It often is a month of mayhem and even the occasional massacre as the nation prepares for warmer weather and more encouraging news. Crimes this month include:

TRAIN STATION TERROR
THE CAMPUS KILLING
CHRISTOPHER SKASE
MR BALDY
THE HODDLE STREET MASSACRE
THE BULLION THEFT
And much, much more!

AUGUST 1

TRAIN STATION TERROR (1997)

Yuksel Atar led a quiet life that revolved around his wife and three daughters. The 57-year-old, who had migrated to Australia from Turkey with his wife in the 1970s, often travelled on trains to visit friends or even just to pass the time away. After midnight on *August 1*, 1997, Atar boarded a train at Dandenong (in Melbourne's east) that would take him via Hallam to Narre Warren, where he had lived for about 20 years. But the diminutive Atar's peaceful train ride in the otherwise unoccupied last carriage was soon disrupted by an unruly, strapping stranger.

Michael Keith Maxwell Clancy, an immature 20-year-old, was in an aggressive mood after being dumped by his girlfriend earlier that day. He had drowned his sorrows for several hours at a hotel in Dandenong and, at one point, insulted the wrong person and was punched in the face. Just before entering the train carriage occupied by Atar, Clancy had unsuccessfully asked two men for money. Without provocation, Clancy attacked the defenceless Atar.

The pair got off the train at Hallam station and, once out of sight, Clancy continued his frenzied attack, viciously assaulting Atar for about half an hour, initially breaking the umbrella Atar had used to protect himself and stealing his watch. The incessant punching, kicking and stomping overwhelmed Atar, who suffered numerous severe head injuries and lost consciousness. Clancy's final act of violence on the helpless older man was to push him off the station platform to the tracks below, where he was left to die.

In sentencing Clancy to 17 years' jail with a minimum of 12 years, Justice Teague told him: "I find that you did not intend to kill Yuksal Atar but only to inflict really serious injury. I make that finding essentially because of the mindlessness and the motivelessness of your actions. Your conduct was affected in some degree by the drinking. I am troubled that there was a one-sidedness in your choice of victim. You were a strapping 20-year-old, yet you picked on a small man nearly 60. There was no provocative conduct whatsoever on his part, but you subjected him to a vicious and terrifying beating over an extended period."

THE BODY IN THE BARWON (1953)

Tall and elegant Mr H.A. Winneke QC (later Sir Henry Winneke, Governor of Victoria), chose his words carefully. Mr Winneke was making an opening address in one of the most sensational murder trials in Victorian criminal history. Mr Winneke said: "Someone has committed a foul and ghastly murder. On *May 13* (1953) the dead man left his home after his evening meal, giving no indication he was not returning. Nothing more was heard of him until a diver recovered the decapitated body from the Barwon River, Geelong, on *August 1*. When the body was recovered the head was sawn off the trunk, and each hand had been sawn off above the wrist. The trunk was in two sacks wired to a 126-pound stone, and the head and hands in a kerosene tin punctured with holes. A post-mortem examination showed the body to be very, very extensively damaged. The trunk had been mutilated – there were six main wounds on the skull and there were underlying fractures beneath three of them caused by heavy blows."

On trial before Justice Martin in the Supreme Court of Victoria at Geelong were Andrew Gordon Kilpatrick, 33, and Russell William Hill, 22, both of Colac, a prosperous rural city in Victoria's Western District. Both had pleaded not guilty to a charge of murdering Donald Brooke Maxfield, also of Colac, on or about *May 13*, 1953. The case was widely known as "The Body in the Barwon" murder and it captured headlines in Victoria for years. Yet, incredibly, only a determined policeman's hunch led to a murder investigation.

The policeman was Detective Sergeant Fred Adam, a well-known member of Victoria's Homicide Squad. Detective Adam had been sent to Colac to investigate a number of mysterious break-ins in the district. It was not a murder investigation and there was not even a hint of murder, at first. Detective Adam's job was to prosecute Kilpatrick and Hill on a charge of assaulting a local constable with a weapon. That case alone drew considerable publicity in Melbourne as Kilpatrick and Hill eventually were found guilty of assaulting Constable George Ross Chester and sentenced to a year's jail each. They have notice of appeal and were released on bail.

However, Adam felt something was wrong and filed a report to police headquarters suggesting there was a conspiracy of crime in Colac which needed investigation. Adam was ordered to proceed with the investigation and, believing that by putting pressure on the younger Hill, he would get further than by questioning Kilpatrick. Hill was young, impressionable and not as worldly smart as Kilpatrick, who had been educated at the exclusive and expensive Geelong Grammar School. In preparing for the investigation, Adam also noted that another man, 22-year-old Donald Maxfield, had gone missing.

Adam looked at the Maxfield file and said later: "It had murder written all over it." Then, when questioned, Hill blurted out: "It's no good denying it. He's dead. He's in the river. We cut him up." Hill then made a confession about how Maxfield was killed because he had told police too much about the break-ins. Kilpatrick had arranged to meet Maxfield in a garage on the night of *May 13*, 1953, hit him on the back of the head four or five times with an iron bar and threw him into the back of a Pontiac car. Maxfield was still alive when Kilpatrick pulled him out of the car, so Hill finished him off with another blow to the head, this time with a .45 pistol.

Hill's statement then said that the two drove to the Barwon River, where Maxfield said that if they cut off the dead man's head and hands no one would be able to identify him. The Hill statement said: "He (Kilpatrick) got out a hacksaw and cut off his hands and then his head." Kilpatrick then ordered Hill to put the head and hands in the kerosene tin, with the body then being thrown into the river from a bridge. Police divers found the body of the unfortunate Maxfield and Kilpatrick and Hill were charged with murder.

The jury at their murder trial deliberated for almost three hours before returning verdicts of guilty. Justice Martin sentenced both men to death and told them: "You have been found guilty of a horrible and cruel murder, of a crime planned in cold blood and completed in circumstances of the utmost barbarity." Asked by the judge whether they had anything to say, Hill replied in the negative, while Kilpatrick, who claimed he had been framed, said: "I am not guilty, sir." The death sentences were never carried out. Hill had his sentence commuted to one of 20 years' jail, while Kilpatrick's was commuted to one of life imprisonment.

THE 'VICIOUS CRIMINAL' (2003)

Mild-mannered pharmacist Emad Youssef, 38, was shot dead outside his shop in the Sydney suburb of Canley Vale on *August 1*, 2003, and robbed of his day's takings. Police later arrested a 33-year-old man and his 14-year-old nephew. The man, who could not be named at the trial for the murder of Youssef for reasons relating to the identity of his nephew, was referred to as "Dudley Hill". The killing of Youssef, shot through the chest, was part of a three-month crime spree by "Hill" and already was serving a 40-year sentence for a gang-rape when found guilty of murder. The spree included another gang-rape and numerous armed robberies.

Youssef's widow, in a victim impact statement submitted to the Supreme Court of New South Wales, said: "I am constantly depressed and have been taking medication. My life has been destroyed by Emad's pointless death." "Hill", who had been in trouble with the law from the time he was ten years of age, told the court that when he was released from jail in 2002 he had tried to "go straight", but went back to a drugs habit when his girlfriend accused him of an assault and had been using the drugs ice and heroin during his crime spree. He also claimed he did now know whether he or Youusef had pulled the gun's trigger as "once he (Youssef) saw the gun he grabbed it". He added: "We were just struggling when the gun went off."

Sentencing "Hill" to life imprisonment, Justice James Wood said the killer "presents a very serious ongoing danger to the community" before adding: "His psychological profile shows very little hope of him being rehabilitated." The judge said that although the murder on its own would have have deserved a life sentence, the overall "criminality" of Hill's crime spree, including gang rape and armed robberies, meant the community needed to be protected.

AUGUST 2

SENTENCED (1871): Ned Kelly sentenced to three years' jail on *August* 2, 1871, for receiving a stolen horse when the actual thief, Isaiah "Wild" Wright, got only three months.

**

HANGED (1926): Convicted murderer Roystan Rennie hanged at Fremantle Gaol on *August 2*, 1926.

AUGUST 3

THE CAMPUS KILLING (1999)

On the morning of *August 3*, 1999, Jonathon Brett Horrocks left Chisolm College on the campus of Melbourne's La Trobe University with mayhem and murder in mind. Horrocks armed himself with a .38 calibre revolver and 45 rounds of ammunition and headed for the Eagle Bar, on the lower level of the university's Union Building.

On his desk at Chisolm College, Horrocks left a note which read: "I'm not crazy. I tried every legal way possible to find justice for being wronged. This is a warning to employers, politicians and corrupt men of authority. The little guy is getting tired of being used and shat upon with no avenues for fair play." There was also a quotation from Shakespeare: "Cry havoc and let slip the dogs of war."

Horrocks, 38, was intent on killing three people he believed had cost him a reduction in his work hours as a part-time barman at the Eagle bar. They were Leonardo Capraro, Sally Mitchell and Kevin Coates, and Horrocks chose his hour carefully as the bar did not open until noon. He therefore knew he could confront the three intended victims with relative ease. However, he knew that if he got involved in a mass shooting, he most likely would have to sacrifice his own life. With this mind-set, Horrocks entered the bar where Ms Mitchell was making herself a cup of hot chocolate. He said "hi Sally" and, when she turned, he fired the handgun at her, hitting her a glancing blow to the chest.

The gunman then walked to Capraro's office and fired five shots at the bar manager, hitting him four times and killing him. Horrocks then started reloading the gun but, in the meantime, Ms Mitchell had scampered for help and people were starting to lock themselves in their offices. A man named Michael Torney, who had an office on the second floor, was trying to lock a door to protect other personnel when confronted by Horrocks. A shot was fired unintentionally, but no one was hit and Torney struggled with Horrocks to get the gun. Then, when other staff went to Torney's help, the gunman was overpowered and held until police arrived.

Horrocks pleaded guilty to the murder of Capraro, the attempted murder of Ms Mitchell and of endangering the life of Torney, and Justice Vincent told him before passing sentence: "It cannot be forgotten that you staged what you declared and intended to be an act of war against specific individuals and, symbolically, against the wider community. This court, representing a community which has experienced other such incidents over recent years, must through the sentences it imposes upon those who act in this fashion express societal denunciation and make it perfectly clear that conduct of this kind will not be tolerated. Those who act in the fashion that you have done must anticipate that, as a matter of just retribution, if committed, very substantial penalties will be imposed."

Meanwhile, a note by Horrocks handed to the judge by his counsel read: "Your Honour, I stand here as your suppliant. I know I have done a terrible, terrible thing and I caused great sorrow and pain to the family the victim. Please believe me that I am very remorseful for any crime and find it difficult to come to terms with. Every day I think of what I have done and still cannot believe what drove me to it. My plea to you, Your Honour, is for leniency despite the degree of culpability of my crime and it is my heartfelt wish to one day be allowed to go back to my small home town and look after my ageing mother and at the same time help the community in any way I can. My life is in your hands." Justice Vincent sentenced Horrocks to life imprisonment, with a fixed non-parole period of 23 years.

AUGUST 4

SHOT DEAD (1992): Underworld identity Alfonso Muratore shot dead in the Melbourne bayside suburb on *August 4*, 1992.

AUGUST 5

CHRISTOPHER SKASE (2001)

Christopher Charles Skase was part of Australian business' greed of the 1980s. His excesses led him to being one of the most disliked identities in Australia and few but his family mourned his death in Spain in 2001. Skase was born into a solid middle-class Melbourne family and was educated at private schools before embarking on a career in financial journalism. Then, at just 27 years of age, he bought the small Tasmanian company of Qintex and built it into one of Australia's largest conglomerates. At one stage, the Skase empire controlled holiday resorts, the Seven television network and, most bizarre of all, the Brisbane Bears AFL club.

Skase enjoyed a lavish lifestyle and guests at Bears' game at Cararra, on the Gold Coast, were treated to the best wine and food. He used private jets to fly around Australia and his parties were renowned for their extravagance. However, by 1989 it was largely a mirage as the Qintex group was in financial difficulties. Skase received a $13.5 million payment without board approval and the matter came to the attention of the Australian Securities Commission. Qintex soon collapsed with Skase $700 million in debt. The tall, flamboyant businessman was arrested and briefly held in custody but, soon after release, fled to the Spanish island of Majorca.

Australian officials tried desperately to have him extradited from Spain, but Skase claimed he was suffering from a serious lung condition and therefore could not travel. The Australian government eventually cancelled his passport and Skase was ordered to leave Spain. However, the Dominican Republic made him a citizen and he therefore was allowed to stay at the luxury home he inhabited in Majorca. The Australian government eventually realised the pursuit of the nation's most wanted fugitive was a futile exercise, but he died on the Spanish island — ironically, from lung disease — on *August 5*, 2001, at 52 years of age.

AUGUST 6

SENTENCED (2003): Bali bomber Amrozi on *August 6*, 2003, sentenced to death.

AUGUST 7

SENTENCED (1821): Bushranger John Wilkinson sentenced to penal servitude for life after being captured on *August 7*, 1821.

AUGUST 8

MERCY FOR ONE (1902)

Soon after August Tisler arrived in the colony of Victoria early in 1900, he settled down to a life of routine and hard work. He was engaged to be married, but then met married woman Selina Sangal and started an affair with the wife of Keysborough market gardener Edward Christopher Sangal. The affair continued for 12 months before Tisler finally confronted the husband. According to Tisler's trial evidence,

Mrs Sangal pestered him to kill her husband. Then, on the night of *August 8*, 1902, she placed a stick in his hand and again suggested Tisler commit murder. Tisler said he hit Sangal with the stick, but the husband hit back and a fight ensued. It was then that Tisler pulled a knife on his adversary and stabbed him to death.

However, Mrs Sangal told an entirely different story, of how she loved her husband and had nothing to do with his murder. She claimed she went to bed with her husband that fateful night and was awakened by Tisler entering the bedroom and rushed to another room. The jury took just two hours to find both accused guilty of murder, although it strongly recommended mercy for Mrs Sangal. Tisler who was executed at Melbourne Gaol on *October 20*, 1902, said: "I only want to say that for anything I have done in this world I am prepared to suffer." Although Mrs Sangal also was sentenced death, this was to committed to imprisonment.

MR BALDY (2005)

The nickname Mr Baldy was given to Brian Keith Jones, who abducted and sexually assaulted six male children between 1979-80. He was given his nickname because he shaved the heads of his victims and dressed them in female's clothing. He re-offended soon after his release from prison in 1994 and was sentenced to a further jail term. Jones was released again in 2005 under strict parole conditions but, after a Melbourne radio station disclosed that he was living in Frankston, his home was attacked. Then, on *August 8*, 2005, the Victorian government applied to the County Court for a 15-year supervision order once his parole term expired. Jones lived in a cottage within a prison at Ararat, but breached his curfew in mid-2006.

AUGUST 9

THE 'DINKY' KILLING (1946)

Little Alan Cooper, just five years of age, liked riding his "dinky" bike in a lane behind his house in the Sydney suburb of Crow's Nest. Alan was riding his "dinky" on *August 9*, 1946, when approached by a youth who later took the little boy to a nearby house. The youth, 18-year-old Alexander William Tipping, took Alan into his bedroom and attacked him, apparently without motive. According to evidence at Tipping's trial, the 18-year-old tried to choke the little boy, later bashing him with a flower pot and then kicking and punching him. Little Alan did not die instantly and was rushed to the Misericordiae Hospital after Tipping himself rang police. Alan was found suffering from severe head wounds under Tipping's house.

Tipping at first told police that he heard moaning and groaning from under the house and, when he investigated, discovered the badly injured boy. However, he then stated: "I'll tell you all about it – I done it. I bashed the kid. When I was lying on my bed I was thinking I would like to do something big and get away with it. I brought the little boy in from his "dinky", sat him on the bed and tried to choke him. But he was too tough. I took him under the house, bashed him with a flower pot and went upstairs. I heard him still moaning, so I went down again and punished him. Then I rang the police."

A jury could not agree on a verdict at Tipping's trial, but the jury at a second trial handed down a verdict of "insanity" and Tipping was detained at "the governor's pleasure". Evidence was given at the inquest into little Alan's death that Tipping had suffered from brain trouble from the age of three and four doctors told the jury at the second trial that the 18-year-old had contracted encephalitis at the age of three. Child Welfare Clinic psychiatrist Dr Irene Sabire told the court a person in Tipping's condition would not be able to distinguish between right and wrong.

LATE JUSTICE (1986)

Samatha Knight was as pretty a nine-year-old as anyone would wish to see, with cute, innocent eyes and long hair. However, she was last seen alive on *August 9*, 1986, after she had bought a toothbrush while waiting for her mother after school. Samantha and her mother Tess had moved to Bondi in 1986 and they had a permanent arrangement in which Samantha would change at home after school and then play with friends until her mother arrived home from work at about 6pm. However, Samantha was last sighted at 5.30pm on the day she went missing and had been seen in the company of a man.

A massive search was launched for the missing girl, but without result. A number of well-meaning people reported possible sightings, but the case went cold for a number of years – until two seven-year-old girls in February, 1996, told their parents about a man abusing them and taking photographs. Police were called in and interviewed the man, Michael Anthony Guider, who then was 45 years of age. Police searched his home and found child pornography and underwear. He was charged with numerous offences regarding the sexual assault of little girls and was sentenced to 16 years' jail.

Police, however, believed they had discovered only the tip of the iceberg and went to other, rented premises and discovered a scrapbook on the Samantha Knight disappearance, along with photographs taken of her naked. There were also photographs of two of Samantha's friends and when police interviewed these now adult women, they knew they were hot on the trail of a pervert who had caused the death of a little girl as they had learned that Guider's modus operandi was to give girls drinks of Coca Cola laced with drugs. They therefore knew little if anything of the assaults and had no idea of him taking photographs.

Guider was in jail for his sexual offences in 2001 when he told another prisoner he had drugged Samantha and that the little girl had died accidentally. The prisoner told police and although Guider denied he had said anything, police knew they were close to solving a long-standing mystery. They therefore called on the assistance of Guider's brother Tim, who was in prison for planning a robbery. The police told Tim Guider that if he could get his brother to put his hand up for Samantha's death, he would get a pardon himself. Michael Guider refused, but eventually confessed to accidentally killing Samantha, who collapsed after consuming the drugged drink. He claimed he buried her body in bush near Cooper Park, but later dug it up and threw it into a dumpster at Kirribilli. Her body was never recovered and Guider told police:

"I never physically harmed the girl. I intended to take her home; it's a very sad thing. It caught me by surprise that the drug had an effect like that. Naturally, I panicked as I knew I was in trouble. I tried to find some way out of the problem, disposing of the evidence I guess. I've blanked all this out of my mind. I can't be much more specific."

A psychologist who spoke with Guider at the Metropolitan Remand Prison at Long Bay said: "He didn't show any remorse. He blamed the mothers all the time for not caring about their children. They were out having a good time and did not care who was with their kids." Guider was sentenced to 17 years' jail for the manslaughter of little Samantha Knight and is not eligible for parole until 2014.

THE HODDLE STREET MASSACRE (1987)

There was nothing to suggest the evening of *August 9*, 1987, would be any different to any other cold Melbourne winter's night. Traffic ebbed and flowed along the busy Hoddle Street near the Clifton Hill railway station, but that all came to a stop when 19-year-old gunman Julian Knight started firing at innocent motorists and passers-by. He killed seven people and wounded another 19 in a night of infamy.

The shooting started soon after 9pm and, within half an hour, there was carnage along one of Melbourne's busiest roads. Knight, who had shown anti-social tendencies from a young age and had been sent down from the Duntroon Military Academy, claimed to have had a nervous breakdown in the lead-up to the massacre. Regardless, he was charged with seven counts of murder, 39 counts of attempted murder and other alleged offences.

Knight pleaded guilty to all charges and the public learned that on the night of the massacre he packed three guns – a .22 semi-automatic rifle, a .38 semi-automatic rifle and a 12-gauge pump-action shotgun – for his murderous mission. He knelt near an advertising billboard and shot at passing motorists and pedestrians. He was sentenced to seven life terms of imprisonment, with a non-parole period of 27 years.

AUGUST 10

MONSTER OF THE WEST (1963)

Eric Edgar Cooke was one of Australia's most infamous killers and, at one stage, sent Western Australia into a state of frenzy during a one-man crime spree in which he not only committed something like 250 burglaries, but was a multiple killer. Cook, born in 1931, first came to the attention of the law as an 18-year-old and, from there, he went further and further downhill, stealing cars and committing burlaries. Then, on the night of *January 29*, 1959, he broke into an apartment in South Perth and stabbed 33-year-old Pnena Berkman to death, It was just the start of an horrific killing spree.

On *January 27*, 1963, while committing a burglary in the Cottesloe area, Cooke shot accountant Brian Weir in the head, leaving him paralysed and blind in one eye. Cooke fled in a stolen car and, at Nedlands, crept into a boarding house and shot dead student John Sturkey. Moving to a nearby house, Cooke rang the front doorbell and, when 54-year-old George Walmsley answered the door, shot him in the head.

Then, on *February 16*, Cooke was committing burglary in a West Perth apartment when 24-year-old Constance Madrill woke, only to find herself bashed unconscious. Cooke strangled her and then had sex with the corpse before he dumped the body in a nearby back garden. However, the spree was far from finished and, on *August 10*, 1963, shot

18-year-old babysitter Shirley McLeod in the head. Police were desperate for a lead in this massive crime spree and their prayers were answered when a couple came across a rifle hidden in bushland near the Swan River. Police set a trap and captured Cooke, who went to retrieve the rifle.

Cooke confessed to numerous killings and, significantly, admitted to being involved in a number of hit-run motor incidents. In one, 17-year-old Rosemary Anderson had been killed on *February 10*, 1963, and her boyfriend John Button was found guilty of manslaughter, After massive legal action, Button eventually had his conviction quashed. Cooke also confessed to the stabbing death of Jillian Brewer on *December 19*, 1959. Deaf-mute Darryl Beamish had been convicted of the murder but, in 2005, the High Court of Australia accepted that Cooke and not Beamish had killed the Perth socialite. Cooke was hanged at Fremantle Gaol on *October 26*. Just before he walked towards the noose, he took hold of a Bible and said: "I swear by Almighty God that I killed Anderson and Brewer."

AUGUST 11

DEBAUCHED BEHAVIOUR (2006)

When the NSW Supreme Court's Justice Michael Grove on *August 11*, 2006, sentenced William Thomas Clare to 25 years' jail for the manslaughter of a three-year-old boy, he said words could not express the "debauched behaviour" of the convited paedophile. Justice Grove, who also sentenced Clare to 14 years' jail for aggravated sexual assault on the boy, said:

"On an objective level, your depravity, manifest in the commission of that offence must attract severe attention."

Clare, who once had been jailed for having sexual intercourse with an intellectually impaired person and also of the indecent assault of a child under 10 years of age, met the boys' mother as she was passing the Croydon rail station in July, 2003. He said he could help mind her son and daughter, and she accepted the offer. Clare, who was paid $30 a day to mind the children, would look after the children until their mother finished work. She then would visit them before they stayed the night in Clare's one-bedroom flat.

On *September 13*, 2003, the mother brought with her a box of party pies for the children to eat and the boy, whom the judge named "J", appeared to eat at least one of these. Then, just after midnight, Clare telephone the 000 emergency number to report that the boy, aged three years and 10 months, had vomited and appeared to be choking. Clare also reported that the boy had not responded to "a little bit of an electric shock" in an attempt to revive him. Justice Grove said that although the application of electric wires did not cause the boy's death, it "plumbed the depths of stupidity". The boy, who had choked on his own vomit, was rushed to the Royal Prince Alfred Hospital, but already was dead.

Nurses at the hospital noticed that the boy's underwear was bloodstained and there was fresh blood in the area of his rectum. Justice Grove told Clare he was "satisfied beyond reasonable doubt that these signs and injuries were caused by the sexual assault which you committed on the child which constitutes the offence to which you pleaded guilty. I am satisfied that that assault consisted of a penetration of the child's anus by your penis".

Clare had pleaded not guilty of the boys' murder, but guilty to the assault and, although a jury found him not guilty of murder, it found him guilty of manslaughter. He will not be eligible for release until July, 2033, when he will be 62 years of age. However, his sentences from this case will not begin until 2015 as he already was serving a term for assaulting the boy's six-year-old sister. Outside the court, the children's father said: "I am just so relieved that society will be able to move on and not have somebody of this nature and character out on the streets upsetting anyone else and their family."

AUGUST 12

MURDER, BUT NO BODY (1997)

It is a common misconception that no one can be found guilty of murder if there is no body. There have been numerous instances in which killers have been convicted without a body being discovered, and this occurred in Melbourne in 1999 after a woman was found guilty of a murder almost two years earlier with no body being found.

Ann Denise Williamson had a relationship with a man named Robert Mock, was also involved with two other women, including one named Edith Eberts. Williamson's involvement with Mock was stormy and each time he left her to live with either Eberts or the other woman, she would stalk him. Williamson would go through his possessions, collect telephone numbers and addresses and even carry out surveillance while sitting in her car.

The possessive Williamson convinced Mock to return to her in June, 1997, but he left her again for Eberts. This set

Williamson on another determined campaign of surveillance and stalking. She made nuisance calls to Ebert's telephone number and tracked Mock down to a flat in the bayside suburb of Balaclava. Then, early in the morning of *August 12*, 1997, she looked through a window to the flat and saw Eberts and Mock having coffee. Mock turned off the light so Williamson could not see them, but she then made further nuisance telephone calls.

Williamson, the mother of three adult boys, eventually left but some time during the day returned and killed Eberts. At her trial, Justice Teague told her: "I am satisfied that you killed her by shooting her. Two spent cartridge cases were found in the flat. Edith Eberts' blood was found on your sports shoe. Edith Eberts' blood was found on a rug at the foot of the bed."

Justice Teague said it was not possible to say how Williamson disposed of the body. But said she might have removed the body in a car. He added: "More likely, you placed it where it would be removed by a garbage man, who would have been unaware of his dumping truck's grisly load." The judge sentenced Williamson, aged 51 years at the time of her trial, to 18 years' imprisonment, with a non-parole period of 13 years.

AUGUST 13

MOONDYNE JOE (1873)

One of Australia's most famous bushrangers was a man known as Moondyne Joe. Whereas many bushrangers were killers, Moondyne Joe was not a violent man, even if he was an incorrigible thief. He was born Joseph Johns in Cornwall,

England, some time around 1828 and, after stealing food, was sentenced to 10 years' penal servitude. It is not known why Johns was transported, but he arrived at Fremantle, Western Australia, early in 1853. His good behaviour earned him a ticket of leave, but he later stole a horse and branded it with his own mark. Johns escaped custody and cut the brand from the horse's hide and therefore had his charge reduced from horse stealing to jail-breaking.

Johns again was released, but could not go straight. He escaped several times from custody and, for some reason, adopted the nickname of Moondyne Joe as he embarked on a series of thefts and bushranging activities. His ability to escape saw him placed in a closely guarded cell at Fremantle jail. Remarkably, however, he escaped yet again and was on the run for two years before being recaptured. He was returned to prison and, after another attempted jail break, was placed in irons. He won his ticket of leave again in 1871, but continued his thieving ways. Finally, however, he developed a form of senile dementia and, on *August 13*, 1873, died at the Fremantle Lunatic Asylum.

THE LUCKY DIGGERS (1917)

Although hundreds of British and Commonwealth servicemen were executed for desertion, cowardice or other military offences during World War I, only one Australian paid the ultimate penalty. Yet Private John King was an Australian serving in a New Zealand uniform, with the Canterbury Infantry Regiment. King, who was found guilty, not of desertion, but of being absent without leave, was executed on *August 19*, 1917. King's sentence of death was confirmed by General Sir Douglas Haig, who had made strong representations that Australian soldiers should also be subject to the extreme penalty. However, the Australian government decreed that none of its servicemen would be executed, regardless of the circumstances, mainly because all its soldiers were volunteers.

Yet two Diggers could have considered themselves fortunate to have escaped the hangman's noose in wartime England. Privates Ernie Sharp and Tom Maguire were absent without leave on the evening of *August 21*, 1917, when they went drinking at the Rising Sun Hotel off the Waterloo Road in south-east London. Ironically, this watering hole now is just a few hundred metres from the Imperial War Museum. Sharp and Maguire started drinking with a petty English crook named Joe Jones and, late in the night, the three of them followed two cashed-up Canadian soldiers, Oliver Imley and John McKinley, into the dark, narrow Valentine Place.

The Canadians, to use an Australian expression, were 'rolled'. McKinley recovered from the injuries he received in the bashing and robbery, but Imley died four days later. Jones, Sharp and Maguire faced possible murder charges. Sharp, who recognised the gravity of his situation, turned King's evidence and, for stepping forward had a murder charge against him dropped and, instead, was handed a seven-year penal sentence. Sharp also insisted that it was English civilian Jones, who had been discharged from the army after twice being wounded on the Western Front, who was responsible for bashing the two Canadians and therefore killing Imley.

Both Sharp and Maguire claimed that Imley had laid into the two Canadians with a police truncheon. Jones denied he had a truncheon and even claimed that the Australians had done all the bashing, but other witnesses said they had seen him with a weapon earlier in the night. Jones' fate was sealed and he was sentenced to death. Maguire, for his part in the robbery that led to Imley's death, was sentenced to eight years' jail. Jones' execution was set for dawn on *February 20*, 1918, and as executioner John Ellis slipped the noose over his head, he mumbled: 'God forgive them.' It is presumed that Jones was referring either to the jury that had found him guilty or to the execution party, including hangman Ellis. Or could he have been referring to the two Australian Diggers, Sharp and Maguire, his partners in crime, if not in murder, that night near Waterloo Road?

AUGUST 14

DOCTOR DEATH (1922)

To all intents and purposes, Dr George Cranstoun was a pillar of society in the Melbourne bayside suburb of Hampton. He and his family lived in an extremely comfortable Queen Anne villa in Station Street, just 50 yards from the Hampton railway station, and had a thriving medical practice. His wife regularly attended the local Congregational Church and their five children went to Sunday school.

Dr Cranstoun, 45, was a pharmacist until he graduated in medicine at the University of Melbourne in 1914; he practised in Gippsland for several years before establishing the practice in Hampton. He was well liked and another Hampton medical practitioner, Dr Garnet Leary, said he "never met a more charming personality". He added: "Everyone who met him liked him."

However, Dr Leary shared one of Dr Cranstoun's darker secrets as just a month after the former pharmacist opened his practice in Hampton, Dr Leary had to treat him for an over-injection of morphia. Dr Cranstoun was unconscious for 16 hours, but then made a full recovery – only to continue his drug addiction. Dr Leary could not possibly have known what Dr Cranstoun's drug addiction would lead to and, on the morning of *August 14*, 1922, Melbourne newspapers trumpeted what they described as the worst domestic tragedy in the history of Victoria. Dr Cranstoun had killed three of his children and a servant and had tried to kill his wife and their other two children before suiciding. The victims were servant Gladys Baylis (22), John Cranstoun (15), Robert (10), Colin (eight). Mrs Cranstoun and daughters Margaret (13) and Belle (six) survived Dr Cranstoun's deadly attacks by hypodermic needle.

The discovery of this enormous domestic tragedy was made by one of the doctor's patients. After she had telephoned with no answer, she decided to make a personal call and arrived at the Cranstoun house, where she peeped through a letter-box and saw the pyjama-clad doctor lying in the hall. Police were called and they found a hypodermic needle on the floor near Dr Cranstoun, who was still alive. They found the other bodies, with Mrs Cranstoun and the two daughters very ill. Dr Cranstoun died in hospital before he could be questioned, but police investigations revealed he had injected his family and Miss Baylis with strychnine, which can be used as a stimulant, but is lethal in large doses.

Apart from his drug problem, Dr Cranstoun was heavily in debt and form guides and race programs were found in his surgery after his death. Police also learned that he had been to Caulfield races the Saturday before killing his three sons and the family servant.

THE BOMB GENIUS (1956)

Residents in and around Paterson Avenue, Kingsgrove, a Sydney suburb, were preparing for a quiet night on *August 14*, 1956, when the peace of the neighbourhood was shattered by a tremendous explosion. Residents ran from their houses as windows rattled and rooms rocked. Residents in the avenue itself could not believe their eyes when they saw a bomb-wrecked car in their quiet suburban street. The car was a dreadful sight. Its bonnet was 50 metres down the street, all four doors had been blown out and windscreen glass was spread for metres.

People crowded the scene and police and firemen had to link arms to keep the area clear before a detailed investigation could be launched into the bombing. The explosion occurred when Dr Edward Brotchie, 50, turned on the car's ignition. Dr Brotchie died in hospital shortly after the explosion and his passenger, his sister Mrs Elsie Foster, 45, died instantly. They were victims of an expertly planned car bombing. Police knew that whoever planted the bomb knew exactly what he was doing.

In fact, the technical officer of the Explosives Department, Mr S.W.E. Parsons, said soon after examining the wrecked car: "To make a bomb of this strength and type, and to be able to place and connect it, would require considerable knowledge of explosives." The bomb, indeed, was the work of an expert, Mrs Foster's husband Henry Foster, who shot himself through the head soon after the bombing. Police did not discover Foster's body, in Dr Brotchie's surgery 100 metres from the bombing, until the next morning. Incredibly, Foster left behind a swag of notes which painstakingly described the bomb's mechanism. He wanted experts to know exactly how the bomb worked so there would be no confusion after his own death.

Foster's note explained everything, right down to the last detail. It seemed he disliked his brother-in-law for failing to treat him to his satisfaction for a back complaint. But, strangely, it seemed consulting and design engineer Foster loved the wife he killed with the hand-made explosive device. The inventive genius killed and died with the efficiency of an analytical scientist.

AUGUST 15

HANGED (1870): Scotsman Andrew Vair hanged at Ararat on *August 15*, 1870, for the murder of Amos Cheale at St Arnaud, Victoria, in January, 1869.

AUGUST 16

THE POLICE KILLINGS (1998)

Victoria Police officers Sergeant Gary Silk and Senior Constable Rodney Miller were staking out the Silky Emporer restaurant near the corner of Cochranes and Warrigal Road, Moorabbin (south-east Melbourne) at around midnight on *August 16*, 1998, when they were shot dead. The killings horrified Melbourne as they appeared to have all the hallmarks of a dual execution. The two police officers were shot at close range and the Victorian government offered a $500,000 reward for any information leading to the arrest and conviction of the killer(s).

Poice had a number of clues, including pieces of glass from the getaway car left at the scene. They tracked these fragments to a late model Hyundai hatchback and, through painstaking investigation, tracked down the registration, to well-known criminal Bandali Debs. Although the police investigation lasted more than two years, Debs and accomplice Jason Roberts were charged on *September 24*, 2001, with murder. They were found guilty and sentenced to life imprisonment.

AUGUST 17

THE SHOPPING MALL MASSACRE (1991)

To all intents and purposes, 33-year-old taxi driver Wade Frankum was a solid citizen who got on well with most people, even if he was something of a loner. He had had a troubled life as his father had died and his mother had committed suicide by gassing herself. He spent most of time reading or watching television at home and no one suspected he one day would be involved in one of the most horrific killing sprees in Australian criminal history.

Frankum on *August 17*, 1991, walked out of his home armed with a self-loading assault rifle and a machete packed in a bag and went to the North Strathfield rail station and bought a ticket to nearby Strathfield. From there, he walked to the busy Strathfield Plaza shopping centre and sat down in the Coffee Pot café and ordered one coffee after another. In fact, he was there for more than 90 minutes when, at around 3,30pm, he asked for the bill.

Suddenly, Frankum produced the machete and started stabbing 15-year-old Bo Armstrong, sitting in the next booth, in the back. The girl started screaming and, with other customers, horrified, Frankum continued his frenzied attack, finally leaving the knife in the innocent teenager's back. However, he was just starting his rampage of death and, after mortally wounding Armstrong, produced the semi-automatic rifle and started firing.

The mad gunman at first turned his attention to a family group sitting near him and other customers dived for cover as shots were fired. Frankum appeared to shoot only at those who were trying to flee the scene but, as he himself withdrew, he was confronted by a woman in a car. Catherine Noyce became the gunman's seventh, and final victim, with another six people wounded. Shot, she later died in hospital. Meanwhile, police were desperate to apprehend Frankum, who had made his way to the car park. They found him dead, the gunman taking his own life.

AUGUST 18

KILLING FOR PLEASURE (2001)

When teenager Melissa Joy Maahs elected to move in with her boyfriend Lloyd Maurice Crosbie, she had no idea that she and her mother soon would be the victims of a truly sadistic and brutal killer. The teenage couple originally lived with 18-year-old Crosbie's father in the Victorian town of Morwell, but later moved to another house in Morwell with 19-year-old Melissa's mother Kaye Lucy Maahs, 54, in April, 2001.

Just a few months later, at around 3am on *August 18*, Crosbie was watching a movie in bed while his girlfriend slept in the double bed next to him. For some reason, Crosbie wore a scabbard containing a skinning knife with a curved blade. Some time during the movie, Crosbie removed the knife from the scabbard and, using his right hand, stabbed Melissa three times in the head. The wounds were not fatal and Melissa woke and screamed. This prompted Crosbie to hold her by the back of the head while he slashed at her throat. Melissa somehow managed to get into a sitting position, but Crosbie kept attacking her, cutting his own hand in the process.

Mrs Maahs, hearing her daughter's screams, left her own bedroom and was confronted by the knife-wielding Crosbie, who stabbed her to the throat and upper back. Mrs Maahs fell to the floor while he slashed and cut at her. She screamed: "Melissa, call an ambulance. I think I am dying."

Crosbie then turned back to his girlfriend and stabbed her again and again in the throat and body. He then paused before he returned to Mrs Maahs, pushing the knife into her throat and then pulling it sideways. Believing Mrs Maahs was still alive, he then struck her several times across the head with a ceramic ornament before going getting an iron from the laundry and smashing her again over the head.

Crosbie made the scene look like a burglary went wrong but, before he left, he committed more ghastly acts. He rubbed his girlfriend's anus and vagina and his penis with lubricant and then had sex while looking at pornographic magazines placed on Melissa's back. He ejaculated twice and then removed his clothing to take a shower. Crosbie then caught a cab to the Morwell station and caught a train to Melbourne before moving on to his father's house at Wangaratta, in northern Victoria.

While on the run, he made calls to fantasy sex lines with Melissa's mobile telephone before throwing it into a creek.

Police apprehended Crosbie on *August 20* and, at the Wangaratta police station, he made admissions about killing Melissa Maahs and her mother.

He pleaded guilty to two charges of murder and the prosecution argued that he had killed for the "sheer pleasure of killing". Justice Kellam, in the Supreme Court of Victoria, told him: " There is not a scintilla of evidence to suggest that either of your victims had given you any cause or provocation or reason for anger which could in any way explain your murderous behaviour towards them. The depravity with which you treated the body of your victim Melissa after her death is not only an aggravating factor but it demonstrates a total lack of remorse by you at that time."

He added: "The two murders to which you plead guilty before me were particularly callous and brutal. Your victims must have suffered painful and terrifying deaths. The only explanation for your behaviour is that the killings took place in a context of sadism involving sexual excitement linked to the murderous acts to which you subjected your victims. There is the aggravating circumstance of your defilement of the body of Melissa. Furthermore, it must be remembered that not one but two decent members of our community have lost their lives at your hands." Justice Kellam sentenced Crosbie to life imprisonment, with a minimum 30 years.

THE UMBRELLA KILLING (2003)

Bricklayer Novica Jakimov left his rented house in the western Melbourne suburb of Westmeadows on the night of *August 18*, 2003, and met up with sex worker Kelly Hodge, either in St Kilda or at the Crown casino. The slightly-built Hodge went back to Jakimov's house and, some time early next morning, was viciously attacked. She was hit many times over the head with the shaft of a rolled-up umbrella and suffered a fractured skull. Hodge also suffered a serious wound to the vagina and the bleeding from this wound, combined with the fractured skull caused her death.

Although Jakimov later declared that Hodge initially had attacked him, he tied her hands together with her bra, wrapped her body in a sheet and blanket and drove to Beveridge, where he dumped the body. A jury at Jakimov's trial was also told that he cleaned his home, burned or disposed of Hodge's clothing – but made one big mistake. He failed to dispose of Hodge's mobile telephone and police used it to track him down.

Although Jakimov had no previous convictions for violence, Justice Teague noted: "I have noted that some matters of which you spoke to the police suggest a capacity on occasions for anger and violence." However, the judge said he was prepared to accept "some degree of remorse" and sentenced Jakimov to 19 years' jail, with a fix non-parole period of 14 years.

AUGUST 19

'I JUST SNAPPED' (2003)

Marc Andrew Rookledge, 39, had had a sexual relationship with Rosehanie Marilyn Holmes for several years before he contacted her on *August 19*, 2003, and later visited her at her flat in the bayside Melbourne suburb of Hampton East. Rookledge and Holmes bought liquor together, while Holmes bought a carton of cigarettes. Some time during the night,

Rookledge suggested he swap the cigarettes for amphetamines. Then, when he returned from the nearby suburb of St Kilda, they both used the drugs intravenously and watched television before Holmes went to bed.

Rookledge went to lie beside her and in his own word, "snapped" while thinking about his life. He hit Holmes over the head with a heavy object and then stabbed her repeatedly, inflicting 17 wounds. In an attempt to cover his crime, Rookledge ransacked the flat to make it look as if there had been a burglary and stole credit cards. Holmes' body was not discovered for six days but police almost immediately wanted to talk to Rookledge and arranged to meet him.

At the Homicide Squad office, Rookledge said: "You don't have to look any further. I'm the one you're looking for … I just snapped." Rookledge pleaded guilty to Holmes' murder and Justice Smith told him: "The offence was extremely serious and specific and general deterrence must be reflected in the sentence to be imposed. I am satisfied, however, that this long standing abuse of drugs was a factor in the commission of the offence and to a limited extent reduces the level of moral culpability." He sentenced Rookledge to 17 years' imprisonment, with a non-parole period of 12 years.

AUGUST 20

THE RAPE OF A MAID (1837)

Nursery maid, Martha Emily Cadman, was brutally treated by a succession of masters but, after running away in 1837, was sentenced to a house of correction for three months. The 16-year-old was placed in the care of a police constable for her

20-mile journey to Sydney. She then was handed over to another constable, George Nutter, who placed her in a room with other men on the night of *August 20* at a public house in Sutton Forest . One of Nutter's companions, Patrick Brady, dragged her onto his bed and raped her, with Nutter in the same bed. When the girl eventually reached Sydney, she told her mother of her experience and, within quarter of an hour, she was given a medical examination, which revealed she was "labouring under a loathsome disease", even though she had had no previous sexual experience. Brady was charged with rape, while Nutter was charged with aiding and assisting in the rape. A jury found both men guilty and they were sentenced to death.

THE 'REVOLTING' ASSAULT (1985)

Michael John Alexander moved to Sydney from Narrabri to start a new life after battling drugs and alcohol. The 24-year-old moved into a home with 42-year-old Mrs Susan Kirk and her three-year-old daughter. Mrs Kirk, who was separated from her husband, was grateful she had someone to help her with the rent. However, she and Alexander had a row about the rent on *August 20*, 1985, and he was so enraged he went to a garage, grabbed a length of rope and returned to strangle Mrs Kirk.

Then, just as he was covering the body, he was spotted by three-year-old Stephanie Kirk. Alexander therefore struck her with a length of wood before stabbing her through the heart. The killer hid the murder weapons and went to work, where he confided in a female co-worker that he had committed murder. By coincidence, police visited the factory on a separate and far less serious matter and were told of

Alexander's "confession". He passed it off as a joke, but police took him to Mrs Kirk's house, where he told them he did not have any keys.

Alexander was allowed to return to work, but he then went back home and placed the two bodies, wrapped in a curtain, under the house. The police eventually were handed keys by a real estate agent, but found nothing at the house. They then visited Alexander again at work and told him he was being charged with having caused a public mischief. This time he confessed, took the police back to the house and pointed to the bodies.

Alexander pleaded not guilty at his trial before Justice Slattery and a jury and although he did not contest that he had been responsible for the deaths of Mrs Kirk and her daughter Stephanie, he sought to raise the partial defence of diminished responsibility. This was rejected by the jury and he was found guilty of the murders of mother and daughter.

Justice Slattery pointed out: "The post mortem reports and photographs in evidence disclose the ferocity of his acts. Not content with this sneaky, cool and calmly executed act, he stabbed her (Mrs Kirk) with considerable force in the chest, puncturing her lung and aorta. His attack upon her was vicious and probably executed with all the feelings and frustration and anger that he had been brewing within him for days, if not weeks.

"When three-year-old Stephanie innocently came upon him in the garage where he had taken her mother, he bashed her twice in a savage and brutal manner on the forehead and the back of the head. He also stabbed her in the heart. The treatment of the young child was uncaring and brutal. It was a revolting and horrifying assault upon a young, innocent child. Undoubtedly, the reason for her death was because she stood in the way. She was a person who could identify him. He regarded her a brat who had to be killed along with her mother."

Alexander was found guilty and sentenced to two life terms. Then, in 1995, he and another prisoner escaped from Grafton jail and were at libery for two days before being captured. In 1999, Alexander applied for redetermination of the two life sentences and, in the Supreme Court of New South Wales, Justice Kirby set a total minimum term of 28 years, with the double killer not being eligible for parole until August, 2006.

AUGUST 21

A POINTER TO DEATH (1931)

Roderick Davies, his wife Dorothy and five children in 1931 were living on a dole of two pounds and nine shillings (about $4.90) a week. Davies, 36, had been unemployed for months, but no one knew that this had depressed him to the point of suicide. On *August 21*, 1931, neighbour Samuel Knifton found a note on the back door of the three-bedroom Davies home in the Perth suburb of Carlisle.

The note read: "Mr Knifton, please open the door." Knifton believed the note was part of an elaborate joke, but once he stepped into the house he realised that the note had been a pointer to death. Mrs Davies, 35, was dead in a bed in the kitchen, a bullet through her head. Next to her, sitting in chair, was the body of her husband, who also had a bullet wound to the head and had a revolver in his right hand. Knifton did not want to see any more and rushed to the police, who discovered the bodies of the five Davies children – Rita (14), Robert (12), Dorothy (10), John (six) and Alfred (five months) – in two of the house's three bedrooms. The bodies of John, Rita and baby Alfred were in one room, with the bodies of Dorothy and Robert on stretchers in another room. All had bullet wounds to the head and there were no signs of struggle.

Detectives concluded that Mr and Mrs Davies had made a suicide pact, with Davies shooting the children and then his wife before turning the gun on himself. Detectives reasoned that Mr and Mrs Davies had dragged a bed from the back porch into the kitchen and that the husband then sat by his wife's side before killing her and then himself. Police also believed the children had been drugged before being killed. Police found 19 discharged cartridges in the house but, strangely, not one neighbour had heard a single shot. The nearest house might have been more than 15 metres away, but the shots which wiped out an entire family exploded without notice or comment. The house had been well stocked with food, but the Great Depression had taken its toll on Mr Davies' mental health and pride. Sadly, it was 14-year-old Rita's birthday the day she and her family died.

AUGUST 22

THE PARRAMATTA ROAD RAPE (1833)

A number of men — William Black, Robert Watson, George Matthews, Joseph Hawley, John Brickfield and Richard Coghlan — were found guilty of being involved in the rape of Isabella Yeomans on the Parramatta Road on *July 7*, 1833.

But, whereas Black, Matthews and Hawley were charged with "ravishing" Isabella Yeomans, the other three were charged with aiding, abetting and assisting in committing a rape. The *Sydney Herald* edition of *August 22*, 1833, refused to give details of the crime and merely stated that "the details must not sully our pages". The six men were all sentenced to death.

AUGUST 23

THE GRANNY KILLER (1998)

Adrian Douglas Porter and some mates watched a video of the film *Freeway* some time in August, 1998, and the action in this movie somehow planted the seed for a terrible crime little more than a week later, in the early hours of *August 23*, 1998. The movie, featuring Keifer Sutherland, told the story of a serial killer who had intercourse with the dead bodies of his victims. Based loosely on the old Red Riding Hood fairy tale, Sutherland's character also kills and then has sexual intercourse with his girlfriend's grandmother.

Porter, on Saturday, *August 22*, drank heavily at a number of venues in Frankston (bayside Melbourne) and eventually was ejected from a nightclub. He had no money on him by this stage, so started walking to his grandmother's home in Frankston as it would have meant a two-hour walk to his family home at Pearcedale. The 22-year-old Porter, on reaching his grandmother's house in Deane Street, found a rear window slightly ajar and climbed through.

Porter's mother the next day rang her mother to make arrangements to go to church, but there was no answer. She then asked her brother to call their mother but, despite numerous calls, there still was no answer. Finally, Porter's uncle went to the Deane Street home and still was unable to get a response. He therefore climbed through the back window and discovered his mother dead on her bed. She had been strangled.

Police immediately were called and noted that the 69-year-old pensioner was lying naked on her back with her legs spread. Her throat and the area around her eyes were bruised and two scarves were wound around her neck and tied to the bed-head. A post-mortem revealed that the woman had suffered fractures to the larynx and hyoid bone, consistent with strangling. There were no bruises or injuries to the genitalia, but swabs indicated sexual intercourse had taken place, telling police the grandmother had been sexually assaulted after death.

Police interviewed Porter the following day and he told them that, after climbing through the window so that he could have a bed for the night, he bumped into his grandmother in the dark. He said she started screaming and that he manually strangled her to keep her quiet. However, she twice recovered and he finally tied scarves together and strangled her with the ligature.

Porter pleaded guilty to the murder of his grandmother and Justice Cummins, in the Supreme Court of Victoria, told him it was a "terrible situation" for the Porter family. Justice Cummins, who suggested that "a seed had been planted" after Porter had watched the *Freeway* video, said: "The fact that your grandmother was in the security of her own house is an aggravating factor in this case. What you did to her after her death was an act of depravity." He sentenced Porter to 19 years' jail, with a 15-year non-parole period.

AUGUST 24

AXED TO DEATH (1939)

When Dulcie Summerlad left her farmhouse at Tenterfield, New South Wales, to visit her mother in January, 1939, she had no idea she would return a few days later to a scene of absolute horror. Miss Summerlad returned to her orchard property on the morning of *February 4* and was surprised when no one approached her with the usual family greetings. It was deathly quiet. Miss Summerlad lived with her brother Eric, 26, and sister Marjorie, 33, with Eric running the property and Marjorie acting as her brother's housekeeper.

Dulcie Summerlad opened the front door of the farmhouse and stepped inside. She immediately saw the blood-stained body of her sister and, in horror and fear, started calling for her brother. There was no answer. Fearing the worst, Dulcie immediately headed for the verandah, which her brother used as a bedroom. There, Eric, was on a bead, his head soaked in blood. The young farmer was not dead, but critically wounded. Dulcie called the police and an ambulance rushed her brother to hospital, where he was admitted in a life-threatening condition.

The murder weapon obviously was an axe found leaning against the front of the house. It also was obvious that the brother and sister had been savagely hit with considerable force, Marjorie dying immediately. It also was thought her brother would not survive the axe attack. Police, meanwhile, soon realised that farmhand John Trevor Kelly was missing, along with the Summerlad utility. Police launched an immediate search for Kelly, 24, and notified police stationed in a wide radius of the murder scene.

Kelly had driven from Tenterfield to Brisbane, where he rented a room in the suburb of Spring Hill. A wanted man, he was too scared to venture from his room, but was arrested just 14 hours after the axe attacks. Kelly originally told police that Eric Summerlad had sacked him on Friday, *February 3*, and this led to the axings. However, Kelly later changed his account of events and said he attacked Dulcie first after he had made sexual overtures to her, even though she was engaged to be married to a local farmer. Dulcie called for her brother and Kelly hit him with his fists before going outside and returning with an axe.

Summerlad made a remarkable recovery and told police he could not recall the attacks as he was sleeping at the time. Kelly had been drinking on the night of the murder and his plea at his trial was that of insanity. He told the jury: "I am sorry for what I have done." However, he was found guilty and sentenced to death. The case was appealed to the High Court of Australia, but the sentence stood. Kelly's last chance was for the State Cabinet to give him a reprieve, but the Cabinet, under the leadership of Premier Alexander Mair, stood firm. Kelly was hanged at Long Bay jail on *August 24*, 1939.

AUSTRALIA'S CHARLES MANSON (1973)

The British public was outraged late in January, 2004, when serial killer Archie McCafferty was fined just 50 pounds for striking a police officer and sentenced to a 12-month community order. It was nothing more than a slap on the wrist for the man known as 'Mad Dog' for his murderous spree and infamous behaviour as a prisoner on the other side of the world in Australia.

McCafferty was born in Scotland, but migrated to Australia with his family when he was just 10 years of age. The McCafferty family first settled in Melbourne, but then moved to Sydney, where young Archie soon found himself in trouble with the police. The tough young Scot's family believed Archie would settle down after his marriage to Janice Redington in 1972, especially when the couple announced they were going to be parents. Son Craig was born in February, 1973, only for the McCafferty joy to be short-lived. Little Craig lived just six weeks, dying on *March 17* in truly tragic circumstances when his mother rolled on top of him after falling asleep while breastfeeding him. An inquest exonerated the young mother, but McCafferty accused his wife of killing their son. The death of baby Craig appeared to tip McCafferty over the edge and although he admitted himself to a psychiatric institute, he checked out again a few days later. McCafferty threatened violence against his family, but no one could have known the extent to which he was prepared to go in his lust for blood.

His brief but dreadful reign of terror started on *August 24*, 1973, when he teamed up with girlfriend Carol Howes, 16-year-old psychiatric patient Julie Todd and teenagers Michael Meredith, Richard Whittington and Rick Webster to kill World War II veteran George Anson. The gang had been looking for someone to 'roll' for easy money, and the drink-affected Anson appeared to be the perfect victim. However, the assault went way beyond a robbery with violence.

McCafferty kicked Anson several times to the head and chest before repeatedly plunging a knife into the 50-year-old's chest and neck. Most of McCafferty's young gang were too shocked to make any comment, but Webster asked the heavily-tattooed Scot why he had gone berserk. McCafferty replied that he had reacted to Anson swearing at him.

Just three nights later, on *August 27*, McCafferty took his gang to the Leppington Cemetery to show them his little son's grave. The gang then retreated to a nearby pub, only for McCafferty to insist on returning to the grave site. Todd and Meredith went their own way, but McCafferty, Howes, Whittington and Webster went back to the cemetery. Then, at the cemetery, a car pulled over near Craig McCafferty's grave. Todd and Meredith had returned to the group with a victim, 42-year-old Ronald Cox, at gunpoint. They had been hitchhiking in the rain when the miner — on his way home from work — gave them a lift.

McCafferty ran over to where Todd and Meredith were holding Cox and ordered Meredith to kill the terrified father of seven. Both Meredith and McCafferty shot Cox to the back of the head. McCafferty, who later claimed he had heard voices in his head telling him to kill seven people, the following day ordered his gang members to find him another victim. Todd and Whittington went hitchhiking and were given a ride by young driving instructor Evangelos Kollias. However, Whittington then produced a rifle from under his coat and ordered Kollias to lie on the floor while Todd drove back to McCafferty's unit. McCafferty then drove away and ordered Whittington to kill Kollias. The youth did as he was told and shot the driving instructor through the head. Then when ordered to shoot again, Whittington fired into Kollias' head again. The body was dumped in a nearby street.

Meanwhile, McCafferty seemed determined to do what the voices had instructed — 'kill seven' — and high on his hit list was his wife, her mother and one of his gang members, 17-year-old Webster, who had questioned him over the brutal killing of Anson. However, a gang member alerted Webster to McCafferty's plans and he decided to act to save his own life. Webster, an apprentice compositor with the *Sydney Morning Herald*, called the police from his workplace.

Detectives arrived to interview him, but Webster had spotted McCafferty and his gang in a car outside and was too terrified to leave the building. Armed police therefore surrounded the car and arrested McCafferty and Whittington. Although McCafferty admitted to police that he had killed Anson, Cox and Kollias, he pleaded not guilty at a committal hearing, as did Howes, Meredith, Whittington and Webster. The gang was sent to trial, with newspapers referring to McCafferty as 'Australia's Charles Manson', the American hippie leader who organised a gang to commit multiple murders in the late 1960s.

Everything revolved around the question of whether McCafferty was insane or not and, near the end of the trial, he read a statement from the dock which, in part, stated: "I would like to say that at the time of these crimes I was completely insane. The reason why I done (sic) this is for the revenge of my son's death. Before this, I had stated to a doctor that I felt like killing people, but up until my son's death I had not killed anyone. 'My son's death was the biggest thing that ever happened to me because I loved him so much and he meant the world to me. And after his death I just seemed to go to the pack. I feel no wrong for what I have done because, at the time that I did it, I didn't think it was wrong. 'I think, if given the chance, I will kill again for the simple reason that I have to kill seven people and I have only killed three, which means I have four to go. And this is how I feel in my mind, and I just can't say that I am not going to kill anyone else, because in my mind I am."

The jury rejected the insanity plea and found McCafferty guilty as charged on all counts. He was sentenced to be imprisoned for life, with Meredith and Whittington sentenced to 18 years in prison and Todd for 10 years for the murders of Cox and Kallios. Webster was given four years for the manslaughter of Cox. Howes, who was pregnant with McCafferty's child when the verdicts were announced, was found not guilty.

McCafferty, who married and then divorced a woman named Mandy Queen while in jail, proved to be one of the most difficult prisoners in NSW penal history and was transferred from one jail to another until, to the horror of NSW police and public, he was given parole. He was deported to his native Scotland in 1997. However, McCafferty could not stay out of trouble and was involved in a number of incidents, including threatening police officers. He settled in Hampshire and remarried Mandy Queen, but then fled to New Zealand when he faced a charge of assaulting a police officer.

McCafferty was arrested immediately he returned to the United Kingdom but, to the amazement of the British public, escaped with that 'slap on the wrist' fine and community order. The court had been told that the man known as 'Australia's Charles Manson' was a changed man and had even taken up painting to 'calm him down'. Indeed, lawyer Simon Moger said his client's work was 'of a very high standard which could sell commercially'. McCafferty, who once had threatened to kill seven people, therefore was left to continue family life, despite once being told he would never be released from jail for the three murders he committed.

BASHED AND BURIED (2000)

Raymond John Prior had been married for 12 years before he and his wife separated over his reliance on drugs, particularly heroin. He went to live in the New South Wales town of Lismore, while his wife remained at the family home in Tenterfield. During this separation, the wife decided she wanted a relationship with someone who was not a drug-user and started seeing a Queensland truck driver, Colin Booth. Prior, who also was a truck driver, confronted Booth but resorted only to slashing his love rival's truck tyres. Then, when Prior visited Tenterfield in late August, 2000, his wife allowed him to sleep in a caravan at the back of her home.

Early in the morning of *August 24*, Prior went into the house to use the toilet and then confronted his wife. She told him she did not love him any more and he attacked her with considerable fury. The woman suffered severe facial injuries and, more than likely, was also strangled. Prior wrapped the body in a blue tarpaulin and bound it with electrical tape before driving it into bushland 17 kilometres away and burying it in a shallow grave. When Prior's wife failed to turn up for work, police became suspicious and questioned Prior. Finally, a friend advised him to turn himself in and, after making a statement, Prior was arrested.

At Prior's trial in the Supreme Court of New South Wales at Grafton, Justice Michael Grove said after Prior had been found guilty of murder: "My conclusion is that the genesis of the prisoner's offence was his uncontrolled rage at being discarded by his wife for her new lover. I am, however, persuaded that the probability is that the prisoner is genuinely remorseful for what he has done, and in this regard I have paid careful attention to letters which he has written and the candour with which he has expressed his remorse." He then sentenced Prior to a prison tem of 16 years, with a non-parole period of 12 years.

AUGUST 25 (1824)

'I RIPPED HIS BOWELS OPEN'

Convicts William Allan and William Saul escaped from custody at Macquarie Harbour on *August 25*, 1824, with Allan returning by himself two weeks later. He claimed that he and Saul had been set upon by aborigines and that his companion had been speared to death. As Allan was wearing some of Saul's clothing, this explained their torn condition. Then, while in the hospital at Macquarie Harbour, Allan confessed to another prisoner: "I am very uneasy in the mind; the devil terrifies me both night and day, so that I never have a moment's rest." He then told an extraordinary story of Saul catching a snake and offering him only a small part to eat. Then, when Saul refused him a bigger portion, Allan attacked him with a knife. He said: "Blood ran down his clothes and Saul cried out 'oh, Allan do not murder me – you may take all my clothes, but don't kill me'." The final part of Allan's chilling remark was: "I then struck my knife into his heart, and ripped his bowels open."

An examination of Saul's body revealed that not only had Saul been stabbed, but Allan had cut off his penis. The dispenser of medicine at the Macquarie Harbour hospital, George Eldridge, said at Allan's trial that when Allan's body had been found, the stomach had been cut open and, indeed, the penis had been removed. Allan was found guilty of murder and executed on *February 16*, 1825.

AUGUST 26

EXECUTED (1953): The "Rampaging Rumanian", John Balaban, executed in Adelaide on *August 26*, 1953, after being found guilty of the murder of Zora Kusic.

AUGUST 27

THE DANCE OF DEATH (1925)

The band had just started an encore of a new and unfamiliar foxtrot, *Follow Yvette*. It was Perth's glittering social event of the year – the St John of God Hospital Ball at Government House. It was just past the witching hour on *August 27*, 1925, and as couples started gliding around the polished floor, a tall and beautiful young woman in a blue evening dress walked slowly but purposely towards one of the couples. She touched the man on the shoulder, but he brushed her aside with the sneering comment: "Oh, go away! Can't you see I'm dancing?" The woman responded by pressing the trigger of a revolver she had hidden behind a handkerchief. The dashing young man in the dinner suit crashed to the floor, a crimson stain spreading across his white-starched shirt. Some women screamed, while others rushed to the scene to see what had happened. The young man had been mortally wounded, shot through the heart, and the woman who had killed him stood staring into space.

The shooting of Englishman Cyril Gidley by the woman he had spurned became one of the most celebrated cases in Australian criminal history. Its Government House setting and its aura of melodrama created headlines around the country for months; the public devoured every word written about this sensational killing and, for example, the now-defunct Perth *Mirror* shrieked the headline BALLROOM HORROR.

The shooting, of course, brought the ball to an abrupt end and the band played *God Save the King* as stunned revellers filed out of the ballroom. Perth had never seen anything like the shooting at Government House. Audrey Campbell Jacob had shot her man dead and her photograph was splashed across the front pages of just about every newspaper in Australia. Dark-haired, vivacious and pretty, Audrey Jacob would have been every young Australian's dream girl of the 1920s. But her man had done her wrong, and she had shot him down in front of a dancing throng of revellers.

When a policeman took Miss Jacob by the arm to lead her away, she told him: "It's all right; I know what I have done." She then was placed in a chair before being taken to a nearby lock-up for questioning. Miss Jacob, a mere 20 years of age, was charged with the murder of 25-year-old Gidley, who had arrived in Australia as a fourth engineer on a British steamer in 1923. Although he had a family in the north of England, he decided to leave his British ship to take employment as an engineer on a coast vessel, the *Kangaroo*. It was during one of his many stops at the port of Fremantle that he met the lovely and innocent Miss Jacob.

Gidley, blond and dashing, was a man of the world and Miss Jacob fell head over heels in love with him. In fact, she broke every rule of her convent upbringing to give herself – body and soul – to the man she loved. Although she had been engaged to another man, she broke off the engagement to suit Gidley and even left home so that she could see him whenever he was in port. However, Gidley obviously had a roving eye and there were other women in his life. His carefree attitude cost him his life.

Miss Jacob stood trial before Justice Northmore just six weeks after the shooting. It was the cause celebre of the year, if not the decade, and there were long queues outside the Criminal Court when Miss Jacob was due to give evidence. Miss Jacob told of how Gidley was "the living embodiment of the Sheik" a clear reference to Hollywood movie idol Rudolph Valentino. The former Catholic convent girl also told of how Gidley had told her he would be on his way to Singapore on the night of the ball. A friend convinced her to go to the ball regardless and she immediately saw her lover there. He refused to recognise her, so she went home and undressed.

It was then that she saw a revolver given to her by her previous fiancé for protection, so she decided to dress again and go back to the ball – armed with the revolver. However, on the way back to the ball, Miss Jacob stopped at the Catholic Cathedral and prayed. There was no doubt that the public believed Gidley had inadvertently caused his own death and evidence was presented at Miss Jacob's trial that he was a cruel arrogant womaniser. Miss Jacob, who told the court she never wanted to harm Gidley, was acquitted of murder. It was an enormously popular decision and Miss Jacob left Perth almost immediately, presumably to make a new life for herself under another name in another state

AUGUST 28

DEATH OF A CALL GIRL (1998)

Soon after Graeme Leslie Green, 23 years of age, had been released from Beechworth Prison on *August 28*, 1998, he caught a bus to Wangaratta and booked himself into the Gateway Motel. After serving a two-month sentence for theft and related offences, Green had a few drinks in the motel cocktail bar, won more than $200 on pokies and made several telephone calls for the services of a call girl. That girl was 24-year-old Tracey Holmes, the mother of a three-year-old son, and she arrived at Green's motel room at 8.40pm, along with an escort agency driver, who also acted as her security.

Then, when Ms Holmes had been in Green's motel room for about 20 minutes, she telephoned the agency to say that the original booking was to be extended from one hour to two hours. However, when Ms Holmes did not meet her driver at 10.40pm, he and the motel manager went to Green's room, where they found Ms Holmes' naked body on the floor; she had been strangled to death. Green had fled through a window, taking his and some of his victim's belongings. After another drinking and gambling session, he was arrested by police at 5.30am. In a record of interview with police, Green said he sat on Ms Holmes' stomach and grabbed her by the front of the neck and choked her to death.

Green was tried at Wangaratta, but this trial could not be completed. He then was convicted of murder at a second trial, but this was set aside in the Court of Appeal and Green therefore faced a third trial, in which he again was found guilty. Justice Osborn, before handing down his sentence, told Green: "The killing of Ms Holmes was totally unjustified …

the circumstances of the killing and your conduct thereafter were particularly callous. After an initial confrontation you prevented your victim from escaping and you deliberately strangled her with your bare hands until she was dead ... more, significantly, perhaps, you did not seek help for her as you might have done at the time of or after fleeing the motel." He sentenced Green to 18 years' imprisonment, with a minimum term of 14 years.

AUGUST 29

THE BULLION THEFT (1887)

When the mail ship *China* docked at Galle, Ceylon (now Sri Lanka), on *August 29*, 1887, bank officials expected to find 5000 pounds in newly-minted coins which had been placed in strongboxes in Sydney. However, when they opened the boxes, there was nothing but sawdust. The bullion originally had been placed aboard the steamer *Avoca* in Sydney, amidst tight security. Then, in Melbourne, the boxes were switched to the *China,* again with tight security. However, once the theft had been discovered, shipping officials realised the bullion had gone missing between Sydney and Melbourne.

Soon after, the *Avoca's* carpenter Martin Weiberg retired to a property in Gippsland, Victoria. It was there that his sister-in-law found gold coins hidden in soap. The woman took the coins to police and, following a search of Weiberg's property, they found a considerable number of gold coins. Weiberg, meanwhile, made a run for it and nothing was heard of him for months. Finally, however, he was tracked to Waratah Bay and he was sentenced to five years' jail. On release, he bought a boat and told anyone who cared to listen that he was going to sail to New Zealand to start a new life. That boat eventually was washed up on a beach at Waratah Bay, with no sign of Weiberg. Many assumed he had drowned, but there also were suggestions he had fled with the 4000 pounds still missing from the great bullion theft.

AUGUST 30

DEATH OF A HERO (1923)

Constable Joseph Delaney, of the Victorian mounted police, was one of the most highly respected members of the Swan Hill community. A tall man, Constable Delaney dispensed justice along with Murray River with tremendous authority and the backing of a thankful rural community. In fact, Constable Delaney was regarded as something of a hero as he had been awarded the Military Medal in France during World War I. He and another soldier were engaged in laying lines at Villers Brettoneux when they were surprised by the enemy. The other soldier was shot, but Delaney completed the task and then carried his mate to the safety of the trenches.

Police had been called to a farmhouse at Tyntynder, about eight miles from Swan Hill, on *August 28*, 1923. There had been a break-in during the absence of the owner, Mr William Crick. Police suspected a young farmhand from a neighbouring property had taken advantage of Mr Crick's absence and he was questioned over the break-in. However, Constable Delaney decided to interview the suspect himself on *August 30*. He went straight to the house where the youth was living and, once inside, noticed a movement from behind a door. The police officer then was shot in the chest from point-blank range.

The youth was seen running out of the house and neighbours who went to investigate found Constable Delaney lying in a pool of blood. He was still alive and conscious and told the men who found him what had happened. One man stayed with him while the other jumped onto Constable Delaney's horse to notify other police. A doctor and a police officer arrived two hours later after being bogged in a quagmire and feared they would be too late. However, Constable Delaney was still alive and arrangements were made to have him taken to Swan Hill and later, at the Swan Hill Public Hospital, his condition was reported as "serious". Police scoured the country for the gunman and finally tracked him down to a farmhouse a few miles from the scene of the shooting. Later, at the Swan Hill police station, police charged 15-year-old Frederick Smith, a ward of the state, with intent to murder.

Meanwhile, the police surgeon, Mr G.A. Syme, was flown from Melbourne to Swan Hill to perform an emergency operation on the wounded constable. However, Constable Delaney's death was announced on the morning of *September 4*. The whole of Swan Hill went into mourning and Constable Delaney was given a hero's farewell, with his coffin draped by the Union Jack. Smith eventually faced trial at Bendigo for the police officer's funeral and the court was told that the 15-year-old had waited behind a bedroom door before ordering Delaney to "put his hands up". Instead, Smith claimed, Delaney rushed him and that the shooting was an accident. Smith was found guilty of the lesser charge of manslaughter, although Justice McArthur indicated that he believed Smith had lied to the court. He added: "The court must declare that the promiscuous firing of guns – whether by young or old – has to be put down with a firm hand." He sentenced Smith to five years' jail and a private whipping of at least 10 lashes of the birch.

AUGUST 31

'DON'T DO IT MY HEART' (1999)

Mustafa Acikoglu migrated to Australia from Turkey in 1992 with his wife, but found it difficult to settle in Australia. He worked as a fruit picker near the northern Victorian town of Shepparton, was separated from his wife. He met Adelet Demir at about this time and they made plans to move away together as Acikoglu knew she was having marital problems.

Acikoglu and Demur moved into a house in the northern Melbourne suburb of Reservoir, but the relationship lasted just a few months. However, Acikoglu drove Demir's children to school and did much of her shopping while they were estranged, even though the relationship was fragile. Acikoglu disapproved of Demir smoking marijuana and said she was trying to humiliate him.

Finally, on *August 31*, 1999, the 39-year-old Acikoglu telephoned Demir to ask about picking up her children. As there was no reply, he went to the house and an argument developed. Acikoglu again accused Demir of trying to belittle him and then left the house to go his car. He collected a gun from the glove box, returned to the house and accused Demir of trying to make him "a man without honour". He then fired a shot into her chest, prompting Demir to say in Turkish: "Don't do it, my heart. Don't do it." About 30 seconds later, he shot her a second time, this time at very close range to the head. Acikoglu fled the scene, disposing of the gun and ammunition as he drove to Shepparton, where he wanted to see his children before he was arrested.

After being found guilty of murder, Justice Bongiorno said: "For sentencing purposes, I characterize this murder as one carried out with a degree of anger and with only such premeditation as is necessarily implied in your deliberate retrieval of your hand gun from the motor vehicle parked in the street, which necessitated your leaving the scene of your argument with the deceased, going to the car and returning. It is thus distinguished, if only to a minor degree, from a cold blooded execution. After obtaining the gun your actions in shooting the deceased twice in the presence of her four-year-old son and in the circumstances where, after the first shot she pleaded for her life, are horrendous indeed." He sentenced Acikoglu to 18 years' jail, with a minimum of 14 years.

SEPTEMBER

Australia over the years has been rocked by some of the most foul murders imaginable and many of these have occurred in the spring-type warmth of September. Bodies have been discovered in culverts, in the outback and even in a suburban lake. There have been robberies, rape and every imaginable type of offence. Crimes this month include:

THE PYJAMA GIRL

ARSENIC AND BULLETS

THE GREAT BANK ROBBERY

THE BACKPACKER MURDERS

THE REMAINS IN THE LAKE

SET ALIGHT

And much, much more!

SEPTEMBER 1

THE PYJAMA GIRL (1934)

Young farmer Tom Griffiths was walking along the Albury-Howlong Road in the Riverina on the crisp, sunny morning of *September 1*, 1934, when a prize bull he was leading became restless. As Griffiths approached a culvert, the bull pulled away. It was then that the young man spotted a bundle and, when he went to investigate, he was horrified to see the body of a young woman badly damaged by fire. Police in Albury, just four miles away, rushed to the scene.

The body of the woman had been pushed up the entrance of a water pipe and police knew from the state of the body that identification would not be an easy task. She had been battered about the head and there was a bullet wound near the right eye, apart from the burns. Clues included a burnt bag and towel used to cover the body and, most important of all, cream and green pyjamas with a large dragon motif. It therefore was only natural that the dead woman became known as "the Pyjama Girl".

Police knew the women was in her mid-20s, was well-nourished and had had considerable dental work on her teeth. However, police just could not identify the body, despite seeking the assistance of forces around the world. Police even moved the body to Sydney University and had it placed in a special formalin bath for preservation. Hundreds inspected the body, but there were no positive leads. Several people told police the dead woman resembled Linda Agostini, nee Platt, the wife of Italian migrant Antonio (Tony) Agostini. Although Agostini admitted his wife was missing, he said the body was not that of Linda.

A coroner's inquest was held at Albury in January, 1938, and information on the dead woman was provided by Professor A.N. Burkitt, professor of anatomy at Sydney University, who said the Pyjama Girl was probably English or European and aged about 25. After hearing the evidence, the coroner, Mr C.W. Swiney, said: "I find that between *August 28*, 1934, and *August 31*, 1934, a woman whose name is unknown, aged about 25 years of slight build, height around 5ft 1in, with brown hair and bluish-grey eyes, whose partly-burnt body was found at a culvert on the Albury-Corowa Road, about four miles from Albury on *September 1*, 1934, died from injuries to the skull and brain apparently maliciously and feloniously inflicted upon her, but where and by whom such injuries were inflicted does not enable me to say."

The break in the case came 10 years after the discovery of the body when Police Commissioner William J. Mackay assigned a new team of detectives to re-examine the file on the murder mystery. An old photograph of a group of women led to the name of Linda Agostini resurfacing and in March, 1944, Police Commissioner Mackay now believed Tony Agostini, a waiter at the fashionable Romano's restaurant, had some involvement in the Pyjama Girl mystery. Mackay asked Agostini to see him and the waiter went to police headquarters as soon as he finished work. When confronted, Agostini, who had arrived in Australia in 1927 and had married English woman Linda Platt three years later, admitted he had been keeping a secret for 10 years. He made a statement which said he and his wife had argued and after he had gone to bed, she produced a gun and held it to his head. There was a struggle and the gun went off. Agostini said he panicked and decided to drive off with the body, with "no plans ... just running".

However, the statement did not say how Linda Agostini suffered such serious head wounds and, after being taken to the culvert in Albury where the body was found, Agostini said he had dropped the body, hence the injuries. A second coroner's inquest was held at Albury and, despite claims that the body was that of a woman named Anna Morgan, Agostini was committed for trial.

That trial opened in the Supreme Court of Victoria in Melbourne on *June 19*, 1944, before Justice Lowe. Agostini's defence was that he did not intend killing his wife , but that she died accidentally. The jury deliberated for two hours and found Agostini not guilty of murder, but guilty of manslaughter. He was sentenced to six years' jail, but the judge commented: "I think the jury were merciful to you." Linda Agostini finally was laid to rest at the Preston Cemetery on *July 13*, 1944, just 13 days after her husband was sentenced to prison. Agostini served three years and nine months of his sentence and then was deported to Italy.

THE PAYROLL KILLING (1938)

Brothers Frederick and Clarence Sherry had started a small shoe-making business in the inner Melbourne suburb of Abbotsford in 1924 and, despite the Great Depression, this business flourished and, by 1938, the Sherry Shoe Company had more than 30 employees. This, of course meant a substantial payroll in an era before pay cheques, direct entry or even security services. On the other hand, Melbourne was a much quieter, more peaceful city in those days and armed robbery was relatively rare. The Sherry brothers therefore were confident they would be able to draw the wages from their bank and deliver it to employees without any trouble. That view changed dramatically in March, 1938, when two masked men tried to hijack the Sherry wages. One of the men drove a car alongside the Sherry car and the other masked man leaned out of a window and pointed a pistol at Clarence Sherry, "Hand over your money," the bandit shouted as he waved the gun. Sherry sped away and, for several months, a police escort was used for the delivery of wages.

Time passed and the brothers felt the attempted hold-up had been a one-off incident and they therefore decided to discontinue the use of the police escort. It proved to be a fatal mistake for 46-year-old Frederick Sherry, a father of six. On *September 1*, 1938, Sherry and company secretary Henry Thomas drove to the Northcote branch of the Commercial Bank and withdrew more than 600 pounds. Thomas stuffed the notes into his coat pocket and threw a large number of coins into a bag. Sherry and Thomas left the bank and were confronted by a youth. However, neither was aware there would be another hold-up and got into their small brown car. They were followed by a blue tourer with two men in the front.

Sherry drove his car down High Street and around a curve along a railway line into Queen's Parade, not far from the factory. The blue tourer pulled alongside and Sherry and Thomas saw two men with handkerchiefs pulled over their faces. The two shoe factory men must have thought they were in some weird Hollywood drama, with the men in the car playing the baddies in a Western movie. They were forced to pull over and asked to hand over the bag. When Thomas pressed his hand on the horn to attract attention, the man holding the pistol fired a shot which pierced the window and cut Thomas about the face. Sherry bravely grabbed the gunman's hand and struggled for several seconds before opening a car door and running down a street.

The gunman followed him and, when Sherry fell, shot him through the heart from almost point-blank range. The bandit turned to a gathering crowd and, waving the pistol, warned them to keep away. He then rushed back to the blue tourer, insisted Thomas hand over the bag and made his escape with the driver. Sherry had been fatally wounded and, after struggling a few paces, fell onto the pavement with blood spurting from his chest wound. The blue tourer later was discovered in a northern suburb, torched to destroy clues.

Police had a fair idea of the identity of the bandits and, five days later, made their first move. A 22-year-old, Selwyn Wallace, admitted he had been involved in the hold-up, but insisted he had not been responsible for shooting Sherry. Then, with Wallace's help, they tracked down a man in Queensland and labourer Herbert Jenner, 23, and Wallace were charged with murder.

They stood trial before Justice Gavan Duffy at the Criminal Court just three months after the shooting. Although Jenner was the man who fired the fatal shot and Wallace was still in the car at the time of the cold-blooded shooting, both men were found guilty of murder and sentenced to death. However, the judge told the jury that its recommendation of mercy because of the youth of Jenner and Wallace would be conveyed to the Executive Council. Both sentences were commuted to life imprisonment, with no benefit of remission. Both men spent alsmot 20 years in maximum security at Pentridge before Jenner was transferred to the Corriemungle prison camp in Western Victoria, while Wallace was transferred to the French Island prison farm in 1958. Both were freed in October, 1959.

SEPTEMBER 2

THE BIKIE BATTLE (1984)

There was no love lost between the Comancheros and Bandidos bikie gangs, but no one expected the massacre that would occur at Milperra on *September 2*, 1984. The Bandidos was founded after a faction broke away from the Comancheros and there had been considerable bad blood between the two gangs, with both declaring matters would come to a head that brutal day outside a Sydney pub.

A spare parts meeting had been organized and, with hundreds in attendance when the two gangs faced off. When the shooting and mayhem finished, six men and 14-year-old Leanne Walters, who had been selling raffle tickets, were left dead or dying. Police charged more than 43 men with murder, but some charges were dropped and only nine were found guilty of murder, the rest being found guilty of manslaughter.

The court case following the massacre at the time was one of the biggest and most expensive in Australian criminal history. The leader of the Comancheros, William "Jock" Ross, was accused of being responsible for the decision for gang members to go to the Viking Tavern armed and ready for violence. He was sentenced to life imprisonment, along with seven other bikies. Sixteen other men were sentenced to 14 years' jail for manslaughter.

**

BEHEADED (1857): Chong Sigh and Hing Tzan executed in Melbourne on *September 2*, 1857, for the decapitation murder of Sophia Lewis.

SEPTEMBER 3

EXECUTED (1860): Scotsman John McDonald executed in Melbourne on *September 3*, 1860, after being found guilty of the murder of his wife in a drunken rage at Iron Bark Gully, near Bendigo.

**

HANGED (1928): Convicted murderer Clifford Hulme hanged at Fremantle Gaol on *September 3*, 1928.

SEPTEMBER 4

SENTENCED (2005): Dudley Mark Aslett sentenced to 40 years' jail for the gang rape of a 16-year-old girl in Sydney on *July 17*, 2003, but, on appeal on *September 4*, 2005, this was reduced to 30 years' imprisonment, with a minimum of 22 and a half years. Accomplices Christopher Bonham, Stephen Aslitt and a 17-year-old youth who cannot be named because of his age, also handed lengthy sentences.

SEPTEMBER 5

THE KILLING OF A SON (1989)

Norman Edward Wilson, 44, could see his life disintegrating when his wife Janelle left him in June, 1989. The couple had five children but, when Mrs Wilson left the family home at Inverill, New South Wales, only 18-year-old Dean and 14-year-old Melissa were left to live with their father. Just two months later, Dean told his father that he had been successful with an application to join the NSW Police. This appeared to upset Wilson, but this was never raised as a motive for the killing of the teenager who had applied to be a police officer.

On the morning of *September 1*, 1989, Wilson tricked Dean into accompanying him to a dirt track about 13 kilometres from Inverill. The two argued, mainly about Mrs Wilson leaving him, and the father shot his son in the upper left arm with a .22 rifle. Wilson then attacked his son with a rock, smashing his head so violently that the boy suffered massive brain damage and skull fractures. Wilson then covered his son's body with branches and leaves and drove back to Inverill, where he went shopping with his daughter Melissa.

Wilson reported his son missing and, two days later, asked police if they had heard anything of his son. He then broke down and told them where they could find Dean's body. He said in a statement that he "should have shot myself instead". He said Dean grabbed the gun and that it "went off". He also said: "I just went bang and when I saw blood, I just went mad. I couldn't stop. I just kept going and hitting him, hitting him with anything I could get my hands on, with a rifle, rock, anything." Wilson was convicted of murder in June, 1990, and Justice Finlay imposed a life sentence. Then, in 1999, Justice Dunford re-sentenced him to a minimum term of 15 years from the time of being apprehended on *September 5*, 1989.

SEPTEMBER 6

MASS KILLING (1971): Clifford Batholomew murdered his wife, their seven children (ages ranging from four to 19), his sister-in-law and her two-year-old son at Hope Forest, South Australia, on *September 6*, 1971.

SEPTEMBER 7

EXECUTED (1861): Aborigines Nilgerie and Ticherie executed at Fowler's Bay, South Australia, on *September 7*, 1861, for the murder of two people.

SEPTEMBER 8

THE COBBY COPYCATS (1988)

Sydneysiders were still getting over the horrific rape and torture killing of Anita Cobby in 1986 when, just two years later, a copycat gang abducted a young woman and subjected her to vile sexual assaults before killing her. The gang, comprising 23-year-old Stephen "Shorty" Jamieson and teenagers Bronson Blessington, Mathew Elliott and Wayne Wilmot decided on *September 8*, 1988, that it would be a good idea to steal a car. They then decided that the Sutherland railway station would be the idea place to find the right vehicle and, if the opportunity presented, abduct a woman. That woman turned out to be 20-year-old Janine Balding, who was engaged to be married the following March.

The gang abducted her in her own car and Elliott raped her at knifepoint in the back of the car as it travelled along the F4 freeway. The car was driven by 15-year-old Wilmot, with his girlfriend Carol Arrow in the front passenger seat. Balding was raped repeatedly and dragged to the edge of a dam at Minchinbury. Then, their sexual energy spent, the gang tied her up and dragged her to the dam water, where she drowned. All members of the gang eventually were arrested and charged with abduction, rape and murder. However, it was decided that Arrow and Wilmot would go to trial only on charges involving Balding's abduction and the theft of her engagement ring, jewellery and money. Wilmot was sentenced to 10 years' imprisonment, while Arrow was released on a three-year good behaviour bond after spending a year and a half in custody.

A trial against the other three was abandoned when two of the accused claimed police had arrested the wrong "Shorty". Finally, at a second trial, the jury took just two hours to find Jamieson, Blessington and Elliott guilty on all charges and, on *September 19*, 1990, Justice Newman sentenced them to life imprisonment, with no possibility of parole. He said: "To sentence people so young to long terms of imprisonment is, of course, a heavy task. However, the facts surrounding the commission of this murder are so barbaric that I believe I have no alternative. It is one of the most barbaric killings in the sad criminal history of this State." Jamieson repeatedly has protested his innocence, claiming another man known as "Shorty" was involved.

SEPTEMBER 9

KILLED OVER A FISH (1824)

As in the previous cases, two convicts – Francis Oats and James Williamson – escaped from Macquarie Harbour, Van Diemen's Land, on *September 9*, 1824. Like Allan and Saul in another case, both men were wracked by hunger while on the run. When Williamson caught and ate a fish without giving Oats a share, there was a violent argument. Oats admitted when captured on September 13 that he hit his friend with a stick and, when he fell, "the back part of his skull was split by a stump".

Oats even led authorities to the corpse, but Macquarie Harbour hospital medical dispenser George Eldridge said Williamson's skull was fractured nine times, with pieces embedded in the skull. He insisted the wounds could not have been caused by a stick. Although Oates had claimed the two men had fought and that Wiliamson's death was an accident, there were no marks on him. Oats was found guilty of murder and executed on *February 16*, 1825, along with William Allan of a previous case and another convicted murderer, Thomas Hudson.

THE UNWANTED PREGNANCY (2000)

Daniel Vance Mizon, a science graduate from Monash University, met Lucille Rosalie May through the Save Albert Park movement in protest against the Australian Grand Prix being held in that part of Melbourne. That was in 1995 and they had an on-off relationship for several years, even though

Mizon at one stage left Miss May to live with a another woman.

Then, in March, 2000, May, 40, visited Mizon, 41 at the time, at work to tell him she was pregnant and that he was the father. Several months later, on *September 9*, Mizon visited his first wife and was told that she was concerned about child maintenance payments for their son. Next day, he visited his mother and she told him she had spoken to May and that she had told her of the pregnancy. Enraged, Mizon headed to May's home in the bayside suburb of Highett and killed her.

May's mother and sister rang her the following day and, when there was no response, paid her a visit. The front door was locked, but they used a key to gain entry to the house and found May's body in a pool of blood on the rear living room floor. There also was blood in the kitchen and bathroom and a post mortem later revealed that the woman, seven months pregnant, had been stabbed in the neck and that there had been an attempt to strangle her.

Police interviewed Mizon, but he at first denied any knowledge of May's death and, in a second interview, said he went to May's back door, found it open and discovered her body on the living room floor. However, a jury found Mizon guilty of murder and Justice Bongiorno said the likely motive was the financial and social inconvenience to Mizon of May's pregnancy.

The judge, in sentencing Mizon to 21 years' imprisonment, with a minimum of 17 years, said: "The most significant aggravating factor so far as sentencing in this case is concerned is the fact that at the time you killed her, Lucy May was pregnant. She was accordingly extremely vulnerable. From time immemorial, society has regarded pregnant women with particular solicitude. That this is so is beyond argument. It needs no elaboration. I regard Lucy May's pregnancy as a significant aggravating factor in this case."

SEPTEMBER 10

SENTENCED (2003): Imam Samudra, the "field commander" in the Bali Bombings on *September 10*, 2003, sentenced to death.

SEPTEMBER 11

ESCAPE (1863): Bushranger Captain Thunderbolt (Fred Ward) escaped from Cockatoo Island on *September 11*, 1863.

SEPTEMBER 12

ARSENIC AND BULLETS (1903)

Butcher John Baker was in love with a woman named Nellie Smith, who went to live with Chinese trader Tim Ah Doo at Cootamundra, NSW. Baker on *September 12*, 1903, went to a chemist's shop and bought sixpence worth of arsenic "to poison cats and dogs". The following night he went to Ah Doo's house and shot his enemy in love, once through the head and once through the heart. Ah Doo died almost instantly, but Baker then went into the house and fired at Smith, hitting her in the hand.

Baker then told her: "I will do for you as I have done for the other." Then, after being wounded in the hand, she begged Baker to spare her life. The lovelorn butcher then told her: "No, I have only put three (bullets) into it (the revolver)." Baker then jumped over a house fence and, as he left, he told Smith: "I suppose I will swing for this." He later was found with bullet wounds to the head and neck and died in hospital several hours later. He also had taken some of the arsenic he had purchased the night before. An inquest jury returned a verdict of wilful murder against Baker.

THE DEADLY MISTAKE (1953)

Shirley Collins, just 14, might still be alive if it had not been for one tragic mistake. Instead, she suffered a terrible death at the hands of a monster. Worse, that monster has never been brought to justice for his savage crime. Shirley Collins, whose real name was Shirley Hughes, lived with Mr and Mrs Alfred Collins in the northern Melbourne suburb of Reservoir. Her real mother, Mrs Leila Hughes, had shifted to Queensland and although Shirley kept in touch with her, she referred to Mrs Collins as her mother.

A quiet, shy girl, Shirley took a job as a shop assistant in the city when old enough to leave school. An invitation from a store employee, Ronald Holmes, 21, to attend a party at Richmond on the night of Saturday, *September 12*, 1953, was the first innocent step to tragedy. Shirley, with Mrs Collins' blessing, accepted the invitation and Holmes arranged to meet the young girl at the Richmond rail station. Unfortunately, Shirley was confused about the meeting place that there were two other rail stations in Melbourne bearing the name Richmond. Shirley, used to travelling to work in the city on the Reservoir line, passed through the West Richmond station each working day and obviously believed she had to meet Holmes at the West Richmond station, and not the Richmond station. It was a fatal mistake.

Holmes waited at the Richmond station for Shirley, parking his car nearby. However, Shirley did not turn up and after a long wait Holmes went to the party believing she had decided not to go to the party after all. However, Shirley had left her home shortly after 7pm to catch a train. Shirley Collins was murdered that night, but her body was not discovered until the following Tuesday morning.

Incredibly, the girl was murdered some 40 miles from Richmond, at the popular seaside resort of Mt Martha. The body was discovered by Mr Lionel Evelyn-Lairdet, who was out walking his dog. Other passers-by had seen the body in the driveway of a vacant holiday cottage, but believed it was a girl suntanning herself. Meanwhile, Shirley's foster mother had already alerted police over the girl's disappearance as the 14-year-old had been told to be home by midnight.

Police were shocked when they examined the body. It was a terrible sight, the girl being battered to death. Shirley had walked up the drive of the holiday cottage with her murderer and hit over the head with three full bottles of beer. The murderer than smashed Shirley's face in with heavy slabs of concrete guttering and her features were unrecognisable, her face smashed to pulp. The murderer also removed Shirley's panties, stockings and girdle, leaving the girl's skirt above her shoulders. She was not sexually assaulted but the murder horrified Melbourne.

Police were told a light-coloured car had been spotted near West Richmond station on the night Shirley disappeared, but would Shirley have entered the car willingly? One theory was that she knew the driver, but nothing was conclusive. Police also traced the batch numbers on the the labels of the beer bottles, but without any significant lead. The police even reconstructed the abduction, using a model, with the now-defunct *Argus* newspaper running a photograph to try and prompt someone's memory. Again, there were no leads and this horrific murder remains a mystery.

SEPTEMBER 13

SEATED ON THE GALLOWS (1826)

Although the case of two aborigines, Jack and Dick, seemed straight forward, it sparked considerable debate in the colony of Van Diemen's Land. The two had speared stock-keeper Thomas Colley to death at Oyster Bay in 1826 and, after being found guilty, were sentenced to death. However, the *Colonial Times* of *June 2*, 1826, noted: "We are aware of the legal dogma, that all persons on English land become subjected to English law. Good. But as far as these poor wretches are concerned, it is not quite clear, that as relates to them it is English land." Jack and Dick, were set to be hanged on *September 13*, 1826, along with five others – William Smith, Thomas Dunnings and Edward Everett for murder, and John Taylor and George Waters for robbery.

The *Colonial Times* of *September 15*, 1826, reported that the aborigine named Dick "received the Sacrament" on the morning of his execution but, because of "a loathsome cutaneous (skin) disease", had to be carried to the scaffold. He then was seated on a stool while the noose was placed around his neck and then "plunged into eternity". The other aborigine, Jack, went to his death unmoved. The *Colonial*

Times reported: "The old black (Dick) died very hard" before noting that the younger aborigine, Jack, "bled profusely from the nose".

THE HIT-MAN (1990)

Richard Hanmer and his wife Mildred ran a hardware shop at Mordialloc and, as part of the business, also had an agency for the State Savings Bank and a dry cleaning depot. On *September 20*, 1982, Mrs Hanmer drove her two daughters to school and then opened the family business for trade as her husband was recovering from hernia surgery. She was holding $2569 in bank deposits when, at about 12.50pm, she was shot in a hold-up. A woman next door heard a loud "bang", the sound of Mrs Hanmer taking a shot to the right chest between the second and third ribs. The gunman fled, but not before taking the money. Mrs Hanmer rang her husband to say she had been shot and told him: "Dick, I've been robbed and I'm dying" and later she told him "It's all right – here's the ambulance."

Mrs Hanmer was rushed to the Alfred Hospital and, while still conscious was able to describe the gunman as about 25 years of age, Australian, about 5ft 7in and having ginger hair. He was carrying a sawn-off rifle which had been used to shoot her from the front. The coroner, Dr J.H. McNamara, subsequently found that Mrs Hanmer died from a haemorrhage caused by the gunshot wound. There were no witnesses as no one else was in the shop at the time and, despite their best efforts, police were unable to track down the killer.

Then, in August, 2000, a convicted murderer stepped forward to say he had killed Mrs Hanmer. Gregory John

Brazel, who was 28 years of age at the time of the shooting, was a career criminal with a terrible record of violence and dishonesty. He had been convicted of the murder of a prostitute at Barongarook, western Victoria, on *September 13*, 1990, and of the murder of another prostitute at Sorrento, on the Mornington Peninsula, in the same month. He was sentenced to a cumulative term of 30 years but then incurred other sentences while in prison and was not to have been released until February, 2024.

Brazel might have stepped forward to confess to the murder of Mrs Hanmer, but it took police almost two years to verify his claims that he had been paid to kill the woman in the hardware shop. He claimed he was acting as a hit-man after being approached with a $30,000 offer for the killing, half to be paid in advance and the rest on completion of the job. He said that when he went back to the instigator after the killing, he was told "well done".

Justice Cummins, who had sentenced Brazel for the murder of the two prostitutes, said in the Supreme Court of Victoria in April, 2003, that the convicted killer stepped forward "to tell the truth". The judge told him: "It was to seek to purge, partially, your guilt. It was, in your words, to confront your demons. I am satisfied that there was not a collateral or hidden reason for your coming forward. The only benefit you sought to gain was the partial expurgation of your guilt. You well knew that the consequence of your coming forward would be a significantly increased term of imprisonment upon the already lengthy terms you were then serving."

Brazel pleaded guilty to the murder of Mrs Hanmer and Justice Cummins, before passing sentence, told him: "There is a cluster of mitigating factors in your present situation and which is relevant to the proper sentence to be imposed upon you. First, after nearly 20 years you have come forward wholly of your own volition and confessed to the crime. Second, your coming forward and confession was motivated by contrition and true remorse. Third, the authenticity of that motive is not deflected or derogated from by any collateral purpose or seeking by you of advantage. Fourth, your confession has solved a long unsolved crime. Fifth, it has brought some partial finality to the suffering of the living victims; but they will suffer for as long as they live. Sixth, you have pleaded guilty to the crime. Seventh, you have genuine and plenary remorse. Eighth, you have not at any time since you came forward and confessed, sought to avoid full responsibility for your actions. You also waived the benefit of possible indemnity. Ninth, you told the truth to the police, involving as that did the placing of this crime in the most serious category of murder, a paid execution. Tenth, you have been in continuous custody since September, 1990, and face lengthy further imprisonment and you are in a state of poor health".

The judge directed Brazel, who once had been in a serious altercation with the notorious Mark "Chopper" Read, to serve a minimum term of 27 years before being eligible for parole and he now will not be released until at least 2030, when he will be 75 years of age.

SEPTEMBER 14

KILLED OVER A DEBT (1999)

When George Rakos was experiencing financial difficulties, he approached workmate Darren McArdle to help him get a bank loan. Rakos' credit rating was poor, so they devised a plan in which they would tell a bank Rakos was planning to buy McArdle's car and a bank cheque therefore would be made out to McArdle. Rakos handed McArdle a bank cheque for $7000 and the money should have remained in the bank. However, McArdle withdrew the money and gambled it away on poker machines.

After the two had worked a night shift finishing on the morning of *September 14*, 1999, Rakos asked McArdle if he could have some of the money. Arrangements therefore were made for McArdle to make a withdrawal when the bank opened and he left his workmate watching television at Rakos' Ferntree Gully home. McArdle went to drive off, but noticed a car steering lock in the car. He picked up the lock, took it into Rakos' home and struck his workmate to the head five times.

McArdle cleaned up after the killing, left the home and threw the lock away. However, he was always the chief suspect and, after being arrested, pleaded guilty to Rakos' murder. Justice Teague, in the Supreme Court of Victoria, noted that although McArdle had a serious gambling problem, he had worked hard and kept out of trouble with the law. The killing was described as "inexplicably out of character" and the judge noted a "high level of remorse". He sentenced McArdle, 38 years of age, to 17 years' imprisonment, with a non-parole period of 12 years.

SEPTEMBER 15

THE GREAT BANK ROBBERY (1828)

Former convict Charles Dingle, who had been given his ticket of leave in 1827, came up with the idea in 1828 of robbing the Bank of Australia building in Sydney. Dingle realised it would be no mean feat as the building was solidly constructed on thick sandstone foundations. However, he believed any effort would be worth it as the bank was believed to contain vast sums of money placed there by Sydney's elite. Dingle was keen to get his hands on this money and believed that he could get to it by drilling a tunnel from a storm-water drain into the strongroom. He realised he would need help and, for his daring plan, recruited former construction worker Thomas Turner, experienced blacksmith William Blackstone and another villain in George Farrell.

The gang started its work in August, 1827, but Turner opted out early as he believed that the tunnel work would make him a prime suspect. Dingle therefore recruited another convict, a man named Clayton. They worked week after week to set their plan in motion and, on *September 15*, 1828, breached a bank wall. The men packed 140,000 pounds in bank notes, 750 pounds in coin and British and Spanish silver and gold into bags and made their escape. The only problem was that many of the notes were old and unacceptable at legal tender, while the gold and silver coins were too "hot" to handle. Dingle therefore took some of the notes to a well-known Sydney fence, who exchanged the old notes for new ones. The fence, Thomas Woodward, conducted the switch operation himself, but then disappeared.

Then, three years later, Blackstone was arrested on a separate theft charge and taken to jail on Norfolk Island, then regarded as hell on earth. Blackstone confessed to his part in the great bank robbery in an effort to win his freedom. Dingle, Farrell and Woodward were arrested and sentenced to 10 years' jail each. Blackstone won his freedom, but again fell foul of the law and was taken back to Norfolk Island. However, most of the loot was never recovered and the Bank of Australia struggled until it closed its doors in 1843.

'I JUST KILLED MY MISSUS' (2001)

Taxi-driver Desmond John Waddington, 46, had been drinking beer and watching football on television at his New Town, Tasmania, flat on *September 15*, 2001, and was in good spirits as he prepared a meal for himself and 52-year-old de facto wife Diane Ellen Mudge. However, Mudge started making telephone calls and this upset Waddington, who often complained about her telephone calls, especially at meal times.

During Mudge's telephone conversation with friend Georgina Males, Waddington was heard to yell: "Get off that fucking phone. I've been putting up with it for the last 10 years. I'm sick to death of the fucking phone." Males rang back, but Waddington shouted "fuck off" down the line to her and hung up. Males, concerned for her friend, went around to see her friend, but Waddington refused her entry to the flat. He then headed off to a hotel but, after just one drink, went to the Liverpool police station and said: "I've just killed my fucking missus."

Waddington had held a pillow over Mudge's face and smothered her for about three or four minutes until she died.

He pleaded guilty to a count of murder and was sentenced to 17 years' jail, with a fixed non-parole period of 12 years. However, on appeal, the none-parole period was reduced to 10 years.

SEPTEMBER 16

THE 'DEMENTED' FATHER (1902)

The *Age* newspaper of *September 16*, 1902, reported "a terrible domestic tragedy", probably sparked by heavy gambling at the races. Country traveller John Joseph Peadon was not his usual self on the Sunday night before the *Age* report and could not settle at his Gloucester Road weatherboard home. When his wife asked him if there was any problem, he merely replied that he had a cold. Mrs Peadon eventually dozed off, but was awakened by a blow to the head. Her husband continued to attack her with an iron bed key, but she finally managed to ward him off. Son Lancelot, hearing the commotion, rushed in to see what was happening and also was hit about the head.

Lancelot Peadon said his father looked like a "wild animal" as he left the bedroom in search of other members of the family. He slashed seven-year-old Nancy so savagely across the throat that he almost severed her head and killed 18-month-old Beatrice with a slash across the throat. Three-year-old Morton also was slashed but survived, along with three-year-old Alexander who was battered around the head. Peadon, 45, later held a gun in his mouth and put a bullet through his head. Mrs Peadon, Lancelot, Morton and

Alexander survived their wounds and the only member of the family who was not attacked was eldest daughter Rokeby.

SEPTEMBER 17

THE CHILD KIDNAPPER (2003)

When Dennis Raymond Ferguson was jailed in 1989 for 14 years, the sentencing judge said the chances of rehabilitation were "nil". Ferguson was jailed for kidnapping three children from their homes in New South Wales and molesting them for three days. He was convicted on charges including kidnapping, sodomy, gross indency and carnal knowledge. These offences were committed with his girlfriend Alexandria Brookes, who was sentenced to 11 years' jail, and Ferguson was released in January, 2003. But, just eight months later he was sentenced to another 15 months' jail, with no parole. The *Bulletin* magazine edition of *September 17*, 2003, reported: "Convicted paedophile Dennis Ferguson is back behind bars after he allegedly failed to tell police of a new job which may have brought him into contact with children."

SEPTEMBER 18

UNSOLVED (1997): Sydney grandmother Pauline Gillard, 57, brutally murdered on *September 18*, 1997, and the case is still unsolved.

SEPTEMBER 19

THE BACKPACKER MURDERS (1992)

Australians recoil with horror at the very mention of Ivan Milat's name and with good reason. He will forever be remembered as one of the nation's worst mass murderers, with seven known victims. The word 'known' has special significance as there are many who believe the number of victims could be well into double figures. Yet Milat, the Backpacker Murderer, could have been apprehended much earlier in his bloodthirsty spree around the Belanglo State Forest area south of Sydney.

It probably will never be known when Milat turned to murder, but his first known victims were British backpackers Caroline Clarke and Joanne Walters. Both 22 years of age, their bodies were discovered in the Belanglo State Forest on *September 19*, 1992, five months after being reported missing after leaving Sydney for Melbourne. Both women had been stabbed, but Clarke also had been shot numerous times in the head. In fact, forensic examination revealed that Clarke had been shot from different angles, suggesting she had been used as target practice. Indeed, the wounds of both young women were horrific, with Walters slashed to the neck, chest and head with a large hunting knife. Clarke also had been stabbed. NSW police were horrified but, despite a number of clues, were unable to determine a suspect.

Then, just three week after the bodies of Clarke and Walters were discovered, English tourist Paul Onions accepted the offer of a lift by a man driving a silver four-wheel vehicle. The young Englishman was on the Hume Highway when approached and was on his way to work at the fruit orchards in Mildura. The four-wheel driver, who had a large, bushy moustache and introduced himself as 'Bill', slowed down just outside Mittagong and then pulled over to remove some item. 'Bill' by now had started to act aggressively, so the concerned Onions got out of the vehicle on the pretence of stretching his legs.

However, 'Bill' barked at him to get back into the car. Onions obliged, but then had a black revolver pointed at his head. Terrified, Onions immediately jumped out of the vehicle and ran down the road. A shot was fired while the Englishman tried to flag down a passing car. 'Bill' eventually caught up with Onions and grabbed him, only for the young man to again break free. Onions waved down a car carrying two women and five children, jumped into the vehicle, locked the door and told the woman behind the wheel to drive off as the man who had been attacking him had a gun. The driver, Mrs Joanne Berry, dropped Onions off at the Bowral police station where an officer took down details. Then, incredibly, Onions was given directions to the railway station.

He caught a train back to Sydney and stayed in Australia another six months, his near escape never far from his mind, although seemingly far from the minds of Bowral police. Back in England two years later, Onions read in a newspaper about bodies being found in the Belanglo State Forest. Perturbed, he went to his local police station and then was advised to contact the Australian Embassy. Onions eventually reached the task force investigating the Backpacker Murders.

Police by now were dealing with the appalling fact that seven bodies had been discovered and, despite every effort, they seemed no closer to solving the murders. They accumulated files on dozens of suspects, including Milat. He once had owned a silver four-wheel vehicle, had a bushy moustache and sometimes was known as 'Bill'. Police decided to have a closer look at Milat's background, especially after learning that he had a long criminal record and once had been charged with rape after picking up two girl hitchhikers along the Hume Highway in New South Wales. The two girls alleged that Milat had threatened to kill them, but he was found not guilty. However, his profile both alarmed and appalled the police investigating the Backpacker Murders.

Finally, police read Onions' claim that he had been threatened when hitchhiking along the Hume Highway. His description was too much of a coincidence so, after being flown to Australia, Onions was asked to pick out his attacker from photographs of a dozen other suspects. He picked out Milat without hesitation. This was just the break the police needed, so they raided Milat's home at Eaglevale, near Liverpool. Significantly, the house was close to the Hume Highway, the road to death for so many.

Milat was arrested on *May 22*, 1994, and when police searched his home they had no doubt they finally had nabbed the Backpacker Murderer. The evidence they gathered was overwhelming and, for example, they found the .22 rifle that had been used to kill Caroline Clarke, as well as the dead woman's camera. Milat was charged with the murder of seven backpackers and the attempted murder of Onions.

His trial started in March, 1996, and lasted more than three months. Jurors heard from more than 100 prosecution witnesses and had to deal with more than 300 exhibits and photographs, many of them gruesome in the extreme. Justice David Hunt in his summary said: 'It is sufficient here to record that each of his (Milat's) victims was attacked savagely and cruelly, with force which was unusual and vastly more than was necessary to cause death, and for some form of gratification. 'Each of two of the victims was shot a number of times in the head.

A third was decapitated in circumstances which establish that she (German backpacker Anja Habschied) would have been alive at the time. The stab wounds to each of the other three would have caused paralysis, two of them having their spinal cords completely severed. 'The multiple stab wounds to three of the seven victims would have been likely to have penetrated their hearts. There are signs that two of them were strangled. All but one appear to have been sexually interfered with before or after death. 'The jury deliberated for three days before returning on *July 27*, 1996, for their verdict of guilty on all charges.

Milat was sentenced to life imprisonment on the seven counts of murder and to seven years' jail on the charge of attempted murder. Then, in 1998, the NSW Court of Criminal Appeal rejected a Milat appeal and declared that he was to spend the rest of his life behind bars. However, several questions remain, with many police convinced that Milat did not act alone in at least some of his murders. Also, were there other victims of the Backpacker Murderer? It is doubtful whether these mysteries will ever be solved.

SEPTEMBER 20

THE REMAINS IN THE LAKE (1906)

Melbourne was horrified on *September 20*, 1906, when human remains were found floating on the Albert Park Lagoon (now Lake). It was a gruesome discovery and police were baffled. They did not know whether it was murder or a practical joke. The news created enormous interest among residents near the lagoon and, when police dredged the area, they had to contend with the macabre interest of bystanders hoping to get a glimpse of even worse discoveries. Reports of the discovery of the human remains paint an extremely interesting picture of Melbourne and the operations of the Victoria Police at the turn of the twentieth century. The now-defunct Melbourne newspaper *The Argus* ran this report, in great detail, in its edition of Saturday, *September 22*, under the headlines: ALBERT-PARK TRAGEDY, PATHOLOGICAL EXAMINATION, MURDER THEORY STRENGTHENED, INTERESTING DSCOVERIES:

"Yesterday's investigation into the discovery in Albert Park Lagoon of mutilated pieces of a man, though they did nothing to remove the mystery that surrounds the case, materially strengthened the presumption that a particularly foul and horrible murder has been committed.

"Mr C.H. Mollison M.R.C.S. (the government pathologist), examined the remains yesterday afternoon. He found that in addition to the lower front portion of the abdomen, they included all, or parts of all, the internal organs. The heart was whole, and had still attached to it portion of the left lung. The right lung was separate. The liver had been damaged a little. The kidneys had been cut away and flung separately into the package. A large gap had been torn in the stomach and portion of the small intestine was missing, though a lot of it and the whole of the large intestine were there.

"When a decomposed body is found, it is always difficult to determine the length of time that has elapsed since death. When only portions of a body are found that difficulty is greatly increased, and in the present case it is almost impossible to form any accurate estimate. So many things that are unknown require to be taken into account. Though some portions of the parts found are much decomposed, others are but little affected, especially parts protected by cuticle. The fat, for instance, is quite fresh, and the flesh underlying it, too, is but little affected. This might lead to the conclusion that the murder had occurred recently: but the remains were found floating in water, and decomposition in water is much slower than in air. Yet allowance cannot be made for this because it is not known how long the parcels were in the water. They may have been there only 24 hours. They may have been there 24 days.

"After careful examination, Mr Mollison yesterday concluded that the remains were probably about a fortnight old; but they might be three weeks. The murder has certainly been committed within the last three or four weeks.

"A point which is most important in the work of the elucidation is the time when the parcels were actually placed in the lagoon. The boys who found them assert that the parcels were not there when they passed the spot a couple of hours before; but this is very unlikely. It is more probable that the packages, which were tightly rolled and small, escaped their notice. Of course, it is also possible that during the absence of the boys the parcels drifted in to the little bay in which they were found, or that, impelled by the gases generated in them, and confined by the brown paper, they had just risen to the surface.

"It is, indeed, almost certain that these two parcels had been present in the little bay for over a week before they were noticed, and taken out. This is shown by a curious piece of evidence. For the last few days fish had been taken near where the parcels had been found. The fish are not, as a rule, caught there, but over a week the boys who were fishing there have every day got three or four good-sized perch. It is fairly evident that the fish must have been drawn to that spot by something, and those who know the lagoon well are convinced that the two grim packages were the attraction. It is hardly conceivable that the parcels, if they had been floating on the surface all the time, could have escaped observation. It is much more likely that they were lying on the bottom, and rose to the surface only on Thursday afternoon.

"When this is admitted, it seems quite feasible that other packages containing other portions of the man's body are still in the lagoon. It may be urged that a murderer who was so careful and so astute as to cut his victim up into small pieces would be much too clever a man to throw all the parcels into the one lake. He would throw some into the sea, some into the river, and dispose of other parts in the sewers or by burning. This is, of course, very probable; but there remains after all the great chance that the murderer was not a genius, and that he may have made the great mistake of separating the body only to unite it again by dropping all the parts into the lagoon. It is through mistakes of this sort that crimes are discovered and their authors punished.

"Detective Burvett, who has been placed in charge of the case, clearly recognises the necessity for thoroughly dragging and searching the lagoon. Early yesterday morning the water police, under Senior Constable McDonald, together with four constables from Russell Street barracks, set to work to drag the lake in the vicinity of the little bay in which the parcels were found. All day they rowed about, trailing the drags, but they found nothing except the green silk neck scarf, which most probably has no more to do with the case than the rest of the rubbish, old tins, and debris that hooks brought up from the bottom. The drags which the police are working, however, are inadequate. The lagoon has a surface of several hundred acres, the water being 2ft. to 3ft. deep. The whole of this will have to be dragged and the only applicances for the work that the police possess are a couple of ordinary drags — weighted hooks at the end of a long line.

"Detective Burvett tried yesterday to obtain a proper sweep that would cover 20ft. or 30ft. at a time. There is no such thing in Melbourne, however, and the men today will continue the disheartening business of trailing the hooks about in aimless fashion. Another method of thoroughly searching the bottom would be to use a heavily-weighted Seine net. None of the police, however, are anxious to undertake the manipulation of a net, and it is probable that if this method is resorted to a couple of fishermen will be hired. The lagoon is kept full mainly by storm-water from the surrounding land, but provision is also made for pumping water in from the Yarra. There are outlets also which enable the water to be run off into the sea, and it is not impossible that this — the only really effective way of discovering what may be lying at the bottom of the lagoon — may be resorted to if other measures fail.

"It has been suggested, as is always done when pieces of a body are mysteriously found, that it is all a ghastly joke perpetrated by medical students. The medical student has a reputation for grim levity that causes him to be regarded as capable of anything. It would, however, be an almost impossible task for a student to secrete from a body in the dissecting room, such a number of organs as were found on Thursday (*September 20*). Then again, all the organs of every body that is opened are carefully dissected.

"In none of the organs have been detected so far any signs that would indicate the cause of death. The heart is flabby, and very thin-walled, but nothing can be argued from that. The exterior parts that were found in the parcels have about them nothing distinctive, and beyond the fact that the thick coating of fat below the skin shows the man to have been in good condition, nothing whatever is known about him. His age cannot even be guessed at, and if other parts of a body were found today in another suburb there would be nothing to surmise to connect them with the organs found. The murderer has thrown into the lagoon what are probably the most unidentifiable parts of a man's body.

"It is well known that a body which has not been disembowelled is most difficult to dispose of in water. It invariably bursts away from weights attached to it, and rises to the surface. To dispose of it effectually it must be disembowelled and the organs themselves, if they are to sink, must be opened. The murderer in this case seems to have been aware of these facts, and acted accordingly, for most of the organs have been cut so that they could not form reservoirs for gas.

"A crowd of several hundred persons assembled yesterday at the side of the lagoon, close to where the police were at work dragging. Some excitement was caused when it became known that a blood-stained seat had been discovered on the other side of the lagoon, immediately opposite the spot where the two parcels had been found.

"The seat is an ordinary hardwood plank about 6ft. long, set on two uprights. The stains were discovered by Mr John Bousie, of Cecil Street, Albert Park. Detective Burvell and Sergeant Williamson examined the seat. There were about 20 splodges of what was undoubtedly blood; but they had evidently fallen from a height of a foot or two, and it was plain they had been caused by a bleeding nose or a cut of some sort; besides, the blood looked not more than a day or two old. Had the bloodstains been connected with the tragedy they could have been caused only by the murderer resting on one of the parcels on the seat, and then the stains would have been extensive, and not have presented the appearance of fresh dropping blood.

"Nevertheless, Detective Burvett, who believes in leaving nothing to chance, obtained a chisel and chopped out several of the stains. The wood will be submitted to the Government Analyst (Mr Percy Wilkinson) for analysis. There were also on the seat a number of reddish hairs; but these are probably of some cow that has rubbed against the seat.

"Never a week passes but the police are notified that at least four or five men have disappeared from their homes. Warrants are taken out for some as wife or child deserters, and they are generally traced, and sometimes brought back. The rest are merely put down as 'missing friends', a formal notification appears in the *Police Gazette*, and in most cases that is the last that the police ever hear of the case.

"Often the man returns to his home, and proffers explanations of his absence that are accepted by the family. Either because these explanations might be laughed at by the police, or just from sheer remissness the man's return is seldom notified to he police, and the man remains on the list of missing friends till he drops out by effluxion of time.

"When a tragedy like the present one comes to light the keenest interest is naturally taken in the list of those missing. In the present case, several men have been reported as missing during the last month and, of course, there is a faint possibility that the murdered man is one of them. It is, however, impossible to effect anything by inquiries. Such men, if they are alive, have their reasons for remaining missing, and would no doubt welcome the chance of being set down as murdered. The missing men themselves will not therefore help by coming forward and proclaiming themselves. The only investigation work that could be done by the police therefore is to inquire as to the probability of any one of the missing men having been murdered.

"Such inquiries would, however, at the present juncture be altogether fruitless, for there is always the impossibility of identification to be remembered, At present the remains in the hands of the police cannot be identified as being part of any particular person. The police cannot even commence to build up a case until some additional parts of the body, such as the head or a leg or an arm, have been found.

"At the present time, the police know of five men who are missing, and general inquiries are being made about them. One of these men is Thomas McCulloch. He is a bricklayer's labourer, 29 years of age, of fair complexion and of medium build. One evening about a fortnight ago he left his home in Ross Street, Richmond, after telling his wife he would be back soon. He has not been heard of since, though his friends know of nothing that would cause him to stay away of his own accord. He was working, at the time of his disappearance, on a building in St Kilda Road.

"Yesterday, the police were told of the disappearance of another man named Macklin, who lived near the St Kilda railway line, not more than a mile from the end of the lagoon, where the parcels were found. He, too, is a fair man, and about 35 years of age."

The mystery captured the public's attention and *The Argus* followed up with another report the following Monday,

September 24. Alongside a report of how Carlton defeated Fitzroy in the 1906 VFL Grand Final, the newspaper ran the following under the headlines ALBERT PARK TRAGEDY, DRAGGING THE LAKE, MISSING MEN TRACED:

"Investigations are being steadily conducted into the tragedy which was brought to light last Thursday evening by the discovery of portions of the body of a man in the Albert Park lake. As the case stands at present, most of the attention of Detective Burvett is being confined to the dragging of the lake. No proper case can be built until some other portions of the body are found, and the first place in which the rest of the body must be sought is in the lake. Superintendent Sainsbury and Detective Burvett are both determined that the search of the lake shall be thorough, so that whatever result may be obtained it shall be definite.

"All day on Saturday the water police under Senior Constable McDonald were engaged in dragging operations. The puny drags with which they were working on Friday were discarded, and two big hay-rakes, about 4ft. wide, were used from two boats, while the third boat, directed by the senior-constable himself, used an ingenious contrivance, invented by the Detective Office and made in the Police Barracks. This is a piece of timber 8ft. long with a curved iron frame depending from it to a depth of about 2ft. The frame is covered with wire-netting, and its lower edge trails along the bottom of the lake, throwing into the curve of the netting any objects that may be lying there. A few old rags and tins were caught up in this manner, but nothing that could possibly be connected with the tragedy.

"Yesterday — especially in the afternoon — the dragging operations were watched by a large crowd of the curious. They followed the boats up and down the banks, and eagerly inspected the articles brought up by the dregs. These consisted of an old coat, a broken umbrella, a hat or two, and usual miscellaneous collection of tins and rubbish. Though the new methods of dragging are more effective than those first used, they are very unsatisfactory. It is not improbable that more definite results will be sought by the employment of a weighted fishing net several hundred feet long. It is hoped that in this way everything on the bottom will be picked up.

"Ever since the tragedy was first reported detectives have been at work tracing the whereabouts of men reported as missing. The murdered man was fair, so no notice has been taken of dark men or grey-haired men who are missing. With the exception of two, the missing men have been all accounted for, and their whereabouts ascertained. The two exceptions are William Macklin and Ernest Alfred Cutler.

"Macklin is 43 years of age, 5ft. 6in. in height, of thin build, slightly stooped, with a wrinkled, slightly weather-beaten face. He had fair hair and a fair moustache. Macklin for 16 years worked for Mr Elliott, the manager of Walla Walla Station, at Culcairn, in New South Wales. He came to Melbourne from Culcairn on *August 25* last. He obtained work as a driver for Messrs. Williams and Parker, of Regent Street, Prahran, and was to have taken a team and a wagon to Ballarat on *September 1*. At a quarter to six o'clock on the morning of that day he left his home in Fitzroy Street, St Kilda, to walk to Prahran and take charge of the team. He has never been heard of since. He did not go to his work, and another driver had to take his place.

"Mrs Macklin (he has a wife and three daughters)did not expect him back from Ballarat for a week, and until that time has elapsed, did not feel anxious. When the discovery at Albert Park was made the police were at once informed of his disappearance. Yesterday Detective Burvett saw Mrs Macklin and showed her the hair that was found on the remains. She stated that it was not at all like her husband's hair, and it is now thought that Macklin has quietly returned to Culcairn, probably tired of the city.

"It is also regarded as highly improbable for Ernest Alfred Cutler to be the murdered man. He is the author of his own mystery, since three days after he disappeared he was seen and spoken to at a football match in South Melbourne. The two men who saw him and the one who spoke to him have known him for 20 years and are certain that they have made no mistake. The police look on Cutler's disappearance as due probably to a temporary weakness of intellect. He was ill the day before he disappeared, and he had previously told a resident of Rowena Parade, Richmond, that he was going to Broken Hill. Unless more positive evidence is obtained, he cannot be connected with the tragedy.

"Chemical and microscopical examinations of the remains found in the lake will be made today, and on their result the future actions of the detectives in a great measure depend. In the meantime the chief efforts are being put out at the lagoon, where it is hoped the solution of the mystery will be obtained."

The mystery remains, despite every police effort and, more than a century later, almost certainly will never be solved.

SEPTEMBER 21

SENTENCED (1988): Sidney Justin Bowtell sentenced to life in 1989 (with a minimum of 21 years), for manslaughter, with Justice Mathews describing the case as one of the worst she had come across. Bowtell's offence occurred on *September 21*, 1988, when he was just 17 years of age. His victim was an 81-year-old woman who was throttled to death and had her jaw broken. He stole small change from her purse and dumped her naked body in an industrial waste bin. On appeal, Bowtell's sentence was reduced to 21 years, with a minimum term of 15 years.

SEPTEMBER 22

A GANGLAND MURDER (1933)

Well-known criminal James John, who lived in the inner Melbourne suburb of Collingwood, was a gambler and a stand-over man with few friends and many enemies. John, 24 years of age, had been at a gambling club in the city early on the morning of *September 22*, 1933, and decided to walk to his lodgings through the Exhibition Gardens. He was with a group of men, but two of them left John and another man, Jack Chrisfield, at the top of Nicholson Street.

John and Chrisfield kept walking through the dimly lit streets of grimy Fitzroy when they noticed a cream-coloured car about 100 yards behind them. The car appeared to be cruising behind them and, every time the two men stopped, the car also would stop. John and Chrisfield therefore decided to "lose" themselves in a narrow, tree-lined street which offered them plenty of cover in case there was trouble.

The two men therefore walked into Gore Street and watched in horror as they saw the car's headlight beams turn the corner in their direction. The car moved to within yards of the two men, but Chrisfield decided that discretion was the better part of valour and stepped aside. John was left alone as a man jumped out of the car from the front passenger seat and, with a handkerchief over his face, started firing at him. John had no chance of escape and was riddled with bullets, the gunman even pumping three bullets into John as he lay in the gutter. Chrisfield watched in horror as the gunman climbed back into the car and the driver sped away.

Police were called to the scene, but John was in a critical condition and died under examination at the Melbourne Hospital. Later, at the inquest into his death, government pathologist Dr C.H. Mollison said John had been shot five times. One bullet had pierced his right side and had passed through his chest and liver, another had passed through the middle of his back, the third had lodged in the middle of the back, the fourth had entered the left buttock and the fifth in the right buttock.

Chrisfield told coroner Mr Grant PM that he was unable to identify the gunman or the driver of the car. However, Chrisfield knew he had to be extremely careful about what information he gave to the police and coroner and, when asked at the inquest whether John had any enemies, he replied: "I do not know." Police already had a suspect, well-known criminal James Robert Walker, and Chrisfield was asked if Walker looked like the gunman. Chrisfield had no hesitation in replying "no".

The inquest was also told that salesman Henry Mitchell had made a statement alleging that Walker and a man named Bert Adams had approached him at the Mentone racecourse on *September 23* (the day after John's killing) and asked him if he would like to earn 100 pounds. He alleged in the statement that Walker asked him to get rid of a gun, but later recanted that statement. Walker also had an alibi and the coroner had no option but to declare that John's killer could not be identified.

Walker, one of the most infamous criminals of his era, was given a life sentence in 1953 for the shotgun death of a man in St Kilda and, just one year later, shot himself dead during an attempted escape from Pentridge. He left behind numerous notes, a chronicle of crime. In these notes he referred to John's killing and said he confronted the young gambler with "an ice-cold rod in my right hand". Police therefore were able to close the file on John's killing, even though they already knew Walker was the gunman in the cream-coloured car.

DEATH OF A GANGSTER (1974)

Jack Regan was one of Sydney's most notorious underworld identities for many years to his death in 1974 and was feared by many. He had been involved in robberies and other crimes from the time he was a young man and, in 1968, it was suggested he was involved in the shooting death of fellow underworld identity Barry Flock. He was also said to be implicated in the shooting death of SP bookmaker Jack Clark, making Regan an even bigger target for his rivals. Regan, born in 1945, started out as a pimp and graduated to the role of standover man and assaulting those who refused to do "business" with him.

When he left home on *September 22*, 1974, he had no idea he would never return. He was shot dead in Chapel Street, Marrackville. The coroner concluded that the Sydney gangster had died of gunshot wounds which had penetrated the chest, liver and head. The killer(s) was never apprehended, but few mourned the death of one of Sydney's most violent criminals.

THE GIRL IN WHITE (1969)

Beautiful Anne Zapelli was one of the most popular identities in the West Australian town of Morawa. Anne, 20, had a pleasant personality and was well-liked by all her neighbours in the quiet country town. In fact, the whole of Morawa had its fingers crossed that Anne would put the town right on the national map by winning the prestigious Miss Australia quest. Anne was due to appear in nearby Geraldton in late September, 1969, for the regional judging and, from all accounts, she had a good chance of going all the way in the quest. However, violence robbed Anne of her dreams – and her life.

Anne went to Geraldton on the Monday before the Miss Australia judging for an examination as part of her job as a telephonist. She was due to return to Morawa before going back to Geraldton for the judging. Anne booked into a guest house in Geraldton on Monday, *September 22*, with her thoughts entirely on the two big forthcoming events in her young life. Anne went to the local drive-in theatre that night with another telephonist and two young men, one of them a police constable. However, Anne said she was bored with the film and said she was going to walk back to the guest house.

Dressed in white, Anne set off on foot, the other three staying at the drive-in to watch the end of the movie. They did not see Anne alive again. Constable Graham Batt, one of the three with Anne at the drive-in, reported Anne missing early in the morning when he and his friends were surprised to find no trace of her at the guest house. Anne had vanished and a search was launched. Her body was found the following day in brush and scrub 50 yards from a roadway. She had been battered, raped and strangled.

A number of witnesses told police they had seen a girl dressed in a white mini-dress walking from the drive-in that night and some even told police they had seen a suspicious man, or men, in the vicinity. One witness even told police that a light coloured car pulled up near the girl in white. However, no witnesses could be explicit enough and police ran into a dead-end in their investigation. Anne, whose rape and murder shocked Geraldton, was the victim on an unknown killer or killers. Police, who found scuffle marks near the body, reasoned Anne had put up a struggle but was strangled with a rope or cord for her efforts. The murder weapon was missing and, strangely, so too were Anne's pants and pantyhose.

Police tried everything in an effort to bring the killer(s) to justice but all efforts failed. A reconstruction by an ABC television outfit, with a policewoman playing the part of Anne Zapelli, also failed to lead to the killer(s). An inquest was held in 2001, more than 30 years after Anne's death and, for the first time, a possible killer was named. However, with most of the forensic evidence lost or destroyed, WA coroner, Mr Alastair Hope, was unable to make a conclusive finding.

SEPTEMBER 23

THE WEDDING ROW (1957)

The quiet city of Adelaide was shocked on *September 23*, 1957, when the three members of a Greek family were shot dead in their own home. The Greek community was outraged when one of their own community members was later charged with murder. They felt that the killings had brought shame on them. Dead were Mr Tom Galantomos, his wife Anna and daughter Ploheria (Ritsa). A 24-year-old Greek, Stalianos Athanaisidis, was charged with the murders. The Galantomos killings created enormous interest in Adelaide, with a Romeo and Juliet drama unfolded in the courts.

Stalianos Athanaisidis had migrated to Australia from the Greek island of Rhodes three years earlier and worked in Adelaide as an electrician. The Galantomos family also had come from Rhodes and Athanaisidis started courting 17-year-old Ritsa and then asked for her hand in marriage. The Galantomos' agreed and everyone seemed more than happy. In a 14-page statement to police, which Athanaisidis titled "The First Step to the Wedding", he wrote of everyone's joy and how everything seemed perfect for the wedding.

The couple was married in a registry office on *April 27*, 1957, and in the eyes of the law they were man and wife. However, they did not live as man and wife because they were awaiting the Greek religious ceremony. Meanwhile, the Galantomos family bought their new son-in-law a Ford Mainline car valued at 2000 pounds, but he later was upset when he discovered it had been bought on hire purchase, with 1800 pounds owing. From then, according to his statement, "things automatically changed". He also was convinced Mr and Mrs Galantomos were planning to take their daughter back to Greece to be married to a young doctor.

Athanaisidis snapped, killed Mr and Mrs Galaltomos and then, according to his statement, made a suicide pact with his beloved Ritsa. He pumped 11 bullets into her and then shot himself. Although he had mortally wounded Ritsa, he was rushed to Royal Adelaide Hospital and survived. Athanaisidis was tried twice, being found guilty of murder both times. He was sentenced to death at his first trial, but an appeal to the High Court resulted in a new trial. He again was found guilty and again sentenced to death, which later was commuted to life imprisonment.

SEPTEMBER 24

KNIFED FOR NO REASON (2003)

Hani Ghaleb Jaber was walking with two friends, Hassain Hussain and Alexandra Berry, on the south bank of Melbourne's Yarra River towards the Crown Casino on the night of *September 24*, 2003, when they were approached by another group. The initial contact between the two groups seemed amiable but, when Hussain was asked if he wanted to have a knife fight, Jaber suggested he and his friends continue their walk.

The three friends, to avoid further confrontation, walked across a footbridge, but were followed by the other three, Bollus Angelo Athuai, William Angok and Birag Kuat. Athuai approached Jaber and started wrestling him. Much taller and stronger than Jaber, Athuai was unable to restrain the young man he had attacked and pulled out a knife.

Athaui stabbed the 17-year-old Jaber, who fell to the ground wounded. Athaui then lent over his victim and stabbed him three more times before leaving the scene. Incredibly, Athaui smiled as he turned to look at what he had done. Jaber had three wounds to the left side of his face and had two stab wounds to the upper part of his back, with one of these gashes piercing the aorta. Another stab wound had penetrated Jaber's heart.

Justice Kaye, at the 17-year-old Athaui's trial, told him: "Your attack on the deceased man was particularly cowardly.

You had a superior advantage in height and reach. Both you and Angok were larger and stronger than the deceased man. You used a weapon. Your victim was unarmed. You used that weapon with the maximum of surprise and ferocity, depriving your victim of an opportunity at all to defend himself. It is not surprising that the pathologist did not find one single defensive wound on the body of the deceased man. He did not get any opportunity to raise his hands in self-defence, let alone strike out at you …

" … Your brazen and totally unjustified attack on the deceased man and his two companions going about their lawful business was utterly unacceptable. Your use of a knife was a contravention of a basic standard and value of our society. You took the life of an innocent and decent young man. Your conduct violated the most fundamental norm of civilised behaviour."

Athaui was born in Sudan but he and his family were forced to flee because of civil war and arrived in Australia in 1997. The family originally lived in Queensland and moved to Melbourne in 2003. At the time of the stabbing, Athaui already was on bail on two charges of occasioning actual bodily harm and, a month later, was arrested again and charged with armed robbery, with an allegation that he had used a knife.

In sentencing Athaui to 22 years' imprisonment, with a minimum period of 17 years, Justice Kaye said: "The murder by you of Hani Jaber was committed in circumstances which were particularly callous. Your demeanour during the killing, the defenceless nature of the victim, the savagery of the blows inflicted by you, and tne entire lack of reason for you to attack him cause me to have some reservations in evaluating your prospects of rehabilitation."

SEPTEMBER 25

HANGED (1883): Robert Francis Burns hanged at Ararat on *September 25*, 1883, for the murder of Michael Quinlivan at Wickliffe in July of that year.

SEPTEMBER 26

TAKING THE RAP? (1923)

Bank clerk Thomas Berriman was carrying almost 2000 pounds in notes in the Melbourne suburb of Hawthorn in October, 1923, when was confronted by two men. When Berriman refused to hand over the money he was carrying, he was shot dead. Career criminal Angus Murray was arrested and charged with Berriman's murder but the other man, Richard Buckley, managed to avoid custody for more than seven years. There were some who believed that Murray might have taken the rap for the notorious Leslie "Squizzy" Taylor or, a least, Taylor had planned the robbery. Regardless, Murray was found guilty of the murder of Berriman and was sentenced to death.

If Taylor had been directly or indirectly involved, Murray did not let on, not even in the final minutes before his execution at the Melbourne Gaol on *April 14*, 1924. The *Sun News-Pictorial* reported: "He (Murray) might have gone on to revile his misfortune or to blame a confederate. He did not. He turned to his executioners as they fastened the noose around him: 'Pull it tight,' he said. This was his second remark to them. In his cell, when he first met the masked faces that, by their appearance before him, conveyed to him the final hopelessness of reprieve, he made to them his last request in life – 'make it quick, friends'. Perhaps they were. Murray's death was as instantaneous at their hands as the switching on of an electric light."

The newspaper reported that 1000 people knelt in prayer outside Melbourne Gaol in the lead-up to Murray's execution. Then, as the crowd waited for the "clang of prison bell" to announce Murray's death, they knelt and recited the Lord's Prayer. An inquest into Murray's death was held immediately and, with unintentional black humour, it concluded that he did not suffer from brain disease. Buckley, meanwhile, eventually was apprehended by police and convicted for his part in the fatal hold-up. He was sentenced to life imprisonment, but was released after just 15 years. "Squizzy" Taylor and another underworld identity in "Snowy" Cutmore killed each other in a gunfight in the inner Melbourne suburb of Carlton in 1927.

Murray was the last man hanged at the Melbourne Gaol and executions in Melbourne then took place at Pentridge. However, the first man executed at Pentridge was not a murderer, but a sex offender. David Bennett had been convicted of criminal assault on a four-year-old girl and was executed on *September 26*, 1932. Bennett proclaimed his innocence to the last and his final word was "goodbye". The other 200 prisoners at Pentridge had to wait in their cells until Bennett's body was been cut down from the gallows.

SEPTEMBER 27

SET ALIGHT (2000)

Although Claude Monks had been living with his de facto wife Viola Kelin at the Victorian town of Kyabram for a number of years, he became increasingly disenchanted with the relationship. The couple had a son, seven-year-old Grant, while Monks had an adult son and Klein a son, Ashleigh. Monks complained that Klein did not feed Grant well enough and also told her he believed his step-son treated Grant roughly.

Monks, 58 years of age, eventually assaulted Ashleigh on *February 21*, 2000, and Mrs Klein, 48, obtained an intervention order against her de facto husband. Monks therefore left the family home and went to live elsewhere in the fruit town of Kyabram. It was then that Monks started describing Klein to friends as "a slut". He also intimated that he was going to kill her with one friend telling him: "You're mad, that's rubbish. You'll go to jail for that."

Then, on *September 27*, 2000, Monks asked Klein and Grant to help him clean up a caravan. They agreed but, when they got to Monks' house, he told Grant to stay in the lounge room. After about 10 minutes, little Grant heard screaming, just before Monks ran through the back door with superficial burns to the face, hands and the left leg. Monks had set the caravan alight with petrol and a cigarette lighter.

Mrs Klein took the full fury of the fire and was engulfed by flames, with burns to all parts of her body except the right foot. She screamed: "Help me, please, help me. I'm burning. God's punishing me. I don't want to die. I've got to live for my kids." She eventually lapsed into unconsciousness and was rushed to Kyabram Hospital, where she died of her burns. Monks, who was treated for his burns, said at the hospital that Klein had been in the caravan when a can of petrol had been knocked over while he had lit a cigarette and there then was an explosion.

However, a jury found Monks guilty of murder and Justice Coldrey, in the Supreme Court of Victoria, told him that his insistence that Klein's death was an accident "deprives you of the benefit of any remorse". He said: "On any reasonable view of the evidence, the offence was premeditated. It involved not only the dispersion of petrol *throughout* the caravan but the luring of Mrs Klein to come to your house and to enter the van. Having caused her to be engulfed by flames, you left her there to suffer in agony until, perhaps mercifully, the depth of her burns destroyed the nerve endings beneath the skin." He sentenced Monks to 20 years' imprisonment, with a minimum period of 15 years.

SEPTEMBER 28

KILLED (1917): Euginia Falleni, who lived as a man, killed her "wife" Annie Birkett in Sydney on *September 28*, 1917.

SEPTEMBER 29

A KILLER OF BOYS (1984)

On Saturday, *September 29*, 1984, 12-year-old Mark Mott and 11-year-old Ralph Burns disappeared from the Griffths (NSW) Showgounds. Mott's body was found almost 12 months later at Lake Wyangan, while Burns' skeletal remains were found in the bush three months later. Then, on *June 21*, 1986, eight-year-old John Purtell was reported missing after a football match at Griffith. This time, however, a man had been seen loitering near the change rooms and a photokit portrait showed a likeness to convicted paedophile Michael George Laurance. Police interviewed the 36-year-old and he eventually confessed to killing the three boys. He said he drowned Mott and Burns in a bath and throttled Purtell. At his trail, Laurance pleaded not guilty on the grounds of diminished mental repsonsibility, but was convicted and sentenced to life imprisonment, with a recommendation that he never be released. Laurance hanged himself at Lithgow jail on *November 16*, 1995.

SEPTEMBER 30

A BONZER KID (1948)

Charles Louis Havelock le Gallion, 52, ran a successful motor engineering business in the Sydney suburb of Crow's Nest. A big, burly man, Charles le Gallion was separated from his wife and family of four sons, but the successful engineer still paid his family's living expenses, even the grocery bills. The youngest of le Gallion's four sons, 17-year-old Charles believed his father should have been providing more money and went to see him about this on the night of *September 30*, 1948.

Young Charles told his father: "Mum is sick and you should provide for her." However, his father replied: "Mind your own business. I'm after a divorce." He then indicated that he had made a will and would leave everything to le Gallion's typist, Betty de Groen.

Police discovered le Gallion's body later that night after Miss de Groen had tried to telephone him. The engineering wizard had been stabbed and was slumped against a table in the office. The post mortem revealed that he had been drinking before he had been killed and that death was caused by a wound on the left side of the chest which had penetrated the chest wall and into the front of the heart. Police arrested young Charles on *October 4* and the 17-year-old was committed for trial. He pleaded not guilty at the Central Criminal Court although he admitted visiting to ask about household payments. However, he said his father had grabbed him by the throat and that his father was stabbed in a scuffle. The boy said his wounded father told him to go home and not to worry about a doctor. Young Charles then broke down when shown the pen knife that killed his father.

The jury deliberated for 105 minutes before handing down its verdict – guilty. Mrs Heather le Gallion gasped at the announcement and later described her son to newspaper reporters as "a bonzer kid". The "bonzer kid" was sentenced to life imprisonment, but was released in August, 1960. However, the le Gallion tragedy did not end there as Mrs Heather le Gallion died in a blaze at a Melbourne milk bar she had bought just two weeks before her death on *July 30, 1965*.

OCTOBER

Australia might bask in the warming sun of October and delight in the new spring foliage, but it also has been shocked by any amount of horrific crimes in this otherwise gentle month of green and dappled sunlight. From bushranger times to modern acts of violence, October has seen more than its share of bloodshed, lust and theft. Crimes this month include:

THE HOUSE OF HORRORS

THE FARADAY KIDNAPPING

THE ACID WOMAN

THE GENTLEMAN BUSHRANGER

THE RICHMOND BORGIA

DUMPED IN THE BUSH

And, much, much more!

OCTOBER 1

THE WRONG BODY (1933)

William Griffenhagen was a quiet young man who desperately wanted to get married to his sweetheart and settle down at his bush allotment a few miles from the old Victorian mining city of Bendigo. He lived in a hut on the property with his uncle, James Pattison, a well-known local prospector. Griffenhagen, 26, spent most of his time clearing the land of scrub. Pattison, 68, was a dedicated fossicker who lived in the hope he one day would come across a nugget as big as his fist.

Both men were seen on Sunday, *October 1*, 1933, and Griffenhagen's friends became worried when they had not seen him for several days after that date. Police were informed and two constables went to Griffenhagen's hut, only to find it had been severely damaged by fire. Inside, the constables found a huge pile of ashes in the centre of the log and mud hut. There, under the charred and fallen corrugated iron roof, they found a body. But was it that of Griffenhagen or that of his uncle?

The local police informed the CID and Detective Bill Sloan took charge of the investigation. His first task was to sift the ashes for clues to enable him to identify the body. Police found a pair of badly damaged spectacles, a ring, a watch, a rabbit trap and several misshapen household items. The ring was an obvious clue and several people identified as belonging to the old man. The spectacles, however, puzzled police and locals. Neither Griffenhagen nor his uncle wore glasses. Besides, the old man had only one eye. It therefore was impossible to identify the body as it had been reduced to a blackened skeleton. The discovery of the ring therefore assumed critical importance and, because of its identification as Pattison's, police assumed that the body found in the ashes was that of the old man.

Pattison was buried with all due ceremony, but locals questioned the identification. This prompted Detective Sloan to investigate further, especially as there was no sign of Griffenhagen. Had he, too, been murdered? If so, where was his body? Was robbery the motive? Had the old man found a nugget and had Griffenhagen murdered him for financial gain? Or had someone murdered them both? There were many, many questions to be answered, but police first had to positively identify the body.

Detective Sloan made further inquiries and police and 50 volunteers scoured the surrounding countryside and re-sifted the ashes. Their efforts were rewarded with the further clues, including the metal buckle from a belt worn by Griffenhagen and three brass caps from shotgun cartridges. Police now were convinced there had been a case of mistaken identity, especially when they learned Griffenhagen did, in fact, wear glasses but had tried to keep this a secret. Finally, Pattison wore false teeth and none had been found in the ashes.

Then, on *November 9*, Axedale bee-keeper Fred Bennett discovered a man's body in scrub along the banks of the Mosquito River, a few miles from Griffenhagen's hut. The body was identified as that of Pattison. It was badly decomposed, but the thumb and forefinger of the right hand were missing and Pattison lost these digits in an accident many years ago. A suicide note revealed that he had shot himself. But why? Had he killed his nephew in a rage? Pattison, in his suicide note, made no mention of his nephew.

That might have been the end of the "Wrong Body" case if it had not been for a strange confession several months later by a young man who claimed to be Griffenhagen. The young man walked into the Swan Hill police station and told the wife of a senior constable that he was "wanted for murder". She tried to detain him but he rushed out of the police station and said: "I cannot wait any longer; I have to do myself in."

The man claiming to be Griffenhagen went straight to the flooded Murray River, boarded a motor launch and jumped into the river mid-stream. He drowned but police discounted the possibility that the young man was Griffenhagen as there was a big difference in height and build. Griffenhagen almost certainly was shot by his uncle, who then turned his nephew's hut into a funeral pyre. But why? And who was the mysterious young man who drowned himself in the Murray River? These mysteries are unlikely ever to be solved.

OCTOBER 2

THE MAD DENTIST (1865)

On the evening of *October 2*, 1865, Sydney dentist Louis Bertrand was at the home of wife Jane's lover Henry Kinder. Some time during the night, Kinder collapsed, shot in the head. It was at first thought that bank teller Kinder had shot himself, but the gunshot wound did not kill him. In fact, he seemed to make a complete recovery, even sitting up in bed and smoking a pipe. However, he died on *October 6*, and the verdict at a subsequent inquest was "suicide while emotionally insane". Bertrand, who was known as "the mad dentist of Wynyard Square" because of irrational behaviour, became involved in a blackmail scandal over Kinder's death eventually went on trial for murder. He was tried in February, 1866, but the jury failed to reach a verdict as there was no evidence whether Kinder had died of his gunshot wound or of poison. Bertrand was tried a second time, found guilty and sentenced to death. He appealed successfully and his sentence was commuted to one of life imprisonment. Bertrand was released after serving 28 years.

OCTOBER 3

THE MUTILATION KILLER (1998)

Nurse Stacey Anne Rhodes took a telephone call from friend Martin James Giles just after 10 o'clock on *October 2*, 1998. Giles, who had been drinking for several hours, asked if he could get a lift from the Diggers Rest rail station on Melbourne's north-western outskirts. The 20-year-old Rhodes agreed to meet Giles, whom she had known for two years, and after picking him up she drove to a bypass on the Bulla-Diggers Rest Road. They intended to smoke marijuana before she drove him home. Then, when she tried to drive off, the car would not start because of a faulty battery. An argument developed and Giles later walked from the car and made his way home alone. A passing divisional van from the Sunbury Police Station took note of the parked car at about 6.20am the following day, *October 3*, and police officers went to investigate. It was then that they found Rhodes' mutilated body.

The young woman had been strangled with a draw-string from a windcheater, her stomach had been slashed and there were other horrific mutilations. Police tracked down Rhodes' address through motor registration details and Rhodes' mother then told them that her daughter had taken a call from Giles the previous evening. They therefore made their way to Giles' home, but saw him walking down a street. Giles at first denied he had seen Rhodes the previous evening but, when taken to Homicide Squad headquarters, admitted much of what happened to the young woman. However, he denied slashing her stomach or mutilating her body.

He eventually pleaded guilty to the murder and rape of Rhodes and Justice Cummins, in the Supreme Court of Victoria, told him before sentencing: "These were wicked crimes. The fact that your victim was unconscious during the infliction of the rapes upon her does not, and cannot, constitute any diminution of the objective gravity of the offence of rape. The more so as her state of unconsciousness was directly brought about by a grievous — and soon fatal — attack by you upon her." He sentenced Giles to a total jail term of 26 years, with a non-parole period of 21 years.

THE HOUSE OF HORRORS (1978)

Mick Lewis was what was known in rural Australia as a "gun shearer". In fact, he was so good at his job that his workmates nicknamed him "Tricky Mickey" and he often sheared more than 200 sheep a day. Mick worked hard, and played hard. He had a big thirst and loved a gamble. In fact, it was said that if he had a good win on the horses he sometimes would have his pockets stuffed with notes. Lewis, 25, was married to a typical country girl, Sue Lewis, a 27-year-old who had a much quieter personality and was devoted to their two children, five-year-old Tania and three-year-old Michael. In October, 1978, the Lewis family was living near the southern New South Wales town of Jerilderie, in an old homestead picturesquely named "Summerfield". It was a typical

Australian country homestead, with a high-pitched corrugated iron roof and a surround verandah. Early in its days it must have been something of a mansion; in 1978 it became a house of horrors.

On the morning of Tuesday, *October 3*, 1978, telephonist Mrs Nola Evans was asked if she could check the Lewis telephone line at "Summerfield". A switchboard operator in the nearby town of Hay had been trying to connect a call, but a little girl kept answering the telephone. Mrs Evans rang the number and a sad little voice told her that her "mummy and daddy were asleep". Mrs Evans called the Jerilderie police and talked to the girl until they arrived at the homestead.

The police officers, Sergeant Paul Payne and Senior Constable Ken Waterhouse, walked straight into a ghastly scene – they found Lewis dead in the kitchen, his head in a pool of blood. The police officers moved further into the house and turned their noses up at a foul odour from the main bedroom. They walked in and discovered Sue Lewis' decomposing and maggot-infested body in a double bed. The Lewis children, grubby but unharmed, had been caring for themselves in the house where their parents had been killed and left to rot.

Police at first believed Lewis had been bashed around the head, although they were convinced his wife had been shot in the head. They found a spent .22 cartridge in the bedroom, where her body was found, but had not found any bullet wound to her husband's head. They also were puzzled by the different condition of the bodies. Lewis' body showed little sign of decomposition, yet his wife's body was in a terrible state of putrefaction. It finally was realised that Mrs Lewis' electric blanket was turned on the "high" position and this explained the state of her body.

There seemed little doubt the Lewis couple had been executed, but what had been the motive? Police at first thought that Lewis might have had a successful punting spree and robbed. However, this theory was quickly discounted as the murders appeared to have been extremely well planned. Careful examination of the house of horrors turned up the first clue – a small tear in a flywire door to the kitchen. It was precisely the same size as a .22 bullet hole and a post-mortem examination of Lewis' body showed that he died of a single gunshot wound to the head, behind the right ear. Mrs Lewis had been shot twice in the head.

Forensic tests on the .22 calibre cartridge and a bullet taken from Lewis' skull revealed that the murder weapon was an Australian-made Fieldman rifle. This information proved vital, as the Melbourne manufacturer was able to narrow it down to a batch of 750. Police also pricked their ears at local gossip which suggested that Lewis had been planning to "write off" his car so that he could collect $5000 in insurance money. This information also proved vital and another link in the chain of evidence was forged when police questioned people in Lewis' telephone contact book. One of those listed was a Shepparton painting contractor and part-time insurance representative, John Fairley, who had previously arranged motor insurance for Lewis. When police discovered that one of Fairley's friends had lent him a .22 Fieldman rifle to "shoot a couple of bunnies", they were convinced they were close to solving the gruesome double murder. Fairley's friend, Raymond Rafferty, told police the part-time insurance agent had borrowed the rifle only days before the Lewis couple was shot dead.

Fairly, 40, pleaded guilty at the Central Criminal Court before Justice Yeldham and Detective Sergeant Donald

Worsley told the court that Lewis had paid Fairley $295 as part-payment on a premium for his car. However, Fairley had kept the money and Lewis' car therefore was not insured. Lewis expected an insurance payout and Fairley decided that the only solution was to kill Lewis and his wife. He borrowed the rifle and shot Lewis dead before walking through the old homestead to kill Sue Lewis. Fairley, who had never previously been in trouble with the law, was sentenced to two terms of life imprisonment. Worsley, who headed the team, later was presented with a special prize for the most outstanding phase of police duty of 1978.

OCTOBER 4

HANGED (1853): Bushrangers George Wilson and William Atkins hanged in Melbourne on *October 4*, 1853. They had been involved in a robbery with violence at Avoca, pistol-whipping one of the passengers. They headed into the bush but were traced to their hideway by blacktrackers. They were responsible for a number of crimes in the area.

OCTOBER 5

THE FARADY KIDNAPPING (1972)

Australians were horrified on *October 6*, 1972, when news hit the airwaves that six primary school children and their teacher were being held for ransom after being abducted from a tiny old school at Faraday, about 100 kilometres from Melbourne. Two men, one carrying a sawn-off shotgun, the previous day

— *October 5* — barged into the schoolroom and ordered teacher Mary Gibbs and her pupils into a van waiting outside the school. No one heard anything from the two men and, when parents went to collect their children from 3.30pm there was no one there to greet them. Police were informed and soon discovered a note inside a desk. It told of a $1 million ransom and warned of the "annihilation" of the abducted teacher and children.

The note was so threatening that Victorian Education Minister Lindsay Thompson said his government would meet the ransom demand as long as no one in the abducted group would be harmed. He even told the kidnappers that he personally would take responsibility and act as their contact. Thompson then was told to take the money to the Woodend Post Office at 5am on *October 7* but, after doing this, there was no one there. Meanwhile, the 20-year-old Miss Gibbs kicked out a panel in the van and led the children to a bush trail where they came across a shooting party. At last, they were safe.

Police then launched a massive hunt for the kidnappers and, on *October 10*, arrested Edwin Eastwood and Robert Boland. Eastwood was sentenced to 16 years' jail, and Boland 15 years. However, the kidnapping drama did not end there as Eastwood escaped from prison and, on *February 14*, 1977, walked with gun in hand into the Wooreen Primary School in Gippsland and abducted a teacher and nine children. It was a carbon copy of the Faraday kidnapping, even to the extent that he bundled teacher Robert Hunter and the children into a van. Then, when the van crashed into a truck, the gun-wielding Eastwood forced the two men from the truck into the van. Later, Eastwood flagged down a bigger van and forced two women into the back before transferring his nine hostages in with them. The group spent the night in bushland before truck driver Robin Smith managed to escape and raise the alarm. Eastwood was recaptured following a gun battle and, again, his hostages set free without physical harm. Thompson later became Victoria's Premier and retired in 1982.

OCTOBER 6

THE ACID WOMAN (1909)

When Martha Rendell moved in to live with Thomas Morris in 1906, she inherited a young family. However, the presence of step-children Anne, Olive, Arthur and George sparked feelings of jealousy as her new husband showered his children with affection. Anne, Olive and Arthur Morris died in suspicious circumstances, but Rendell was charged only with the death of Arthur. It was alleged she had swabbed his throat with hydrochloric acid after he had complained of a sore throat. Morris also was charged with the boy's murder, but was found not guilty.

Rendell was found guilty in the Supreme Court of Western Australia and this sparked enormous controversy as many wanted her to hang while others argued it would be wrong to hang a woman. Besides, there were serious doubts about her guilt and there were moves to have the heavily-set Rendell's sentence commuted to one of imprisonment. However, these arguments fell on deaf ears and Rendell was hanged at Fremantle Gaol on the morning of *October 6*, 1909.

OCTOBER 7

THE TRUCK CARNAGE (1985)

Truck driver Douglas John Edwin Crabbe was drinking in the Inland Hotel in Yulara, the Northern Territory, on *August 18*, 1983, when he was refused service. The bar staff believed he was intoxicated and was ejected from the hotel soon after midnight. Then, according to witness Martin Fisher: "Crabbe then manouevered the 25-ton semi and trailer, at speed, around a blind bend, through a car park, around a mini-bus, turned and drove it through the bessa brick wall into the crowded bar, crushing the people there. Leaving the engine running, he then got out of the truck, smiled down at one of his victims, stepped over some bodies and ran. This was at 1.10am. It had been 40 minutes between being thrown out and driving the truck into the bar."

Crabbe ran into the bush, but soon was captured and charged with murder. He had killed five people and seriously injured another 16. His trial was held in March, 1984 but, after being found guilty of murder, he successfully appealed to the High Court of Australia, which ordered another trial. The jury in the second trial, which opened on *October 7*, 1985, also returned a guilty verdict and Crabbe was sentenced to life imprisonment.

OCTOBER 8

THE BODY IN THE BOOT (2000)

Married couple Patrick and Mary Joiner went to the wedding of Mrs Joiner's cousin at the Greek Orthodox Church in Redfern, an inner Sydney suburb, on *October 8*, 2000, even though they were having counselling over marital problems. They went for a drink at the Brighton RSL before the wedding reception and had another argument. Mrs Joiner stormed out and was not seen alive again.

Patrick Joiner later claimed he caught up with his wife and the couple drove south from Sydney, only for the argument to flare again. He said he accidentally struck Mary to the side of the face and, after she screamed, punched her. However, he claimed, she then had spasms and fell to the ground. Joiner said he was unable to revive her and put her in the boot of the car he was driving, a VW Golf. He also claimed he ran out of petrol and had to call the NRMA for assistance before driving to Redfern and then walking to the church where the wedding had taken place earlier in the day before returning home.

Mrs Joiner was reported as missing and Joiner even went on national television with pleas for his wife to return or let authorities know where she could be located. Indeed, he played the upset husband for what it was worth before police on *October 26* opened the boot of the VF Golf left in Redfern. Inside, they found the badly decomposed body of Mrs Joiner, who had been severely assaulted. A post mortem revealed she had a deep laceration to her upper lip, extensive bruising around her jaw, a cut above the right eye and severe tears to the scalp as if she had been kicked or hit with a heavy object like a rock.

However, Joiner was the major suspect when police not only learned of his violent behaviour towards his wife, but also that he had called the NRMA for assistance when the VF Golf found in Redfern earlier had run out of fuel. Then, amazingly, Joiner suggested his wife might have died as a result of an epileptic fit or blackout. He was found guilty of murder and sentenced to 18 years' jail, with a non-parole period of 13 years and six months.

OCTOBER 9

ESCAPE (1959): Kevin Simmonds and Leslie Newcombe escaped from Long Bay, NSW, on *October 9*, 1959, and a massive manhunt was launched.

OCTOBER 10

THE 'HIDEOUS KILLING' (1985)

Sydney teenager David Jack Glen had recently been introduced to his 10-year-old cousin Kylie Corbett on *October 10*, 1985, when the little girl left home to go to school. She was carrying a bag of old clothes she had collected for a charity drive at school when she came across 19-year-old Glen, who invited her into his flat on the pretext that he had some clothes for her. When Glen lured little Kylie into his bedroom he grabbed her by the neck and threatened her with a knife. He pushed her onto a bed, removed her clothes and inserted a finger in her vagina before tying her up with rope. Glen then left her on the bed while we went shopping and playing pinball machines in Parramatta. Then, when he returned, he continued his disgusting attack on the defenceless girl.

Glen took the girl to have a shower to wash her vagina and then allowed her to read her school books before he produced a baton and pushed it under her chin so violently that she choked into unconsciousness. Finally, Glen tied a cotton belt around her neck and hanged her from a bar in his wardrobe before leaving the flat. A search was mounted for the little girl and police found her body in Jack's wardrobe the following day.

A post-mortem revealed horrific injuries, apart from the marks around her neck. Her vaginal walls were lacerated and part of her anal passage was torn and gaping. Death was caused by asphyxia due to hanging and shock, and Glen was arrested almost immediately. When asked whether he intended to kill Kylie with the baton he replied: "No, I did not intend to kill her with the baton. I was going to kill her with a knife, but I couldn't get the courage up to stab her, so I then took the baton and choked her."

At his trial in December, 1985, Glen pleaded not guilty of murder, but guilty of manslaughter. This plea was rejected and Glen, who did not give evidence, made an unsworn statement in which he said: "Ladies and gentlemen of the jury, I am not guilty of murder. I am sorry about what has happened. As I said in my record of interview, I wish this hadn't happened at all.

"When I asked Kylie around to my flat I didn't have any intentions to hurt her. I just wanted to give my wife's maternity clothes to her because my wife left me 12 days before and I thought I wouldn't see her or my daughter again. I don't know why I sexually harassed Kylie. I didn't plan for that to happen. After I did that, I didn't know what to do; that's why I tied her up. I didn't want to hurt Kylie in any way, even though I said 'if you scream or cry, I'll kill you'. I had a knife, but I didn't use it to hurt her, but just to cut the rope when she said it was too tight. I didn't put any part of my body or anything into her anus. When I put the baton on her neck I didn't want to kill her or hurt her badly. In fact, I don't know why I did that at the time and I don't know now.

"When I put Kylie in the wardrobe, I tied the cotton belt around her neck to stop her falling off the chair as she was unconscious at that time. I didn't do that to hurt her, to kill her. I didn't think it would cause any more harm. All I can say is that I'm truly sorry for what I have done. I mean that, but I have done what I have done and there is nothing I can say, but to say that I am sorry and I don't know how it happened. Thank you."

Justice Wood described the killing as "hideous" and the "worst case of murder" over which he had presided. Glen, who had a disturbed childhood and entries for offences ranging from burglary to malicious injuring, had been unemployed since he was 16 years of age and was an occasional user of alcohol, cannabis and LSD. He was sentenced to life imprisonment.

OCTOBER 11

THE DEATH WALK (1964)

Sunday, *October 11*, 1964, had been a quiet, pleasant day for the Ganino family in the northern Melbourne suburb of Fawkner. It had been like many Sundays, spent in quiet relaxation and family activities. Dominic Ganino, 15, had spent the morning at Mass and Communion, then spending the afternoon looking for bits and pieces of motor cars at a nearby rubbish tip. He returned home in time for an early dinner and washed up the dishes for his mother.

Dominic, a student at Fawkner Technical School, did not feel like watching television with his brother and sister after dinner but elected to take his dog Lassie for a walk. It was still a pleasant spring day and Dominic could not have known that his day would end in death. He stepped into Sydney Road, immediately outside his home, without a worry in the world. Dominic did not return from his walk and his parents became worried almost immediately. It was unlike Dominic to stay away for long without telling his parents. When it became obvious he was not with friends or relatives, the family contacted police.

A description of Dominic was flashed to police patrols soon after 10pm and Dominic Ganino officially became a missing person. What now particularly worried Dominic's family and police was that the boy's dog had returned home by herself soon after 7pm An intensive police search the next day failed to find any trace of the missing boy.

Two weeks later, on Monday, *October 26*, a security officer at the Ford motor works (six kilometres from the Ganino house) was searching swamp country behind the works. He was looking for hollow logs, and eventually spotted what he might have been after. However, Mr Alexander McCann also discovered the body of Dominic Ganino under a tree trunk. The face was immersed in about ten inches (16cm) of water and the boy's clothing was disarranged. Dominic had been murdered and police immediately launched a massive investigation. Forensic examination later showed that

Dominic had died of asphyxiation due to strangling. However, the post mortem also showed that that boy had been homosexually raped. Dominic obviously had struggled with his attacker but because the body was not discovered until two weeks after his disappearance, the trail to the killer was cold.

Police had few clues. There were footprints and car tracks near where the body had been found but they were too old to be of much use. A blue comb was also found near the body, but this proved to be a negative clue. Police decided that the public had to help in inquiries and thousands of people in the Fawkner and Broadmeadows area were questioned and interviewed. In fact, police launched a doorknock campaign, speaking to everyone in the neighborhood. Residents were asked if they had seen the boy on the night he was murdered. Dominic had been wearing dark jeans, a check shirt and a grey school pullover. He was just 5 ft 3 in (160cm), was slightly built and dark.

Several sightings were given, the most useful being by a 14-year-old neighbour, who told police that he had seen Dominic in Sydney Road but on the opposite side of his home, Dominic obviously crossing busy Sydney Road. It seemed that the whole Italian community of Melbourne mourned the death of Dominic Ganino. His funeral, on *November 5*, was a mass display of grief, with hundreds of schoolmates, friends, relatives and sympathizers moving from St Matthew's Church, North Fawkner, to the Fawkner Cemetery. Dominic's killer was still free. Police continued their investigations, convinced that someone had abducted the boy and driven him to the lonely swamp country at the back of Ford's. One theory was that the killer offered to give Dominic driving lessons 'away from the traffic'. The boy was interested in cars and desperately wanted to learn to drive.

Although police never arrested anyone over Dominic's killing, it has been alleged that a notorious paedophile Catholic church worker might have been implicated. Robert Charles Blunden, known as 'Bert', was living at the St Matthew's presbytery at the time of Dominic's death and is known to have been abusing children and young men. Police interviewed Blunden soon after Dominic's murder, but had no information at that time of his sexual activities. Indeed, they knew nothing of this until a victim stepped forward in 1996. Blunden was 79 years of age and in poor health when police were told of his background and, in 1997, he was jailed for four years after pleading guilty in the Melbourne County Court to 27 charges of indecent assault and buggery between 1964-70.

Significantly, Blunden used a ruse of offering boys a lift on the pretext that he would give them driving lessons. But, although questioned by police in 1996 about Dominic's death, Blunden refused to make any admissions. Blunden died in 1998 at 81 years of age.

OCTOBER 12

THE POLICE KILLER (1902)

Police Constable Richard Johnson was shot in broad daylight in Milton Street, St Kilda, on the morning of *October 12*, 1902. The police officer was just about to arrest a man wanted for the murder of a police officer in the Sydney suburb of Redfern the previous July. In the Sydney killing, on the night of *July 19*, Constable Denis Guilfoyle and another policeman had followed two men who had been passing counterfeit coins. Guilfoyle, in attempting to make an arrest, placed a hand on the shoulder of the man nearest to him and said: "What's your name?" The man replied that it was "Wilson" and, at the same time, fired two shots into the policeman's body. Sadly, the Melbourne slaying of a police officer echoed what had happened in Sydney. However, this time the killer turned his gun on himself and committed suicide.

The killer's body eventually was identified as that of George Shaw, who went under such aliases as Yates and Raingill. The deputy governor of Darlinghurst Gaol, Sydney, a Mr McKenzie, travelled to Melbourne to specifically identify Shaw's body. Mr McKenzie asked for the body to be placed in a sitting position for easier identification and, after examining the dead man's face from several angles, said there was not the slightest doubt it was that of George Shaw, whom he had discharged from the Maitland Goal just a few months earlier. "There is not the slightest doubt in my mind that it his body," McKenzie declared.

OCTOBER 13

THE GENTLEMAN BUSHRANGER (1846)

William Westwood was regarded as a "gentleman bushranger" who dressed like a dandy and treated women with respect. Westwood had been a clerk in England, but was transported to the colony of New South Wales in 1837 for forgery and theft. He was sent to a property near Goulburn, but escaped and took to bushranging. He held up numerous coaches and raided a number of stores, but finally was caught at Berrima in

1841 and sent to Darlinghurst jail. Known as "Jackey Jackey", he escaped again and this time was sent to Cockatoo Island.

Westwood tried to escape by swimming to the mainland at Balmain, but was caught again and sent to Port Arthur, Tasmania. However, he escaped yet again to return to his old bushranging ways. He eventually was captured in Hobart and sentenced to death. This sentence was commuted to one of life imprisonment on Norfolk Island. It was there that he was involved in a convict mutiny in which he murdered three men. Westwood again was sentenced to death and, this time, was executed. He was hanged on *October 13*, 1846, at 26 years of age.

OCTOBER 14

BODY DUMPED (1997): Gerard Ross, 11, was taken from a street in the southern Perth suburb of Rockingham on *October 14*, 1997, and his body found 15 days later in a pine plantation at Karnup.

OCTOBER 15

DEATH OF A TEENAGER (2003)

Shaun Francis Finnigan, 17, lived with his mother Gillian and her de facto husband Boriss Vjestica at the northern Victorian town of Wodonga. However, the teenager apparently was in fear of Vjestica, especially after rejecting a job as a bricklayer arranged for him in Melbourne. On the morning of *October 15*, 2003, Finnigan and some of his friends were working on a motor vehicle in the driveway of the family home when Vjestica pulled up in his car. Finnigan and Vjestica walked towards each other and, after words had been exchanged, Finnigan was shot in the chest with a crude pistol made from a sawn-off .22 rifle. Vjestica had pulled the gun from the waist band of his trousers after Finnigan apparently had called him "a big man".

However, Vjestica said at his trial that he had gone into Finnigan's room that morning "to see if there was something there that shouldn't be". He was referring to drugs and said he had found some foil with powder in it and a gun. Vjestica also claimed he decided to confront Finnigan about the gun, put it in his waist-band and, during the confrontation, the gun discharged accidentally. Vjestica drove away without waiting to see how seriously Finnigan had been wounded.

Although the boy did not immediately fall to ground, he later died of the gunshot wound. However, a jury found Vjestica guilty of murder and Justice Bongiorno in the Supreme Court of Victoria told him: "It (the jury) found that the discharge of the gun was a deliberate act on your part with the intention of either killing Shaun Finnigan or at least inflicting really serious injury upon him." He sentenced Vjestica to 21 years' jail, with a minimum of 17 years before being eligible for parole.

OCTOBER 16

GATHER YE ROSEBUDS (1930)

Elderly widow Mrs Elizabeth Little was devoted to her grown-up family of a son and two daughters. She lived with one of her children, veterinary surgeon George, on the family's 80-acre farm near the tiny Victorian township of Stratford. Mrs Little was well known in the district as her father had been a prominent Gippsland grazier. The family was well liked and respected by the entire community. It was a happy family and, on the afternoon of *October 16*, 1930, Mrs Little collected roses from her garden for a visit to one of her daughters. Sadly, Mrs Little, who was not in the best of health, was never able to deliver the roses as she was strangled in the middle of her preparations for the visit.

The alarm was raised by 15-year-old farmhand Daphne O'Brien, who told Sale police that she had been attacked by another farmhand, 18-year-old Herbert Donovan, who had rushed into the farmhouse and demanded to know there Mrs Little kept her money. Miss O'Brien told police that Donovan then went into a bedroom and took three five-pound notes from a bag before attacking her and then forcing her to harness Mrs Little's horse to a buggy. He drove off in a cloud of dust and Miss O'Brien called police.

Mrs Little's body was found in a cowshed on the property. Her hands were tied behind her back by a cow halter and her legs were also tied. There were facial wounds, but police were unable to tell at first how Mrs Little had died. Their immediate concern was to apprehend Donovan, who had abandoned the horse and buggy outside a house in Sale. Police believed he had caught a late afternoon train to Melbourne and police throughout Victoria were given his description.

The first break in the hunt for Donovan was when a taxi driver told police he had driven a young man answering Donovan's description to Melbourne. The driver, Norman Buntine, told police that he found the young man sitting in his cab outside the Star Hotel in Sale at 5.15pm on the day of

Mrs Little's death. The young man asked Buntine to drive him to Melbourne and was told that the charge would be one shilling a mile. The youth made no objection to this, but later asked Buntine to pull over at Berwick so that he could hitch a ride to the city. A truck driver, Eric Craig, told police that he had taken the young man to the Dandenong railway station and it was assumed that Donovan caught a train to Melbourne from there.

Police launched a massive manhunt in Melbourne and, at one stage, three police groups were investigating sightings of the wanted young man. Then, on the morning of *October 18*, two days after the killing, two police officers noticed a dishevelled young man coming out of the Exhibition Gardens close to the city. They watched the youth for several minutes before apprehending him and taking him to police headquarters.

Donovan made a statement confessing to killing Mrs Little and was charged with murder. Evidence was given at his trial at the Criminal Court, Sale, that he struck Mrs Little six times around the head before she died of asphyxiation caused by a handkerchief place in her mouth. Donovan was found guilty of murder and was sentenced to death. However, this sentence later was commuted to one of life imprisonment after killing a frail widow for just 15 pounds.

OCTOBER 17

THE ESCAPE GONE WRONG (1826)

Nine prisoners – George Lacey, Samuel Measures, John Ward, John Williams, John McGuire, John McMillan, William

Jenkins, James Kirk and James Reid – made a bold bid for freedom at Macquarie Harbour, Van Deimen's Land, on *October 17*, 1826. They planned to use a catamaran, made by Williams, for their escape and, during the breakout, took a constable, George Recks, as hostage. However, the catamaran later started sinking and Recks was drowned, with one witness saying that he heard "a gurgling sound as of water getting into a man's mouth". The prisoners eventually were rounded up and all were charged with Recks' murder. A witness, James Cock, told the Supreme Court of Van Diemen's Land that he heard someone say: "Why didn't you keep the bastard down?" One of the arrested men, Lacey, also was reported as saying that he would rather hang than work in irons. A jury deliberated for only a few minutes before finding all nine prisoners guilty of murder. They were sentenced to death and, when the judge said "And may the Lord have mercy on your souls", one of them – believed to be Lacey – added "Amen".

OCTOBER 18

THE MISSING GIRL (2002)

Niamh Maye, 18, had just finished her Higher School Certificate and decided on taking a break before starting tertiary studies at the University of Technology, Sydney. She telephoned her mother to tell her she had booked on the road express from the fruit-picking area of Batlow, where she had been working, to Cootamundra and then on to Sydney. However, her ticket was never used and she was last seen between Tumut and Gundagai on *March 30*, 2002. The Armidale teenager simply disappeared and a number of bushland searches failed to find her. One of the last to see Niamh was a friend, Jason Paul Nichlason, who had dropped the teenager off after giving her a lift. Nicklason was arrested on *October 18* following the bashing rape of a women in Brisbane, but fell to his death when being escorted to a Brisbane jail cell.

OCTOBER 19

DEATH IN A CARAVAN (1989)

Raymond John Rosevear had a dispute with his wife on *October 19*, 1989, and pushed her on to a bed at the caravan they shared at the Rivergum Caravan Park in the southern New South Wales town of Corowa. Rosevear grabbed her by the throat and seemed to black out from there. However, his wife suffered burns to 65 per cent of her body when the caravan caught fire and died three days later in hospital from cardiac failure as a consequence of the shock from her burns. Also, a post mortem revealed that there were findings consistent with attempted strangulation.

Rosevear was charged with murder and, at his trial, police gave evidence that the bed clothes in the caravan had been deliberately lit after being soaked with methylated spirits. Rosevear, an alcoholic who consumed a carton of beer a day, said he did not light the fire, but was found guilty of murder and sentenced to life imprisonment. Rosevear, in the Supreme Court of New South Wales in 1999, sought determination of a minimum term and Justice Studdert set a period 15 years.

A FAMILY ROW (2001)

Julie Calway was close to her mother, even though she did not get on with her mother's de facto, Michael Pitts. Calway's mother was seriously ill in mid-2001 and moved in to help look after her at her home in the western Melbourne suburb of Newport. Calway and Pitts had a row on August, 2001, when she complained that he was smoking in her mother's room; he reacted by punching Calway in the face. Calway's mother died a couple of months later and Calway was upset by Pitts' behaviour as Calway, a sister and an aunt went through the dead woman's belongings.

On *October 19*, Calway drove from her East Malvern flat to Newport and was involved in a fight with Pitts. She suffered several bruises, but Pitts died from severe head injuries, a post-mortem revealing 16 linear lacerations to the scalp and a fractured skull. Calway was tried for murder and, at her trial, Justice Teague said "the indications are that it (the killing) was done with a brick or rock or garden form that happened to be on hand". In sentencing Calway,

Justice Teague told Calway: "There is not sufficient basis for a finding that the killing of the deceased was premeditated. I sentence you, therefore, on the basis that it was not." Calway was sentenced to 15 years' imprisonment, with a non-parole period of 10 years.

OCTOBER 20

THIRD TIME 'LUCKY' (1932)

It is most unusual for anyone to face three trials on the one charge – especially a murder charge – as 48-year-old Walter James Henderson did in Melbourne in 1932. Henderson had been a farmer at Lake Boga, but had shifted to the Melbourne bayside suburb of Albert Park at the suggestion of his mother, Mrs Sarah Jane Henderson, in 1932. The home Mrs Henderson found was in one of Melbourne's most fashionable streets, St Vincent's Place, which was close to where Mrs Henderson's daughter lived, in Kerferd Road.

Henderson, who had been married but was living apart from his wife, was at home on the afternoon of *July 27*, 1932, when he found his mother seriously injured at the foot of the stairs. He called to next door neighbour Mrs Elizabeth Meurillian for help and advised her to get a doctor. Mrs Henderson died in hospital that evening, but this was no surprise as the 63-year-old had suffered horrific head injuries. Although Henderson said his mother obviously had fallen down the stairs, police were suspicious as a broken, bloodstained hammer was found in the home and there was blood everywhere, with clothing scattered about the floor.

An inquest was told that Mrs Henderson had suffered five lacerations to the left side of the head and there was a laceration of the brain, even though the skull was not fractured. Henderson was sent for trial before Justice Mann and jury at the Criminal Court, and the jury deliberated for more than five hours before sending a message to the judge that it could not agree upon a verdict. Despite asking the jury to persist in trying to come to a decision, it returned an hour later to say there was no agreement.

The retrial was heard in October before Justice Wasley and the evidence presented was almost identical to what was presented at the first trial, with Henderson insisting he had done nothing to cause his mother's death. The jury retired at 1.25pm on *October 20* and returned six hours later to say it could not agree on a verdict. Henderson was remanded for a third trial at the Criminal Court the following month.

Henderson's third trial was before Justice Macfarlane and jury, with most of the same evidence paraded again. By this time the Melbourne public had tired of the mother-son case and little of the evidence was reported. After all, the public had read it all before. The third trial lasted three days and, in his summing up, Justice Macfarlane told the jury that it had been the responsibility of the Crown to prove that Mrs Henderson had died in the way alleged. Henderson again gave evidence and said he had heard his mother fall and had gone to her aid, hence the blood on his clothing. Two highly qualified medical experts also gave evidence that Mrs Henderson's injuries could have been caused by a fall down the stairs. The jury retired at 5.45pm on *November 23* and returned three hours later with a "not guilty" verdict.

OCTOBER 21

KILLED (1818): Bushranger Michael Howe killed by troopers Worrall and Pugh on *October 21*, 1818.

OCTOBER 22

THE RICHMOND BORGIA (1894)

Martha Needle, an extremely attractive young woman, was "unfortunate" enough to lose her entire family through "serious illnesses". She won enormous sympathy from friends and neighbours who could not believe that one delightful, frail, intelligent young woman could have so much bad luck. What the friends and neighbours did not know, until years later, was that Martha Needle was a mass poisoner. In fact, she was so adept at poisoning with arsenic that she was dubbed the "Richmond Borgia".

Pretty Martha Needle was raised in Adelaide, but moved to Victoria soon after her marriage to carpenter Henry Needle in 1881, Martha was just 17 and Henry Needle was regarded as an extremely fortunate man. It seemed an ideal marriage and the couple was blessed with the birth of daughter Mabel. However, Martha dreamed of running a boarding house, but where to get the capital? That problem was solved by the death of Mabel, who was just three years of age when poisoned by her mother in 1885. Martha had laced her daughter's food with a preparation called Rough on Rats.

Naturally, no one suspected the attractive young mother of killing her own daughter, a death certificate was issued and Martha collected 200 pounds from little Mabel's insurance policy. Martha Needle's trail of death was just starting, with her husband next on the death list. Martha, who had given birth to two more daughters – Elsie and May – spiced her husband's food with the same brand of rat poison and watched him die in agony. His death was certified as having been caused by "inflammation of the stomach" and Martha again collected 200 pounds from an insurance policy.

Next to die were little Elsie and May, both of whom were insured. Elsie, just four years of age, died of a "wasting disease" and Martha this time collected 100 pounds. Little May, just three years of age, then died in October, 1891, the insurance this time netting just 66 pounds. Widow Martha Needle, free of her daughters, then renewed an old friendship with the Juncken brothers, Otto and Louis, in Adelaide. Louis took ill and died, while Otto planned to marry Martha. Another brother, Herman, objected to this planned marriage and took ill after drinking a cup of tea. He recovered but, after visiting the widow and drinking more tea, he became ill again. He saw a doctor and, at long last, arsenic poisoning was suspected and a trap was set for Martha Needle.

Herman again visited Mrs Needle and, when offered a cup of tea, called in police and handed them the drink. An analysis revealed poison and the bodies of Mrs Needle's husband and daughters showed signs of arsenic poisoning when exhumed. Louis Juncken's body also was exhumed and this again revealed arsenic poisoning. Martha Needle, who killed five people, was hanged in Melbourne on *October 22*, 1894. She refused help on her way to the gallows and told the hangman that she wanted to die quickly and with dignity.

OCTOBER 23

THE MULTIPLE KILLER (1948)

Eric Thomas Turner won notoriety as one of Australia's worst and most depraved killers when, on *October 23*, 1948, he killed his girlfriend Claire Sullivan and then her father Frank Sullivan. The 20-year-old Turner strangled 15-year-old Claire as she lay on a settee at her family home in the Sydney suburb of Liverpool. Turner then axed her father to death. Turner, who claimed he was drunk when he killed the Sullivans, was sentenced to death, but this was commuted to life imprisonment.

He was released from jail in 1970 and, just three years later, killed again in a fit of rage, also while he was under the influence of alcohol. Turner, a man who could not control his rage when crossed, savaged his mother-in-law Harriet Field with a carving knife. Even more tragic was the killing of Turner's 11-year-old stepson John Pilz, who was stabbed while attempting to defend his grandmother. Turner was sentenced to two terms of life imprisonment and he therefore, at the time of this book's publication, had spent 54 of the past 57 years in jail, with four deaths from two drunken rages on his conscience.

OCTOBER 24

HANGED (1892): Leonardo William Moncardo hanged in Brisbane on *October 24*, 1892, after being found guilty of murder.

OCTOBER 25

THE CEMETERY KILLINGS (2005)

Stockman Terrence Laurence Dann, 37, was sentenced to life imprisonment on *October 25*, 2005, after pleading guilty to hanging his two stepchildren in a cemetery. He will serve a minimum of 22 years for the murder of a 14-month boy and a four-year-old girl. The children were hanged in a cemetery in Derby, in Western Australia's far north, on *April 23*, 2005. Dann also admitted assaulting the children's 29-year-old mother Jacinta Djiagween just minutes before her children were killed.

The Supreme Court of Western Australia was told that, after drinking at the Spinifex Hotel, Derby, Dann started arguing with Ms Djiagween. He kicked her and broke three ribs, puncturing a lung. Dann then drove the children to the cemetery and tied a "hanging" knot in one of the trees there. He hanged the boy first, and then the girl before driving himself to the Derby police station to tell officers of what he had done. He referred to the killings as "payback time".

OCTOBER 26

EXECUTED (1885): Walter Gordon executed in Brisbane on *October 26*, 1885, after being found guilty of murder.

OCTOBER 27

LESLIE "SQUIZZY" TAYLOR (1927)

Leslie "Squizzy" Taylor might have been a short, weasel-featured dandy, but he was one of Australia's most notorious criminals who terrorized Melbourne in the 1920s. Born on *June 29*, 1888, in the bayside Melbourne suburb of Brighton, Taylor's father Benjamin was a coach-builder who fell on hard times. As such, the family was forced to move to the far less salubrious suburb of Richmond. A runt all his life, Taylor became an apprentice jockey and rode at pony meetings around Melbourne, all the while racking up a record for petty crime which mainly involved theft and picking pockets. From there, he graduated to blackmail and extortion. He eventually became one of the leaders of a "push" known as the Bourke Street Rats. The gang was notorious for its "badger trap" scheme, of using young women to entrap married men and the woman's "husband" then rushing in to demand payment for silence.

Taylor's crimes became more and more audacious and was acquitted of murder in 1916 of the murder of taxi driver William Haines. His name also was linked with the robbery and murder of commercial traveller Arthur Trotter on *January 7*, 1913. He also was thought to be involved in the slaying of bank manager Thomas Berriman in Hawthorn on *October 8*, 1923. He was charged with being an accessory to murder, but never faced trial, while two other men faced the full wrath of the law. Career criminal Angus Murray was executed on *April 14*, 1924, for the Berriman killing, while Richard Buckley was sentenced to life imprisonment and held for 15 years.

The cunning and elusive Taylor was involved in almost every criminal activity imaginable, but specialised in sly-grogging, armed robbery and illegal gambling. He was involved in a massive diamond heist and was the chief suspect in the torching of a grandstand on the eve of the 1922 Caufield Cup. Finally, however, the pock-faced gangster met his end in bizarre circumstances in a shoot-out with another criminal, John "Snowy" Cutmore, in a house in Barkly Street, Carlton.

There was no love lost between Cutmore and Taylor and, when Cutmore returned from a stay in Sydney, Taylor wasted no time in visiting him at the Carlton house to ask of his plans. When Taylor walked into Cutmore's room on *October 27*, 1927, a gun battle raged and both men were mortally wounded. Cutmore died almost immediately, but Taylor died later in St Vincent's Hospital. However, some speculation remains as police found Cutmore's revolver — the one used in the killing of Taylor — 200 yards away under a picket fence. There has been speculation down the years that someone else killed both Taylor and Cutmore.

OCTOBER 28

THE 'AILING RAPIST' (2000)

Elles John Pont was 63 years of age when convicted of rape on *October 28*, 2000, but the offences took place more than 30 years earlier, between January 1, 1968, and September 9, 1971, at Yarraman, Queensland. A Dictrict Court in Brisbane sentenced Pont to eight years' jail on each of two counts of rape, with no recommendation for parole. However, he appealled the sentence, with his case going to the Queensland Court of Criminal Appeal, where the bench was told Pont suffered high blood pressure and depression and was partly disabled by back, knee and elbow pain. However, his application for leave to appeal was rejected.

The first of the two rape charges was perpetrated on a girl, who was just 10 years of age at the time. She was riding her bicycle home after having run an errand for her mother when Pont, who worked with her father, offered her a lift in his utility. He put the bicycle into the back of the utility but, instead of driving the girl home, he stopped on a country rode and raped the girl in the back of the utility. The girl said the offence was repeated, but could not recall particulars, except for an occasion in 1970. The girl told Pont that she was having her period, but he said this did not matter and he placed her on some hessian bags in a shed and raped her.

DUMPED IN THE BUSH (1996)

Sung Eun Park arrived in Australia from Korea as a boy, married Chinese-born Qian Qin and had two children with her, son Andrew and daughter Amy. However, there were problems with the marriage as Park was a chronic gambler and also entered into a relationship with another woman, 19-year-old Korean So Yung Hwang (known as Demi). Park, 26, left his family home in the Sydney suburb of Eastwood in July, 1996, to live with Hwang in a flat in Ashfield. However, Mrs Park did not know of this relationship for several months and eventually went to the Ashfield flat to confront Hwang.

The two women quarrelled so fiercely that police had to be called, upsetting Park, who was only too aware that his girlfriend had extended her visa. To make matters worse, Park received a letter from the Child Support Agency on *October 17*, 1996, stating that although he did not earn enough to be responsible for the support of his family, this could change in the future.

Park went to the Eastwood flat and killed his wife and then his children. He bound their hands and feet with rope and stockings and placed plastic bags over each victim's head, thereby suffocating them. Park then rang Hwang to tell her he had sorted out his domestic problems and that they now could travel to Korea. Then, two nights later, he drove Hwang to a beach and suggested they suicide together. Even more significantly, he looked at the stars and told his girlfriend that his children were up there, "peacefully".

Park went back to the Eastwood flat a few days later and placed the bodies of his wife and children in large suitcases and dumped the bodies in the bush at Watagan State Forest, near Cessnock. He told Hwang that his wife and children had moved to Queensland and he then travelled with his girlfriend to Korea on *October 28* after he got wind that the police were investigating the disappearance of his family. His family had already been dead almost a fortnight then, but the bodies were not discovered until fire fighters back-burning in the Cessnock area made a truly gruesome discovery.

After police had completed their investigations, Park eventually was arrested in Korea in March, 1998, and extradited to Australia. He was sentenced to an overall term of 26 years' jail, with a non-parole period of 19 and a half years.

OCTOBER 29

TRIAL OPENS (1880): The trial of Ned Kelly opened on *October 29*, 1880, while his mother, Ellen Kelly, was serving a three year prison term. (Refer to *November 11*)

OCTOBER 30

THE BABES IN THE CAVE (1950)

Little John Ward and Albert Speirs, like all young boys, liked carnivals. They were looking forward to a day at the Portland, New South Wales, carnival on *October 30*, 1950. They were expected to enjoy all the fun of the fair and the two seven-year-old playmates were as excited about the carnival as any children in Portland. The two little boys did not return home from the carnival, their day ending in murder. When the boys failed to return home at a reasonable time after the carnival, John Ward's father, John Alfred Ward, notified police.

A huge search was launched and thousands of miners and quarrymen joined police and other volunteers. It was to become one of the biggest searches in Australian history, searchers even carrying torches at night to investigate the possibility of the boys being lost in a quarry cave. Unbeknown to the searchers, they went within less that 100 metres of a gruesome sight on the first night of the search. Hopes faded quickly of finding the boys alive as the search dragged on to a fifth day. Then, on the morning of *November 4*, 23-year-old Herbert Hutchinson, acting on a hunch, decided to search a cave where he had looked for pigeon eggs as a boy. Hutchinson was horrified in finding two small bodies.

Police were shocked. The huddled bodies were a tragic sight, partly because of their very youth, but also because the bodies had been partly eaten by rats. Police appeared to have a case of murder on their hands, although there were initial suggestions that the boys had been lost and died of exhaustion. However, expert medical examinations later showed that the boys had died of suffocation, with evidence that shock was a contributing factor.

The man police wanted to interview was John Kevin Seach, a 26-year-old quarryman with the reputation of being a heavy drinker. Seach had left the town of Portland soon after the boys were reported missing and John Ward's elder brother, nine-year-old Richard, also identified Seach as the man he had seen walking away from the sports ground with his brother and little Albert Speirs on *October 30*. Seach had headed for Tamworth, taking a job under the assumed name of John Larsen for the short time that he was missing. Police questioned him at Tamworth and he confessed to killing the two boys.

Seach had told the boys he would take them home, but took them to the quarry cave instead. He interfered with them and immediately panicked. A statement he made read: "I grabbed the little bloke and smothered him by putting a handkerchief over his nose and mouth. As soon as he went limp I just let him fall back. I grabbed the other one and did the same to him." He added: "I was frightened to let them go because they would have told what I had done."

Seach stood trial at the Central Criminal Court in March, 1951, and pleaded not guilty to murder on the grounds of insanity. However, a jury took just half an hour to find him guilty of John Ward. Seach was sentenced to death, with Justice Street saying: "It needs no words of mine to speak of the abhorrent and detestable crime of which you have been found so rightly convicted. There is only one possible sentence. You are sentenced to death."

OCTOBER 31

THE PHAR LAP SHOOTING (1930)

The big chestnut affectionately was known as "Big Red" but, officially, he was Phar Lap. He was the idol of Australian sports fans in an era of severe depression. Phar Lap's magnificent turf achievements created headlines every time he ran. He undoubtedly was Australia's greatest racehorse and, in the lead-up to the 1930 Melbourne Cup, punters would not hear of his defeat in the big race. After all, the New Zealand-bred horse (by Night Raid out of Entreaty) had won most of Australia's big races, including the AJC Derby and the VRC Derby, and had finished third in the 1929 Melbourne Cup (won by Nightmarch).

Phar Lap (his name was Thai for "wink of the sky", ie lightning) and bookies stood to lose a fortune if the favourite won the 1930 Melbourne Cup. Phar Lap's owner, American David Davis scratched his horse from the lead-up Caulfield Cup and rumours swept the racing world on *October 31*, 1930, that there had been a massive 100,000 pounds plunge on an Amounis-Pharl Lap cups double. Amounis duly won the Caulfield Cup and bookmakers therefore stood to lose a fortune if Phar Lap completed the double.

"Big Red", also known as "the Red Terror" was entered for the Melbourne Stakes on Saturday, *November 1*, 1930, as a lead-up to the Melbourne Cup the following Tuesday. Phar

Lap's strapper Tommy Woodcock saddled the great horse for one last training gallop early on the morning of the Melbourne Stakes and, riding a grey pony, led Phar Lap down a street for that last hitout at the Caulfield track. It was just 6am and Woodcock was alerted to the sound of a car. He spotted a big, black Studebaker and noted there was something strange about it as the front number plate was covered by mud. Woodcock therefore took Phar Lap down a side street, but the car followed him, the pony and Phar Lap. Finally, with horn blaring, it pulled alongside Woodcock, who bravely pushed the champion racehorse onto a narrow footpath. A double-barrel shotgun appeared from a window and two shots were fired. Although Phar Lap briefly was "spooked", he was unharmed.

News of the shootings shocked Melbourne even though there was no doubt the gunman intended to harm, not kill, Phar Lap to have him scratched from the Melbourne Cup. Police found a cartridge case and several shotgun pellets, but never apprehended the gunman. Phar Lap won the Melbourne Stakes by three lengths and then was taken into hiding before reappearing for the Melbourne Cup. Phar Lap arrived at Flemington racecourse just 40 minutes before the big race, but thrilled the 72,000 spectators by winning in a canter, sending many bookies broke. Phar Lap was taken to the United States and Mexico in 1932, but took ill and died in California on *April 5*, that year. His death remains a mystery, but many believe he was accidentally poisoned by grazing on pasture which contained lead through spraying of crops. Phar Lap started 51 times for 37 wins, three second and two thirds and, at the time of his death, was the third highest stakes-winner in the world.

NOVEMBER

November brings with it the usual companions of murder, rape, robbery and crimes so horrific that the public is gripped by every detail. Crimes this month include:

THE POLICE STRIKE
THE BROWN-OUT KILLINGS
NED KELLY HANGED
THE CONVICT CANNIBAL
THE GREAT MANHUNT
And much, much more!

NOVEMBER 1

THE CEMETERY MURDER (1997)

Mersina Halvagis, a 25-year old with a Greek background, went to the Fawkner Cemetery, a northern Melbourne suburb, on *November 1*, 1997, to place flowers on her grandmother's grave. She walked to the grave and, as she was about to place the flowers in an urn, was stabbed to death. Her killing seemed senseless as it was committed in broad daylight and with no apparent motive. Miss Halvagis, engaged to be married, led a quiet, ordinary life and all she wanted on that day was to remember her grandmother. Police therefore believed she was the victim of a thrill killer who had been searching for a victim.

Police later interviewed convicted killer Peter Dupas over Miss Halvagis' murder, especially as his grandfather's grave was just 100 metres from that of Miss Halvagis' grandmother. Police spent several hours questioning him on *August 6*, 2001, but he refused to say anything more than "no comment". In February, 2005, a reward of $1 million was offered for information leading to the conviction of Miss Halvagis' murder.

THE SKATING GIRL MURDER (1974)

Michelle Allport was no ordinary skater. When Michelle, 13, pulled on her white skating boots a transformation came over her and was so good at her hobby that she became the New South Wales Under 13 roller skating champion. However, she was never able to progress her ambitions as she was strangled and buried in a bush grave after disappearing from a roller skating rink at Mittagong on *November 1*, 1974. Michelle had gone to the rink, in a shopping centre, with her brother Philip but went off on her own. She told him she would be back soon, but she did not return and was never seen alive again.

Her father, Williams Allport, reported to police that his daughter was missing and they interviewed children and others who were at the centre that night. The first break came a couple of days later when Michelle's brother-in-law found part of Michelle's yellow slacks near a road outside Mittagong. Police, sensing they were close to solving the mystery disappearance, checked out a bush track about five kilometers from Mittagong. Their worst fears were realised when they discovered a bush grave, concealed by heavy timber, about three kilometres along the track.

A post mortem showed that Michelle had been strangled. Police working on the case said they were lucky in tracing Michelle's body so quickly and added that they believed the killer virtually had left signs telling them where to find the body. They also said a chainsaw had been used to cut down several trees which had been used to hide the bush grave. The killer also threw tree logs and branches over the grave before trying to set them alight. The grave virtually was "marked" for police, who otherwise might have had difficulty in making their gruesome discovery. Michelle's body had been partly burned in the grave. She was buried at the Bowral cemetery on November 7, on the same day police charged Bowral labourer Kenneth William Johnstone with murder.

At the committal hearing at Moss Vale Court, Detective-Sergeant A. McDonald alleged that Johnstone, 36 years of age, had admitted strangling the girl. He told the court that Johnstone had said to him: "I did kill Michelle. I have been having an affrair with her for 18 or 19 months. Last Friday she told me she was pregnant and I could not face that at her age or mine. So I strangled her with a bit of rope and tried to burn her. But she would not burn, so I buried her." Johnstone, who knew the Allport family well, pleaded not guilty at his trial at the Central Criminal Court. However, the jury took only one and a half hours to find him guilty and, after the seven-day trial, he was sentenced to life imprisonment.

NOVEMBER 2

DEATH OF A FATHER (1995)

William Peter Victorson's life, by his own admission, was "a complete mess" after his mother died in November, 1995. Victorson was devoted to his mother, but also should have been grateful to his father who bailed him out after losses in the futures market. Victorson wallowed so heavily in a combination of Valium, marijuana and alcohol that his father limited supplies of money to his son.

On *November 1*, 1997, while his father was out with a lady friend, Victorson's thoughts turned to murder. After drinking heavily and using drugs, Victorson, 24, thought he heard voices in his head suggesting he should kill his father. Then, when his father returned to the family home in the suburb of Eastwood early on *November 2*, he struck him with a heavy metal pipe as he entered the back door. There were repeated blows and a post-mortem later revealed that the dead man had suffered massive head injuries, extensive fractures of the skull and the destruction of brain tissue.

Victorson removed money and credit cards from his father's pockets, washed his blood-stained clothes and went to the Darling Harbour Casino, throwing the credit cards into the water. Then, when he returned home at 5am, he dialled 000 and later told police that because he had owed a considerable amount of money for drugs, dealers had killed his father in a case of mistaken identity. However, Victorson eventually pleaded guilty to murder and was sentenced to a total of 18 years' jail, eventually being eligible for release in 2015.

NOVEMBER 3

THE MERCY KILLING (1969)

When middle-aged Max Enkhardt heard the squeal of car tyres early one night in 1968, he had no idea that the motor accident he had heard a couple of blocks from his Bentleigh home would turn his life into a nightmare. Max Enkhardt's wife Anna was seriously injured in that accident and spent the following 45 days in hospital recovering from head injuries and a broken pelvis. Indirectly, the accident led to her death, with her husband being charged with her murder.

Enkhardt, a German who arrived in Australia in 1928, married Anna in 1936 and, until the accident, they led a blissful life. Then, however, Anna was racked by pain and her condition slipped dramatically. She suffered from stomach upsets and was convinced she had cancer. There was no doubt her husband suffered with her and, 16 months after the accident, Enkhardt acted. On the afternoon of *November 3*,

1969, he shot his wife dead. Max 59, said later that he killed Anna, 69, because he loved her and that it was a mercy killing.

Enkhardt was charged with murder and was tried at the Criminal Court the following year, the case attracting enormous public interest. Enkhardt said Anna often would tell him she wished she could "end it all" and that he kissed her before shooting her. He said: "I loved her. I only did it for me. Believe me, I didn't come here to grovel for anything. She was my love … my only love for 35 years … she didn't nag me, she loved me. I couldn't bear to see her suffer."

The jury found Enkhardt guilty of murder and Justice McInerney sentenced him to death. However, the Victorian Executive Council later commuted the sentence to 20 years' imprisonment, with a minimum of 15 years. Enkhardt became a model prisoner and won numerous art and public speaking awards while serving his sentence. He was released in August, 1978, after serving eight years and eight months of his sentence. Ironically, he died from injuries he received when hit by a car in Elsternwick in September, 1979. Not long before his death Enkhardt said: "All that's left to say is my conscience is clear. I can make my Maker, He knows."

NOVEMBER 4

THE VIOLENT HUSBAND (2003)

Mother of three Thao Thi Tran endured beatings by her husband Chung Manh Tran, but boiled over with rage after his final attack, on *November 4*, 2003 — Melbourne Cup day. Mr Chung's attack was so violent that neighbours had to restrain him. However, what upset Tran most was that her husband had smashed a sacred Buddhist shrine she kept in memory of her late mother. Tran rang her husband, who was at a neighbour's home, and asked him to return. She then stabbed him five times, including one wound to the heart.

Tran insisted she had acted in self defence and, in April, 2005, a Victorian Supreme Court jury acquitted her of murder although it convicted her of manslaughter. However, Justice Stephen Kaye imposed a suspended three-year sentence, which meant Tran walked free. Justice Kaye said Tran had been the subject of a "brutal and cruel beating" and told her: "By its verdict, the jury accepted that an ordinary person might, in the same circumstances, have reacted in the same manner in which you did." He said he had taken into account several mitigating circumstances, especially the care of Tran's three children, aged nine, seven and six. Justice Kaye said: "It would be an affront to common sense and human decency for a sentencing judge to ignore such a factor."

**

DROWNING MURDER (1895): Melbourne mother Emma Williams executed on *November 4*, 1895, after being found guilty of drowning her two-year-old son at Sandridge (Port Melbourne). She tied a piece of cloth around the boy's waist, fastened it to a rock at the other end and pushed him off a pier.

NOVEMBER 5

THE POLICE STRIKE (1923)

Melbourne newspapers on the morning of Monday, *November 5*, 1923, trumpted the chaos sparked by the Victoria Police strike. One newspaper, *The Age,* reported "unprecedented scenes" of looting and rioting and ran headlines about "hoodlums and criminals" smashing windows to steal valuables. There even was a death, of a former World War I soldier, a victim of looters when he tried to intervene. The police had gone on strike over what they considered to be low wages and even lower morale, as well as the scrapping of their superannuation scheme. Also, Chief Commissioner Alexander Nicholson had introduced a system of supervisors, reporting on other police officers. These plain clothes operators were known as "Spooks" and were despised by the rest of the force. The Victoria Police force at that time had 1750 officers, but 636 of them demanded that the "Spooks" be removed, or they would be on strike.

That strike came into effect on the night of *November* 2, 1923, just as a large crowd had gathered in the city following late night shopping. The aftermatch was one death, 237 people hospitalised and looting and robbery offences by the hundreds. The Victorian government "sacked" the striking police officers and civilians had to be sworn in as "special volunteers". The Federal Government also gave assistance by posting detachments of the military to Melbourne. Mobs derailed trams in the heart of Melbourne as anarchy reigned. The 5000 "specials", as they were known, eventually restored peace and calm after a number of running battles with the mobs and the Victorian government started recruiting and training police officers to replace those who had gone on strike. The strike cost the Victorian government an estimated 78,000 pounds, not to mention the cost to business.

NOVEMBER 6

THE THURGOOD-DOVE KILLING (1997)

Mother of three Jane Thurgood-Dove was shot in the driveway of her own home in the north-west Melbourne suburb of Niddrie on *November 6*, 1997. The killing shocked Victorians, especially as Mrs Thurgood-Dove was gunned down in front of her three children, Scott (11), Ashley (six) and Holly (four). The gunman had chased her around her car and, when she slipped a fell, shot her dead before running to a car stolen in the inner suburb of Carlton several days earlier.

Scott Thurgood-Dove told police there was another man in the car but, despite a fairly good description of the gunman, the mystery remains, even though Victoria Police offered a pardon for the man who drove the car. Mrs Thurgood-Dove's father, John Magill, said: "To take a life is odious in itself. And I see the person who murdered Jane as a faceless, craven coward." Police have never been unable to find a motive for the killing and, in 2003, the Victorian Government offered a $1 million reward for information leading to the conviction of the killer.

NOVEMBER 7

NED KELLY'S TEACHER (1891)

Old rogue Harry Power was regarded as the man who taught Ned Kelly the black art of being an outlaw. An Irishman who sought his fortune on the Victorian gold fields, he was arrested for shooting a trooper in 1855, but escaped from Pentridge prison on *May 7*, 1896, just before the completion of his sentence and embarked on the life of a highwayman in northern Victoria and just over the Murray in New South Wales. He had a hideout near the King River and was befriended by the Kelly family. In return, Power taught young Ned the tricks of his trade. While Kelly and his gang went on to achieve infamy, Power was sentenced to 15 years' jail at the Beechworth prison. He served the full sentence, but drowned in the Murray River while on holiday at Swan Hill on *November 7*, 1891.

BURIED UNDER GRASS (1974)

Little Svetlana Zetovic (known as Lana), just six years of age, was a strikingly pretty girl with beautiful straw-coloured hair. She lived with her parents and eight-year-old brother Danny in the western Sydney suburb of Guildford. Her family had migrated to Australia from Yugoslavia in 1970 and, four years later, had settled into a quiet routine in their adopted country.

However, Lana did not return home from school on *November 7*, 1974, and Mrs Barbara Zetovic immediately called police, who launched a massive search for the missing girl. The search was two days old when police made the discovery they hoped they would never make. They found

Lana's body under a pile of grass clippings, rags and rubble in the backyard of a house just three doors from the Zetovic home. Lana had been choked, stabbed through the heart and sexually assaulted. Police charged 45-year-old labourer Noel Edward Holden with the murder of the six-year-old girl.

At a committal hearing, Police chemist, Inspector J. Goulding, said hairs taken from the girl's body and from a pair of Holden's trousers were the same, "beyond reasonable doubt", while evidence also was given that a knife taken from Holden's house could have been the one used to stab Lana. Holden was sent for trial at the Central Criminal Court before Justice Isaacs and, although he pleaded not guilty, a jury took just 90 minutes before announcing its verdict – guilty. The judge, in sentencing Holden to life imprisonment, described the murder of little Svetlana Zetovic as a "horrible crime".

NOVEMBER 8 (1889)

HANGED: Arle Pres hanged at Fremantle Gaol on *November 8*, 1889, after being found guilty of murder.

NOVEMBER 9 (1942)

THE BROWN-OUT KILLINGS

Melbourne was a dark city in the autumn of 1942, the city's residents preparing for what they believed would be a long, cold war-time winter. It was during the autumn of 1942 that what came to be known as the "Brown-out Killings" started, on *May 3* when the body of a middle-aged woman was found in the doorway of a house in Victoria Avenue, Albert Park, a beach suburb only three miles from the heart of the city. The woman had been bashed and strangled. Part-time barman Henry Billings, who discovered the body, later said: "At about 3am I saw an American soldier stooping in the doorway of a shop next to the hotel. He might have heard me because he got up and walked towards the corner, turning into Beaconsfield Parade. When I came to the doorway, I saw what I thought was a woman lying there. I struck a match. It was a woman. She was naked. Clothes had been ripped from her body and her legs folded back. I then roused the hotel and telephoned the police."

The police were horrified. The body was a pitiful sight, the poor women being terribly wounded. Her legs were bruised and the left temple had been fractured. The dead woman was identified as Mrs Ivy McLeod, 40, a woman described by friends as easy-going and happy. Mrs McLeod had been visiting friends in Albert Park and was on her way to East Melbourne, on the other side of the city. She was waiting for an all-night bus in Victoria Avenue when the killer struck.

Police were still puzzling over the murder when they were confronted by a second killing. This time the body was found almost in the heart of the city, in the doorway of a residential building in Spring Street, Melbourne, on the morning of *May 9*. Nightwatchman Henry McGowan noticed a bundle in the doorway at about 5.30am and immediately investigated. His horror can be imagined as he realised that the bundle was the corpse of a woman. As in the killing of Mrs McLeod, the second victim's clothing had been ripped and the dead woman was identified as Mrs Pauline Coral Thompson, 32, the wife of a Bendigo police constable. Mrs Thompson had seen her husband off to Bendigo that night and later was seen in the company of American servicemen.

Police investigating the killings now had a real lead, although finding the killer still was like looking for the proverbial needle in the haystack. There were thousands of American servicemen in Melbourne and the best lead police had was that the man they wanted to interview was "baby-faced". Then, the killer struck for a third – and last – time, on the night of *May 18*, nine days after the previous murder. The body of 40-year-old Gladys Hosking was discovered in Royal Park, just outside the city proper. Again, the dead woman's clothing had been ripped. The victim, who worked at the University of Melbourne as a secretary with the School of Chemistry, had been strangled.

Hosking's body was lying on its face, which was half-buried in a yellow mud and slush produced by rain on heavy clay-like soil. This proved to be an excellent lead and an American solider had been apprehended to a camp entrance at Camp Pell, Royal Park, with yellow mud on his uniform. Police went to interview Private Edward Joseph Leonski, a 24-year-old who was quiet and unassuming when sober, but everyone's buddy when drinking. The baby-faced Leonski was something of a mother's boy and his family had a history of mental problems. Also, Leonski had been charged with rape in San Antonio, Texas, and although found not guilty, that acquittal led to his freedom and therefore indirectly led to the death of three woman halfway across the world.

Leonski's court martial was not as dramatic as might be imagined. There were no histrionics and only the press and invited guests were allowed to attend. Leonski admitted the killings, but his defence hinged on a plea of insanity. It was argued that he behaved perfectly when sober, but was the opposite when drunk. The court martial therefore was suspended for 30 days while three US Army psychiatrists examined Leonski to determine whether he was sane. However, he was found guilty and sentenced to death. He was hanged by American authorities at Pentridge on *November 9*, 1942. A report in the Melbourne *Herald* read: "Leonski came onto the scaffold and a black cap was put over his head, while his legs and hands were shackled. He maintained such an attitude of calm indifference to the end as to leave everyone associated with him aghast and amazed, Certainly no other murderer in the memory of Australian students of criminology was so obviously uninterested in his own fate." Leonski's body was shipped to the United States for burial.

NOVEMBER 10

THE CESS PIT MURDER (1883)

Mah Poo was a short young man who settled in Adelaide after briefly living in Melbourne following his arrival from China as a teenager around 1873. He was jailed for theft soon after arriving in Adelaide and used this time in learning to read and write. This later led to an extraordinary confession in the killing of compatriot Tommy Ah Fook, who ran a café in Adelaide's Hindley Street.

The death of Ah Fook came to light when, in August, 1883, three men were cleaning a cess pit at the City Hotel in Hindley Street and noticed a body among the filth and excreta. They hailed a patrolling police officer and, with the men's help, dragged the body out of the mire. It had been there for several days, but a local doctor was able to identify the body as that of Ah Fook, who had been missing for a week. His head had been bashed in and he also had been shot.

Police originally had three suspects — Poo and two other occupants of Ah Fook's café. However, police honed in on Poo who had been seen wearing a pin belonging to Ah Fook. Besides, he recently had bought a revolver from a pawnbroker and was known to have argued with Ah Fook. The revolver had been found by two boys in nearby grass and Poo subsequently was charged with murder. He pleaded not guilty at his trial and although the evidence was largely circumstantial, the 26-year-old cook was found guilty of murder and sentenced to death.

There were fears that there might have been an injustice as the prosecution evidence was threadbare, to say the least, but Poo saved legal embarrassment when he wrote a confession in English. It read: "As I am about to suffer the extreme penalty of the law, I sincerely and solemnly declare that I murdered Tommy Ah Fook. He was always cursing and swearing at me and finding fault with everything I did. My temper was such that I could not control it. I fired the shot that killed Tommy at five or six yards' distance, and he fell mortally wounded. I threw him down the closet." Poo was executed at Adelaide Gaol on the morning of *November 10*, 1883, and in the lead-up to the hanging he was heard to say: "Me shoot Tommy, he die. You hang me; me no 'fraid to die."

DEPRAVED LOVERS CAPTURED (1986)

A semi-naked 16-year-old girl sprinted into a Willagee supermarket on *November 10*, 1986, with a terrifying story of abduction and rape at the hands of an evil couple living nearby. The hysterical teenager told police she had been walking in the well-to-do Perth suburb of Nedlands the previous afternoon when she was dragged into a car by a man and woman, driven to their house at 3 Moorehouse Street, chained to a bed and raped twice by the man. She managed to escape after the man had gone to work and the woman unchained her. Police promptly arrested David Birnie, 35, and his defacto wife Catherine, 32, who soon confessed to the sex murders of four young women – aged 15 to 31 – who they buried in bushland during a five-week rampage.

The Birnies were originally teenage lovers who teamed to commit a spate of burglaries before being sent to different detention centres and leading separate lives. When the pair reunited almost two decades later, Catherine was a married mother-of-six, but it didn't take long for Birnie, a sadistic sex-addict, to convince her to abandon her family and devote herself entirely to him.

Although David Birnie dominated their relationship and was the more violent of the duo, Catherine Birnie was no shrinking violet in the attacks on their unsuspecting victims (the first of which took place on *October 6*), taking explicit photographs as macabre mementoes of their depraved exploits, and when her 'husband' seemed to be smitten by a victim they kept as a sex-slave for several days, she flew into a jealous rage and ordered her execution.

On *March 3*, 1987, after a mere half-hour trial in which they offered no defence for their atrocities, the Birnies were sentenced to life in prison, with the judge recommending that David Birnie never be released. Birnie hanged himself in his cell at Casuarina Prison on *October 7*, 2005, at the age of 55. His 'widow' is behind bars at Perth's Bandyup Women's Prison.

NOVEMBER 11

NED KELLY HANGED (1880)

Ned Kelly, Australia's most infamous bushranger, was hanged at Melbourne Gaol at 10am on *November 11*, 1880. His execution was the final act in a turbulent life that spanned only 25 years yet, to this day, incites passion, provokes debate and polarises opinion. To many, Kelly was simply a mad-dog cop-killer whose death at the end of the hangman's noose was fitting final to a wasted, miserable existence. But to many others, he was a folk hero who rebelled against class oppression and police harassment, a natural icon of mateship and courage who ultimately entered the realm of martyrdom.

The epic, far-reaching story of Ned Kelly had humble origins. His father, John Kelly, from Tipperary, Ireland, was 20 when he was convicted of pig stealing on *January 7,* 1841, and sentenced to seven years' transportation to Van Diemen's Land (Tasmania). After serving his sentence, Kelly crossed Bass Strait to Victoria and, on *November 18*, 1850, married Irish migrant Ellen Quinn, 21. Edward, or Ned, the third-born of their eight children, arrived between December, 1854, and June, 1885 (no official record of the birth exists).

John Kelly died of dropsy on *December 27,* 1866, at the age of 46, leaving Ned to become the man of the house at the tender age of 12. At 14, Kelly was acquitted of a charge of assaulting a Chinaman with a stick. At 15, he became a bushranging "apprentice" to notorious highwayman Harry Power and, despite his obvious guilt and the prospect of a lengthy prison term on the serious charge of robbery under arms, was again acquitted. However, Kelly's luck ran out just months later when he was jailed for three years for receiving a stolen horse, while the actual thief — a mate named Isaiah "Wild" Wright — inexplicably copped just 18 months.

Upon release, Kelly and his new stepfather, Californian George King (just five years his senior), observed a successful horse-stealing ring, which a Constable Alexander Fitzpatrick single-handedly tried to smash in the early evening of *April 15*, 1878. Fitzpatrick, who was later dishonourably discharged from the police force as a liar, arrived at the Kelly homestead drunk. A fight ensued and Fitzpatrick reported that Kelly had shot him in the wrist. Kelly and his youngest brother Dan went to a bush hideout, but Mrs Kelly and two men who weren't present at the fracas were jailed for their role in the attempted murder of Fitzpatrick.

Over the following 26 months as fugitives in Victoria's north-east, the four-man Kelly Gang, comprising Ned and Dan and mates Joe Byrne and Steve Hart, on *October* 26, 1878, killed three plain-clothes police in a gunfight at Stringybark Creek, near Mansfield, robbed banks at Euroa *(December 10*, 1878) and Jerilderie, NSW *(June 26*, 1880), and killed ally-turned-police informer Aaron Sherritt *(June 26*, 1880) before staging their world-famous shootout with police at Glewnrowan *(June 26-28*, 1880). In a siege that lasted about 12 hours, Ned Kelly received 28 gunshot wounds before being captured, while the remaining gang members were killed.

On *October 29*, 1880, Kelly was found guilty of the murder of Constable Thomas Lonigan at Stringybark Creek and was duly sentenced to death. Kelly's final words have been variously quoted as "such is life" or "ah well, I suppose it had to come to this". Whatever the truth, while Kelly's drop from the scaffold terminated his physical being, the legend/myth/enigma lives on.

TOO YOUNG TO HANG (1863)

Elizabeth Scott, an Englishwoman who had migrated to Australia with her family after a year in New Zealand, was just 14 years of age when, in 1854, she married 36-year-old Robert Scott, a hard-drinking gold prospector. She bore him four children before she was 20 years of age, but only two survived. They lived in a shack near Mansfield, north-east Victoria, and Elizabeth despaired as her husband turned increasingly to drink. He ran a grog shop from his shanty, but seemed to drink more than all his customers combined. Meanwhile, Elizabeth became entangled romantically with young farm labourer David Gedge. To complicate matters, Malay labourer Julian Cross was infatuated with Elizabeth.

Matters came to a head on the night of *April 11*, 1863, when Robert Scott was shot in the head while in a drunken stupor. Elizabeth claimed it was suicide, but she, Gedge and Cross were charged with murder. At the trial at Beechworth the following October, Cross told the jury that Elizabeth had given himself and Gedge a shot of brandy each while they prepared to get rid of the drunken Robert Scott. All three were found guilty and hanged together at the Melbourne Gaol on *November 11*, 1863. Elizabeth Scott, who believed she would be given a last-minute reprieve because of her sex and age, was just 23 years of age when executed.

DEATH OF AN INFANT (2001)

From all accounts, two-year-old Lewis Blackley was a happy little two-year-old and his mother Daisy De Los Reyes was a good and attentive mother. However, Ms De Los Reyes had the misfortune to take up with a man named Haemon Gill. The relationship had existed for about three months to

November 11, 2001, when Ms De Los Reyes was preparing an evening meal at her Norlane home in the suburb of Geelong, with Lewis yelling and screaming. Lewis ate his dinner in a high-chair, but started crying again.

Ms De Los Reyes and Gill had been drinking and smoking marijuana and, after little Lewis had cried himself to sleep, his mother went to bed. She found her son cold and blue in the face the next morning, despite a blanket being placed over him; the boy was dead. When Ms De Los Reyes was told a week later that her son had died of head injuries, she attributed this to Lewis banging his head.

However, Gill later admitted that Lewis' death was his fault and stated that he had bit him on the lip and then tried to conceal this by punching the affected area. The boy's post-mortem revealed that the fatal injuries could not have been caused by head banging and, in an interview with police, Gill said: "I intended to let him (Lewis) know who was boss 'cos he's a little shit. He was demanding, he was terribly demanding - demand, demand, demand. Just cry, sook, try and get his own way and usually Daisy would give up and give him his own way."

Justice Coldrey told Gill: "The jury were satisfied that at the time of you inflicted the fatal blow or blows you did so with the intention of causing him really serious bodily harm." The judge added that although he did not think the killing was premeditated, Gill "refused to fully accept responsibility for Lewis' death" and that his "state of mind falls well short of genuine remorse". He sentenced Gill, 30, to imprisonment for 19 years, with a fixed period of 14 years.

NOVEMBER 12

HANGED (1888): Two men, one known as Sedin and the other, Edmund Duhamel, hanged in Brisbane on *November 12*, 1888, after being found guilty of murder.

**

MURDERED (1979): Alleged Great Bookie Robbery ringleader Raymond "Chuck" Bennett murdered outside the Melbourne Magistrate's Court on *November 12*, 1979, before he was to face a commital hearing for a $69,000 payroll robbery in the western Melbourne suburb of Yarraville.

NOVEMBER 13

THE CONVICT CANNIBAL (1823)

When convicts Alexander Pearce and Thomas Cox escaped from the Macquarie Harbour penal settlement, Van Diemen's Land, on *November 13*, 1823, they would have had no idea that they would become part of Australian folklore. The two men ran into the bush armed with an axe, but with no food. Several days later, they came across the King's River but, because Cox would not swim, Pearce flew into a rage. He struck his companion several times with the axe and, as he was about to cross the river, Cox shouted to him: "Put me out my misery." Pearce turned back and again struck Cox over the head, killing him. Pearce, who was desperately hungry, saw his dead companion as a source of food and then committed the unthinkable. He cut a piece from Cox's thigh, roasted it and ate it before cutting off another slice for sustenance once he had crossed the river.

However, the remorse of turning cannibal saw him hailing a schooner and he then confessed to both murder and cannibalism. He said he was "willing to die for" for his actions. A search party was sent to look for Cox's body and, when it was found, the head and arms were missing, along with parts of the thighs and calves. When asked about the head, Pearce said he had left it on the body. It was found several yards away, but the hands were never found. Pearce also said that after eating part of a thigh, because "no person can tell what he will do when driven by hunger", he threw the rest into the river. Pearce was found guilty of murder and sentenced to death. His execution on *July 19*, 1824, was watched by a large crowd, with a Rev. Conolly addressing those assembled before the drop. The minister told the crowd that Pearce, standing on the edge of eternity, wanted to acknowledge his guilt. Finally, he asked the crowd to offer their prayers and beg the Almighty to have mercy upon him.

NOVEMBER 14

KICKED TO DEATH (1944)

When two young Brisbane men, Stan Smith and Neville Hansen, entered a dark alley on the night of *June 19*, 1944, to retrieve a bike, they were horrified at what they saw stretched on the ground. It was the half-naked body of a young woman and it was obvious she had been bashed or even kicked to death as her face had been badly battered. Meanwhile, her killer had left behind a vital clue — a American paratrooper cap. The woman quickly was identified as Doris Roberts, who had been seen in the company of several American serviceman at a nearby café. A Private Avelino Fernandez, who had been seen without his cap, was apprehended just a few hours after the discovery of Roberts' body. He admitted he had been with a woman for sex in the laneway but added that he was leaving when he saw another man and woman enter the lane.

Finally, however, Fernandez admitted "hitting the dame". He even admitted to kicking and belting Roberts "all over" because she had made him feel cheap in asking for money. Private Fernandez was tried by court martial and although he insisted he was affected by alcohol, he was found guilty of the murder of Doris May Roberts. Fernandez' heavy military boots were produced at the court martial to show how much damage could be caused by repeated kicking while wearing these boots.

Although he was sentenced to death, Alverez believed he would escape the noose as capital punishment had been abolished in Queensland in 1922. However, he was transferred to New Guinea, away from Queensland jurisdiction, and was told on the evening of *November 14*, 1944, that he would be hanged at dawn. Alvarez later that night attempted to commit suicide by cutting his throat with a dinner knife. However, the wound was stitched and he was executed the following morning.

THE GREAT MANHUNT (1959)

When Kevin John Simmonds and Leslie Allan Newcombe escaped from Long Bay jail on *October 9*, 1959, New South Wales police believed they would be recaptured within hours. However, Simmonds remained at large for 36 days and created an aura of invincibility, always being one step ahead of those hunting him down. As such, he became almost a folk hero and reports of his deeds and sightings, real or imaginary, were splashed across the front page of almost every daily newspaper in Australia. It was the largest manhunt in Australia and many who followed the saga believed, and even hoped, police would never get their man.

Symmonds had been in trouble with the police from just 14 years of age and graduated from petty theft to armed robbery. In 1959, he was sentenced to 15 years' jail for various offences ranging from car stealing to burglary. Then, in Long Bay jail, he met up with Newcombe, who was serving a relatively minor sentence. They made their escape by breaking into the jail chapel, crawling through a ventilator duct and then scaling a wall before leaping to freedom. Symmonds and Newcombe commandeered a car and, two days later, killed to ensure their freedom. They battered 40-year-old Emu Plains jail prison warder Cecil Mills with a baseball bat and stole his pistol. Police were more determined than ever to recapture the two convicts, but the task was made more difficult when Symmonds and Newcombe decided to separate.

Whereas Symmonds headed to the bush, Newcombe decided to stay in Sydney and was recaptured in Paddington two weeks after the escape. The more dangerous Symmonds, however, was still at large and led police a not so merry chase. He bailed up two rangers, stole their car and smashed through a road block. Public interest was phenomenal and, finally, the fugitive was spotted in scrubland, hungry and desperate. Symmonds, the most wanted man in Australia, meekly surrendered on *November 14*, 1959, and he and Newcombe later were tried for the murder of Mills. They were found guilty of manslaughter, with Newcombe sentenced to 15 years' jail and Symmonds for life. However, Symmonds hanged himself in jail in 1966, 10 years after Australia's greatest manhunt.

NOVEMBER 15

A RAZOR ACROSS THE THROAT (1836)

A man named James O'Neale was delivering mail from Bungonia to Marulan, New South Wales, on *September 22*, 1835, when he came across what he thought was someone sleeping by the side of the road. However, when he took a close look, he was horrified. He had discovered the body of a man, John Haydon, whose throat had been slashed so that "his head fairly turned back". O'Neale immediately notified nearby sawyers who, in turn, notified authorities. Witnesses testified that the dead man had been seen in the company of a man named James Smith and that Haydon was seen trying to get change for a one-pound note from the Bungonia Bank. Another witness said that Smith had passed a one-pound note from the Bungonia Bank for his lodging at a Sutton Forest hostelry. Smith was arrested and indicted for the murder of Haydon.

Surgeon Francis Murphy told the Supreme Court of New South Wales he examined the body on the day of death and added: "The throat had been cut by a sharp instrument; all the vessels around the neck had been cut through to the bone; the vertebrae was partly cut; it was quite impossible that he minded for him to have done it himself. There was a wound below the left eye, which had broken the bone, another upon the left ear. These wounds were severe, but not quite sufficient to cause death. The body was then warm and the wounds fresh; a razor was lying across his breast with which I think the wound on the neck must have been inflicted." Smith pleaded his innocence, but was found guilty and sentenced to death and that his body then be delivered to surgeons for dissection.

The *Sydney Gazette* of **November 15**, 1836, reported on Smith's execution: "Yesterday the utmost penalty of the law was carried into effect upon William (James) Smith, convicted on Friday last of a wilful and atrocious murder. Smith was a native of the colony, about 30 years of age, of a very strong and muscular frame. He was attended in his last moments by the Rev. Mr. M'Encroe, being of a Catholic persuasion. He made no public statements as to his guilt, and every arrangement being completed, the drop fell, and he was launched into eternity. His struggles, before animation ceased, were long and violent."

THE BODY IN THE ACID (1997)

Tony Kellisar arrived in Australia from Iran in 1990 and, three years later, met Svetlana Podgoyetsky. They eventually moved in together and despit their stormy relationship, married in April, 1996. The marriage did nothing to cement the relationship and, if anything, they bickered more and more. So much so, in fact, that they separated in September, 1997. That could have been a simple end to yet another failed marriage, except that Kellisar heard that under Australia law all property would be shared on divorce. It appears that Kellisar then decided on a course of action that would see his wife killed and her body disposed of in the most horrific circumstances imaginable.

Kellisar was able to put his murderous plan into action when he learned his wife would leave Sydney to attened a travel agents' conference in Melbourne. Ms Podgoyetsky was staying at the Crown Casino and Kellisar told her initially that he could be joining her in Melbourne. This, it seems, was so he could be sure she would not share a double room with another conference member. However, Kellisar later told her he would not be going to Melbourne after all and she subsequently decided she would have a quiet evening watching a video on the night of Saturday, *November 15*, 1997.

Meanwhile, Kellisar hired a Budget car fast enough for him to drive to Melbourne within seven or eight hours so that no one would notice he was missing from Sydney. He spent the Saturday at work and started driving to Melbourne at 6pm, sometimes exceeding 190 kilometres an hour to make good time. Then, as soon as he arrived at the Crown Casino, he called his wife from a public telephone to tell her he was in Melbourne after all and could she meet him outside the casino. His wife agreed to this meeting and unwittingly walked to her death.

No one knows for sure what happened after the couple met, but Kellisar said they drove to Queensbridge Street, near the Crown Casino, and started arguing. He claimed his wife launched an unwarranted attack and that he acted in self defence, without intending to hurt her. Regardless, Ms Podgoyetsky was killed and Kellisar put her body into the back of the hired car and drove back to Sydney as fast as he could.

However he ran into problems, especially when he was pulled over for speeding by a New South Wales police officer at Yass. Kellisar, with his wife's body in the back of the vehicle, had to produce his driver's licence and knew then that the police would know he had left Sydney and that any alibi no longer would stand scrutiny. He also realised that there would be video footage of him through security cameras outside Crown Casino. He therefore knew he had to act with even greater haste and he put the final part of his plan into action. Once back at his workplace, Metropolitan Radio Repairs, he put his wife's body in a wheeled plastic rubbish bin and filled it with hydrochloric acid he had ordered a week earlier.

Police, alerted to Ms Podgoyetsky's disappearance, soon became suspicious of Kellisar, who had left a trail of clues, apart from the video footage. The police eventually tracked down the hire car and found that it had been cleaned of stains at the Polaris Car Spa. Finally, police found what was left of his wife's body — two legs protruding from the drum of acid, part of the lower left arm and hand and some organs.

Kellisar was charged with murder and although he pleaded guilty to manslaughter, this was rejected and after a 22-day trial, a jury found him guilty of murder. Justice Vincent told him: "Your conduct constitutes a particularly serious example of a very grave crime. It was committed after careful deliberation and involved a considerable measure of cynicism and deceit. I wonder what thoughts passed through your mind in the course of more than seven hours which were occupied in your journey to Melbourne. You were highly unlikely to have been troubled by conscience or remorse as there is, in my assessment, nothing which even remotely suggests that you experienced any such such emotions at any later stage. Even on your own and rejected version of events, your major pre-occupations following the death of your wife concerned your own situation. Your treatment of the body ...

belies the presence of any proper sense of respect for her or regret for what had occurred."

The judge sentenced Kellisar to 22 years' jail, with a minimum period of 18 years. Kellisar appealed against this sentence, but this appeal was dismissed.

NOVEMBER 16

THE BOLTING HORSE (1906)

Two youths who stopped a horse bolting with a cart behind it in North Adelaide on the night of *August 13*, 1906, inadvertently turned the spotlight on one of the city's most sensational murders. One of the youths noted blood stains in the back of the cart and therefore notified a police officer, who believed the horse and cart belonged to Natalla Habibulla. When he went to Habibulla's house, the police officer noted a large pool of blood in the backyard.

Habibulla, an Afghan, was not at home at the time, but later turned up at the local police station and explained that a blood-stained shirt found in the back of his cart was caused by a nose bleed. He also was at pains to explain that the horse had bolted after being frightened by a new-fangled motor vehicle and that he was at the station because he had heard police had taken control of the horse and cart. However, police were concerned about the amount of blood found in Habibulla's backyard and questioned him at length about this. Meanwhile, police made further investigations at the house and discovered that there were human fragments among the blood.

Police launched a massive search for Habibulla's wife, even using black trackers. Then, after scouring the Torrens River, they found a hessian bag which contained the lower part of a human corpse. The other half was found some time later and Habibulla was charged with murder after the body was identified as that of Edith Ellen Mary Habibulla, who had married the accused just a few months earlier. It was not a happy marriage and at one stage Habibulla threatened to stab his wife. Instead, according to medical evidence given at his trial, he strangled his wife and taken into Habibulla's backyard where she was chopped in half, the pieces placed in hessian bags and driven by horse and cart to the Torrens River and dumped like a dead cat.

The jury at Habibulla's trial took less than an hour to consider its verdict – guilty. Although there was a strong recommendation of mercy, he was sentenced to death. He was hanged at the Adelaide Gaol on *November 16*, 1906.

NOVEMBER 17

THE $1.5 RANSOM (2003)

Building developer Alexander Yang Su hatched a quick way to raise $1.5 and put his plan into action on *March 3*, 2001. Sitting in his ex-wife's car in the eastern Melbourne suburb of Glen Waverley, he and two other men monitored the movements of 20-year-old University of Melbourne student John Lin. Then, when Lin parked his car outside his home, he was tackled by Su's accomplices and subjected to "shots" from an electric spark gun. He then was forced into the back of a car and told to be quiet. Su then tried to contact Lin's mother, but was told she was overseas and would not be back until the following day. Lin then was driven to a residential garage and was told he would be shot if he tried to escape as he was put into another vehicle and taken to another house.

Lin was forced to live in a bare room for several days , with his arms tied at the front and a hood over his head. Su told Lin he wanted $1.5 million from the victim's family and advised him to cooperate. Su eventually telephoned Lin's mother Rachel and told her her son had been kidnapped and that although the ransom demand was $1.5 million, he was trying to get this reduced to $800,000. Other calls followed, Lin was transferred from the house to one motel after another. An arrangement was made for the collection of the ransom money but Su quickly realised that his plan was falling apart and police eventually found Lin in a motel room. Su was quickly arrested and, on *November 17,* 2003, was sentenced to a total of 16 years' jail, with a non-parole period of 11 years.

NOVEMBER 18

HANGED (1881): William Nugent hanged at Adelaide Gaol on *November 18*, 1881, for the stabbing death of Police Trooper Harry Pearce on *May 17*, 1881.

NOVEMBER 19

THE KIDNAP RAPIST (1999)

Leslie Cuncliffe came up with a bizarre plan to solve his money problems, of kidnapping a young woman and demanding $1 million as a ransom. Cunliffe put his plan into operation on *May 10*, 1999, by following a young woman as she drove towards her university in the Victorian town of Geelong. He pulled her car over, introduced himself as a police sergeant and accused her of speeding. He then told her that, after checking, she had done nothing wrong and let her go. Then, a week later, the woman again was intercepted and this time accused her of having drugs in her car. Cunliffe then handcuffed her, pulled a handgun and forced his victim into his car. He then drove her to a shed where he led her to an alcove padded with foam and lined with thick plastic.

Cunliffe then put into operation his complicated ransom bid by taping a device with wires to the woman's chest and photographing her, blindfolded, gagged and tied to a chair. He then wrote a ransom note demanding $1 million, plus $1000 "interest" per day if payment is late. He said the devices under the woman's chest and at her feet were "all connected to a modem via a phone, which can detonate all or at any package at my demand". Cunliffe then put the note and the photograph in an envelope and took it to a designated telephone box where the package later was found by the woman's mother and 14-year-old brother.

Meanwhile, Cunliffe raped the woman, who said in her victim impact statement: "I thought he was going to mutilate me and I knew he was going to rape me. He never spoke to me again (after cutting away my trousers). The anticipation of the rape was worse than the rape itself. I've always been a modest girl and lying there with nothing covering me was a nightmare. I was dying inside … The rape made me lose all hope of survival; I gave up all hope of living. I even tried to will myself to die. If he raped me, no doubt he would kill me, I thought. When it was all over I was left shivering uncontrollably. I've never felt so empty and cold in my life; it was almost like part of me had died then and there. I remained in a miserable, black daze for a long time afterwards."

The woman eventually was able to work her arms free and be able to remove the tape from her mouth. She then "screamed and screamed and screamed", her pleas heard by the proprietor of a nearby fish shop. The police were called and the woman rescued from her horrifying experience.

Justice George Hempel on *November 19*, 1999, sentenced the 51-year-old Cunliffe to 20 years, with a minimum of 16 years on charges of false imprisonment, rape, extortion and making a bomb threat and the judge told him: "To say that these are extremely serious offences is a gross misunderstatement. The kidnapping and blackmailing were carefully planned. The method you adopted was persistent and calculated to produce as much fear in the victim and her parents as possible. It is hard to describe the terror and agony which your actions caused." On appeal, Cunliffe's sentence was reduced to 15 years' jail, with a minimum term of 12 years.

NOVEMBER 20

A DRUNKEN RAGE (1997)

Ian Edward Hoare and de facto wife Sally Anne Lorraine Hansen spent much of *November 20*, 1997, drinking and undoubtedly were under the influence of alcohol. On their way back home to a property known as *Ardroy*, Hansen went into the Longwood Hotel to buy some beer. However, she returned soon after to ask someone to call the police because

Hoare had become abusive. Hoare, in return, threatened violence with anyone who interfered with him and/or Hansen.

Hoare started attacking Hansen on the 15 kilometre trip back to the property and Hansen even went to a neighbour's house to get help. However, there was no one home and Hoare became increasingly violent. The ferocity of his onslaught was incredible as Hansen's entire scalp was bruised, with other serious injuries. In fact, Hansen's brain injuries were so severe that it was noted that they usually occurred in motor vehicle accidents.

Justice Vincent, in the Supreme Court of Victoria, said: "Miss Hansen sustained a subdural haemorrhage and damage deep in the brain which involved the tearing of the linkages between the two hemispheres. Professor Cordner, whom it must be borne in mind is an extremely experienced and highly qualified forensic pathologist, had not encountered an injury of this last type that was not associated with skull fracture and a motor vehicle accident." The judge told Hoare: "It is evident that you attacked the deceased, unleashing drunken uncontrolled rage. Although you did not intend to kill your victim, the jury has, understandably, found that you intended to inflict really serious physical injury upon her.' He sentenced Hoare to 16 years' imprisonment, with a fixed non-parole period of 12 years.

NOVEMBER 21

BLOOD AND BONES (1931)

Farmer Bernard Cunningham was mustering sheep near Bungendore, about six miles from Canberra, on *November 21*, 1931, when his dogs yapped and ran into a hollow. Cunningham went to investigate and came across the remains of a huge log fire. He at first thought it was a swaggy's camping site, until he noticed the dogs tugging on bones at the bottom of the ashes. Cunningham bent over, retrieved a bone from one of his dog's mouth and immediately recognised it as human.

Cunningham called police and Detective Sergeant Tom McRae and a team of investigating officers rushed to the scene. They verified that the blackened bones were human and started sifting ashes. Police worked in relay, sifting and re-sifting, looking for even the tiniest clue. Their task looked hopeless, especially when hours of work netted them just a handful of objects, including the molten remains of a gold watch, a belt buckle, a few teeth, a button, several coins and the barrel of a small calibre rifle.

Meanwhile, forensic experts told police the human remains were male and that death had occurred on or around *October 27* – more than three weeks before Cunningham's dogs had tugged at the bones. Police had little to work on, so decided to re-sift the ashes and this time they found a small key. More importantly, it carried a code number which, under microscopic examination gave a reading and eventually led to the identification of the body. However, was it murder or suicide? Police at first thought it was murder as the bones were found under logs used in the fire but, if it was suicide, the man would have had to shoot himself and ask an accomplice to stoke the fire for him. It sounded an implausible theory, but police had to keep an open mind on this intriguing case.

Police eventually discovered that the key had been made in Britian but, undeterred, called in Scotland Yard and police eventually were able to trace the key to the Sydney YMCA, who had given the key to a young man for a locker. It had been used by 21-year-old Sidney James Morrison, captain of the club's basketball team. Significantly, Morrison had not been seen since October. Police, convinced that the remains at Bungendore were those of Morrison, asked Professor A.N. Birkett of the Sydney University's Aanatomy Department to make a study of the bones. He reported that they were of a young man of approximately six feet and well built – precisely Morrison's physical description.

When detectives started questioning Morrison's friends, they learned that the missing young man had resigned his job as a clerk on *October 6*, 1931, and had told friends he was going to the bush to prospect for gold. It seemed out of character for Morrison but, even more disturbing Detective Sergeant McRae was told Morrison had been receiving psychiatric treatment. It seemed the young man had an inferiority complex and kept telling relatives he lacked personality.

Police again turned to the suicide theory and suggested that Morrison had lit the huge fire before killing himself so that he would fall back into the flames. This theory gained favour when police investigations proved that Morrison had bought the rifle at a well-known Sydney sports store at the time of his resignation from work. It therefore appeared Morrison might have planned a bizarre suicide. The problem with this theory was that there were logs found across

Morrison's blackened bones and traces of blood were found on dry branches several yards from the fire. And what about tyre marks near the scene? Who would have driven a car to and from the death scene?

Police painstakingly continued their investigations, but could not trace Morrison's movements over the last weeks of his life. The only sighting of him in the two weeks before his death was by an old prospector who had seen him with two men in a car about 20 miles from the death scene. Police were never able to trace these men and although an inquest was held into Morrison's death, the coroner returned an open finding. The mystery remains: suicide or murder?

**

HANGED (1927): William Henry Francis hanged at Adelaide Gaol on *November 21*, 1927, after being found guilty of the murder of his wife.

NOVEMBER 22

RELEASED (1872): Bushranger and horse and cattle thief Frank Gardiner, who had terrified parts of New South Wales during the gold rush era of the 1850s and early '60s, was arrested in Queensland in 1862 and, after being taken to Sydney for trial, was sentenced to 32 years' jail. However, he served just 10 years before being released on *November 22*, 1872. One condition of his release was that he leave the colonies. He therefore moved to California, where legend has it that he died in a bar room brawl.

NOVEMBER 23

THE RAZOR GANG BOSS (1948)

George Wallace might have looked like American comedian Oliver Hardy, but there was nothing comic about his activities. Wallace was one of Sydney's most ruthless criminals and revelled in his role as leader of "the Razor Gang". The hefty Wallace was a standover merchant who operated with seeming impunity throughout most of the 1930s. If you crossed Wallace or any of his gang, you invariably left with their trademark razor scar across the face. Wallace was suspected of many vicious crimes, but was not alone as other razor "experts" included Norman Bruhn, Frank Green and "Snowy" Cutmore, who was shot dead in a gunfight with Leslie "Squizzy" Taylor in Melbourne in October, 1927. Bruhn was shot dead a few months before in an ambush at Darlinghurst on *June 22*, 1927.

Wallace managed to survive the savage gang wars for more than 20 years, but the razor expert died in ironic circumstances in Perth on *November 23*, 1948, when he was stabbed to death while visiting a nightclub. It was a classic example of living by the sword and dying by the sword and few mourned the death of one of Australia's most vicious criminals. The dapper Green survived longer than any of his gangland contemporaries, but was stabbed to death by a girlfriend in Sydney in 1956.

NOVEMBER 24

HANGED)1964): Glen Sabre Valance hanged at Adelaide Gaol on *November 24*, 1964, after being found guilty of the shooting death of former employer Richard David Strang at the Kooroon Station on *June 16*, 1964.

NOVEMBER 25

SENTENCED (1825): Convict Richard Leary sentenced to death on *November 25*, 1825, for breaking and entering and the attempted rape of a woman near Sydney. He was hanged the next month, on *December 12*.

NOVEMBER 26

SENTENCED (1982): Satan worshippers Bob Reid and Peter Luckman sentenced to life imprisonment on *November 26*, 1982, for the brutal murder and torture of 13-year-old Peter Anston.

NOVEMBER 27

THE EVIL COUPLE (1987)

If Valmae Fae Beck was an unattractive woman, her husband Barrie John Watts was even less appealing. While Beck was dumpy with a pot belly, Watts was a curly-haired, shriveled creature with rodent-like features. They might have been opposites in appearance, but shared sexual fantasies. Watts dreamed of raping and killing young virgins, while Beck was more than willing to satisfy this sick and evil fantasy. They put their plan into operation on *November 27*, 1987, with Watts telling his wife of one year: 'Today is the day. It's on.' Beck and Watts, like spiders in a web, waited in their car on Queensland's Sunshine Coast for a victim. Tragically, pretty, blonde 12-year-old Sian Kingi was riding her bike at Tewantin, Queensland, when the evil couple called her over to their car to ask her if she had seen a poodle.

They abducted Kingi, with Watts grabbing her from behind and, with her arms bound and mouth taped, was taken to a nearby forest where Watts raped her while Beck watched. Watts then stabbed the innocent young girl a dozen times before slashing her throat and then strangling her with his wife's belt. Watts' lust had been satisfied and, almost unbelievably, he and his wicked wife went home and had a bath before watching television and then going to bed.

The discovery of Kingi's body outraged Queensland and, when Watts and Beck eventually were brought to justice a lynch mob greeted them, with some people carrying banners and placards which read 'Hang Them'. Although Beck and Watts had separate trials, both were sentenced to life imprisonment. During the sentencing of Beck, Justice Jack Kelly said: 'No decent person could not feel revulsion at what you did — and a woman with children of your own (she had six children from previous marriages).' He also described the woman prepared to watch an innocent girl raped and killed just to please her husband's sick fantasies as 'callous and cruel'.

Incredibly, Beck gave evidence at her trial that Kingi 'never cried, never shed a tear, she never uttered a peep, she just did everything we told her'. Watts was described at his trial as 'a thoroughly evil man devoid of any sense of morality'. Even more amazingly, Beck later claimed she was not as evil as she had been painted and had even become a born-again Christian. She said: 'I am not a repeat serious crime offender. I have no sex or violence offences on my record.' Although she made an appeal to have a lower security rating, this move failed.

However, Beck insisted that she had found God and would be applying for parole, much to the horror of little Sian's parents, Barry and Lynda Kingi. There therefore was outrage in Queensland in 2000 when Beck, (who changed her surname to Cramb) applied for work release, home detention and parole. The application was denied, but a friend said that everyone deserved forgiveness and added: 'If I had a daughter, I hope I would be big enough to try and forgive her, but I probably wouldn't. She was a victim of an obsessive love relationship with her husband.' Queensland Premier Peter Beattie, when told that Beck was seeking parole described the murder of Kingi as 'shocking' and added: 'Just because someone applies for parole does not necessarily mean they will get it.'

NOVEMBER 28

THE CHALK-PIT MURDER (1946)

"Connoisseurs" of murder might be puzzled by the title of this segment, for the "Chalk-Pit Murder" is one of England's most infamous cases. However, it deserves its place in this book of Australian crime because one of the accused was a leading

Australian politician. Thomas John Ley was a former New South Wales Minister for Justice and a controversial character in the world of political intrigue during the 1920s.

Ley, known as "Lemonade Ley" because of his temperance beliefs, left Australia at the end of his political career and took up residence in England. He lived in semi-retirement with his long-suffering mistresss Mrs Maggie Brook, who was considerably fitter than the grossly overweight Ley. Both were aged 66 but Mrs Brook was a relatively attractive woman, whereas Ley was a mountain of fat. This caused Ley much heartache as he became insanely jealous, regarding Mrs Brook as something of a personal possession. It might have been due to Ley's eventual impotence but, whatever the cause, the obsession led to murder.

The former politician believed that several young men were interested in Mrs Brook but particularly accused 35-yearold barman John Mudie, who had the gross misfortune to share the same lodging house with Mrs Brook at one stage in 1946. Mudie left the lodgings by the time Ley's jealousy had flared, but the former Australian political figure traced the harmless young barman to his new work place at Reigate, Surrey.

Ley then lured Mudie to a "party" in London on *November 28*, 1946. Mudie attended the "party", but discovered he was the only guest. Ley and two paid thugs, John Smith and John Buckingham, attacked Mudie, covering his head with a blanket before being left at Ley's mercy. A rope around Mudie's head apparently killed him, although it was not certain whether this was by design or by accident. Regardless, Mudie's body was placed in a shallow trench in a chalk-pit near Woldingham and the body was discovered two days later.

Ley and Smith were later charged with murder and both were sentenced to death. However, Ley by this time was desperately ill and escaped the hangman after being declared insane. He died a few months after his trial, while Smith's death sentence was commuted to life imprisonment.

NOVEMBER 29

DEATH ON A TRAIN (1966)

Sales demonstrator Pamela Blair was returning to her St Peters home in Sydney on the night of *November 29*, 1966, but never reached her destination. Mrs Blair caught a train at Hurstville station at 8.11pm, intending to leave at the Sydenham station 22 minutes later. However, she was attacked on the last leg of her journey home. She was bashed about the head with a heavy brass door lever, wrenched from a carriage, and left to die. Mrs Blair, who suffered terrible head injuries, was discovered by fellow passenger Cecil Johnson, who tried to help the injured woman by putting a handkerchief to her head wounds. The woman was partly conscious, but largely incoherent and therefore was unable to give Mr Johnson or the train guard any information on her attacker.

Mrs Blair was rushed to hospital but did not recover from her head wounds and died, despite emergency surgery. A mysterious young man was seen on the train on the night of the murder and one witness said that the "aggressive" young man made a sort of "growling noise" as he moved about the train. The killer has never been brought to justice, despite massive police efforts and the New South Wales government offering a reward for information on the woman's death

THE SWIMMER WHO DROWNED (1996)

When Tattslotto agent Ian Freeman drowned at the Cairn Curran Reservoir, near Bendigo, in November, 1996, his adult children reacted with disbelief. Son Paul and daughter Claire kept asking themselves how their father could have drowned in water less than a metre deep. After all, he was a strong swimmer and a proficient and experienced windsurfer.

An autopsy at the Bendigo Hospital revealed that Freeman indeed had drowned and that seemed the end of the matter, despite problems Paul and Claire immediately had with their stepmother. Sue Freeman had arranged for her husband's body to be cremated, without even discussing it with her stepchildren. Then, to compound problems, Sue Freeman told Paul and Claire that there would be a small private funeral with only a handful of guests. This horrified Paul and Claire, who eventually discovered their father's most recent will, made three months before his death. This will named them as his beneficiaries and they eventually had their own way, with a well-attended funeral service. Sue Freeman was furious, but there was nothing she could do about it.

Then, the day after Freeman's funeral, a woman contacted Bendigo police with the amazing claim that Sue Freeman had been asking local identities whether they could have her husband killed. The woman even gave police a name — Ian Richard Brown — and said he knew something about Freeman's death. Police launched an immediate investigation, but were partly stymied by Freeman's cremation the previous day and had to rely on the original pathology report that death was caused by asphyxia, or drowning. To make matters worse, there were no photographs of Freeman's body at the hospital as the mortuary camera had been sent away for repairs. However, police did have a photograph of Freeman's Mitsubishi Colt car hanging over a ledge above shallow water and another photograph of the body immediately after it was discovered on the morning of *November 29*.

These photographs, in conjunction with the telephone call they had received, finally made police extremely suspicious that a murder had been committed. Police therefore contacted Brown, who told them Sue Freeman once had told him she wanted her husband killed. She even asked if he knew anyone who would murder her husband. She wanted rid of him because, she told Brown, he no longer showed interest in her and, besides, she suspected him of giving Paul and Claire Tattslotto 'scratchy' tickets.

Brown told police he then came into contact with Greek motor mechanic Emmanuel Chatzidimitriou, who was known as Max Chatz, and told him about Sue Freeman's determination to have her husband killed. Chatz was interested, for a $10,000 down-payment and another $40,000 on completion of the job. Chatz and Sue Freeman met to discuss 'business' and, on the night of *November 28*, he launched his murderous plan.

Ian Freeman, who also worked at the Adult, Community and Further Education Regional Council, left this job at close of business and arrived at the Tattslotto agency to relieve his wife just before 7pm. Freeman, according to security records, left the shop at 9.39pm and was not seen alive again. Chatz, it later was argued in court, abducted Freeman at gunpoint and forced him to drive his Mitsubishi to the reservoir. Chatz then tied his victim's hands behind his back, pushed him into the back of the car and drove it into the water. It also was claimed in court that Chatz told a prisoner while on remand that he pulled Freeman out of the car and then held his head under water until he was dead. Freeman's hands then were untied and the body floated on top of the water. Meanwhile, police had to prove their case and their whistle-blower was a self-confessed drug addict — hardly an auspicious start to their case in proving murder.

Police therefore interviewed Brown and after he gave them details of the Freeman-Chatz pay-for-murder arrangement, launched an under-cover operation. Brown subsequently had several meetings with Sue Freeman, all taped. Finally, Brown met up with Chatz and, despite the motor mechanic frisking him, Brown managed to hide a bugging device.

Police arrested Chatz and four days later, Sue Freeman and her solicitor went to the police. Neither Chatz nor Sue Freeman made any admissions, but police were able to build a strong case, especially as they found money in a drawer at Chatz's home. However, Chatz insisted that, in fact, Brown had killed Ian Freeman. Eventually, Chatz and Freeman went to trial separately for murder, Chatz in Bendigo and Freeman in Melbourne. Both were found guilty of murder.

Freeman, at her plea hearing, was portrayed as a hard-working woman whose husband had been violent towards her. However, Justice Hempel said: 'This is not a case of a desperate, trapped woman or a case of highly emotionally charged circumstances in which some people react and kill … This is a case of a plan to kill, when each of you had ample time to do."

NOVEMBER 30

SENTENCED (1994): Robert Lowe on *November 30*, 1994, sentenced to life imprisonment, never to be released, for the murder of six-year-old Sheree Beasley at the Victorian coastal resort of Rosebud.

DECEMBER

The month of December might be highlighted by Christmas, but even this sacred celebration has been marred by murder, mystery and mayhem. It has been a gruesome month in the Australian crime calendar and, in fact, probably poses more questions of guilt than any other month, including the possibility of a wrong man being executed. Crimes this month include:

THE NGUYEN HANGING
THE QUEEN STREET MASSACRE
PERVERT 'DOLLY' DUNN
THE HUMAN GLOVE
THE GATTON MYSTERY
THE GUN ALLEY MURDER
And much, much more!

DECEMBER 1

"LABELLED" FOR CHILD RAPE (1825)

When William Creswell was indicted in 1825 for an alleged assault and attempted rape of an eight-year-girl, the Supreme Court of New South Wales' Judge Stephen told him it was an atrocious crime that rarely came before the courts. A 10 year-old boy, the girl's companion, gave evidence against Creswell and a medical examination at Wooloomooloo further told against the charged man. He was found guilty and was sentenced to a year's jail. Further, he was ordered to stand pilloried in Sydney, with labels stating his offence, on two separate days — *December 1*, 1825, and one year later.

THE TAMAN SHUD RIDDLE (1948)

A simple headstone in the West Torrens cemetery, Adelaide, says simply: "Here Lies the Unknown Man Who Was Found at Somerton Beach – *1st Dec.* 1948." The body of the middle-aged man was buried in the grave in June, 1949, more than six months after being discovered on the Somerton sands. The body had been embalmed and this more than anything else suggested that South Australian police were unwilling to give up early on this mystery, known either as the Somerton Sands Mystery or the Taman Shud Riddle.

The body was embalmed so that it could be examined on any future exhumation. It was said at the time the body was buried that it would be well preserved for many years. However, there has been no lead in police investigations to warrant an exhumation and the mystery remains and no one even knows whether the man died of natural causes or was murdered.

The mystery developed on *December 1*, 1948, when Adelaide jeweller John Lyons was walking along Somerton beach. He had been there the previous night and had seen a man slumped against the esplanade steps. Mr Lyons therefore was shocked to see the man still there the next morning. In fact, the man was dead and the police were called. However, there was nothing to identify the body – no letters, no passport, no note. There was just a scrap of paper bearing the words "Taman Shud". Police had no idea of what it meant and originally believed it was part of a foreign language.

Dr John Dwyer, a vastly experienced pathologist, examined the body at the Adelaide morgue and was struck by the man's superb physical condition. The subject was about 45 years of age, about 5ft 11in, strongly built and apparently in perfect health before he died. All organs were normal and Dr Dwyer concluded that death was caused by heart failure, but that in itself presented another mystery as there seemed no reason why the man's heart should fail and there was no trace of poison, although he noted that not all poisons could be traced in the body.

Police, meanwhile, concentrated on their Taman Shud clue, being told that the words were from Omar Khayyam's *Rubaiyat*. The words had a macabre significance as they meant "the end". Once the meaning was discovered, a doctor came forward to say that he had found a copy of the *Rubaiyat* on the back seat of his car while it was parked at Somerton on the night of *November 30*. The page bearing the words Taman Shud was torn from the book and matched the paper found on the dead man, who must have realised he was near his own end. The book found by the doctor also had a series of capital letters pencilled on the last page and they read:

MRGOADARD

MTBIMPANETP

MLIABOAIAQC

ITTMTSASTGAB

There was a cross over the letter O on the third line, but what did it all mean? Police called in code experts, but no one was able to unravel the message if, indeed, it was a message.

Finally, a tailor told police that the man's clothing had been made in America and when police found a suitcase at the Adelaide rail station, the clothes inside matched those on the dead man. There also was a laundry mark bearing the name Kean or Keane, but all police leads petered out.

At an inquest into the mystery man's death, coroner T.E. Cleland concluded that murder could not be ruled out and that (1) The identity of the man was unknown (2) Death was not natural (3) Death was probably caused by poison and (4) Death almost certainly was not accidental. The coroner also concluded that there was not sufficient evidence to warrant a finding. However, police later noticed that a woman dressed in black placed flowers on the grave every December for years. Police interviewed her but although she claimed to have known the man, they were not convinced. So, the riddle remains.

DECEMBER 2

TWO INNOCENT CHILDREN (1865)

George Johnson left his home near Glenorchy, Tasmania, on the morning of *September 12*, 1865, to cart materials. Later, wife Emily, leaves the family home with daughter Mary to cut firewood on the opposite side of a stream. Two smaller children, Sarah (six) and George (eight), are left on their own to play outside. However, Mrs Johnson had not gone long when a man named William Griffiths started searching the home for goods he could sell to raise money for alcohol. Sarah and George spotted him and ran off to signal an alarm. However, Griffiths caught up with them and bashed them violently with a hammer. Sarah died instantly from wounds to the head, while George lingered until he died late at night.

Griffiths fled to Hobart, but was captured in the Kings Arms hotel the day of the murders. Griffiths, naturally, denied all knowledge of the murders and even swore he would get even with the police for handcuffing him. The itinerant worker was charged with the wilful murder of the two children and claimed: "I am quite innocent of the crime brought against me. I would not take life away for anything. I haven't the heart to do it. That is known in the neighbourhood well." However, numerous witnesses gave incriminating evidence against Griffiths in the Tasmanian Criminal Court.

Before sentence, Chief Justice Sir Valentine Fleming told the prisoner: "You must look for a more enduring mercy in another world. For you who have mercilessly deprived two innocent children of their lives, it would be a mockery to suppose that any mercy could be extended to you … it is now my duty as the mouthpiece of the law to pronounce upon you the sentence which it provides for your crime, and which is that you be taken from the place from whence you came, and then to a place of execution, and that you there be hanged by the neck until your body be dead, and may the Lord God have mercy upon your soul." Griffiths was hanged on the morning of *December 2*, 1865, and was reported to have cried bitterly on his way to the gallows.

THE 'SON' WHO KILLED (1969)

Officers at the Moonee Ponds police station in suburban Melbourne could not believe their ears when a man claimed on *December 2*, 1969, that he had a body in his car. Detective Ken Smith spoke to the young man and police then examined a car parked outside the police station. The body of a young woman was lying across the front seat. Police then went to a house in the nearby suburb of Niddrie and discovered the body of a younger woman. The dead women were sisters, and the man who had walked into the police station had been engaged to the older woman. Police had twin killings on their hands but at least they did not have to launch a search for the killer.

The dead sisters were Lynette (19) and Anthea (16) Ainsworth. Douglas Alfred Mauger, 24, was charged with having murdered the sisters. It was a tragic case as Mauger had moved into the Ainsworth family home two and a half years earlier and Mr Bernard Ainsworth, father of the dead girls, said he treated Mauger "like a son". Mr Ainsworth said he believed Mauger had been deprived as a youth and "wanted to give him the things he missed". Mauger and Lynette Ainsworth became engaged in November, 1961. Mauger moved into a pet shop business early the following year, but that venture indirectly led to his troubles as the business failed and he was declared bankrupt. The engagement therefore was called off in October, 1962.

The engagement was an "on-off" affair and the young couple made several attempts to reconcile their differences. However, it seemed they would never really get together again. At least that is how it appeared to Mauger, and he was determined not to lose the girl he loved. The matter came to a head on the night of *December 1* when Mauger watched his former fiancée talking to another young man at the Ainsworth home. It was an innocent enough conversation, but it was the turning point for Mauger.

He spoke to Lynette in her bedroom that night and told her he did not want to lose her. But even then Lynette could not have known that Mauger would go to such extremes. He loaded a .22 rifle, went into Lynette's bedroom again but did not pull the trigger. He just could not kill, not at that stage, anyway. Mauger, soon after nine o'clock the next morning, went into Anthea Ainsworth's bedroom and shot her in the body and then in the head. He then battered the girl about the head with a hammer as he was convinced she had had something to do with his broken engagement. Mauger then drove to the Ainsworth garage business, picked up Lynette and drove to an area near Anthea's school in Essendon. A struggle developed and Mauger shot Lynette five times in the head and then drove to the police station.

Mauger pleaded not guilty to two charges of murder and his counsel entered a plea of insanity on his behalf. However, the jury took just an hour and a half to find him guilty. Mauger was sentenced to death, but this later was commuted to 50 years' imprisonment and the State Executive Council ordered that he not be eligible for parole until he had served 40 years.

THE BODY IN THE BATH (1998)

Craig John Whittle had boarded for a couple of weeks at the home of Judith Fowler in Narre Warren and visited her on the night of *December 2*, 1998, along with two other men. It was a social visit but, during the night, Fowler offended Whittle by pointing to one of his friends that he had taken a can of beer which did not belong to him. Whittle, 35, felt Fowler, in her 30s, had "dobbed" on him and, after leaving the house with his friends, returned and confronted Fowler.

He punched her several times in the face before she went from the kitchen to the bathroom, where he ordered her to undress. Whittle punched her again, causing several injuries, and then strangled her with his hands. He then took her to the bathroom, placed her in a bath and filled it up with water. Whittle cleaned up as best he could and left the house.

The body of Judith Fowler went undiscovered for five days and although Whittle at first denied any knowledge of what had happened to the woman, he finally admitted that he had killed her. In sentencing Whittle to 17 years' jail, with a minimum term of 13 years, Justice Teague told him: "I weigh in your favour that the murder of Judith Fowler was not premeditated. You did not, at the time you first went to her house or when you went back to her house, intend to kill her. Your plan on returning only was to remonstrate. As events developed, your intention changed. It is of great concern that your relatively spontaneous reaction to circumstances was so terrifying and so brutal."

THE NGUYEN HANGING (2005)

Nguyen Tuong Van, an Australian who was born in Thailand of Vietnamese parents, was in financial difficulties in 2002 and therefore accepted an extraordinary offer to wipe out debts he and his twin brother Dang Khoa had incurred. It is believed that Nguyen himself had debts of around $20,000, while his brother owed about $12,000.

The debts stemmed mainly from costs incurred by Dang Khoa on drug charges and, with the deadline for the payment of the loan in full approaching, Nguyen contacted a friend for assistance. He then was told to make contact with another man, who told him he could wipe out the debts if he transported packages from Cambodia to Australia. Nguyen agreed, and it cost him his life.

Nguyen arrived in Phnom Penh on *December 3,* 2002, and eventually was taught how to tape packages to his body. Then, on *December 12,* he set out for his return to Australia. However, he triggered a metal detector while at Singapore's Changi airport while awaiting a connecting flight to Australia. Airport officials investigated and noticed a strange lump on Nguyen's back. They asked him to strip down and found packages of heroin. Nguyen then told them he had another package in his luggage and eventually confessed to possessing 396 grams of heroin, which was more than 15 times the amount for a mandatory death sentence.

After Nguyen had pleaded guilty to possessing the heroin, the Singapore High Court on *October 20*, 2004, sentenced him to death. The sentence sparked outrage in Australia and the Australian government pleaded with Singapore for clemency. All pleas fell on deaf ears and Nguyen was hanged at Singapore's Changi Prison at 6.07am on *December 2*, 2005.

His body was released to his family four hours later and taken to the Marymount Chapel of the Good Shepherd Convent in Singapore. From there, his body was taken to Australia four days later and a requiem mass was held at St Patrick's Cathedral, Melbourne, on *December 7*, attended by an estimated 2000 mourners.

DECEMBER 3

A BEER BOTTLE THROUGH THE HEART (1971)

Maureen Bradley, 14 years of age, was not the type of girl to run away from home. She had regular habits and, before she disappeared on her way home from her Sydney school on the afternoon of *December 3*, 1971, she had telephoned her mother from Hornsby railway station to say she would not be long. It was the last time Mrs Bradley heard her daughter's voice. Despite every effort and one of the biggest searches in Sydney for many years, no sign of Maureen Bradley was found over the following 10 days.

The naked body of the pretty blonde eventually was found in a disused septic tank at McKell Park, Brooklyn. She had been stabbed through the heart with a broken beer bottle and there was such outrage that the New South Wales government offered a reward of $10,000 for the arrest of Maureen's killer.

Police eventually made an arrest on *January 16*, 1972, when a 20-year-old man was charged with the attempted rape of a woman at the northern suburb of Cowan. Labourer Bruce Kenneth McKenzie stood trial at the Central Criminal Court from *June 5* that year and the court was told he had confessed to murdering Maureen Bradley. Detective-Sergeant Albert

MacDonald said McKenzie had told him he had waited near a bush track as Maureen was walking home from school. He then grabbed her by the neck, dragged her to his car and locked her in the boot before driving to Brooklyn, about 14 kilometres away. He then backed the car into the bush and, with the girl's neck locked in his arms, marched her to the septic tank where he made her undress before he indecently assaulted her.

Then, when McKenzie heard someone shout "hey", he thought someone had seen him. He therefore picked up a beer bottle, smashed it and drove it twice into Maureen's chest, piercing her heart. A jury took just 10 minutes to find McKenzie guilty of murder and he was sentenced to life imprisonment. When Justice Slattery asked him if he had anything to say, McKenzie replied: "I am sorry for the trouble I have caused the girl's family and my own, and I just wish to do what is right in the future."

DECEMBER 4

NOT GUILTY (1998): Unemployed mechanic Greg Domaszewicz on *December 4*, 1998, found not guilty of murdering 14-month Jaidyn Leskie at Moe, Victoria, on *January 1*, 1998. (Refer to *January 1*)

DECEMBER 5

KILLED (1952): Adelaide prostitute Zora Kusic was killed, her throat slashed, in Adelaide on *December 5*, 1952. Her killer, Rumanian migrant John Balaban hanged on *August 26*, 1953.

DECEMBER 6

LAST SEEN (1994): Melbourne woman Elizabeth Membrey last seen after she left her job at the Manhattan Hotel, Ringwood, at approximately 11.45pm on *December 6*, 1994.

DECEMBER 7

HANGED (1868): Thomas Woods hanged at Brisbane on *December 7*, 1860, and aborigine "Billy" hanged in Brisbane on *December 7*, 1868.

DECEMBER 8

THE GREAT RAILWAY BLAST (1941)

Workers for the New South Wales railways were paid in cash in years gone by and, in 1941, more than 1000 of these workers were expecting wages of more than 10,000 pounds when their "pay express" left Sydney on *December 8*. The money was in a large safe welded to the carriage chassis. Paymaster Fred Walker was in charge of handing out the cash but, as the train approached a bridge near the Hume Highway not far from Bowral, there was a loud explosion. The railway carriage had been blown onto one side and driver George

Rendall and guard Alfred Philpott were killed almost instantly. Paymaster Walker was critically injured and died later in a hospital in Bowral.

Police were investigating one of the state's worst crimes, and a rare one at that. Not only had the thieves planned a rail robbery, but had killed three men. Police found wires leading from the rail line to a wire fence on the side of the track. They also found bank notes scattered all over the countryside and, despite some being pilfered, most of the money was recovered. An inquest was held into the death of the three rail employees, but the coroner found they had been killed "by persons unknown". The culprits have never been brought to justice.

THE VIOLENT HUSBAND (1997)

Dale Wesley Barry had a stormy relationship with his wife Sharon after marrying on *September 19*, 1992. In fact, he was found guilty of assaulting her just months before their wedding and even assaulted her on their wedding night. Sharon Lee-Anne Barry had two children, a boy and a girl, from other relationships and then, in February, 1995, had son Jaimyn together.

However, the violence continued and, after Barry struck his wife on the jaw in November, 1996, she took out an apprehended violence order, which later was extended. Despite this, husband and wife got back together, until they separated again in October, 1997. Then, two months later, Mrs Barry told her husband he no longer would have access to the children. Finally, on the night of *December 8*, 1997, Barry made his way to the family home after a drinking session at the Boomerang Hotel, Lavington. He had keys to the house, which he entered at around 2am and became embroiled in an argument with his estranged wife.

Tara Barry, just 12 years of age, saw and heard them arguing before returning to her own bedroom. While standing at the doorway facing the hall, Barry headed in her direction and stabbed her in the upper abdomen, the knife penetrating several centimetres into the right lobe of her liver. He then forced Tara and his wife to the kitchen and stabbed Mrs Barry at least four times, three of these thrusts into her right breast, penetrating a major vessel in her lungs.

Tara managed to make her way back to her bedroom and waited there until her step-father had left the house. She then went to the bedroom of her six-year-old brother Benjamin and asked him to get the help of a neighbour. However, that neighbour found Mrs Barry already dead in a pool of blood. Tara survived her stabbing, but only through the expertise of surgeons and her 39-year-old stepfather was charged with murder and maliciously wounding the 12-year-old girl.

Barry, who had previous convictions for crimes of violence, was sentenced to 18 years' imprisonment for the murder of his wife and 12 years for maliciously wounding his step-daughter. He will not be eligible for parole until 2021.

DECEMBER 9

THE QUEEN STREET MASSACRE (1987)

Australian newspapers on the morning of *December* 9, 1987, had room on their front pages for just one report, of a masscre which horrified the nation. A crazed gunman late on the previous afternoon (*December 8*) had run amok in the heart of

Melbourne, killing eight people and wounding another six before jumping to his own death. The gunman was 22-year-old law school, dropout Frank Vitkovic, who wrote a note to his family before embarking on his horrific mission of carnage.

Vitkovic entered an Australia Post building in Queen Street and stepped out of the lift on the fifth floor, at the office of the Telecom Credit Co-Operative, and announced that he was there to see an old school friend, credit officer Con Margelis. However, Vitkovic produced a semi-automatic rifle and pointed it at the young man he had known for about seven years. The gunman fired at Margelis but, incredibly, it misfired and Margelis was able to make his escape. Vitkovic, meanwhile, shot 19-year-old Judith Morris before making his way to the twelfth floor of the builing.

He entered an Australia Post office and started firing indiscriminately, killing Julie McBean, Warren Spencer, Nancy Avignone before heading down one floor and killing Michael McGuire, Catherine Dowling, Marianne Van Ewyk and Rodney Brown. Vitkovic could have continued his killing spree if it had not been for accounts employee Tony Gioia, who struggled with the gunman in an attempt to disarm him. However, Vitkovic managed to get away and jumped out a window.

DECEMBER 10

'MAD MOSSY' (1925)

The man known as "Mad Mossy" was a burly swaggie named Albert Andrew Moss, who was born at Narromine in 1885 and first came to the attention of police when he was just 17 years of age. From there, it was a downhill run all the way and whenever arrested for one misdemenour or another, he would plead insanity and either would be sent to jail or an ayslum. For example, on *December 10*, 1925, he was certified insane and committed to the Darlingurst Reception House, but declared sane and released just four days later.

To all intents and purposes, Moss embarked on a murderous spree some time in 1933 with the killing of another swaggie, 41-year-old William Henry Bartley. The rampage was brief, but Moss eventually was charged with the murder of Bartley and two other itinerant workers, 55-year-old Timothy O'Shea and 65-year-old Thomas Robinson. He was found guilty of the murders of O'Shea and Robinson and sentenced to death. However, this was commuted to life imprisonment and, while in Long Bay Jail, bragged that the actual number of murders — purely for financial or worldy gains like a horse and buggy — was more like 13 or 14. "Mad Mossie" died in jail on *January 24*, 1958.

DECEMBER 11

'DEPRAVED' (2002)

When Victorian County Court Judge Bill White on *December 11*, 2002, sentenced sexual predator Andrew Timothy Davies to a nominal sentence of 11 years' jail, he told him his conduct delved the depths of depravity. Davies had been convicted of stalking, abducting and digitally raping two six-year-old girls in a Victorian town. The judge told the 34-year-old Davies: "It could be said that words are inadequate to describe your ciminal conduct. The girls were forced to endure disgraceful sexual abuse in order to satisfy your depraved sexual desires ... The crimes have led to the breakdown of the marriage of one of the girls' parents and damaged the victims, families and their small community.

The judge also told Davies he could apply to the court for parole after the completion of his sentence, but that his prospects looked dim. Davies had been given the maximum penalty available in Victoria but, on appealing to the Court of Appeal, his sentence was revised to one of 16 years with a minimum term of 12 years. The court suggested that after at least 12 years behind bars, Davies might change his mind about having sex offender treatment.

DECEMBER 12

THE LAMBING FLAT RIOTS (1860)

Many of the men who rushed to the goldfields during the 1850s viewed their Chinese counterparts with suspicion and resentment. In a blatant example of racism, a group of white miners on *December 12*, 1860, attacked the Chinese quarter at Lambing Flat in the Burrangong region in New South Wales, ostensibly to clean up opium and gambling dens. Several Chinese miners were killed and, eventually, most of the Chinese were forced to flee the area. Then, when the Chinese returned, there was another outbreak of violence, on *June 30*, 1861.

THE WORST OF THE WORST (2004)

When Geoffrey Robert Dodds faced a Queensland District Court for sentencing on *December 12*, 2004, he was described as Australia's worst paedophile. Dodds, who molested an estimated 150 girls aged between one and 15 years over a period of 30 years, was handed an indefinite jail sentence, a reflection of the extent of his horrific crimes. Yet Dodds, who pleaded guilty to 116 child offences, was arrested only because of his own depravity. He had had his home wired so that he could videotape his activities. Then, after he took his video camera for the repair of a tape jam, he was arrested in Melbourne. There were more than 500 hours of video and Dodds' indefinite sentence was intended to protect the community. He appealed to the Queensland Court of Appeal, but this was dismissed. Dodds, whose victims included his daughter's friends and his wife's friends' daughter, tried to cover his tracks by burning two 44-gallon drums of evidence which included videos, photographs and girls' clothing. Married, Gibbs was a member of two church groups and a gymnastics coach.

DECEMBER 13

HANGED (1865): Rudolf Momberger hanged in Brisbane on *December 13*, 1865.

DECEMBER 14

THE INFERIORITY COMPLEX KILLER (1950)

Good-looking Ronald Newman Cribbin was educated at one of Melbourne's best Catholic colleges, but ended up a cold-blooded killer. Young Cribbin started his criminal career as a hold-up man, robbing taxi drivers of their hard-earned fares. He got away with this for some time, but eventually was caught red-handed and sentenced to 18 months' jail, serving his time at Pentridge.

Cribbin left jail with an enormous chip on his shoulder and the 21-year-old, who already had exhibited an inferiority complex, soon showed an extreme tendency to believe that everyone considered him worthless. He always had the impression that people were laughing at him. This wasn't true but Cribbin nurtured these feelings and they festered inside him. Those feelings helped turn him into a killer.

Cribbin's short-lived career as a killer started in Sydney on *December 14*, 1950. After being released from Pentridge, Cribbin headed for New South Wales, obviously intent on leading a life of crime. He struck pay dirt almost immediately when he robbed 72-year-old widow Mrs Edith Hill of 15,000 pounds worth of jewels and killed her in the process. Mrs Hill, who lived alone in a flat in Macquarie Street, Sydney, was bashed and, severely wounded, was discovered on the evening of *December 14* by her daughter, Mrs Sibella Brooker. However, Mrs Hill later died of her wounds.

Just two days after killing Mrs Hill, Cribbin hailed a taxi driven by 36-year-old father of five, Norman Cecil Dickson. Cribbin told Dickson to stop after a short journey and immediately produced a gun. Dickson resisted and was shot for his trouble. Cribbin later claimed the gun "went off" but he also admitted that he then "shot at his head to put him out of pain".

Cribbin then drove the taxi, with Dickson's body in the back seat, due west. He was only a few miles out of Bathurst when a motorcycle policeman stopped the taxi because he could not notice any passengers. Senior Constable Reg Lowe then dodged a bullet as Cribbin fired at him from the driver's seat. Lowe fired back, but Cribbin was able to escape in the taxi.

Cribbin later crashed the taxi but immediately sped off on foot, leaving Dickson's body in the back. It was a frantic rush for freedom and Cribbin even swam across a river in his bid to escape his pursuers. However, his efforts proved futile and police arrested him at gunpoint. Police obviously wanted to talk to Cribbin about the death of the cab driver and therefore were horrified when he confessed to the murder of Mrs Hill.

The 21-year-old was found guilty of Mrs Hill's murder despite pleading insanity. It was obvious he had planned the robbery in great detail and although he claimed he struck the widow with a rifle because she "kept fighting" him, the jury obviously believed he knew exactly what he was doing. Cribbin was sentenced to death, but this was commuted to life imprisonment.

DEATH IS NO JOKE (1987)

A number of people were drinking on the southern banks of the Murray River, near Tocumwal, at the fortieth birthday party of a man named Greg Baldwin when aborigine Wayne Jackson and others started telling racist jokes. Jackson even told a story against his own people and this offended New

Zealander Glen Ian Ford. Jackson, knowing Ford was a Kiwi, then told a joke offensive to New Zealanders. As a result, Ford tried to pick a fight with Jackson, but the aborigine and some friends decided to leave the camp site where the party was held on *December 14*, 1987.

Ford followed them, still wanting a fight, and when he caught up with Jackson, who was lagging behind his friends, said he would stab the aborigine — not in the back, but in the chest. Jackson threw a can of beer at Ford, who then grabbed hold of the man he considered had been offensive and stabbed him three times, with one wound penetrating the heart. Jackson was rushed to hospital, but died as a result of his wounds.

Ford, meanwhile, left the camp, took off the blood-stained t-shirt he was wearing and washed himself in the river. He also went back to the camp and kicked dirt over the blood left by Jackson's wounds. Ford then tried to drive away, but was arrested by police and charged with murder. Justice Barr, in the Supreme Court of New South Wales, said: "I think that the only explanation of the offender's extraordinary conduct which led to the killing of the deceased is a combination of the ingrained desire to control others and the disinhibiting effects of the alcohol he consumed. There is no evidence of precisely how much he had had to drink, but I think it must have been a significant amount." Ford, who had had convictions for offences of violence, was sentenced to 16 years' jail, with a fixed non-parole period of 12 years.

DECEMBER 15

THE U-TURN TO DEATH (1996)

When Brian Morgan Hall went fishing with a friend on *December 15*, 1996, he would not have known that the pleasant Sunday afternoon would lead to a night of tragedy, a charge of murder and a long jail sentence. Hall, 22, arrived at Birkenhead Point, New South Wales, after the fishing trip and started drinking at the local tarven in Roseby Street. He and his friend left there at closing time at 10pm and headed for their car in the multi-level car park next door. Then, when Hall drove over a low barrier separating the car park from the footpath, he was subjected to taunts from several onlookers.

Hall, upset over some of the comments, replied with an outburst of his own and was invited to get out of his car by a man named Mark Webber. Hall took up the invitation, but Webber got the better of him before they separated. Although Hall got back into his car, Webber punched him in the face through the open window. Hall then drove off but, at the next intersection, did a U-turn and drove to where Webber and others were still standing. The car struck Webber and another man, Wayne Piper. People rushed to the injured men's aid and these included Webber's sister Brooke and a man named Paul Allen.

Hall, after reaching the bottom of Roseby Street, turned and drove back up the street and his car hit Brooke and Mark Webber, and Allen. Although Allen was not seriously injured, Brooke Webber died of her injuries a week later in the Royal Prince Alfred Hospital. Hall was charged with murder and a number of other serious offences. A jury found him guilty of the murder of Brooke Webber, maliciously wounding Mark

Webber with intent to do him serious bodily harm and seriously inflicting grievous bodly harm on Wayne Piper with intent to do grievous bodily harm

In a record of interview with police hours after the incidents which led to Brooke Webber's death, Hall was asked why he did a U-turn and he replied: "I suppose it was out of anger just 'cause I had the shit kicked out of me and I just wanted to get them back, I suppose." Hall, whose blood alcohol level at the time was .170, appeared to have several gaps of memory in relation to the incidents. However, Justice Hidden said it was a "wonder" how "a young man of his character could have embarked upon such a dreadful criminal enterprise". The judge sentenced Hall to 19 and a half years' jail for the murder of Brooke Webber, with a minimum of 14 years and six months. On the charges of maliciously inflicting grievous bodily harm with intent to do grievous bodily harm, the judge sentenced Hall to concurrent fixed terms of 10 years. Hall will not be eligible for release on parole until late 2013.

**

PAINFUL DEATH (1875): An inquest on *December 15*, 1875, into the death of bushranger James Duncan revealed that he died in agony from an abscess on the liver. London-born Duncan was serving a 10-year sentence at Melbourne's Pentridge for the burglary of a jeweller's in Bourke Street, Melbourne, when he died.

DECEMBER 16

HANGED (1907): August Millewski hanged in Brisbane on *December 16*, 1907, after being found guilty of murder.

DECEMBER 17

ESCAPE (1834): Bushranger Edward Boyd, who operated in the Monaro district of New South Wales in the early 1830s, was captured after raiding a property near Cooma on *December 14*, 1834, but managed to escape. Then, on *December 17*, he shot dead overseer Charles Fisher while on the run. Boyd himself was shot dead the next month.

DECEMBER 18

DUAL KILLER (2002)

When Robert Sievers was sentenced to lif imprisonment for the shooting murder of estranged wife Dianna Sievers in Newcastle, NSW, in 1980, it was believed the 51-year-old life of crime was over. However, he was released on parole 12 years later and, after eight years of freedom, killed again. This time he stabbed girlfriend Michelle Campbell to death during at argument in their Sydney suburban home of Lakemba. He was sentenced to another term of life imprisonment on *December 18*, 2002, and this time he is unlikely ever to be released.

DECEMBER 19

PERVERT 'DOLLY' DUNN (2004)

A judge once described sexual predator Robert "Dolly" Dunn as one of Australia's most notorious paedophiles and "would remain a danger to children until the day he died". A former Marist Brother primary school teacher, pervert Dunn in 2001 was sentenced to 30 years' jail, with a non-parole period of 22 and a half years for 24 sexual offences against young boys over a 10-year period to 1995, and on three drug charges. He pleaded guilty to all charges and although he appealed on the grounds that he was deceived into making these pleas, he lost his case. However, on *December 19*, 2004, he won an appeal on the severity of his sentence and he consequently was ordered to serve 20 years' jail, with a non-parole period of 18 years. At 65 years of age, Dunn is unlikely to be released.

DECEMBER 20

SINGLE PAY FOR TWO EXECUTIONS (1916)

Police constable George Duncan was sitting in his office at the Tottenham (about 100 kilometres east of Dubbo, New South Wales), police station on *September 26*, 1916, when he was shot through a window. Two brothers, Roland and Herbert Kennedy and their friend Frank Franz were arrested and charged with murder, with Franz turning king's evidence. He claimed that he was present when the shot was fired, but did not fire the bullet that killed Duncan. The three were members of the Industrial Workers of the World movement and the prosecution argued that the motive for the killing was tied up with international anarchy.

Herbert Kennedy was found not guilty, but his 20-year-old brother and Franz were found guilty and sentenced to death. There was considerable public animosity towards the elder Kennedy and Franz as 1916 was the mid-point of the Great War and Franz also had the misfortune of having a German father. They were executed at Bathurst jail on *December 20*, 1916, but not before the hangman requested double payment for his services. In normal circumstances he was paid five guineas for a hanging but, as he had to execute two men at the same time, asked for double payment "in view of the disagreeable nature of the duties involved". The NSW government refused on the basis that "when two or more criminals are hanged on the same day they are executed simultaneously" and, therefore, "they stand on the platform together and fall at the same time". The hangman had to do with a single payment, while it is believed Franz, 28 years of age, was the first man hanged after giving king's evidence.

DECEMBER 21

THE HURSTBRIDGE TORTURE MURDER (1958)

William John Pill was a hard-working market farmer who lived alone and hoarded his money. He was renowned for his excellent tomato crops and made considerable amounts of money through his hard work. Late in 1958, realising he was in ill-health, he sold 13 acres of land and decided to move in with his sister-in-law Mrs Ada Pill. The 64-year-old Pill had lived all his life in two shacks, one of them used as a kitchen and the other as a bedroom.

Pill had sold his land for 800 pounds and although this might have been a tempting figure for robbers, the agents had received only a deposit of 10 per cent and none of this had been passed on to Pill when he was brutally tortured and murdered on *December 21*, 1958.

Pill had been seen working on his tomatoes on *December 21*, but was not seen the following day. A neighbour, Herbert Funnell, became suspicious when he noticed a delivered newspaper was untouched outside one of Pill's two shacks. Funnell peeped inside and, after taking one glance, ran to notify police. Pill was dead, tied to the foot of his iron bed. Clothed only in a shirt, he was bound and gagged in a kneeling position at the foot of the bed, with his head on the mattress.

Police were shocked by the brutality of the murder as the old man had been viciously tortured, his killer(s) obviously trying to find where Pill had hidden his money. There were 287 different bruises on Pill's body, the old man lashed with a metal-ended razor strop and burned with strips of lighted sheeting. He must have suffered terribly, but whoever was responsible missed the cache of money (870 pounds) hidden in a cavity behind a fireplace. Police interviewed a number of people in an effort to solve the murder mystery but were unable to charge anyone over Pill's death, even though a 1936 Oldsmobile or Pontiac car was seen parked near the Pill shacks on the night of the murder.

DECEMBER 22

THE KROPE CASE (1977)

It is difficult to think of a more sensational case than the one involving the family of a reigning Miss Australia beauty queen, Gloria Krope, in December, 1977. The death of Miss Krope's father, Frederick Krope, in the quiet northern Melbourne suburb of Glenroy made newspaper headlines around Australia for many months. The news of Frederick Krope's death was broken in the *December 22*, 1977, edition of the Melbourne *Herald*, which ran a huge photograph of Miss Krope in her Miss Australia regalia, was headlined: "17 rifle shots kill Miss Australia's father." The report also carried a photograph of the Krope home, where Frederick Krope was shot to death in a hail of bullets. The home, in Sims Crescent, could have been any humble home in Melbourne suburbia – small, neat and unpretentious. However, it had not been a happy home for the Kropes.

Frederick Krope met his future wife Josephine in Yugoslavia in 1947; they married 18 months later and decided to migrate to Australia in late 1951. The Kropes settled in Melbourne and, in May, 1954, Rosemary, the first of their three chidren, was born. Gloria was born 18 months later and William in May, 1957. The family moved into the Sims Crescent house in July, 1955. Krope worked as a fitter and turner, but the wages from this job were supplemented by sales from small metal production items made in the family garage. Krope was a chronic gambler and the family's financial fortunes fluctuated from week to week, from one race meeting to the next. To make matters worse, Krope had a violent temper and would fly into a rage at the slightest provocation.

He was, in fact, a family bully and his wife and three children lived in fear of him. He also used to watch his own daughters through a peephole he had made for himself to the family bathroom.

It was against this background that young William Krope, just 20 years of age, became involved in tragedy. He could no longer tolerate a situation in which he, his mother and sisters were beaten and, late on the evening of Wednesday, *December 21*, 1977, he shot his father dead with a .22 Ruger semi-automatic. William had waited inside the house with the gun cocked and ready to fire as soon as his father walked through the back door. Earlier, William had been disturbed in the garage while trying to get his father's gun. William believed it was a case of kill or be killed and was convinced his father was carrying a gun. Frederick Krope eventually walked through the door and was shot repeatedly.

Both Mrs Krope and Rosemary were in the house at the time of the shooting (Gloria no longer was living at home) and immediately rushed in to see what had happened. They saw Frederick Krope dead on the floor in a pool of blood. Mrs Krope then walked to the telephone and called police. William gave himself up and told police exactly what had happened. The police inspected the body and noted that Frederick Krope was lying face down. There were numerous bullet wounds, including several to the head. They also found a number of .22 calibre cartridges in the entrance foyer and surrounding area. William made a statement and, with extraordinary courage and character, assumed full responsibility.

William was charged with murder and, in an unsworn statement read at his trial, he told of life under Frederick Krope:

From an early age I have heard my father calling my mother a bitch and slut and yelling at her. He used to terrify us with stories of how he killed people during the war and at times he had us in tears of fright and I've seen Rosemary run out of the house. From the time I first went to school I wasn't treated like the other boys. I wasn't allowed to bring them home or go out and play with them, except when he wasn't there I did it.

He also told of his father's foul mood on the day of the shooting. He said in the unsworn statement:

The day he died he was in one of the worst moods I had ever seen. I'd heard my mother asking for extra money for Christmas and I heard him say, 'not for you bloody bastards'. I heard Mum pleading with him, saying we could have a nice, peaceful Christmas and that she might be able to get Gloria to come home, and his saying things like 'not a bloody cent'. And 'get that bastard to work or I'll have him crawling on the ground like a rat'. I heard my mother pleading with him but he just got in a rage. I heard him telling my mother she was a stupid bitch and if she wanted money to get out and work for it and get me to work ...

He came home again about 7pm and my mother gave him his meal, which he ate on his own. He was listening to the wireless and he was using the phone for his betting. He seemed to be in the same bad mood as earlier. I heard him abuse Mum because I hadn't helped her in the garage. He was going on about how useless we all were to him and saying things like as far as we were all concerned we were finished. When I was watching the TV my mother was in the kitchen. I went out on a couple of occasions and put my arm around her, and tried to comfort her and brighten her up. She was still cooking because she said she had to have something to do to keep her mind off things. When I was with her in the kitchen my father came out, gave us one of his mad, threatening looks and said something like: 'I'll figure something out for you.' I was sure he was going to do something to us that night. I thought of his gun and how I could get it away from him. I couldn't bring it in through the house as he would have seen me. That's why I took the flywire off the window, to get out and bring the gun in through the window and hide it in my room. I did this and went to the garage to get his gun to take back.

When I was in the garage I got the gun out of the trunk and just then my father was coming with the torch. I left the gun and walked straight out and ran into the house in fear and got my gun, and got out of the window as I knew once he had seen me with his gun, that would be it. I would be finished. When I got out the back I saw him through the window in the garage where the rifle had been and I thought he was getting it. I got terrified and ran back into the house and hid in the lounge. I heard my father come in from the garage into the house. The lounge light was off and the TV room dimly lit. I was absolutely terrified of him and all the fear I had of him over the past times took control of me and I was just certain he was going to kill me – Mum, me and Rosemary. I believed he had the gun and I thought I had to kill him first. I was that frightened and I shot him. At that time in my mind there was nothing else I could do to save us. I don't know what made me shoot him so often; it must have been fear. I've no clear memory of how often I did it. I was so panicky. I'd often thought over the years that if he attacked me ir Mum I would have to kill him. This is the sort of thing that had been going through my mind for years because of his threats and cruelty towards us.'

One of the most poignant parts of William's statement was when he said: "No one could believe what we've been through and what sort of man he was. If you had lived in the house with us and him for even only a week you would have known what fear was and how it was with us all the time. I believe that he was truly mad."

The jury deliberated for seven hours to decide whether William was guilty or not of murder and whether Mrs Krope was guilty or not of conspiracy to murder and, when it finally announced verdicts of "not guilty", mother and son hugged each other, their ordeal over. The decisions proved enormously popular with the public and the Kropes finally were able to get on with their lives.

DECEMBER 23

HANGED (1878): South Seas islander "Johnny" hanged in Brisbane on *December 23*, 1878.

DECEMBER 24

KILLED: Prison escapee Peter Walker, who broke out of Pentridge with Ronald Ryan, killed tow-truck driver Arthur Henderson in a toilet block in the Melbourne bayside suburb of Elwood on *December 24*, 1964.

**

BEATEN TO DEATH (1991): Retired fruiterer Santo Ippolito beaten to death at his home in the south-eastern Melbourne suburb of Springvale on *December 24*, 1991.

DECEMBER 25

THE HUMAN GLOVE (1933)

There have been few more gruesome murder cases in Australia than the notorious "Human Glove" case, which was a sensation during the Depression years. The drama unfolded on *December 25*, 1933, with the discovery of the body of a middle-aged man in the Murrumbidgee at Wagga. The body, which had been in the water for several weeks, was so badly decomposed that facial identification was almost impossible. The only other hope of early identification seemed blocked when it was discovered that the skin was missing from both hands, making fingerprints impossible.

Police were still trying to solve that problem when they had the luckiest possible breakthrough. They discovered a "human glove" in the same river and immediately concluded it was missing skin from the decomposed body. They were right! A policeman volunteered to use the "glove" over his own hand for a set of fingerprints to be made, police then identifying the body. The dead man was bushman Percy Smith, who lived with another river identity named Edward Morey.

Police charged Morey with murder and the case was expected to reach an uncomplicated conclusion. However, during Morey's trial, at which evidence was given that Smith was killed with an axe found in Morey's possession, one of the prosecution witnesses was shot dead. The victim was Moncrieff Anderson, who was the husband of a woman in love with Morey. Morey was found guilty of murdering Smith and although sentenced to death, the penalty was not carried out. Mrs Anderson, who claimed that her husband had killed

Smith, later was convicted of manslaughter and sentenced to 20 years' jail. Mrs Anderson was trying to protect Morey by claiming that her husband was the real murderer. Her bid to clear him only added to the already tragic aspect of the case.

DECEMBER 26

THE GATTON MURDERS (1898)

The Christmas period in Queensland in 1898 was one of the hottest on record. The inland area west of Brisbane was baked mercilessly under a flaming orange sun and drought ravaged even the best crop and grazing districts. The area around the tiny town of Gatton (population 450), 30 or so miles east Toowoomba, resembled a dustbowl and only the truly hardy ventured into the midday sun. However, Christmas was Christmas, drought or no drought, and the large Murphy family celebrated as if the drought was about to break and there soon would be prosperity for all. Daniel and Mary Murphy, as Irish as the shamrock, had 10 children – six sons and four daughters – with only one of them, Polly, married. Daniel and Mary Murphy had been married in Ireland, but had established themselves at Blackfellow's Creek, where they became relatively prosperous and well known in the Gatton district.

Michael Murphy, a 29-year-old police sergeant, and his sisters Norah, 27, and Ellen 18, had been to Mt Sylvia races on *December 26*, 1898, and had decided to attend a dance at Gatton that night. They returned home for a meal before Michael hitched family horse Tom to a sulky and drove his sisters to the dance at the Provisional Board's Hall in Gatton.

The three Murphys passed their brother Patrick, who was on horseback, at about 8.15pm and arrived at the hall just after 9pm. However, there was no sign of activity and the dance eventually was cancelled because there were not enough women. The Murphys turned around to go home and again ran into brother Patrick, who chatted with his brother and sisters for several minutes. The four met only about a mile from an area known as Moran's Paddock and Patrick Murphy never saw his brother or two sisters alive again. It had been a brilliantly bright evening, but three of the Murphy clan met gruesome deaths under starlight.

The alarm was raised early the next morning when there was no sign of Michael, Norah or Ellen at the Murphy farm. Mrs Murphy sensed something was wrong and William McNeil, married to Polly and staying with the Murphys over the Christmas period, saddled a horse and rode to Gatton. He was shocked when told the three missing Murphys had headed towards home before 10 o'clock the previous night. McNeil decided to retrace their route to Gatton, an easy task as the Murphy sulky had a wobbly wheel which left a distinctive mark on the dusty ground out of tiny Gatton. He followed the wheel marks to a sliprail at Moran's Paddock, a couple of miles out of Gatton, and decided to investigate.

McNeil at first believed the track would lead to a farmhouse. He also was convinced that the sulky or horse had broken down and that his three in-laws had decided to stay there overnight. He certainly was not prepared for what he found just one minute's ride into the paddock, where he discovered the bodies of the three Murphys; the horse also had been killed, shot through the head.

The bodies of Michael and Ellen were back to back, with the dead horse nearby. Norah's body was about eight yards away behind a large gum tree. McNeil, at a Magisterial Inquiry in January, 1899, said in evidence that he noticed ants crawling over Norah's face. He said: "Her jacket was pulled up at the back." It was obvious that both the Murphy girls had been sexually violated. Their hands were tied behind them and their heads battered with extreme savagery. Norah Murphy had a leather strap from the sulky tied around her throat and Michael Murphy, it was later proven, had been shot in the head.

McNeil rushed to the police and the officer in charge, Sergeant William Arrell, telegrammed more senior officers about the gruesome discovery before the bodies were removed to the Boru Hotel in Gatton, where government medical officer Dr William von Lossberg conducted post mortems. He noted that Ellen's face and body were smeared with blood and that the brain protruded from the right side of the head. There were fingernail marks on the body and abrasions on both hands. The skull had been severely fractured and the doctor concluded that the girl had been bashed several times over the head with a heavy, blunt instrument. The girl also had been sexually assaulted as there were traces of semen in her vagina.

Norah Murphy had been savagely beaten about the face and the strap around her neck was so tight that it had stopped circulation to the brain. In fact, it was so tight that it cut into her flesh and could barely be seen. There was a cut (made by a knife) near the right eye and there were fingernail marks on her breasts, arms and hands. Dr von Lossberg also determined that there were fingernail marks on the dead woman's vagina and anus and that she also had been raped. The doctor examined a piece of wood retrieved from the murder scene and said that he found traces of blood, hair and brain on it. It undoubtedly was the murder weapon. Dr von Lossberg suggested that both women had been hit when they were in a standing position and had been raped before they had had their heads bashed by the heavy piece of timber.

The post-mortem examination of Michael Murphy's body was not so straightforward. Dr von Lossberg noted that there was a bloody wound behind the right ear and, after washing the blood away, was convinced he would find a bullet in the dead man's skull. The doctor probed with his fingers, but stopped to wash his hands in disinfectant after pricking a finger on a sharp piece of bone. On resumption of his probing, he felt his hand go numb and realised he had been poisoned. He asked a local chemist to continue the probe, but no bullet was found. Dr von Lossberg's blood poisoning caused him more than three months of illness and a considerable amount of anguish.

However, he finally determined that Michael Murphy also had been bashed around the head by the heavy piece of timber, but said that this was after death. He originally believed that Murphy had been shot in the head, but as he was unable to find the bullet, he therefore assumed the wound had been made by a stick. Then, in a second post-mortem conducted on *January 4*, 1899, government medical officer Charles Wray, from Brisbane, found a bullet in the skull.

So who killed the Murphys? Police, of course, had their suspects, including a known criminal who had been in the Gatton area at the time of the killings. In fact, police concentrated their efforts on this suspect, who recently had been released from jail after serving a sentence for a sexual offence. The suspect, Richard Burgess, was even remanded for eight days, but was able to provide an alibi. Burgess, who died many years later in Western Australia boasted about killing the Murphys, but the evidence suggested otherwise. The other suspect was a young man named Thomas Day, who was working in the Gatton area at the time of the killings. Day, an army deserter, was seen with bloodstained clothes soon after the tragedy and had been seen near Moran's Paddock at least twice before that fateful night of *December 26*, 1898.

Police were unable to solve the Gatton murders and a Police Inquiry Commission noted in November, 1899: "We feel constrained to acknowledge that great mystery surrounds the Gatton murders, and it does not follow that if the police had been in the highest state of efficiency that the murderer or murderers would have been discovered. That there was inertness and dilatoriness at the outset cannot be gainsaid, but after the matter was fairly taken in hand the officers and men acted individually with zeal."

Police were never able to solve the Gatton mystery and, in New South Wales in 1973, a 95-year-old man made a death-bed confession to two elderly sisters that he was the killer. Then, after the old man's death, the sisters went to Murwillumbah police and said he had confessed. He even had told the sisters where he had hidden the revolver used to shoot Michael Murphy. The sisters, Mrs Margaret Rutherford and Mrs Violet Russell, insisted the old man had given them extremely detailed information and were convinced he was telling the truth. However, police found numerous discrepancies in his story and assumed he could not have been the Gatton killer. The mystery therefore remains.

DECEMBER 27

THE BOWLING PIN KILLING (1997)

Christopher Andrew Robinson and a friend, Andrew Newman, had been drinking before they went to the Central Railway Station, Sydney, on the night of *December 27*, 1997. Police arrested Newman for drinking at the station and he was locked up for three hours. When he eventually returned to where Robinson and girlfriend Summer Morris were living, Robinson walked in carrying a bowling pin wrapped in a plastic bag. More ominously, the bag also contained a knife which appeared to be stained with blood.

Robinson then told Newman an incredible story, of how he met a man "where the coaches go" and agreed to go back to the man's home. There, he hit the man over the head "a couple of times" with the bowling pin, which he found on the floor. Robinson then told Newman: "He dropped to the floor and was gasping for air. I got the knife and gave him a good going over. It took him a while to die. I cut down the stomach. There was heaps of blood and it stank." Adding that he thought "killing was liberating", Robinson told Newman he would kill him if he went to the police.

Police found the body of Trevor John Parkin at his unit in Glebe on *December 29* and Robinson was charged with his murder. Parkin indeed had been hit over the head with a heavy object and had had his chest cavity sliced open. Even more gruesome was the fact that the man's left testicle had been removed and was found in the kitchen sink. Parkin's hands had been tied with an electrical cord and the pathologist who performed the post-mortem indicated that the mutilation of Parkin's body had occurred after death.

Parkin had convictions for sexual assaults, but Robinson said he had no knowledge of his victim being a paedophile and that the only reason he went to Parkin's unit was that sometimes when he needed money for heroin he would pose as a male prostitute. Regardless, Robinson's attack on Parkin was brutal in the extreme and Summer Morris, who had started dating Robinson about 10 months before the killing, told of incidents in which her boyfriend showed a sadistic nature. In one, he set a cat's tail alight while he held a plastic bag over its head.

In another incident, Summer Morris said: "I caught a cat and was patting it. Me and Chris got into a fight but I can't recall what it was about. Chris grabbed the cat and was looking at it. He then got out a pen knife out of his pocket; I think it was a flick pocket knife and started cutting the cat's ears off; he cut its tail off and then cut the cat's toes off. The cat was still alive and then he cut it straight down the stomach. I could tell that it was a mother cat and was breast feeding. My mother breeds cats and I know a lot about them. When he cut the stomach open he just started pulling its stomach contents out. I was in shock from the time he first started cutting up the cat and was frozen scared."

Robinson pleaded guilty to Parkin's murder and Justice Adams said: "I have, with some reluctance, come to the conclusion that the murder of Mr Parkin was deliberate and unprovoked. The blows to the head were extremely violent. The offender intended to kill, and not merely to disable. The mutilation of the body must have extended over a considerable period of time and required a great deal of physical effort. The offender told a friend 'do you know how strong those tubes and things inside you are? I do not know how doctors operate; they must have some really sharp knives.

Do you know how long it takes to cut all those organs and those tubes that connect everything together. I can't believe it, man'."

The judge added: "I consider that the offender did not mutilate Mr Parkin's body in order to kill him, although this must have occurred if he were not already dead, but primarily because doing so satisfied some deep-seated need or provided an unimaginable pleasure." The judge sentenced Robinson to 45 years' jail, with a non-parole period of 35 years. This means Robinson, 17 and a half at the time of the murder, will not be eligible for release until 2034.

**

HANGED (1853): Joseph West hanged in Melbourne on *December 27*, 1853, after being found guilty of the rape of a girl at Forest Creek.

**

KELLY DEATH (1866): John "Red" Kelly, father of the notorious Ned, died of dropsy on *December 27*, 1866.

DECEMBER 28

'GOD BLESS YOU' (1861)

Bushranger John Peisley got himself involved in a brawl at Bigga, New South Wales, on *December 28*, 1861, and attacked an old friend, William Benyon, with a knife. Benyon's brother Stephen intervened and, in the brawl, Peisley shot William Benyon in the neck. Benyon died a week later and Peisley was charged with murder. He was found guilty and was hanged at Bathurst Gaol on *April 25*, 1862. He said on the gallows that he was proud of the fact that he never used violence as a bushranger and blamed only himself for his life of crime and his death sentence. His final words were: "Goodbye, gentlemen, and God bless you."

DECEMBER 29

THE BUNGLED KIDNAPPING (1969)

Brothers Arthur and Nizamodeen Hosein had delusions of grandeur, way beyond their modest means as pig and chicken farmers in Hertforshire, England. They wanted to be seriously rich, so came up with a plan to kidnap the wife of Australian newspaper magnate Rupert Murdoch. The brothers followed the Murdoch Rolls Royce on *December 29*, 1969, and abducted the woman driver. However, the limousine had been lent to the Murdoch company deputy chairman Alick McKay and it was his wife Muriel who was at the wheel that fateful day.

The Hoseins initially demanded a ransom of 500,000 pounds and then doubled it as police launched a massive search in snow and sleet for the missing Mrs McKay. Arthur Hosein was arrested near where the ransom money was due to be collected and, although Muriel McKay's body was never found, the Hosein brothers were found guilty of murder, kidnap and blackmail and were sentenced to life imprisonment. It generally was assumed that the Hoseins fed Mrs McKay's body to their farm pigs.

THE WIFE-SLASHER (2003)

On *December 29*, 2003, former insurance manager Joseph Vella waited outside the family home in the Perth suburb of Kallaroo. Then, when Mrs Vella's boyfriend Alan Susta left the house, he gained admission on the pretext of talking to his wife about possible custody arrangements for the couple's four sons. However, Vella then hit his wife four times over the head with a baseball bat and then slashed her throat from ear to ear with a hunting knife. He had bought the bat and the knife from a sports store just a few days before the murderous attack, which was witnessed by the Vellas' six-year-old son.

The West Australian Supreme Court had been told that Mrs Vella had taken out a restraining order against her husband following a previous attack in which she was left with broken ribs and a punctured lung. In sentencing Vella to life imprisonment, Judge Ralph Simmonds said the murder was one of the worst he had come across and added that the fact that the six-year-old son had witnessed the crime was a serious aggravating factor. However, Vella insisted that he did not know his son was watching the attack on the boy's mother. Detective Senior Constable Brian Hill said outside the court after the sentencing of Vella: "I have only done a number of these (murder cases) and it certainly is the most horrific of the ones I have witnessed".

DECEMBER 30

HANGED (1873): Elizabeth Woolcock hanged at Adelaide Gaol on *December 30*, 1873, after being found guilty of murdering her husband Thomas with poison.

DECEMBER 31

THE GUN ALLEY MURDER (1921)

At about five o'clock on the morning of *December 31*, 1921, a bottle collector stumbled across the naked body of a young girl. The body lay across a grate in tiny Gun Alley, Melbourne. Gun Alley, a lane running off Little Collins Street, at that time was an unsavoury part of the city and the site later was occupied by the Southern Cross Hotel. The dead girl was 12-year-old Alam Tirtschke, who had been reported missing the previous afternoon after running a message for her aunt to a butcher shop in Swanston Street.

Alma had been wearing a navy blue box-pleated tunic, a white blouse with blue spots and a school hat bearing the badge of Hawthorn West High School. Alma had left the butcher shop at about 1pm and then "disappeared", although witnesses later gave various accounts of seeing her in the neighbourhood. Significantly, Alma's body was naked when discovered and, even more significantly, the body had been washed down before being dumped in Gun Alley. Alma had been raped and strangled and the New Year's eve murder captured the imagination and horror of the whole of Melbourne.

A post mortem performed by government pathologist Dr Crawford Mollison revealed an abrasion on the left side of the jaw, another on the left side of the neck, a small abrasion on the outer side of the right eye, a small abrasion on the upper lip and a slight graze on the elbow. There was bruising on the right side of the neck and haemorrhages on the scalp and the surface of the eyes. Dr Mollison's expert view was that the girl had died of strangulation by throttling.

Several witnesses helped police in their investigations and the trail eventually led to Colin Ross, who operated the Australian Wine Bar in the Eastern Arcade. Ross, 26, had bought the wine shop business for 400 pounds but, ironically, the licence on the saloon was due to expire on *December 31*, the very day that Alma's body was discovered. Police interviewed Ross several times and, at the first interview, told police he had seen a girl answering Alma's description, but knew nothing of her death. Then, on *January 5*, 1922, he was interviewed for eight hours and made a lengthy statement in which he referred to a suspicious shop opposite his and later described it as a brothel. Then, on *January 10*, 20-year-old prostitute Olive Maddox was overheard saying she had seen Ross with the 12-year-old. Maddox made this remark to a woman named Ivy Matthews, who gave evidence at Alma's inquest on *January 26* that she saw a girl in Ross' saloon at about 3pm on *December 30* and that the girl "resembled" Alma Tirtschke.

Police went to Ross' home in the western suburb of Footscray and discovered 27 hairs on two blankets and these were identified as being from the dead girl. Ross had an alibi, supported by numerous witnesses, but circumstantial evidence saw him found guilty of Alma's murder. When Justice Schutt asked him if he wanted to say anything before sentence was passed, Ross replied: "Yes, I still maintain that I am an innocent man, and that my evidence is correct. My life has been sworn away by desperate people." The judge then sentenced Ross to death.

Appeals to the State Full Court and the High Court of Australia failed and Ross was due to hang on *April 24*. State Cabinet turned down a request for an appeal to the Privy Council and Ross was hanged as scheduled, spending his last hours with two ministers of religion. As he waited for the noose to be pulled right around his neck, he said: "I am now face to face with my Maker. I swear by almighty God that I am an innocent man. I never saw the child. I never committed the crime and I don't know who did it. I never confessed to anyone. I ask God to forgive those who swore my life away, and I pray God to have mercy on my poor, darling mother and my family." Ross also wrote to his mother protesting his innocence.

Ross' counsel, Mr T.C. Brennan (later Dr Brennan) was so convinced of his client's innocence that he wrote a book about the case and its inconsistencies. Significantly, it was titled *The Gun Alley Tragedy*, Brennan leaving no doubt that he believed Ross to be as tragic a figure as poor Alma Tirtschke. In that book, there is an incredible index, telling of a letter Ross received while waiting for death. The letter read:

Colin C. Ross, Melbourne Gaol,

You have been condemned for a crime which you have never committed and are to suffer for another's fault. Since your conviction you have, no doubt, wondered what manner of man the real murderer is who could not only encompass the girl's death, but allow you to suffer in his stead.

My dear Ross, if it is any satisfaction for you to know it, believe me that you die but once, but he will continue to die for the rest of his life. Honoured and fawned upon by those who know him, the smile upon his lips but hides the canker eating into his soul. Day and night his life is a hell without the hope of retrieve. Gladly would he take your place on Monday (the day of execution) next if he had himself alone to consider. His reason, then, briefly stated, is this: A devoted and loving mother is ill and a shock would be fatal. Three loving married sisters, whose whole life would be wrecked, to say nothing of brothers who have been accustomed to take him as a pattern. He cannot sacrifice these. Himself he will be sacrificed when his mother passes away. He will do it by his own hand. He will board the ferry across the Styx with a lie on his lips, with the only hope that religion is a myth and death annihilation.

It is too painful for him to go into the details of the crime. It is simply a Jekyll and Hyde existence. By a freak of nature, he was not made as other men … this girl was not the first … in this case there was no intention of murder – the victim unexpectedly collapsed. The hands of the woman, in her frenzy, did the rest.

May it be some satisfaction to yourself, your devoted mother, and the memories of your family to know that at least one of the legion of the damned, who is the cause of your death, is suffering the pangs of hell. He may not ask for forgiveness or sympathy, but he asks your understanding.

It now seems certain that an innocent man was hanged, with DNA evidence proving that Ross did not kill Alma Tirtschke.

BEN COLLINS is a journalist and author building a reputation as one of Australia's brightest young writing talents. Collins co-authored *Jason McCartney: After Bali* – the highest-selling non-fiction book by an Australian author in 2003 – which chronicles McCartney's inspirational recovery from near-fatal burns inflicted in the 2002 Bali terrorist bombings to  play one last game of AFL football for the Kangaroos. In 2004, Collins wrote *The Book of Success*, which comprised an enlightening series of interviews with successful Australians from various fields of endeavour including business, sport, entertainment, politics and science. In 2006, he wrote *The Champions: Conversations with Great Players and Coaches of Australian Football*, including Nathan Buckley, James Hird, Robert Harvey, Wayne Carey, Peter Hudson and Ron Barassi. Collins started as a cadet journalist with *The Courier* in Ballarat in 1997 and worked with Fairfax Community Newspapers in Melbourne before joining the Herald & Weekly Times as one of the original reporters on free commuter newspaper *MX*, in 2001. He also writes for the *AFL Record*, the AFL's official game-day program.

OTHER BOOKS BY BEN COLLINS

Jason McCartney: After Bali

The Book of Success

The Champions: Conversations with Great Players and Coaches of Australian Football

JIM MAIN is one of Australia's most respected journalists. He studied law at the University of Melbourne, but preferred to pursue a career as a writer. He worked on the Melbourne *Herald* before spending almost two years on Fleet Street with the *Daily Express*. On return to Australia he combined journalism with studies for his Bachelor of Arts degree (majoring in History) at La Trobe University. Chief football writer on *The Australian* for more than a decade, he has covered Olympic and Commonwealth Games and his byline has appeared from London, Dublin, Tokyo, Los Angeles and even Panama City. The author of more than 50 books, he is a winner of the Sir William Walkley Award (Australian journalism's most prestigious award) and, while in London, a Lord Beaverbrook Award. Inducted into the Melbourne Cricket Club Media Hall of Fame in 2003, his interests are wide and varied.

OTHER BOOKS BY JIM MAIN INCLUDE:

Only the Dead (Fiction)
Murder Australian Style
Murder in the First Degree
Australian Murders
An Australian's Travel Guide to Europe
EJ – The Ted Whitten Story
Honour The Names
Fallen – The Ultimate Heroes (with David Allen)
Pants – The Darren Millane Story (with Eddie McGuire)
Whatever It Takes (with Jim Stynes)
The Encyclopedia of AFL Footballers (with Russell Holmesby)
This Football Century (with Russell Holmesby)
How To Play Cricket (with Greg Chappell)